CHOICES

NUCLEAR AND NON-NUCLEAR DEFENCE OPTIONS

Also available from Brassey's

CARTWRIGHT & CRITCHLEY
Cruise, Pershing & SS-20

CHICHESTER & WILKINSON
British Defence: A Blueprint for Reform

COKER
A Nation in Retreat? Britain's Defence Commitment

COKER
British Defence in the 1990s: A Guide to the Defence Debate

MCINNES
Trident: The Only Option?

WINDASS
The Rite of War

CHOICES

NUCLEAR AND NON-NUCLEAR DEFENCE OPTIONS

Assessed by:

Peter Carrington

Michael Carver

Leonard Cheshire

Denzil Davies

John Finnis

Lawrence Freedman

Richard Harries

Michael Howard

Rebecca Johnson

Anthony Kenny

Bruce Kent

Yuri Lebedev

Robert McNamara

James O'Connell

David Owen

James Schlesinger

Edward Thompson

Caspar Weinberger

George Younger

ORGANIZED AND PRESENTED BY

OLIVER RAMSBOTHAM

BRASSEY'S DEFENCE PUBLISHERS
(a member of the Pergamon Group)

LONDON · OXFORD · WASHINGTON · NEW YORK
BEIJING · FRANKFURT · SÃO PAULO · SYDNEY · TOKYO · TORONTO

U.K. (Editorial)	Brassey's Defence Publishers, 24 Gray's Inn Road, London WC1X 8HR
(Orders)	Brassey's Defence Publishers, Headington Hill Hall, Oxford OX3 0BW, England
U.S.A. (Editorial)	Pergamon-Brassey's International Defense Publishers, 8000 Westpark Drive, Fourth Floor, McLean, Virginia 22101, U.S.A.
(Orders)	Pergamon Press, Maxwell House, Fairview Park, Elmsford, New York 10523, U.S.A.
PEOPLE'S REPUBLIC OF CHINA	Pergamon Press, Room 4037, Qianmen Hotel, Beijing, People's Republic of China
FEDERAL REPUBLIC OF GERMANY	Pergamon Press, Hammerweg 6, D-6242 Kronberg, Federal Republic of Germany
BRAZIL	Pergamon Editora, Rua Eça de Queiros, 346, CEP 04011, Paraiso, São Paulo, Brazil
AUSTRALIA	Pergamon-Brassey's Defence Publishers, P.O. Box 544, Potts Point, N.S.W. 2011, Australia
JAPAN	Pergamon Press, 8th Floor, Matsuoka Central Building, 1–7–1 Nishishinjuku, Shinjuku-ku, Tokyo 160, Japan
CANADA	Pergamon Press Canada, Suite No. 271, 253 College Street, Toronto, Ontario, Canada M5T 1R5

First edition 1987

Library of Congress Cataloging in Publication Data

Choices: nuclear and nuclear-defence options.
1. Great Britain – Military policy. 2. Nuclear weapons – Great
Britain. 3. Europe – Military policy. 4. North Atlantic Treaty
Organization. I. Ramsbotham, Oliver
UA647.C557 1987   355'.0335'41   87–9105

British Library Cataloguing in Publication Data

Choices: nuclear and non-nuclear defence options.
1. Nuclear weapons – Government policy – Great Britain
I. Ramsbotham, Oliver
355'.0335'41   UA647
ISBN 0–08–034763–0 (Hardcover)
ISBN 0–08–035820–9 (Flexicover)

*Typeset, printed and bound in Great Britain by
Richard Clay Ltd, Bungay, Suffolk*

For Ed, Ben, and Zand

Acknowledgements

In addition to the contributors to this book, I would like to thank the following: Ronald Higgins, Stephen Pullinger and Jenifer Wates, for so generously including me in the discussions on defence and security, which they organize as part of the 'Dunamis' enterprise; Scilla McLean, of the Oxford Research Group, for her help and encouragement; Malcolm Dando and Paul Rogers, of the School of Peace Studies, Bradford University, for guiding and advising me; Sir Frank Cooper, Sir Ronald Mason and Sir Michael Quinlan, for giving up their time and allowing me to learn from their experience. I am very grateful to them all.

Without naming them, I would also like to thank the many authors of books and articles, which I have used in drawing up the analysis in Part I. References and a bibliography were included in the original version of this book, but have since been left out on the grounds that they would have overloaded it and diverted attention from Part II.

Contents

PART 2 – ANSWERS

PART 3 – POSTSCRIPT

Introduction

Should we continue to develop and deploy nuclear weapons systems?

This became one of the great public questions of our age very suddenly – on August 6, 1945, when the first atomic bomb was dropped on Hiroshima. It has been an urgent, if not dominant, international issue ever since. Those who are now under 50 will have lived the whole of their politically conscious lives in terms of it, and will have become habituated to the apparently irreconcileable differences of opinion which it arouses. This book is the first part of an extended attempt to understand what is at issue in the debate, to explore the possibilities for agreement or compromise, and to come to terms with the implications of whatever remains unresolved. But, before we say any more about the book, we will see if there is anything uncontroversial that we can say about the nature and significance of the question with which it deals.

The Subject

Whether or not we favour a policy of continuing nuclear weapon deployment, we are likely to agree that, in terms of capacity for destruction, the weapons already deployed pose a uniquely immediate and universal threat to our survival. This is what is said ultimately to underpin our security by those who believe in nuclear deterrence, and to undermine it by those who do not. If currently deployed arsenals were used in their entirety, the destruction would effectively be instantaneous and complete. And the weapons that can do this are already there, based, targeted and manned. It is a shock to see and touch them. In this most straightforward sense, they exist as brute objects, irreducible facts. To that extent, the question of nuclear weapon deployment concerns the most tangibly real of the great global threats that hang over us. There is also widespread agreement that no economic, political or ideological principles can ever rationally or morally justify the deliberate carrying out of that threat in its entirety. In the end the debate derives its immediacy and universality from the fact that it concerns how we are to prevent the immediate and universal destruction of us all. The prevention of all-out nuclear war is recognized to be an overarching global priority, which transcends sectional interest. So we may feel encouraged to hope that, because we now share the same major long-term objective (a state of affairs which has by no means always been the case in international affairs in the past), it should, at least in principle, be possible for us to reach a measure of agreement about how we are to encompass it. After all, whether these weapons are used, or, indeed, whether they even continue to exist, depends upon decisions taken by those who create and control them. They are direct expressions of our will. So the question of nuclear weapon deployment is also, in a particularly literal sense, a question about human intention. The threat is a threat made by human beings against other human beings. We may ask how we have anything to fear from a threat, made against ourselves, which is acknowledged to be so horrifying that we all agree that it must never be carried out. Surely we can find a joint programme which we can be confident will prevent that from happening. This book is part of our search for such a programme.

And yet the threat posed by nuclear weapon deployment is in another sense surprisingly remote. We have had no direct experience of a nuclear exchange to bring home the reality of the danger to us. Neither the bombs dropped on Hiroshima and Nagasaki, nor the nuclear devices detonated in successive weapons tests since then, represent the likely outcome of a breakdown of deterrence. Generations of nuclear weapons have been developed, deployed, and then declared obsolete, without having been used. If the 'brute objects' referred to just now have had an effect, then it has been as a result of our *imagining* what they might do. They themselves have in this sense become symbols rather than instruments. And the same applies to command and control structures, and to the various strategies for anticipating, containing, and fighting a nuclear war. None of them have been tested out in the circumstances for which they were devised. We just do not know what the effect of a nuclear exchange would be. In this respect, and to an extent that must come as a surprise to those who enter the field for the first time, everything that is written on the subject is hypothetical and speculative. For forty years now the nuclear weapons debate has been conducted in an empirical vacuum. Whether or not this is itself a result of nuclear weapon deployment, it poses a serious problem for all those involved in the debate – for advocates of continuing reliance on nuclear deterrence, because deterrent policy depends upon the liveliness of our perception of the reality of the threat, and for critics of deterrence, because it is a failure to appreciate the reality of the threat that is said to encourage the folly of deterrent policy. Each accuses the other of not coming to terms with the realities of the nuclear age. And this puts special pressure on our discussion of the problem. Nuclear deterrence *is* mutual perception. If we all perceive that there is deterrence, then there is. And, if we do not, then there is not. So the debate directly affects what it is about. What is said in it may become a self-fulfilling prophecy. In the absence of direct experience to create the reality of the situation for us (as, for example, the accident at Chernobyl may, obliquely, be said to have done – whatever the conclusions drawn from it), it is the nuclear weapons debate itself which must perform this function. The judgements recorded in the second part of this book are an example of how this function is being performed.

What we have just described is not the case with a number of the other threats that face us. Year by year we have evidence of some of the consequences of overpopulation, gross economic mismanagement, depletion of natural resources, soil erosion, environmental degradation – or whatever other social, political, or spiritual dangers may be said to be threatening us. So there is hope that we may be able to learn from our mistakes as we go along before it is too late, and, in the meantime, redress local breakdown with resources drawn from the unaffected areas. But we cannot expect to have such piecemeal experience of the consequences of a failure of nuclear deterrence, nor to be given the chance to recover from it. Both those who advocate and those who reject nuclear deterrent policies, agree that in this sense we would be wise to treat the threat posed by the deployment of nuclear weapons as all or nothing. It is, among other things, the fear that nuclear war might not be limited that is said by the former to enhance deterrence, and by the latter to invalidate it. This again invests the nuclear weapons debate with a frightening significance. Because we cannot afford to make major mistakes in the actual carrying out of policy, we must try to eliminate them in argument beforehand. We must identify unacceptable risks in advance, and, by anticipating danger, prevent it. There is general agreement that the right policies can give us hope of avoiding immediate disaster, and can offer us the time and opportunity to work towards the creation of a world order in which enough aspirations are satisfied, perceived injustices redressed, and disputes settled, within a framework of accepted procedure, to make recourse to war unnecessary, and, finally, unthinkable. There is also general agreement that the wrong policies are likely to have the opposite effect. But, to a remarkable extent, there seems as yet to be no general agreement as to which are which. This book is the beginning of an attempt to assess how serious this is.

Finally, there can be little doubt that the disagreement has widened and deepened during the last few years. Developments at global, regional, and national levels, which we will not try to analyse here, have led to a polarization of opinion, whose political significance is perhaps only now beginning to become evident. At global level, whatever interpretation is made of the events of Reykjavik, both the leaders of the two greatest nuclear weapon states have placed fundamental questions about the feasibility and desirability of eliminating nuclear weapons, in large measure, or altogether, at the top of the international agenda. At regional level, increasingly powerful criticisms of NATO and Warsaw Pact nuclear and non-nuclear strategy, long relatively dormant, have now been raised again, and have elicited more elaborate defences of current policy in response. At national level, the whole question of Britain's status as a nuclear weapon power, and role within a Western alliance com-

mitted to a nuclear deterrent strategy, has erupted into the centre of the
political arena. British voters are being asked to choose between clear-cut
alternatives, which represent elaborate, thoroughgoing, and apparently
incompatible, interpretations of the situation that we are in. It is important to
understand that the British debate is only a part of the international debate,
and that an informed judgement cannot be made on British policy, which does
not at the same time include an assessment of regional and global issues. This
book is an attempt to set the British debate within such a regional and global
context. It is an attempt to provide the reader with an outline of what the
issues are, and what the proponents of alternative policies are saying about
them.

The Book

But how are we to cope with the flood of material which threatens to engulf
us when we try to fathom this question? We are overwhelmed by the spoken
and written comments, discussions, debates, memoranda, speeches, policy
statements, articles, books, which pour from transmitting stations and presses
throughout the world every day – much of it highly technical, most of it in
need of almost constant revision in the light of the onrush of events, and nearly
all of it bewilderingly controversial. It is hard to find firm ground amid such
a welter.

This book is an attempt to provide such firm ground. The central idea is to
offer readers a simple and comprehensive analysis of what is said to be at issue,
and a representative selection of informed opinion about it. Part I sets out the
analysis, and Part II the response. Because those consulted in Part II have
been asked the same complete set of questions, the premises of their arguments
are laid out and their answers can be compared point by point. And, because
they have been free to criticize the framework of questions as they have gone
along, we have not needed to worry about the fact that the analysis in Part I
has no doubt been presented as too simple a juxtaposition of alternatives. The
purpose of Part I is to clarify the issues for the reader. It can be left to Part II
to show up how misleading that clarification may have been.

So the reader should remember that it is Part II which is important here,
and that Part I is just a lead-in to it. Experienced readers may, therefore,
prefer to jump over Part I altogether, and turn straight to Part II.

PART 1 QUESTIONS

TWO ARGUMENTS
AND AN ANALYSIS

In Part I the reader is offered two outline sets of argument, one against the continued deployment of nuclear weapons, and one in favour, followed by an analysis of the points at issue between them. It is this analysis which has been used as a framework for the responses, which are recorded in Part II.

Preliminary

Definitions

Although the classification of nuclear weapons systems is notoriously imprecise, and, in terms of arms control, controversial, the main thing that the reader needs to remember in what follows is the rough distinction between three classes of *offensive* weapon. There are (i) the STRATEGIC nuclear forces, with which, in particular, each superpower directly threatens the other's homeland. There are (ii) the INTERMEDIATE (INF) or THEATRE nuclear forces, which, in Europe, can reach the countries within that theatre. And there are (iii) the BATTLEFIELD or TACTICAL nuclear forces, which are mainly deployed either side of the European frontier in or near what is thought to be a possible prospective battle-zone. Strategic nuclear forces are usually further sub-divided into the 'triad' of land-based Intercontinental Ballistic Missiles (ICBMs), sea-based Submarine Launched Ballistic Missiles (SLBMs), and long-range bombers. Theatre nuclear forces are usually seen to include the so-called 'Longer-Range INF weapons' (LRINF), such as Soviet SS20 missiles, and NATO Pershing II and Cruise missiles. In addition, there are also *defensive* systems, which include Anti-Ballistic Missiles (ABMs), and the broader programmes of Strategic Defence Initiatives (SDIs) being developed by the US and the USSR.

Arms control and arms limitation negotiations can be similarly classified into (i) the Strategic Arms Limitation and Strategic Arms Reduction talks, (SALT, START); (ii) the Intermediate Nuclear Force (INF) talks; and (iii) the Mutual and Balanced Force Reduction (MBFR) talks, which include conventional forces as well as tactical nuclear forces. In addition, there are negotiations about Strategic Defence.

The reader might also like to remember the rough distinction between ballistic missiles, which leave and re-enter the earth's atmosphere, and cruise missiles, which do not. A 'MIRVed' missile is one which carries 'Multiple Independently Targeted Reentry Vehicles' – in other words, multiple warheads which can be independently guided towards different targets. A 'first strike capability' is, as the term suggests, an ability to strike first; a 'second

3

strike capability' is an ability to strike back having absorbed an enemy first strike. A 'counter-force system' is a system aimed against enemy military, and especially nuclear, forces, rather than against industrial plant or centres of population.

Finally, it is also worth noting the annoying ambiguity which surrounds the word 'strategic'. Traditionally used to refer to strategy in general, it is now also applied to a particular class of nuclear weapon.

The Theory of Mutual Nuclear Deterrence

When, by the 1960s, the spontaneous and uncoordinated build-up of nuclear weapons systems on both sides of the Iron Curtain had reached the point where it was generally recognized that neither could expect to attack the other without receiving unacceptable damage in reply, strategists began to explore the implications of the situation. Some of them, concluding that they could make a virtue out of necessity, proclaimed that this was a fundamentally stable, and therefore desirable, state of affairs. The essential ingredient, they said, was that each side should have an invulnerable and potent strategic nuclear second strike force. In other words, no matter what the other might do, even if he unleashed his entire nuclear armoury in an unexpected first strike, a sufficient reserve force would still be left, capable of inflicting an intolerable level of destruction on him. In fact, to look at it from the point of view of defence, what was said to be critical was not so much that each side should *have* such an invulnerable second strike force (after all, you could only find out whether this was so if deterrence failed), but that each should *think* that he had – and, equally important, that each should think that the other thought that he had. If either were to think that the other thought that he had not, then it might be supposed that the other could be tempted to risk a first strike – and the essential stability of Mutual Nuclear Deterrence would have been lost.

Such was the remarkably theoretical nature of much of the abundant literature on the subject. Nuclear systems were seen primarily as instruments for the psychological manipulation of a potential enemy's intention and will, and only secondarily, and deeply ambiguously, as weapons of war. This was a bewildering reversal of traditional military thinking, in which defensive capabilities had always been seen primarily as means for damaging the enemy and throwing back his invading forces, and only secondarily, and as a strict result of this, as a possibly effective deterrent threat. The ultimate reason for deploying nuclear weapons was now said to be to ensure that they would not be used – and therefore that other weapons would not be used either.

An important corollary followed from all of this. If Mutual Nuclear Deterrence of this kind is good, because it is stable, then whatever threatens to undermine that stability is bad. In particular, two potential developments must count as bad. The first would be for either side to think that the other was acquiring a first strike potential capable of threatening the *invulnerability* of his second strike force. The second would be for either to think that the other was building a defensive system capable of threatening its *effectiveness*. Either or both of these would undermine the stability of deterrence. For some, this was the fundamental theoretical reason for going to such lengths to restrict the proliferation of first strike systems in the SALT negotiations, and to curtail the development and deployment of anti-ballistic missile systems in the ABM talks.

Not all commentators, either at the time or since, have accepted this reasoning. A number of those who support, as well as a number of those who oppose, current nuclear deterrent policies, reject it. But we have begun from this position, because it gives us a clear conceptual framework within terms of which contrasting judgements can be better understood. We can now move on to consider the current debate about the rationality and morality of continued nuclear weapon deployment. Is it *sensible* to go on deploying nuclear weapons – are the risks of not doing so greater than the risks of carrying on? And is it morally *right*?

★   ★   ★

In the two chapters which follow, we consider first the principal tenets of those who oppose the deployment of nuclear weapons and then the case for their continued deployment.

1

The Case Against Continued Nuclear Weapon Deployment

The Argument About Morality

To Use Nuclear Weapons Would be to Cause Unimaginable Suffering to Civilian Populations

In order to understand what would be likely to happen if current nuclear war-fighting plans were put into operation, we can begin by trying to imagine the effect of the small atomic bomb dropped on Hiroshima in August 1945. Energy equivalent to 13,000 tons of TNT suddenly exploded in a fireball of intense radiation in the sky. Light permanently or temporarily blinded those who looked at it. Heat, generated almost instantaneously at ten million degrees centigrade from within the fireball, melted, scorched or burned whatever was exposed to it within a wide radius, searing flesh and igniting anything combustible, such as paper or clothing. The shock from the blast-wave demolished buildings with shattering force and generated a hurricane-strength wind, which uprooted trees and swept people off their feet, together with fragments of debris and suffocating dust. All of this happened within the first few seconds of the explosion. Then followed hours of physical agony, bereavement and shock, intensified by the fact that the medical and fire-fighting services had been overwhelmed in the disaster. It has been estimated that of the 1780 nurses in the city, 1654 were either dead or too badly injured to work, while little could be done to control the great fire-storm, which engulfed the city-centre, sucking in forty-mile-an-hour winds and raging for several hours. Almost nine out of ten of the 30,000 people living in the central square-mile of the city were killed. But what is peculiar to a nuclear detonation is the continuing misery from fear of cancers and genetic deformation engendered by the various kinds of nuclear radiation, which at Hiroshima made up perhaps fifteen percent of the energy yield from the bomb. The whole matter is still not at all well understood, and there is considerable controversy about it. It is true that direct radiation from neutrons and gamma rays probably did not add to the immediate toll of suffering among those who were in any case dead or dying, and that, being an air-burst attack, there seems to have been little early fallout (i.e., dust and dirt particles sucked into the irradiated fireball cloud and later falling back again to earth). But delayed effects from exposure to radiation and other long-term consequences may still be causing well over 1000 deaths a year more than forty years after the original explosion. In any case, enough has been written here to indicate something of the scale of human suffering inflicted upon a largely civilian population when a single bomb of small to moderate yield is detonated over a densely inhabited area.

There is little point in saying much more. If a yield of, say, two represents an explosive power which is twice that of the bomb dropped on Hiroshima, then a single Soviet SS-20 Mod II missile can deliver three warheads, each of which has a yield of twelve; a single British submarine equipped with Polaris missiles can deliver forty-eight warheads, each of yield fifteen; a single United States Ohio class submarine, equipped with the projected Trident D-5 missiles, will be able to deliver up to three hundred and sixty independently targeted warheads, each of which may have an average yield of twenty-five – in other words, each submarine will have a firepower several times greater than that of all munitions fired by all belligerents throughout the course of the Second World War. Even a limited nuclear battlefield duel in Europe would cause vastly more damage to civilian populations than the Hiroshima bomb. Moreover, for tactical reasons, a number of the explosions would be ground-burst, adding the horrors of early fallout, largely absent at Hiroshima, to all the other afflictions endured by the civilian population, with radioactive dust carried by the wind anything from about ten to about a hundred or more kilometers from the point of detonation. The recent accident at Chernobyl gives us some idea of how absurd it is to imagine that the effects of a nuclear exchange could be confined to the battlezone.

As to what would happen if the conflict escalated towards a more general exchange, how can we even begin to imagine the implications for hundreds of thousands or millions of people, or hope to assess the consequences for our children and grandchildren, and for the world that they will be living in? The long-term effects of radiation on that scale are unknown, while recent projections of possible climatic and ecological disasters, such as those that might follow from the so-called 'nuclear winter', or from the destruction by nitrogen oxides of a critical percentage of the earth's vital protective ozone layer, are only guesses at what the results might be. It is not clear that we would recover. Those who cite implausible possibilities of nuclear strikes in which collateral damage is negligible are being unrealistic and irresponsible. It is plainly evident that any use of nuclear weapons would in itself be a crime against humanity, and would, in addition, carry the unavoidable risk of escalation towards universal catastrophe.

Such Use Cannot be Justified as Legitimate Defence

We must now try to dispel a common misconception – that there can be such a thing as legitimate nuclear defence, and that it is an aggressor who will bear full moral responsibility for the consequences of his aggression, if we are forced to retaliate with a nuclear counter-strike. Nuclear weapons are simply not like traditional 'conventional' weapons in being primarily aimed against an opponent's military strength. They are, effectively, counter-civilian weapons. What is called 'nuclear defence' in all its guises – admonitory, preemptive, interdictive, punitive – is in effect an attack on enemy centres of population. It is often said that, although we are not morally justified in ourselves initiating a nuclear attack, we are morally justified in threatening to retaliate if someone initiates an attack against us. But would retaliation in fact be justified, if deterrence failed? Clearly, it would not. It would be as if, when someone threatens to torture our child, we threaten to torture his child. This is not what is meant by 'self-defence'. And, if it turned out that both he and we actually carried out our threat, then nothing that he had done earlier would exonerate us from sharing in the full burden of guilt. A terrorist group does not escape moral condemnation for detonating a bomb in a crowded shopping precinct in a state capital by blaming the government of that state for having previously acted immorally elsewhere. Neither the principle of proportion, nor the principle of discrimination, will allow the preemptive or retaliatory use of nuclear weapons, no matter what the provocation and no matter how great the threat. In the same way, it was wrong to bomb Hiroshima and Nagasaki, whatever the supposed alternatives might have been. Consequentialist computations of likely risk and relative cost are entirely irrelevant here. Human suffering is not to be quantified in this way. Nuclear weapons are not instruments of defence.

To Deploy Nuclear Weapons is to Subscribe to a Declared Policy Which Commits us to Using Them Should Deterrence Fail

We turn now to the way in which nuclear forces have been integrated into the military establishments of the major powers, and so into the fabric of international affairs, since 1945. Many people fail to grasp the fundamental significance of the fact that this involves a publicly declared intention to use these weapons should deterrence fail. It is essential for the effectiveness of our deterrent threat that the potential enemy should know that we have both the capability and the will to invoke the nuclear option if our threat is ignored. There must be seen to be no intentional gap between deployment and use – *if* our threat is ignored, we *will* use our weapons. In order that there should be no doubt about this in the enemy's mind, we commit ourselves to it by the way we dispose of our forces. They are deployed with the express intention that in certain circumstances they will be used. We hope that it will not come to this. We hope that our threat will prevent it. But, if it does not, then we will use them. There can be no doubt about this, and it is an illusion to think otherwise, an illusion not shared by those whose whole training has been to design, manufacture, base, target, service, man, operate, and, if necessary, fire the weapons. For example, British Polaris ballistic missile submarines are permanently targeted on Soviet centres of population (the elaborate Chevaline warhead system has recently been fitted to the missiles with the specific aim of penetrating the defences around Moscow), and the crews are trained to fire the missiles when the order is given.

To pretend that we can somehow separate deterrent threat from conditional intention to use, as some moralists have tried to do, is to be disingenuous. To deploy our weapons is to commit ourselves to their use in circumstances, which, by the nature of deterrence, it will not be in our power to control. In other words, the gap between deployment and use is circumstantial, not intentional. It is not a moral gap. There is no such thing as a fully deployed weapons system which is a bluff.

Such a Policy is Therefore in Itself Immoral

The conclusion is inescapable and must be squarely faced. It is wrong to use nuclear weapons. To deploy nuclear weapons involves a publicly declared conditional intention to use them. Therefore, since a conditional intention to do what is wrong is itself wrong, it is wrong to deploy nuclear weapons. That disposition, deliberately institutionalized to make it irrevocable, and openly proclaimed as such, is already thoroughly and deeply immoral.

These Resources Should be Directed Instead Towards Constructive Social and Economic Goals

In addition to everything that has been argued above, it is economically, socially, and psychologically damaging that such large human and material resources should be devoted to the destructive technologies of nuclear weaponry. If we ask what the connection is between this and the other great scandal of our day, the widening gulf between the affluent and impoverished regions of the world, it is easy to argue that the relationship is tenuous. It is true that the problem of nuclear weaponry is only part of the broader problem of armaments industries in general, and that there are broader causes still for global poverty and starvation. But the fact remains that, if the money and resources devoted to the build-up of nuclear armaments were directed instead towards strengthening the economies of under-developed countries, and alleviating the suffering caused by widespread malnutrition and disease, many of these scourges of mankind could be drastically reduced, and some of them eliminated altogether.

But what is even more immediately outrageous here is that nuclear weapon policies in the so-called 'advanced' countries of the rich north are putting millions of innocent people in the poorer parts of the world at risk. It is monstrous that peoples living in countries which have no say in nuclear weapon policy and nothing to do with the squabbles which are said to justify it, should be directly or indirectly targeted as a result. By what right do a handful of nuclear strategists in the rich, white north impose this terrible threat against humanity? It is an appalling example of man's inhumanity to man. Recurrent protest in the United Nations expresses justified global resentment against such unprecedented disregard for other people's fundamental rights.

The nuclear warhead and the begging bowl are the most potent symbols of our day. They represent the quintessence of human hatred and human need, and their coexistence in the world is what is most deeply wicked about it.

Christian Teaching Is Incompatible With a Strategy of Nuclear Deterrence

For all these reasons Christians must take the same view. No doubt the heart of the Christian message is purely spiritual, but the Gospels clearly teach important lessons about human conduct in this world, and the churches have from the beginning necessarily been concerned with the right ordering of life on earth. Moreover, it is evident that Christ laid great emphasis, not only upon right conduct, but above all upon right intention. So there can be no reconciliation or compromise between the teaching about Christian love enshrined in the Sermon on the Mount or in the Second Commandment, and the kinds of action and intention inevitably involved in nuclear weapon development and deployment. If in their official pronouncements particular Christian churches do not yet say this clearly, it is because the complexity of their relationship with the state forces them to cloud the issue in diplomatic ambiguity. But on Christian grounds there can be no justification whatsoever for the continued possession of nuclear weapons as a deterrent by any state, and the only Christian policy for the citizens of a state which does possess them to adopt is to work strenuously towards their immediate elimination.

The Argument About Rationality

We now turn from the argument about morality to the argument about rationality. In other words, leaving aside any further concern with our own culpability for the possible consequences of our actions, we turn our attention instead to the relative risks which we ourselves run by persisting in them. Does our possession of nuclear weapons make the world a safer or a more dangerous place?

There Can be no Coherent Strategy for the Use of Nuclear Weapons in War

The theory of Mutual Nuclear Deterrence itself lays down as axiomatic that it can never be in the interest of either side to carry out its deterrent threat. At any level below that of full strategic retaliation, the carrying out of the threat would invite unacceptable counter-devastation in fulfilment of the enemy's counter-threat; while, after a full strategic enemy first strike, the original purpose for which a retaliatory second strike was threatened would have been entirely lost. In addition, if the enemy had held back his own second strike forces, our retaliation would only bring down even worse retribution on our heads. The accident at Chernobyl, not equivalent even to the detonation of a single small warhead, has in any case demonstrated conclusively how unpredictable the consequences of a nuclear strike would be. In war-fighting conditions, both sides would be relying on entirely untested capabilities at a time when command and control systems were themselves under fierce attack. All talk of firing a 'warning shot', or of attacking an 'isolated military target', or, more generally, of 'fighting a limited nuclear war', is beside the point. It is not a question of whether or not we can imagine a nuclear war being terminated after the first few exchanges. The fact is that, as everyone agrees, we simply do not know what would happen, and, in those circumstances, no responsible civilian or military commander could possibly contemplate taking such a risk.

Concepts as axiomatic to traditional military thinking as 'defence', 'victory', 'weapon', or 'war', seem empty of meaning in this context. If it came to it, a general nuclear exchange could not be said to constitute a 'defence' of devastated areas, or a 'victory' for either side, nor could the instruments of devastation be called 'weapons' in any recognizable sense. 'Instantaneous mutual destruction' is not 'war'. In short, there can be no sane military-strategic justification for the mutual use of nuclear weapons. In this context, 'nuclear weapons strategy' is a contradiction in terms. Nuclear warheads are not weapons of war.

Therefore There Can Be No Coherent and Credible Strategy for Mutual Nuclear Deterrence Based Upon the Threat of Such Use

In classical, non-nuclear, deterrence theory, an enemy is deterred from acting in a certain way if he is convinced in advance that we have both the capacity to inflict unacceptable damage upon him, and the intention of doing so should he nevertheless proceed. He must believe that in the event we will carry out our threat – that it will be in our interest to do so. The threat must be credible. It must be grounded in credible plans for military action should deterrence fail. But we have seen that this is precisely what the theory of Mutual Nuclear Deterrence rules out. It says that it can never be in the interest of either side to carry out its threat. And both sides know this. So the theory fatally undermines itself. For Mutual Nuclear Deterrence theory to work, each side must be rational enough to recognize that the other might be irrational enough nevertheless to carry out his threat, even though it can clearly never be in his interest to do so. And this must hold true indefinitely, no matter who the future nuclear weapon powers are, or how desperate and confused a sudden and unexpected political crisis may be, or how limited the military options one side is tempted to take up in those circumstances. Mutual Nuclear Deterrence must deter, not only from nuclear war, but from all war between nuclear capable states, because, as has always been recognized, if it ever failed to do this, we would, to put it mildly, be in a far more dangerous position than we would have been in had we not been relying on nuclear deterrence at all. Once again, it is the theory of Mutual Nuclear Deterrence itself which dictates as much. That is exactly the threat that is said to underpin Mutual Nuclear Deterrence in the first place. It is all or nothing. So we are asked to believe that at no point in the future will a nuclear weapon state calculate that it can risk small-scale military action in a desperate situation, because the other will be inhibited from a full nuclear response for fear of retaliation. (The main reason why this has not happened already is because, for entirely different reasons, no two nuclear weapon states have so far found that their vital interests conflict. The political situation has not been as desperate as that. There is no reason to suppose that this will continue indefinitely to be the case.) A good example of all this is provided by the main official justification for Britain's retention of independent nuclear forces. The argument is that these forces are necessary for fully effective deterrence in Europe, because otherwise the Soviet Union might calculate that the United States would be inhibited from the nuclear defence of Europe for fear of reprisal.

So Mutual Nuclear Deterrence theory undermines its own credibility. That is why those who have asked strategists and military commanders to explain the purpose of their elaborate battle preparations have found that their answers are inconsistent and incoherent. Current strategies of Mutual Nuclear Deterrence, ultimately based on the premise that it cannot be rational for either side to expect victory in the context of a nuclear war, are incompatible with current strategies for fighting and winning a nuclear war should deterrence fail. Each depends upon the other, yet at the same time subverts it. This introduces a dangerous and ineradicable instability into the heart of defensive systems said to be constructed around the principle of Mutual Nuclear Deterrence. Loss of credibility of this kind is a spectre that has haunted nuclear strategists from the beginning. It is a spectre that they can never exorcise.

As a Result of This Inherent Lack of Credibility, Strategists are Driven to Embrace Increasingly Unstable Expedients at Other Levels in a Vain Attempt to Compensate For it

But the most serious dangers that we face spring directly and inevitably from the efforts of nuclear strategists to compensate for the lack of credibility of the system. Those who have committed us to indefinite reliance upon the myth of Mutual Nuclear Deterrence for a secure and stable defence, have, as a result, to go to any lengths to restore apparent credibility to the deterrent threat. How are they to do this? We have already seen that one reaction is to encourage proliferation – in this case independent European nuclear forces. They are also forced to adopt one or other version of 'Flexible Response' strategy.

Flexible Response covers conventional as well as nuclear options. So far as concerns the latter, it aims to enhance the credibility of deterrence by deliberately lowering the nuclear threshold and making it seem more likely that nuclear weapons will be used. It aims to convince the enemy that we have the capacity to use nuclear weapons in a whole range of limited military actions, and that if need be we fully intend to do so. In order to remove every shadow of doubt, we commit ourselves to this. We deliberately plan for nuclear war-fighting and base the whole of our military strategy upon it. We blur the distinction between conventional and nuclear weapons. We deploy dual-capable missiles, aircraft and artillery, which can fire conventional and nuclear munitions, with the result that an enemy will not know if he faces the possibility of conventional or nuclear attack. We develop nuclear rockets, bombs, shells, mines, torpedoes, depth charges, of every level of yield, some constructed to maximize heat and blast effects, some, like the neutron bomb, to maximize nuclear radiation. We deliberately scatter large numbers of these in the potential battle-zone among our conventional forces, in some cases no more than twenty miles from the frontier, so that it is inevitable that they must be used before they are overrun. We evolve multiple missile warheads of increasing sophistication and accuracy, some soon said to be capable of falling on average within 150 feet of a chosen target at a range of 8000 miles. This allows us to elaborate targeting options for a wide variety of limited selective strikes. We try to orchestrate all of this within a battle plan made up of a more and more complicated overlapping of computerized command and control systems, in which the flood of material to be processed, fear of preemption, and increasing pressure of time, threaten to squeeze human decision-making out of the process altogether. As reaction times narrow (to within a few seconds of launch, if we are to intercept enemy ballistic missiles during their boost phase, as envisaged in plans for Strategic Defence), so we approach the logical terminus for a policy whose aim is to maximize credibility – Launch on Warning. The response will be virtually automatic. The result of all this is that nuclear war-fighting strategies, which are usually presented as underpinning 'deterrence' when political conditions are in any case fairly stable, are almost certain to precipitate nuclear war in conditions of acute political crisis. In the confused swirl of events, all that is needed to bring this about is for one side to *think* that the other is contemplating a strike of some kind. Neither can possibly allow the other to go first. No matter what the declared policy may be, battle plans on both sides are inevitably committed to striking first in these circumstances. Apart from anything else, technology dictates as much. Accurate counter-force systems targeted on enemy missile silos, *must* be fired before those missiles are launched. There would be no point in hitting an empty silo. Political leaders will lose control to military nuclear strategists at this early stage. Flexible Response policies have made sure that there will be a collapse into war.

So the only way in which we can restore credibility to our deterrent threat is by making nuclear war progressively more likely. Lulled into a false sense of security by the fact that, for political reasons which have little to do with nuclear weaponry, we have so far escaped catastrophe, we foolishly continue to pursue policies which make that catastrophe more and more probable. The situation can be summed up like this: *DETERRENCE DEMANDS CREDIBILITY, BUT CREDIBILITY UNDERMINES DETER-RENCE.* The system is dangerously self-defeating.

Unfortunately, it is also self-reinforcing and self-accelerating. It is important to understand that it is *because* it is fundamentally unstable that it has continually to expand. For example, in the search for security and credibility, each side inevitably contrasts its own peaceful *intentions* with the other's sinister *capabilities*. That is why the idea of 'nuclear parity' is such a dangerous chimaera. In order to guarantee a 'defensive second strike capability', each side needs a preponderance of force which is indistinguishable from preparations for a counter-force preemptive strike. The United States sees Soviet land-based Intercontinental Ballistic Missiles in this way. What to the Americans is 'restoring the balance', and to the Russians is 'catching up', is inevitably seen by the other as a drive for superiority. There is no such thing as a purely 'defensive' nuclear system – even civil defence measures appear aggressive to the other side, while a 'defensive shield', such as the US Strategic Defence Initiative aims to create, is profoundly threatening to the Soviet Union. If two gladiators are armed with swords, the idea of one of them acquiring a shield does not seem at all 'defensive' to the other. Against this background, worst-case analysis, combined with unavoidable force-structure and geographical asymmetries, generate further phases of the arms race. That is why arms control negotiations substantially fail. Each side tries to 'negotiate from strength'. But the 'bargaining chip', intended to force the other to yield ground in exchange, only serves to stimulate further rivalry. The Strategic Defence Initiative, presented in some quarters as a means of bringing the Soviet Union to the negotiating table, in fact forces the Soviets to reciprocate, both by increasing offensive capabilities in order to penetrate the shield, and by constructing their own comparable systems. In the process it threatens to unravel the Anti-Ballistic Missile treaty, and carries with it very dangerous implications for anti-satellite operations, and, eventually, for the creation of offensive battle-stations and the deployment of nuclear weapons in space.

'Mutual Nuclear Deterrence' is the wrong term for all of this. It is simply Nuclear Confrontation. And the most palpable expression of the logic of Nuclear Confrontation is the Nuclear Arms Race.

There is an In-built Momentum to the Nuclear Arms Race Which Ensures the Continuing Proliferation of Nuclear Weapons Systems Unless Checked by a Conscious Change of Policy

The argument so far has shown why reliance on the myth of 'Mutual Nuclear Deterrence' leads to increasingly dangerous attempts to compensate for its inadequacy. In addition, it is important to see how, in the process, it creates the structural and conceptual inertia which perpetuates it. It propagates its own accelerating technologies, spawns its own vested interests committed to their exploitation, and generates its own conceptual justification for their development into fully deployed weapons-systems. The system is self-propelled, self-protective, and self-aggrandizing, which makes it very difficult to slow down, let alone halt or turn back.

Prudent contingency planning demands continual investment in all aspects of new technology in order to keep options open, perhaps decades ahead, so that every possible enemy programme can be matched and uncertain future security needs prepared for. This opens the door to every kind of research project, however dangerous its implications may be. In this way, the highly destabilising technologies of multiple re-entry vehicles, counter-force first strike guidance systems, enhanced radiation warheads, anti-satellite and anti-submarine capabilities, and the host of enterprises loosely covered by the blanket term 'Strategic Defence', have been and are being indiscriminately spawned. The funding is often allotted with undemocratic secrecy, both for 'security' reasons, and on the grounds that, since these are only 'research' programmes, they can be debated publicly later, if and when it looks likely that the systems may become operational.

But, by the time the matter comes to public attention, resources have already been earmarked and some already spent, deeply committed vested interests have been aroused and ministerial reputations are at stake. There is, for example, the institutionalized dynamic of research establishments, the intense rivalry between design and manufacturing consortia, the competing claims and traditions of the various armed services, all hedged around by the inertia of a growing bureaucracy.

The result of all this is that so-called 'public debate' is little more than post hoc rationalization and window-dressing, a public relations exercise, in which the enemy is projected as powerful and malevolent, and the defence measures as therefore essential to national security. Those who argue againt them are branded as ignorant and eccentric extremists at best, and at worst dangerous and subversive fifth columnists. Arguments are picked up and dropped as and when the occasion suits. For example, the moment it became clear that a Comprehensive Test Ban Treaty could no longer be blocked on the grounds of the impossibility of verification, opposition switched to the argument that it would be dangerous if old stock was not modernized or tested for safety. In this way every attempt to achieve substantial cuts, or to secure a Declaration of No First Use, a European Nuclear Weapon Free Zone, a Nuclear Weapons Freeze, and so on, is defeated. Instead, almost any and every weapons system made feasible by the blind development of technology is found a justification, even if it means reversing what had previously been argued. Lethal counter-force first strike systems, like Trident or Pershing II, which would have been seen as highly destabilising a few years ago, are now said to 'enhance deterrence', while, in the inverted mirror-language of Nuclear Deterrence Strategy, the equally dangerous MX missile is called 'Peacekeeper'. Research is approved, which makes it increasingly easy and cost-effective for smaller powers, and even sub-national groups, to acquire nuclear weapons, while an attempt is made to maintain that the arguments which justify the retention of nuclear weapons by existing nuclear weapon powers, do not at the same time apply to their acquisition by others. Most remarkable of all, in order to provide a rationale for the burgeoning technologies associated with Strategic Defence, apologists attempt at the same time to claim that these will enhance deterrence by protecting second strike systems, and dismantle deterrence by rendering them obsolete. They say that both of these outcomes would be good: the former, because nuclear deterrence is moral and safe (Henry Kissinger); the latter, because nuclear deterrence is immoral and dangerous (Ronald Reagan). As a final act of outrageous sophistry, those responsible for the most significant acceleration in nuclear weapons programmes in recent years pose as nuclear disarmers and speak of their desire to rid the world of nuclear weapons.

But there can be no halt to the nuclear arms race, let alone progress towards nuclear disarmament, so long as defence establishments continue to subscribe to the myth of nuclear deterrence, and build and refine nuclear stockpiles as if they were traditional war-fighting armouries. The so-called alternative between 'unilaterialism' and 'multilateralism' is a false one. It is propagated by those who call themselves 'multilateral disarmers', in an attempt to discredit their critics as weak-minded pacifists. In fact, they are not disarmers at all, but nuclear confrontationists, and it is they, not their critics, who are responsible for running down Western defences. They deliberately exaggerate Soviet non-nuclear power in order to justify an indefinite reliance on nuclear weapons, and Soviet nuclear power in order to justify a continuous build up of them. The former leads to a quite unnecessary neglect of Western non-nuclear defences, and the latter helps to perpetuate the cold war antagonism on which the whole system feeds. The only true alternative is between substantial, and, if necessary, unconditional, cuts offered by both sides as part of a broader shift of strategy towards properly effective non-nuclear defence (which the present absurd superfluity of nuclear arsenals makes safe even by the criteria of Mutual Nuclear Deterrence), and a continuing escalation and proliferation of nuclear weaponry, which fatally endangers us all.

2

The Case in Favour of Continued Nuclear Weapon Deployment

The Argument About Rationality

The Question of Nuclear Weapon Deployment Must be Debated With Reference to the World as It Is, Not An Imagined World as We Might Ideally Wish It to Be

The first thing to be acknowledged here is that we live in the nuclear age. Whatever happens, nuclear weapons will remain a potent political fact. They have been an integral part of world politics since the end of the Second World War, and, for better or worse, present arrangements have been constrained, and perhaps in a number of cases shaped, by their existence. Whether we like it or not, global politics has been, is, and for the foreseeable future will continue to be, conducted in terms of them.

Secondly, we must not make the mistake of concentrating so exclusively on nuclear weapons, that we forget the wider realities of international politics and of non-nuclear military confrontation. No doubt, if we could reorganize the world community as we wanted, in order to eliminate conflict and perceived injustice, say under the aegis of a revivified United Nations, then general nuclear disarmament would be a feasible, and, indeed, an integral part of the process. But at the moment this all seems very remote in a century which has seen two world wars, followed by a period of intense rivalry between the main power blocs of East and West, together with innumerable bitter regional conflicts. There is no immediate prospect of a final resolution to these tensions, nor of a reduction in the general level of arms spending – of which the cost of nuclear weapons is no more than a fraction. It is within this context that nuclear weapons evolved in the first place, and it is only against this background that the question of nuclear disarmament can realistically be discussed.

Thirdly, we can argue here only in terms of what Western policy should be. It is idle to speculate upon how the Soviet Union ought or ought not to behave, when we have no control over Soviet strategy. We are faced with the fact that the Soviet Union is a power with an uncongenial ideology, very few internal constraints, and very limited public morality. She has a clear military superiority at non-nuclear level in Europe, and her geographical position alone gives her a massive advantage over the Western allies, whose reinforcements have to be flown or shipped in across three thousand miles of ocean. She also has considerable nuclear forces at strategic, theatre and battlefield levels. It does not really matter whether we regard her as an aggressive and expansionist, or as an encircled and threatened, power – whether we see the invasion of Afghanistan as part of a drive to the Gulf, or as an attempt to prevent a militant Islam from infecting the southern Soviet republics. An insecure regime will often behave more violently than a confident one. Either way, the fact of her colossal military might remains. This again is an inescapable aspect of the world we live in, and the nuclear weapons debate must be conducted with reference to it. To try to ignore it is to be irresponsible and naive.

Nuclear Deterrence Has Played an Essential Part in Preserving World Peace at Great Power Level for the Past Forty Years

Before 1945, open war between the great powers was endemic. Now it seems increasingly unthinkable. Armed conflict has been marginalized to the peripheries, to be fought out through proxies – and perhaps now even that is beginning to die away. No doubt a number of factors have contributed to this remarkable transformation, including the growing cohesion and strength of Western Europe and the firm commitment of American troops to its defence, the monolithic stability of the Eastern bloc, and the fact that the frontier between them has been so clearly and brutally defined. But it is hard not to think that in the dangerous years after the Second World War the Western possession of an actual or virtual nuclear monopoly helped to prevent, first the Soviet Union, then the People's Republic of China, from risking a third world war by using their overwhelming advantage in manpower to occupy the power vacuum left by the eclipse of Germany and Japan. Or that, since then, peace between the superpowers has been underpinned by mutual possession of potent nuclear arsenals.

Deterrence ultimately rests on the possession of an invulnerable and overwhelming second strike nuclear capability. It has never been supposed in NATO, for example, that this will on its own prevent war, but it remains the ultimate and essential anchor at the end of the chain of deterrent options. Without it, an enemy might think that we could be trumped; with it, the traditional idea of an escalating contest in strengths becomes meaningless. At the end lies annihilation. No sane military adviser could recommend to the leaders in the Kremlin that victory lay in that direction. Thus, so long as both sides can remain confident that each retains a sufficient invulnerable reserve force of this kind – and that each knows this, and knows that the other knows it – then the classical military option of complete strategic victory is effectively closed.

In these circumstances, the only basis upon which either side could rationally risk the use of force, even conventional force, would be a belief that for some reason the other would choose to stop rather than go on. It is, for example, possible to imagine that, if the Russians perceived that once they had overborne our conventional resistance the only option that we had left was to destroy their cities and have ours destroyed in return, they might think that our threat was incredible and proceed on that assumption. That is why, almost from the beginning, NATO policy has been to evolve limited force options, be they nuclear or conventional. Flexible response means that there is nothing that the enemy can do that will give him a cheap victory, and leave us with an obviously incredible leap to the next level of resistance.

Elaborate criticism of the 'theory' of nuclear deterrence ignores the simple fact that what has almost certainly deterred the great powers from risking even the most limited acts of direct armed aggression against one another has been the fear that this might set in motion an uncontrollable chain of increasingly catastrophic events – and the knowledge that whether this happened or not would not be in the sole power of either to dictate. The relative likely advantage to be gained from military adventures of any kind can no longer begin to match the enormity of the risks involved in embarking upon them. Each is a permanent hostage of the other. That is why to describe Western conventional and nuclear deterrent strategies as having dangerously 'lowered the threshold between conventional and nuclear war', as so many critics do, is misleading. The important thing that these strategies have effectively done is to *raise* the threshold between peace and war of any kind. The threshold is now so high that neither side dares to step over it. Nuclear weapons represent the *reductio ad absurdum* of armed conflict. At great power level the use of military force is no longer a rational option. War itself has become obsolete. Our policy is to make sure that it remains that way.

Nuclear Deterrence is Likely to Remain Stable for the Foreseeable Future if Present Policies Are Broadly Maintained

In tacit recognition of what has been argued above, most critics of nuclear deterrence claim that the conditions which have so far helped to preserve peace at great power level are not likely to persist. In doing so, they show that they have fundamentally misunderstood the nature of deterrence, and at several points blatantly contradict themselves. What are the dangers that they say we face?

First, they say that new generations of nuclear weapons will be destabilizing, because they threaten a preemptive counter-force first strike. In fact, there is no prospect whatsoever of anything like this being achieved – as critics themselves tend inconsistently to argue apropos of the Strategic Defence Initiative.

The complex array of strategic options now available to both superpowers (including, for example, the continuing near invulnerability of SSBN submarines once at sea, despite recent improvements in ASW technology); the tendency of advances in one area to be balanced, often unexpectedly, by advances in another, so long as neither side unaccountably allows the other an unchallenged ascendancy; the remarkable weight/yield ratio of nuclear warheads, which ensures that almost anything short of one hundred per cent success would still invite a devastating and unacceptable counter-blow – these are some of the reasons why it will remain quite irrational for any power to attempt anything as suicidal as a preemptive first strike. It is an operation of enormous risk, and therefore of enormous improbability, and there is nothing on the horizon which is remotely likely to change that. This is all part of a broader point. Critics often argue that the number and variety of nuclear warheads and delivery systems held by both sides is in itself destabilizing and dangerous. This is quite untrue. There are particular systems that have been said to be unsafe and have been modified or withdrawn as a result, and it is also generally acknowledged that current arsenals are unnecessarily wasteful, which is why both sides are trying to agree substantial mutual reductions. But the mere fact that you have got 10,000 weapons, where 1000 would do, is not in itself dangerous. There is a massive stability to the system. The tolerances are enormous. In fact, it is probably true that exactly the opposite is the case, and that some of the critics' points would begin to have more force if arsenals were reduced too *low*. This would particularly apply to the Western 'extended' deterrent, which has to protect Western Europe as well as the United States. To have too few is, if anything, more dangerous than to have too many.

Similar arguments apply to the American Strategic Defence Initiative. Neither in its most ambitious form (a defensive astrodome protecting civilians from ballistic missile attack), nor in the more restricted version (a screen to improve the survivability of the land-based missile force) can it yet be said to be destabilizing. It is a research programme, made up of a large number of projects that were going on anyway, many of which are similar to comparable Soviet initiatives, and necessary for that reason. There is nothing alarming in the idea that offensive weapons may be totally or partially countered by defensive weapons. Why should our security necessarily be enhanced if the superiority of offence over defence is artificially and indefinitely frozen? Critics, who argue like this, are in fact unwittingly subscribing to the permanent enthronement of the theory of Mutual Assured Destruction. If it turns out that both sides can build a more or less effective shield, and at the same time agree on significant cuts in offensive systems, critics should rejoice. Our efforts will have gone into destroying missiles, not people, and at last the universal fear of nuclear annihilation may begin to recede. If we do no more than protect our second strike forces more comprehensively, then at least we have further reduced the incentive for an aggressor to attack. But at the moment the Strategic Defence Initiative is simply a research programme. We must wait and see what options, if any, it opens up for us, before we start making judgements about whether or not this will enhance our security.

And now we come to a cluster of criticisms, which together make up the central misapprehension about the nature of deterrence. It is said that new generations of theatre weapons and the integration of conventional and nuclear forces make a slide towards nuclear war more likely, while the increasing complexity and vulnerability of command and control structures make inadvertent war more probable, and escalation from limited to general nuclear war almost inevitable once the threshold has been crossed. NATO is said to have adopted a war-fighting strategy. This is entirely to misunderstand the situation. To say that NATO is thinking, not of deterrence, but of war-fighting, is to try to make a nonsensical distinction. Weapons deter only as a result of their capacity for use. The two cannot be separated. In the same way, the fear that armed aggression will trigger a vigorous response, perhaps nuclear, and perhaps escalating towards a more general exchange, is precisely what deters from armed aggression in the first place. Without that fear there would be no deterrence. That is not to say that everything possible should not be done to ensure that war will not break out accidentally or that a limited exchange cannot be contained. If deterrence failed, none of us can know what would happen. The situation might deteriorate, or the shock might soon bring us to our senses. We would all hope that it must be the latter, since it could be in no-one's interest for it to be the former. In those extreme and terrifying conditions, it is hard to see why we have to believe that leaders are more likely deliberately to court their own destruction than to pull back. But at the moment all of this is beside the point. It is the universal fear of what might happen if the worst came to the worst that is most likely to prevent it from happening. And to reduce that fear, as critics want, is to make it more likely that it will happen.

Finally, we are told that, if we do not reverse direction and swiftly abandon our nuclear deterrent policies, we face an alarming acceleration in the nuclear arms race between the established nuclear weapon states, sustained by its own in-build psychological and institutional inertia, and an inevitable and highly dangerous proliferation of nuclear weapons to other as yet non-nuclear or semi-nuclear powers. A parallel is drawn with the years before the First World War. This is a gross simplification of a complex situation. There is no 'nuclear arms race' in the sense of two athletes racing one another around a track, nor what is often described in shorthand as a sinister and all-powerful 'military-industrial complex', dedicated to the indiscriminate and perpetual pullulation of nuclear weapons systems. There have, of course, been examples of unnecessary direct emulation between the superpowers, but there have also been examples of restraint. All sorts of factors govern the evolution of nuclear force structure. It is also true that there are pressures from various directions to deploy what you can build – particularly in the Soviet Union – but there are also any number of pressures in other directions. The Americans, for example, spent less on nuclear weapons in the 1970s than they did in the 1950s, and the overall megatonnage of their arsenal today is lower than it was in the 1960s. This is not a runaway system, and no useful comparison can be made with the entirely different conditions in 1914 (which are often misinterpreted, in any case). Overall, central procurement decisions in the West are guided by strategic requirements, and the great stability of deterrence today is a testimony to the good judgement that has, in general, prevailed.

As to the danger of the proliferation of nuclear weapons to, as yet, non-nuclear powers, the process has been slowed down dramatically during the past twenty years and there seems no reason why it should accelerate again. There are a number of technological, psychological and political factors reinforcing restraint. In any case, nothing that the present major nuclear powers can do on their own will prevent the possibility that the continuing international diversification of nuclear reactor capacity may be employed to manufacture warheads. This is a fact that we have to live with, and is best met by negotiation at national, regional and international levels, as in the past, not by irrelevant appeals for superpower disarmament. In the meantime, the size of the nuclear forces deployed by the superpowers ensures global stability and thus reduces the pressure towards regional proliferation, while, so long as there nevertheless still remains a small but real risk of the eventual spread of nuclear weapons to countries like Libya and Iran, it is essential for the mature and advanced nuclear powers to keep their deterrents.

Immediate Global Nuclear Disarmament Would Increase the Risk of War – Including Nuclear War

But the greatest weakness in the case presented by radical nuclear disarmers lies in their reluctance even to consider the possibility that the alternatives which they propose might carry far greater risks than the policies which they are so busy criticising. In fact, global nuclear disarmament is an entirely unreal fantasy for the foreseeable future. It will not happen. But, since critics of current policies so often refuse to recognize this, it is important to confront them on their own ground, and to explore the implications of their rhetoric. Even if immediate global disarmament were feasible, would it be desirable? The answer can be easily given. No.

At the moment it is Mutual Nuclear Deterrence at superpower level which forces restraint and accommodation between the great power blocs, and means that regional conflicts are contained without threatening world war. It is generally recognized that war between nuclear weapon states is no longer a rational option. This means that, not only nuclear weapons themselves, but also the most potent non-nuclear military forces in the world, are becoming ritualistic and symbolic. There is a widely shared hope that, as a result, they may eventually be seen to be unnecessary, and may be progressively reduced by a natural process of prudent resource management. Under the nuclear umbrella the world community is, perhaps, slowly learning to settle disputes without recourse to military action.

What would happen if there were precipitate nuclear disarmament? All of this would be jeopardized. Without the chief constraint on military aggression, the main long-term motive for reducing non-nuclear forces would have been removed, and war between the great powers would again become a rational option. Particularly, in view of the overwhelming Soviet advantage in non-nuclear forces, chemical as well as conventional, the whole stability of the European theatre would be recklessly undermined. There can be little doubt that there would be a greater likelihood that military solutions would be sought at local level, and that this would be more likely to spill over into war. And we must also remember how terrible a future conventional war would be – something which an obsessive preoccupation with nuclear weapons encourages us to forget. And, once a conventional war had broken out, both sides would almost certainly be racing one another to reactivate their nuclear weapons programmes. No matter what the nature of international law, global nuclear disarmament would increase dramatically the advantages to be gained from cheating – and therefore the incentives to do so. In short, global nuclear disarmament would make nuclear war more, not less, likely. This is the central irony that radical nuclear disarmers seem either unable or unwilling to understand.

We are not even considering here the suggestion, heard in some quarters, that the West should unilaterally give up its nuclear deterrent, or one-sidedly emasculate it by a series of progressive unconditional cuts. It hardly needs to be said that, among other things, this would simply invite Soviet pressure through covert or overt nuclear blackmail, would greatly strengthen the reactionary elements within the Soviet state, and would abruptly, and perhaps permanently, set back the process of stabilization and détente. It would be a policy of the greatest irresponsibility.

So global nuclear disarmament remains a distant goal. But it is only feasible and desirable in a world where the incentive to war has in any case been removed. And critics should remember that, after centuries of bloodshed, culminating in the holocausts of the First and Second World Wars, it is above all the existence of nuclear weapons, which now makes that distant prospect even remotely possible to reach.

The Argument About Morality

In Public Affairs it is Morally Right to Prefer the Policy Most Likely to Maximize Human Welfare and Minimize Human Suffering

Those who criticise current nuclear deterrent strategy on moral grounds like to suggest that we are faced with a choice between right and wrong. Unfortunately, as in most areas of public life, we are dealing with something which is more difficult and more uncomfortable than that. We are being asked to choose between evils. In order to highlight the moral dilemma, we will describe three possible developments. In the first there is unconditional unilateral nuclear renunciation. In the second the renunciation is universal. In the third we carry on with current nuclear deterrent policies.

What would have happened if, during the course of the Second World War, at a point where it was becoming clear that Hitler could not overcome the Allied armies with his conventional forces, and had apparently been thrown back irrevocably onto the defensive, his scientists, technologists and manufacturers had developed an ample supply of atomic bombs for the Luftwaffe, or atomic warheads for his new V-2 rockets? And let us suppose that, at the same time, Allied leaders, who could have developed this technology first, had instead chosen to renounce it on moral grounds. Can we think that Hitler would have felt any scruple about doing to the Allies what the Allies in the event did to Japan? And would the Allies have had any option but to surrender? And what would the result have been for millions of people considered expendable by the Nazi regime? What state would the world be in today? What prospects would there be for the future? Even the horror of Hiroshima is eclipsed by the horror of Auschwitz. We will not attempt to describe it. And would we, in the light of this, be applauding the Allied leaders of the time for the tenderness of their moral consciences? Or cursing them for irresponsibly preferring private scruple to public welfare?

Now let us imagine that the world is as it is today, except that no power is stocking or deploying nuclear weapons. We will ignore the fact that there are chemical and biological weapons. We will also ignore the fact that the present mood of accommodation between the great powers has only been developed within the constraints of nuclear weapon deployment. In several years time, let us say, there is acute political crisis in Eastern Europe, triggered by deteriorating economic conditions and the advent of a new hard-line government in Moscow. In response to unrest in East Germany, and fearing a revival of German nationalism, the Soviet leaders decide to occupy West Berlin, calculating that the immediate gain in terms of the reimposition of Soviet authority over the region outweighs the risk of Western conventional retaliation. In the resulting confusion, the situation deteriorates towards war. Casualties are enormous, and, while the outcome hangs in the balance, both sides feverishly reactivate their nuclear weapons programmes. Precipitate nuclear disarmament has brought the world to the brink of nuclear war.

Finally we return to the situation as it is now. Nuclear weapons continue to be deployed by the great powers well on into the next century. It continues to be recognized on all sides that war between nuclear weapon states is manifest lunacy. As a result, political solutions have to be found to what would have been seen earlier as military problems. There are, of course, political crises, as there have been since the end of the Second World War, but these are contained within the bounds determined by mutual fear of war. Slowly, the world community evolves towards a future in which nuclear weapons, already half symbolic and ritualistic, become decreasingly significant, as conventional armaments are themselves reduced. This does not happen because leaders are all at once converted to the idea that it is wicked to deploy conventional arms, but because current levels of arms spending are seen to be grossly wasteful when the weapons themselves are never likely to be used. We have slowly come to realize that the age of warfare is over. Nuclear weapons have made war itself obsolete.

These are imagined scenarios. But they help to make the central point that IF these were the alternatives, THEN it must clearly be moral to continue to deploy nuclear weapons as a deterrent. And to do otherwise would be, if not immoral, then grossly irresponsible. In fact, in the Argument about Rationality we have shown that a policy of continuing nuclear deterrence of the kind described there is the one most likely to protect our liberties and prevent war, whereas a policy of precipitate nuclear disarmament, whether unilateral or multilateral, is likely to have the opposite effect. So on these grounds the question has already been answered. It is undoubtedly moral for us to continue to prefer a nuclear deterrent policy.

But some critics, who are prepared to accept the Argument about Rationality, nevertheless continue to condemn nuclear deterrent policies, because they say that they infringe certain absolute moral prohibitions, which override all prudential considerations. We must now turn to meet this challenge. Are all possible uses of nuclear weapons morally unacceptable? And is to deploy nuclear weapons to intend to use them in this way?

Our Intention in Deploying Nuclear Weapons is to Defend Freedom and Prevent War

A central argument of those who oppose the deployment of nuclear weapons on moral grounds is that to do so is conditionally to intend to perpetrate a criminal act.

But we no more intend the use of nuclear weapons (which would represent the failure of deterrence) than radical disarmers intend the triumph of totalitarianism and the outbreak of war (which would represent the failure of their policies).

The whole philosophy of intention is notoriously controversial and elusive, and certainly too indeterminate to carry the weight of categorical moral judgement often placed upon it by radical moralists. It is not clear whether there can even be a unified description for the various dispositions of those who are responsible for creating and maintaining our deterrent forces. Can they be said to 'intend' to use these weapons should deterrence fail? Most are no doubt full of uncertainty as to what would or should happen in those terrible circumstances. Nor is this a failing on their part. The central fact in all of this is, once again, that for the first time in history weapons have been developed, which, when mutually deployed, cannot be used to secure military victory in any recognized sense. Their only 'use' is to deter aggression and prevent war, and that alone is what we intend in deploying them.

If Deterrence Were Nevertheless to Fail, Just War Principles Should Govern the Use of Nuclear, as of Other, Weapons

Nevertheless, unlike most radical disarmers, who refuse even to contemplate the possibility that their programme might miscarry, those who support present defence policies are responsible enough to face the question: what if deterrence were to fail? Their attempts to plan for the limiting of a nuclear exchange once the threshold had been crossed, or for the reduction of loss and suffering through civil defence measures, are usually caricatured by unilateralist publicists as 'warmongering'. But these possibilities cannot be imagined away, and it must be recognized that war of any kind between the major powers today will involve such or similar considerations.

For example, radical disarmers must ask themselves an equivalent question: what if nuclear disarmament led to the outbreak of war between the great powers? Hitler's war cost fifty million lives. Was this a price worth paying? What price will be worth paying next time, in view of the destructiveness of modern conventional armaments, and the perpetual possibility of the use of biological, chemical and nuclear weapons? If the principle of discrimination was violated by the dropping of atomic bombs on Hiroshima and Nagasaki, so it was too by the saturation bombing of Dresden and Tokyo, which killed and injured larger numbers of civilians. And, by the principle of proportion, the former can be said to have been better justified than the latter on the grounds that it drastically shortened the war with Japan and saved innumerable lives. Conventional and nuclear deterrents are both based on threat. Current British nuclear deterrence threatens 'key aspects of Soviet state power'. What would a conventional deterrent threaten?

It is dangerous to concentrate our attention exclusively on nuclear weapons, as if other forms of modern armament did not raise comparable questions. Just War principles should govern the use of all weapons.

But let us not forget that the overwhelming factor in favour of a policy of continuing nuclear deterrence is that it makes all of this so unlikely to happen.

Therefore, in Present Circumstances and Within Careful Constraints, it is Morally Right for Us To Continue to Develop and Deploy Nuclear Weapons

We now return to the conclusion that we had already reached at the beginning of this section. We cannot wave a magic wand, resolve all international tension, and uninvent nuclear and other weapons. In these circumstances, a policy of continuing nuclear deterrence is the one most likely to preserve our liberty and prevent war between the great powers for the foreseeable future. A policy of radical nuclear disarmament, on the other hand, is likely to place our freedom in jeopardy and increase the risk of war – including nuclear war.

We have denied that nuclear weapon deployment necessarily involves a conditional intention to perpetrate criminal acts. So there is no absolute moral prohibition to override our earlier conclusion. What in the end matters when we are trying to determine public policy – what is morally central – is not whether particular individuals do or do not have particular motives or intentions, important though this is, but which courses of action are most likely to bring most benefit and prevent most harm to those in whose name the policy is being conducted.

There is No Relevant Connection Between the Development and Deployment of Nuclear Weapons and World Poverty and Disease

The attempt by moralists to link the question of nuclear weapons to the question of deprivation in the world is entirely spurious. Leaving aside more sophisticated analyses of the causes and possible remedies for global poverty, there are two points to be made here. First, if the finger is to be pointed at the richer nations for failing to transfer resources to the poorer, then it is the level of conspicuous consumption in general, not the single, relatively small, expense of nuclear weapon deployment, which is at issue. And, if the complaint is to do with the effects of militarization, then it is conventional, not nuclear, weaponry which should be of most concern. Secondly, if it is true, as we have argued, that nuclear weapon deployment is essential for global security, then it is in the best interest of all nations, rich and poor, that this should continue to be accepted policy. The equation, which moralists try to draw, is a false one.

Christian Teaching is Compatible With Such a Nuclear Deterrent Strategy

Let us first of all recognize that not one of the established churches, Catholic or Protestant, has officially ruled that Christian teaching is incompatible with continued nuclear weapon deployment. This question has been debated again and again during the past forty years with deep soul-searching and scrupulous care by leaders of all denominations. They have studied the factual evidence and weighed all the arguments pressed on either side. And still not one of the churches has come down in wholesale condemnation of the development, deployment and manning of nuclear weapons by Christians. This alone suggests that it is arrogant to claim in sweeping terms that Christian teaching is incompatible with current policies of nuclear deterrence.

Clearly, Christians hope for a time when there will be no further need for nuclear weapons. That will be a time when it is not just nuclear weapons that are done away with, but poverty, injustice and the threat of war. But we live in a fallen world, where evil threatens from every side, and, in such conditions, the only way in which the Christian magistrate can protect the innocent and defend the social and political values of a Christian commonwealth, is by being prepared himself to take up arms. He does this reluctantly, trying to respect the principles of proportion and discrimination, and never losing sight of the Christian ideals he is defending. This is the tradition of the Just War, developed by Christian theologians down the centuries. It is the tradition within which the principles of Just Deterrence are being worked out today. Those who are happy to let others take on the burden of defence, while keeping their own hands clean, are not to be admired. Those who want to forbid Christians to defend themselves in the nuclear age, and are prepared as a result to let evil triumph in this world, are perhaps to be respected for their private consistency, but must be strenuously opposed as publicly misguided and dangerous. Martyrs do not make good statesmen.

3

Analysis

How are we to come to terms with these two sets of arguments? Although at some points they are evidently contradictory, at others they seem to miss one another entirely. The main thrust of the argument about morality in Chapter 1 concerns the wickedness of evil intention, whether or not the action in question is ever carried out; in Chapter 2 it concerns a weighing up of the likely consequences of our actions, no matter what the original intention may have been. In Chapter 1 the starting-point for the argument about rationality is the unacceptable danger for mankind inherent in an indefinite reliance for defence on irrational and unstable nuclear war-fighting strategies; in Chapter 2 it is the need for the West to be able to continue to threaten nuclear retaliation in order to neutralize the Soviet military threat and stabilize global security. How can perspectives, which differ from one another as widely as this, be compared, let alone assessed?

Here, despite these difficulties, we offer an analysis, in which the arguments are laid out beside one another, point-by-point, so that we can see where and how they differ. They are also expanded in order to include a more detailed consideration of NATO and British options. The argument 'in favour' of a continuation of current policy is set out on the left-hand page, and the argument 'against' on the right. This may be thought to be perverse, in view of the usual assumption that it is the political right which favours nuclear weapon deployment, and the political left which does not. But, in fact, in the case of a number of the points being made here, this equation breaks down, so it is probably better not to assume it in the first place.

Each pair of arguments is accompanied by an editorial comment set in a different type face (the fact that the comment is shown on the right-hand page should not be taken to mean that it is to be identified with the argument immediately above it). The set of questions upon which this analysis is based is presented first in outline on pages 32–39. These are the questions to which the contributors in Part II have responded.

OUTLINE ANALYSIS OF POINTS AT ISSUE

PRUDENTIAL CONSIDERATIONS

A. *Global Policy*

  1. *The History of the Past Forty Years*

HAS THE BUILD-UP OF NUCLEAR ARSENALS SINCE 1945 INCREASED OR DECREASED THE DANGERS INVOLVED IN SUPERPOWER CONFRONTATION?

(i) Has it been nuclear deterrence that has kept the peace between the great powers since 1945? OR Has it mainly been other factors?

(ii) Does mutual possession of an invulnerable second strike strategic nuclear force prevent war? OR Does the threat of strategic nuclear retaliation, particularly against a similarly armed enemy, lack credibility and invite sub-deterrent encroachment?

(iii) Have limited nuclear options at strategic and theatre levels enhanced deterrence by dramatically raising the threshold between peace and war? OR Have most military planners from the start been aiming for nuclear war-fighting superiority? Has 'flexible response' dangerously lowered the threshold between conventional and nuclear war?

(iv) Has the size and variety of the nuclear arsenals held by the superpowers stabilized deterrence? OR Has the logic of nuclear confrontation and worst-case analysis generated a dangerous and strategically pointless superfluity of weapons systems?

(v) Has the idea of nuclear balance between the superpowers been essential to stability and have arms-control negotiations helped to achieve it? OR Have ideas of 'nuclear defence' and 'parity' proved illusory and is 'multilateral negotiation from strength' a contradiction in terms? Has 'arms-control' been just another name for the arms race?

(vi) Has force-planning been controlled by strategic thinking? OR Has the self-reinforcing impetus of technology and vested interest dictated policies subsequently justified post hoc?

2. *The Prospect for the Future*

(A) WITH NUCLEAR WEAPONS:
IS NUCLEAR DETERRENCE LIKELY TO PRESERVE PEACE FOR THE FORESEEABLE FUTURE OR IS NUCLEAR WAR INCREASINGLY LIKELY IF PRESENT POLICIES PERSIST?

(i) Does the threat of an enemy first strike remain inconceivable for the foreseeable future? OR Is there an increasing threat from accurate and time-urgent first-strike weapons?

(ii) Are command, control, communication and intelligence facilities likely to remain secure? OR Does the amount of information to be processed, pressure of time and fear of preemption put command and control systems under intolerable strain and make inadvertent war more likely?

(iii) If, nevertheless, there were a limited nuclear exchange would it be likely to end hostilities swiftly? OR Is the idea that nuclear war could be limited once it had broken out a dangerous illusion?

(iv) Do new generations of battlefield and theatre nuclear systems reinforce deterrence? OR Do new battlefield and theatre weapons threaten a dangerous lowering of the nuclear threshold?

(v) Does the Strategic Defence Initiative offer the hope of an effective defence against nuclear weapons? OR Is the Strategic Defence Initiative simply the most recent and destabilizing example of the process outlined in 1?

(vi) Is the threat of 'horizontal' nuclear proliferation best met by a continuation of past policies? OR Is continuing reliance on nuclear deterrence by the great powers bound to accelerate the process of proliferation and make nuclear war more likely?

(vii) Do multilateral arms-control negotiations offer the best prospect for future stability? OR Is 'arms-control' an illusion which diverts attention from the only safe policy – nuclear disarmament?

(B) WITHOUT NUCLEAR WEAPONS:
WOULD GLOBAL NUCLEAR DISARMAMENT MAKE THE WORLD SAFER?

(i) If nuclear arsenals were dismantled would war between the great powers again become a rational option and therefore more likely? OR Would nuclear disarmament remove the incentive for nuclear preemption while not affecting the reluctance of the great powers to initiate a third world war?

(ii) Would a major conventional war be likely in itself to be as terrible as a limited nuclear war? OR Is conventional war, however terrible, preferable to nuclear war?

(iii) Because nuclear weapons cannot be OR As with nerve gases in the last war, uninvented would they not be bound to be used sooner or later once war had broken out? would there be no incentive to resort to capabilities which the other side has as well?

(iv) Is global nuclear disarmament only OR Is to argue that even multilateral feasible in a world where war itself is no longer a possibility? nuclear disarmament is not desirable to give up all hope of a rational world-order?

(v) Is peace only preserved when we OR Do the years before 1914 show what are seen to be prepared for war, as failure before 1939 and success since 1945 show? Under likely future conditions would global nuclear disarmament make war, including nuclear war, more likely? happens when military planning and the arms race control political choices? Do present strategies make nuclear war almost inevitable under likely future conditions? Is global nuclear disarmament the only rational policy?

B. *Nato Policy*

WHICH IS THE MORE SERIOUS THREAT TO WESTERN PEACE AND SECURITY, SOVIET EXPANSIONISM OR SUPERPOWER DOMINATION AND NUCLEAR RIVALRY?

(i) Does the Soviet Union, together OR Are NATO and WTO forces with her Warsaw Pact allies, enjoy a strategically dangerous military superiority in Europe? relatively evenly matched?

(ii) Is the Soviet Union an expansionist OR Is the Soviet Union an encircled power which will take advantage of unilateral Western concessions and is only restrained and forced to accept arms-control agreements by Western determination and strength? and threatened power trying to keep up with Western technology and likely to respond positively to unconditional offers of Western restraint within a general context of detente?

(iii) Is Soviet chemical and conventional OR Is NATO dependence on the early preponderance such that NATO must continue to be able to threaten early use of nuclear weapons? use of nuclear weapons unnecessary and strategically suicidal?

(iv) Does the growing size of the Soviet OR Does the West initiate nearly all nuclear arsenal threaten the delicate theatre and strategic balance? Would Western failure to match Soviet systems be destabilizing? phases of the nuclear arms race and continue to enjoy a substantial lead in most areas? Is the nuclear 'overkill' such that the West could offer a nuclear 'freeze' or unconditional cuts without risk?

(v) Are NATO 'forward defence' and 'deep strike' strategies essential for effective deterrence?

OR Should NATO exploit her lead in 'emerging technology' to explore less provocative alternative strategies?

(vi) Is it the presence of American front-line troops and the tying-in of theatre nuclear forces to the American strategic deterrent that guarantees W. European security? Should American policies therefore be supported?

OR Is it domination by the two superpowers that poses the greatest threat to European integrity? Would Europe be safer decoupled from the super-power nuclear confrontation? Should Europe be made a nuclear weapon free zone?

(vii) Would Western unilateral nuclear disarmament invite Soviet blackmail? Are suggestions that the West should take the lead in offering unilateral disarmament initiatives the thin end of this wedge? Do radical nuclear disarmers consciously or unconsciously serve Soviet interests and threaten to undermine Western defences?

OR Are unilateral initiatives as part of a general programme of nuclear disarmament the only way to reverse the arms race? Is talk of 'multilateral disarmament' insincere in the mouths of those who reject all suggestion of a Comprehensive Test Ban Treaty, a Nuclear Freeze, a European Nuclear Weapon Free Zone, or a declaration of No First Use?

C. *British Policy*

1. *The British Deterrent*

(i) Is Britain's deterrent a weapon of last resort which guarantees her sovereignty and independence and protects her from nuclear blackmail?

OR Would all possible uses of Britain's 'deterrent' be suicidal? Is its only effect to encourage proliferation?

(ii) Are British nuclear forces valuable to European allies because they provide a specifically European second centre of decision making?

OR Is the 'second centre of decision making' an illusion when the weapons are dependent upon the US and there is no independent strategic role to be played? Are European allies unenthusiastic about a parochial British force likely to inhibit her commitment to European defence?

(iii) Does the US favour shared responsibility and do British nuclear forces guarantee full US commitment to Europe and Soviet recognition of it?

OR Are US forces committed anyway and independent British initiatives more likely to trigger Soviet retaliation than US involvement?

(**iv**) Is the cost of the British deterrent small in view of the vital defence role it plays? Are alternatives likely to be more expensive?

OR Can Britain's nuclear forces only be afforded at the expense of conventional strength and of other more important economic priorities?

(**v**) Would unilateral British nuclear disarmament have no effect on other countries and only serve to weaken British influence and allow France unchallenged ascendancy in Europe?

OR Does the British deterrent encourage proliferation and do nothing to enhance British prestige? Would British disarmament within the context outlined in B help to break the nuclear log-jam?

(**vi**) Is investment in Trident the best way to continue to ensure effective British strategic defence into the 21st century?

OR Would commitment to Trident exacerbate all the drawbacks listed above?

2. *Nato Forces and US Bases*

(**i**) Must Britain continue to share responsibility for manning NATO nuclear systems upon which her security depends? Would refusal to do so fatally weaken the alliance?

OR Should British obligations to NATO be met by strengthening conventional forces where necessary within an overall non-nuclear strategy as recommended in B?

(**ii**) Would the forced withdrawal of US nuclear bases from Britain make US defence of the West impossible? Is American interference in British affairs negligible?

OR Do the large numbers of nuclear facilities yielded to the US erode British sovereignty? Would their removal do no more than restore a normal peacetime relationship?

(**iii**) Will Britain continue to be targeted by Soviet warheads whether or not she disarms unilaterally?

OR Is Britain seen as an American aircraft carrier and targeted by the USSR accordingly? Will Britain fall an early victim in any superpower confrontation unless bases are removed?

(**iv**) Can non-nuclear defences only safely be afforded by powers prepared to shelter beneath the American strategic umbrella?

OR In a nuclear-free Europe, decoupled from the superpower nuclear confrontation, would Britain no more expect to depend upon the US 'umbrella' than any other Western ally – or than Eastern Europe upon the USSR?

MORAL CONSIDERATIONS

(i) Is it morally right to pursue the policy least likely to cause human suffering? May this sometimes involve doing things which in other circumstances would be wrong?

OR Are there actions which are in themselves wrong no matter what the situation? Is the alternative to excuse almost any act of barbarism?

(ii) In formulating policy should we weigh up the probability of success and the relative costs in terms of human suffering of alternative nuclear and non-nuclear strategies?

OR Is the only relevant point here that a nuclear exchange of almost any kind would in itself cause unimaginable suffering to largely civilian populations?

(iii) So far as concerns intention, need we look no further than the fact that our sole aim in deploying nuclear weapons is to prevent their use?

OR Is there no such thing as a fully deployed weapons system which is a bluff? Is to deploy nuclear weapons to intend to use them in certain circumstances?

(iv) Are there possible uses of nuclear weapons which are allowed by Just War theory, for example the bombing of Hiroshima and Nagasaki in order to prevent worse suffering? Can there be a theory of Just Deterrence?

OR Is a conditional intention to cause indiscriminate and disproportionate suffering of this kind, whether admonitory, preemptive or retaliatory, ruled out by Just War theory? Was it wrong to bomb Hiroshima and Nagasaki in 1945?

(v) Is there no relevant connection between the development and deployment of nuclear weapons and world poverty and disease?

OR Is it a scandal that such huge resources are devoted to the development and deployment of nuclear weapons and not to the alleviation of suffering?

(vi) Does Christian teaching allow the deployment of nuclear weapons?

OR Does Christian teaching condemn the deployment of nuclear weapons?

Conclusion

Is it morally right for us in present circumstances and within careful constraints to continue to develop and deploy nuclear weapons systems?

OR Is the continuing development and deployment of nuclear weapons systems immoral?

GENERAL CONCLUSION

How do the prudential and moral conclusions relate to one another?

RECOMMENDATIONS

EITHER

(LEFT) SHOULD CURRENT POLICIES BE BROADLY MAINTAINED?

or

(RIGHT) SHOULD ALL OR SOME OF THE FOLLOWING PROPOSALS BE IMPLEMENTED?

A *Global Policy*

As part of a broader programme of economic cooperation, confidence-building and regional security measures:

1 Should there be an immediate and general freeze on the deployment of new nuclear weapons systems?
2 Should there be an immediate and general moratorium on anti-satellite and strategic defence research programmes?
3 Should a Comprehensive Test Ban Treaty be signed at once by all nuclear weapon states?
4 Should there be an immediate and general declaration of No First Use of nuclear weapons by all nuclear weapon states?
5 Should immediate deep cuts be made in existing nuclear arsenals at every level by all nuclear weapon states? Should this include the elimination of ballistic weapons over the next decade at the strategic level, and the zero-zero option at theatre level?
6 Should regional security be decoupled where necessary from nuclear confrontation by the immediate establishment of nuclear weapon-free zones?
7 Should there be immediate and general subscription to the Non Proliferation Treaty?
8 Should all this be part of a process of universal nuclear disarmament to be completed, say, by the end of the century?
9 Should the Soviet Union and the United States retain a minimum or sufficient strategic nuclear force of, say, nuclear armed submarines until it is clear that alternative defence arrangements are mutually secure?

B *Nato Policy*

Within this context, where unconditional unilateral initiatives are offered as part of a general shift to non-nuclear defence:

10 Should Western European members of NATO decline to take part in the American Strategic Defence Initiative?
11 Should NATO make an immediate declaration of No First Use of nuclear weapons?
12 Should NATO announce an immediate freeze on the deployment of new nuclear weapons systems and unconditional cuts in existing nuclear

arsenals with a view to the eventual
   a. discarding of all battlefield and dual capable systems?
   b. phasing out of longer-range theatre systems?
13 Should Britain and France abandon their independent nuclear forces?
14 Should the United States announce a programme for the phased withdrawal of her nuclear and nuclear-related bases in Europe?
15 Should Europe be made a nuclear weapon-free zone? Should there be a
   battlefield weapon-free corridor either side of the frontier?

C *British Policy*

Within this context:

16 Should Britain relinquish her independent nuclear capability?
17 Should the money saved be spent on strengthening conventional forces?
18 Should Britain remain inside NATO and press for a non-nuclear strategy?
19 Should Britain refuse to man NATO nuclear delivery systems and insist
   upon the withdrawal of US nuclear weapons from Britain?
20 In the absence of a change in US and NATO policy should Britain stay in
   the alliance?

EXPANSION AND COMMENTARY
The Disagreement about Rationality

A   *Global Policy*

Before we even begin, we are already involved in controversy. By making a distinction between 'GLOBAL' and 'NATO' perspectives in this way, we are begging a fundamental question. For many of those who argue in favour of a continuation of current policy in the West, we cannot defer the problem of the Soviet threat to a section headed 'NATO POLICY', and begin by taking a global overview. For them there is no such thing as 'GLOBAL POLICY', because there is no such thing as a global state. The starting point for *all* policy, so far as they are concerned, is the prior fact of Soviet military power. Conversely, from a Soviet perspective, it is the threat of US imperialism which constitutes the global problem. How serious this is in terms of international relations can be left to the reader to assess.

This is an important example of the way in which an analytical framework breaks down within the context of a disagreement. What was intended as a map of the debate is found to be constructed on assumptions which are already part of it. There is no way round this, because no analysis is immune from it. But it is not a fatal weakness, so long as we are able to acknowledge that it is there. Indeed, it may be in its breakdown that an analysis can tell us most. It may be *why* it breaks down which is revealing.

1   *The History of the Past Forty Years*

HAS THE BUILD-UP OF NUCLEAR ARSENALS SINCE 1945 INCREASED OR DECREASED THE DANGERS INVOLVED IN SUPERPOWER CONFRONTATION?

(i) Has it been nuclear deterrence   OR Has it mainly been other factors?
that has kept the peace between
the great powers since 1945?

Although often put less unequivocally than this, the implication here is funda-mental to the case for continued reliance on nuclear deterrence. Nuclear weapons have been deployed since 1945. There has been no major war between nuclear weapon states since 1945. These two facts must be causally connected, if there is to be empirical substance to the claim that nuclear weapons deter. The further implication is that, if nuclear deterrence has worked in the past, then there is reason to suppose that it will continue to work in the future.

Critics of current policy want to undermine this. They can do so by qualifying the two statements of fact, by questioning the causal connection between them, or by rejecting the further implication. They can draw a distinction between the period when nuclear weapons may have been a deterrent, because they were only deployed by one side, and the situation today when they are no longer a deterrent, because both sides have them. They can deny that there has been peace between nuclear weapon states. They can refuse to accept single-factor causal historical explanations of this kind. They can point out the danger of assuming that what may have been the case in the past, in one set of political and military circumstances, is likely to continue to be the case in the future, when those political and military circumstances change.

COMMENT:

Clearly, this is an important question to decide. Although, when pressed, sophisticated commentators on both sides may say that there can be no final answer to it, it seems that, unless we lean one way or the other, we are unlikely to come to confident conclusions elsewhere. But it is difficult to see how this can be taken further, because, as in so many examples of historical controversy, it is not obvious what else there is to appeal to.

(ii) **Does mutual possession of an**   OR **Does the threat of strategic**
    invulnerable second strike   **nuclear retaliation, particularly**
    strategic nuclear force prevent   **against a similarly armed enemy,**
    war?   **lack credibility and invite sub-**
              deterrent encroachment?

This represents the essence of the idea of Mutual Nuclear Deterrence. To many it seems self-evident that no sane leader will deliberately court the destruction of his own society by offering a direct military challenge to an adversary known to retain the ability to inflict unacceptable damage in retaliation. It is this mutual knowledge which has in the end imposed restraint on nuclear weapon powers in their dealings with one another in recent years.

Most apologists for current policy concede that a strategic retaliatory force of this kind is not enough on its own to deter from all war. As an all-or-nothing response, it represents too disproportionate a threat to be credible. That is why the additional options dealt with in iii below have for many years been thought to be necessary as well.

Critics point out that this means that both sides can initiate hostilities with conventional forces, knowing that the other will be inhibited from a strategic nuclear response for fear of counter-reprisal. In other words, mutual deployment of nuclear weapons weakens deterrence. This is profoundly dangerous, because, as deterrence fails, mutual possession of nuclear arsenals makes the situation far more unstable than it would have been otherwise.

Many on this side concede that the 'cancelling out' of mutually deployed second strike forces may, at least in principle, prevent nuclear blackmail and protect minimum nuclear forces against cheating. What they deny is that nuclear warheads can be used as weapons of defence. We return to the idea of a 'minimum' or 'sufficient' nuclear force in A2 (A) vii.

COMMENT:

Much of the arguing here becomes remarkably abstract and theoretical. It is perhaps partly for this reason that the substantial disagreement is pushed on to other areas.

(iii) **Have limited nuclear options at strategic and theatre levels enhanced deterrence by dramatically raising the threshold between peace and war?**

OR **Have most military planners from the start been aiming for nuclear war-fighting superiority? Has 'flexible response' dangerously lowered the threshold between conventional and nuclear war?**

With this set of questions we reach the heart of the debate.

★   ★   ★

Since the time of the abandonment of 'Massive Retaliation' in the 1960s, the West's declared deterrent strategy has included limited nuclear options. This has been integral to NATO policy, and seems also to be assumed in Soviet planning. To those who defend current strategies, therefore, the alternative offered here is a false one. It is precisely the *threat* of nuclear warfighting (also sometimes described as a lowering of the threshold between conventional and nuclear war) which *deters*. It is this that prevents either side from being tempted to cross the really critical threshold – that between peace and war.

But critics, as we have seen, do not accept that it is such threats that have deterred from war in the past, or are likely to deter from war in the future. Far from compensating for the inherent lack of credibility in Mutual Nuclear Deterrence, the introduction of limited nuclear options simply compounds it. Since both sides have these 'limited' options, the dangerous instability is just translated down to local level. To pretend that secure defence can be built on plans for fighting and winning a limited nuclear war in this way is an inexcusable deception. Security is not enhanced, it is undermined.

COMMENT:

We have reached a fundamental and bewildering disjunction. The disputants seem to be looking at the situation from either side of a critical conceptual watershed, which is very difficult to bridge. For one, the emphasis throughout is on the effectiveness of deterrence. The stability of deterrence rests on the known risks of what would happen if deterrence failed. So we neither want to reduce those risks (to do so would be to weaken deterrence), nor should we be worried by them (they are unlikely to materialize precisely because deterrence is strengthened as a result). For the other, the emphasis throughout is on the implications of the plans for use. The threat to use nuclear weapons lacks operational credibility, which undermines deterrence. Yet, paradoxically, our commitment to a nuclear war-fighting strategy (which is inseparable from such a threat), means that, as deterrence is seen to weaken, we are therefore more likely to be impelled to use them. Such a strategy is seen to be irrational and irresponsible. One sees a virtuous, the other a vicious, circle. This is a disjunction which lies at the heart, both of the arguing about rationality, and of the arguing about morality. It is not easy to see how it can be resolved.

(iv) **Has the size and variety of the nuclear arsenals held by the superpowers stabilized deterrence?**   OR **Has the logic of nuclear confrontation and worst-case analysis generated a dangerous and strategically pointless superfluity of weapons systems?**

Those who argue like this see the richness of current nuclear arsenals as, in general, stabilizing, because it reduces the likelihood that either side will be tempted to think that it has an exploitable political or military advantage in any one area. They often stress that it is an attempted *political* use of a perceived advantage that could well in the first instance be the more destabilizing. There are greater dangers involved in reducing too low than in building up too high. This is particularly the case so far as concerns Western strategists, who have had to plan for extended deterrence – that is to say, above all, for the defence of Western Europe. So the size and variety of nuclear arsenals has not, in itself, been dangerous. Nor, as seen by each side individually, has it been stategically pointless. On the other hand, there is widespread acknowledgement that it has been *mutually* wasteful. In other words, stability could be preserved at substantially lower levels, and, from the point of view of conserving resources, it would be mutually beneficial if it were.

Critics see the growing size of current arsenals as a monument to the folly of past and present policies. Mutual suspicion and mirrored hostility have fed on themselves to produce the grotesque 'overkill' that there is today. They see this superfluity as dangerous for a number of reasons, some to do with the reciprocal reinforcement of mutual paranoia dealt with in B(ii), others to do with the first strike threat and command-control problems which will be dealt with in section A2.

COMMENT:

Although the divergence is still great, there is agreement in one important respect here, which may offer the hope of a substantial area of compromise. For different reasons, a number of those on each side agree that the size of current arsenals should be cut at strategic, theatre, and battlefield levels. The question of how far and in what way they should be cut introduces the idea of an ideal 'minimum' nuclear force, which is another important concept shared by many (but not all) on both sides. This will be explored further in A2(A)vii.

(v) **Has the idea of nuclear balance**   OR **Have ideas of 'nuclear defence'**
    between the superpowers been   **and 'parity' proved illusory and is**
    essential to stability and have   **'multilateral negotiation from**
    arms control negotiations helped   **strength' a contradiction in terms?**
    to achieve it?   **Has 'arms control' been just**
                                                   another name for the arms race?

This argument does not usually suggest that exact *parity*, system by system, has been essential. Deterrence is seen as having been stable enough to tolerate particular asymmetries. But, within the terms already given, the idea of a generally perceived *balance* of capabilities is thought to be important. One of the main aims of arms control is said to be to help to orchestrate this: to identify areas where mutual restraint would be mutually beneficial, to provide a forum for discussion and reciprocal understanding, and to underpin broader political initiatives. Perhaps not too much should be expected of arms control, but it has achieved important successes, notably the Partial Test Ban Treaty (1963), the Non-Proliferation Treaty (1968) and the Anti-Ballistic Missile Treaty (1972).

Critics are sceptical of the whole idea of 'balance', seeing mutual attempts to 'catch up' as part of the arms race. (Those who recommend an interim minimum deterrent see it as based on the concept of 'sufficiency', a reserve force sufficient to threaten unacceptable retaliation, not an attempt to match enemy dispositions). Arms control is seen as having failed to halt the arms race, and, indeed, as having, if anything, legitimized and institutionalized it. 'Negotiation strength', if mutual, is self-defeating, and 'bargaining chips' turn out to be stages in the process of escalation.

It may be confusing, but it is important to understand that among the critics at this point are also a number of those who are most vociferously in favour of an unfettered adjustment of nuclear forces as seems best to each power individually. There are few who argue like this in Britain, but a number in the United States and perhaps the Soviet Union. They say that arms control is artificial, ineffective, and, if anything, destabilizing. So they reject the principle of Mutual Nuclear Deterrence. What will deter the Soviet Union, for example, is the known strength of the United States. Anything which detracts from this, such as attempts to restrict the development and application of technology, weakens deterrence. Deterrence was perfect when the United States had a nuclear monopoly. Deterrence was dangerously eroded when, as in the 1970s, artificial restraints were put on the evolution of US forces.

This is an example of the way in which common opposition to the same policy can make strange bedfellows of those, who, in other respects, are further apart from one another than either is from the policy they jointly oppose.

COMMENT:

Whether or not arms control is seen as having failed in the past depends upon what is thought of as success. If success means the unfettered creation of a perfect nuclear deterrent, then arms control has been too restrictive; if success means progress towards nuclear disarmament, then it has not been restrictive enough; and if success means the further stabilization of an already existing balance, then arms control has perhaps made a modest, but useful contribution. What seems to be generally agreed here is that arms control on its own can rarely be expected to achieve very much. At best it contributes towards, and at worst diverts attention away from, the broader political initiatives which are needed to give direction and purpose to the shaping of public policy.

(vi) **Has force-planning been**   OR **Has the self-reinforcing impetus of**
     controlled by strategic thinking?   **technology and vested interest**
                                             dictated policies subsequently
                                           justified post hoc?

Those who argue in this way see the evolution of nuclear deterrent strategies since the last war as having, in general, been manifestly effective. Although they concede that present levels of spending on nuclear arms are, in one sense, unnecessarily high, they see a massive stability in the overall nuclear balance, and a resulting caution in international politics, which should on no account be jeopardized. Therefore, although the pressure of technology and vested interest may not always have been resisted as it should have been (particularly in the Soviet Union, where there are fewer political constraints), this can only have had a relatively peripheral effect. The underlying principles of nuclear deterrence, upon which our security continues to rest, have been determined by strategic thinking, and have been shaped and endorsed by all the most responsible leaders of the great nuclear weapon states since the war.

Critics paint a very different picture. Since they find current policy dangerous and incoherent, they cannot see force-planning as having been controlled by rational strategic thinking at all. Instead, they see us as having blundered into the present situation as a result of a long series of short-sighted expedients. Because there has been no overall long-term strategy, technology has been allowed to evolve almost unchecked, and institutionalized inertia has carried us further and further in the wrong direction. Attempts at official theoretical justification for nuclear deterrent policies have been little more than post hoc rationalization.

COMMENT:

If nuclear deterrence has successfully underpinned global security since the last war, then nuclear strategy has been rationally justified. But, if not, then there can be no rational justification for nuclear strategy and it can only be accounted for in other ways. In general, those who believe something to be true do not think that they need any further explanation for why they believe it. But those who disagree with them can only think that there must be some reason why what is patently untrue is nevertheless believed. What to one is an argument *ad rem*, to the other is accounted for *ad hominem*.

It is clear from the arguing in this section, that, in a disagreement, what *has* happened often turns out to be as contentious as what *should* or what *will* happen. Both sides appeal to the past, because this is where the empirical content for their argument is found. History is referred to as fact. So it is bewildering for those who are trying to make their minds up about who is right and who is wrong, to discover that, within the context of the disagreement, the distinction between 'fact' and 'interpretation' seems to be lost. This is not to say that there are no facts, only interpretations, but that what is 'fact' to one is 'interpretation' to the other. (This apparently innocent observation has profound implications, which cannot be followed up in this book).

Interpretations of the past as diverse as this make significant agreement on present action and future direction difficult to achieve.

2 *The Prospect for the Future*

(A) WITH NUCLEAR WEAPONS:
IS NUCLEAR DETERRENCE LIKELY TO PRESERVE PEACE FOR THE FORESEEABLE
FUTURE OR IS NUCLEAR WAR INCREASINGLY LIKELY IF WE PERSIST WITH PRESENT
POLICIES?

(i) **Does the threat of an enemy first** OR **Is there an increasing threat from**
strike remain inconceivable for the   **accurate and time-urgent first-**
foreseeable future?   **strike weapons?**

Those who argue like this have confidence in the colossal stability of mutual
nuclear deterrence. They do not see anything on the horizon remotely likely
to tempt either side to think that it could eliminate the other's entire nuclear
force in a first strike. So they do not need to look ahead to what might happen
were deterrence on the point of breaking down.

But that is where the concern of many critics begins. The danger is seen to lie in each side's *perception* that the other may be contemplating a future strike, and what alarms them is the likely effect on current war-fighting strategies in a time of political crisis of new anti-satellite, anti-submarine, and anti-missile technologies, and of new generations of offensive nuclear weapons. They see it as almost inevitable that in these circumstances military necessity will override political restraint, and that fear of an enemy first strike will convert crisis into catastrophe by precipitating preemption.

(One problem throughout this section for those who argue in this way is that a warning about future danger may suggest that there has been past security).

There is also, once again, the further complication that there are those, particularly in the US and the USSR, who fear the possibility of a first strike, but whose concern is more to do with the danger of an enemy surprise attack than with an unpremeditated collapse into nuclear war – and whose preferred remedy, therefore, is an unrestricted build-up of invulnerable second-strike nuclear forces.

COMMENT:

This is another instance of the way in which the situation is seen from either side of a conceptual watershed between the perceived effectiveness of deterrence, and the perceived dangers of crisis instability. From the former perspective, deterrence is what is most likely to prevent crisis instability; from the latter, crisis instability is what is most likely sooner or later to undermine deterrence. Neither sees the ground upon which the other is standing.

(ii) **Are command, control,**   OR **Does the amount of information to**
    communication and intelligence   **be processed, pressure of time,**
    facilities likely to remain secure?   **and fear of preemption put**
                                          command and control systems
                                          under intolerable strain, and make
                                          inadvertent war more likely?

Those who are confident about the stability of nuclear deterrence may acknowledge that command and control facilities could and should be made more secure, but they do not see this as critical. And they see them as becoming, if anything, more reliable now than they have been in the past. There are also those among them who have argued that in any case a measure of known vulnerability further enhances deterrence, because the potential aggressor will then be more likely to fear that his actions may trigger an uncontrollable response.

And yet, once again, this is exactly what causes such concern to the critics. Their grounds for anxiety range from doubts about the reliability of equipment, which, in decreasing lengths of time, is expected to perform increasingly complex functions for which it can never have been properly tested, to a lack of confidence in human operators, who are likely to be working under conditions of high stress and emotion. The Challenger and Chernobyl accidents are seen to confirm their scepticism.

COMMENT:

As things stand, it is not easy to see how these perspectives can be related, let alone reconciled, to one another. This is a good example of how much room there is for differences of opinion, when there is so little empirical evidence to go on. It is another illustration of the remarkably theoretical nature of what in other spheres would be an area of practical experiment. It is a matter to which a great deal of attention has been paid in the literature, but about which no consensus has yet emerged.

(iii) **If nevertheless there were a**   OR **Is the idea that nuclear war could**
      limited nuclear exchange, would it   **be limited once it had broken out a**
      be likely to end hostilities swiftly?   **dangerous illusion?**

Unless they are themselves involved in detailed military strategic planning, those who support current policies do not regard even a limited nuclear exchange as at all probable – so they do not, on the whole, spend much time trying to work out whether it would be likely to remain limited. When pressed, they tend to say, either that they do not know if it would; or that it is the very danger that it would not that reinforces deterrence; or that, since escalation to all-out nuclear war would clearly be mutually catastrophic, the first exchanges would be likely to bring both sides rapidly to their senses.

For critics, however, this is not something to be brushed aside in this way. It seems to them almost inevitable that, in view of the nuclear war-fighting strategies and the profusion of nuclear weaponry on both sides, any initiation of the use of nuclear weapons would degenerate towards a general exchange. This is a major premise in their whole argument. It is *because* the use of nuclear weapons would be likely to be as self-destructive as this, that nuclear deterrence lacks credibility and strategies based upon it are so unstable and dangerous.

COMMENT:

What is peripheral to one is central to the other. This is a discontinuity of viewpoints, which must be bridged if any kind of dialogue, let alone consensus, is to be achieved.

(iv) Do new generations of battlefield OR **Do new battlefield and theatre
and theatre nuclear systems   weapons threaten a dangerous
reinforce deterrence?   lowering of the nuclear threshold?**

This should be looked at within the context established in A1(ii). It is another
area of possible compromise.

★   ★   ★

As we have seen, proponents of current policy insist on the need for a range
of limited nuclear options in order to enhance credibility. In this sense, to
'lower the nuclear threshold' may be to 'enhance deterrence'. But the argument here is that it would have been destabilizing *not* to have matched Soviet
SS20s with Pershing II and Cruise missiles, and that what lowers the threshold
is a weakening of conventional, not a strengthening of nuclear forces.

But the remarkable accuracy of new generations of longer-range weapons
has persuaded a number of those who argue in this way to suggest that we no
longer need to have forward-deployed, land-based nuclear weapons in Europe,
even for extended deterrence. The same function could be performed by
longer-range systems. There is a belief that nuclear battlefield forces could
and should be reduced, if not, in many cases, phased out by mutual agreement
between the two main power blocks. And, in addition, in both the US and the
USSR, there also seems to be a willingness to negotiate away Intermediate
Nuclear Forces (INF) in Europe. It tends to be West Europeans who object
to the latter, for fear that it would represent a weakening of US commitment
to their defence at that level, and would leave them vulnerable to Soviet superiority in other areas.

For critics, there was no need for either side to deploy new generations of battlefield or theatre nuclear systems, no matter what the other did, and the result has clearly been to endanger rather than enhance our security. In any acute military crisis there will be pressure to use the former before they are overrun, while the latter are seen to be part of a threatened first strike. Accurate Pershing II missiles are counter-force weapons, which can reach the Soviet Union in much reduced flight times, while the dispersal of mobile Cruise missiles on alert will in itself contribute towards escalation and attempted preemption.

COMMENT:

There is evidently room for compromise here, particularly on the building down of battlefield nuclear weapons, and, despite continuing West European scruples, on movement towards the so-called 'zero-zero option' – the elimination of certain classes of Intermediate systems from Europe. But there are still a number of complicated technical difficulties to be overcome. There are problems of verification, which become increasingly testing if the putative agreement is to reduce rather than eliminate particular systems, and if dual-capable weapons are retained. There are problems of definition, for example in determining what should count as 'Intermediate' or 'Euro-Strategic' weapons, in view of the geographical and force-structure asymmetries between the USSR, and the USA and her nuclear-capable allies. There are problems of linkage, to do with how closely agreement in any one area should be made dependent upon agreement in others. And there are broader problems to do with the desirability of an overall 'zero option' for nuclear weapons in the European theatre in the first place, in view of what some see as a continuing and dangerous imbalance in chemical and conventional forces.

(v) **Does the Strategic Defence**   OR **Is the Strategic Defence Initiative**
Initiative offer the hope of an   **simply the most recent &**
effective defence against nuclear   **destabilizing example of the**
weapons?   **process outlined in A.1?**

Here we reach a major complication in the arguing which must confuse many.

★   ★   ★

When President Reagan officially launched the American SDI on March 23 1983, he offered it as a radical alternative to nuclear deterrence itself, which was described as both dangerous and immoral. Defensive forces were to replace offensive forces on both sides – perhaps by mutual arrangement – and, in this way, nuclear weapons themselves were eventually to be rendered obsolete. The aim would be to attack missiles, not people, and to destroy nuclear with mainly non-nuclear weapons. This was a remarkable theoretical volte-face, apparently incompatible with what has been argued down the left-hand side so far. For this reason, a number of commentators rejected it as undesirable, even in theory, on the grounds that, if successful, it would once again make conventional war a rational option. Most also agreed that in any case it is likely to be technically unattainable. So, for them, the possible value of the SDI lies, not in replacing deterrence, but in strengthening it by the protection of second strike forces. One idea here is that this might make it possible at the same time to build down offensive systems and to move away from exclusive reliance on retaliatory forces, with gains in both security and cost-effectiveness. Even this represents perhaps the most radical conceptual shift of emphasis in declaratory policy since the principles of Mutual Nuclear Deterrence first became orthodox. Others, in conciliatory vein, have defended the SDI on the grounds that the Soviet Union is in any case engaged in similar enterprises, that this is just a research programme which will not infringe existing agreements, and that, if and when it comes to deployment, this will only be done through negotiation both with allies and with the Soviet Union. Others again, more aggressively, see merit in capitalizing on technological advantage wherever possible, in order, either to force concessions from the Soviets at the negotiating table, or to drive them towards bankruptcy if they take up the challenge.

Critics reject all of these rationales. But the conceptual incompatibility between them threatens to duplicate itself in a corresponding inconsistency in their refutation. It is difficult to criticize what is presented as a rejection of nuclear deterrence without seeming to be defending it – which is why many critics welcome the spirit behind President Reagan's Initiative, while nevertheless rejecting its substance. Their list of charges is comprehensive. The SDI, in all its guises, is dismissed as: covertly imperialistic (threatening to fund American technological hegemony); politically divisive; hugely expensive; technologically unfeasible; in the long term provocative (threatening a first strike capability, forcing an expansion in enemy offensive systems, carrying all the dangers of the militarization of space); in the short term destabilizing (undermining the ABM treaty, blocking arms control agreements); and in any case unnecessary (there is no 'window of vulnerability' threat to second strike forces, and Soviet strategic defence technology is rudimentary).

COMMENT:

The Initiative seems to be both defended and attacked by a bewildering swarm of often barely compatible arguments. It is borne down by a heap of assailants and then encumbered with help as it is revived. The stirring of the conceptual pot has provoked a frenzied realignment of rationales.

In these circumstances, the reader may be forgiven for concluding that it would be better to come to a decision with reference to what is argued elsewhere, and then to assess the SDI within those terms. A further justification for doing this would be the arguments of those who see the American SDI a blanket term for a complex of enterprises, most of which were going on in any case before it was announced, and many of which would almost certainly be carried on even if it were abandoned.

(vi) **Is the threat of 'horizontal'**   OR **Is continuing reliance on nuclear**
    nuclear proliferation best met   **deterrence by the great powers**
    by a continuation of past policies?   **bound to accelerate the process of**
                                                 proliferation?

We will assume that there is general agreement that the further proliferation of nuclear weapons to as yet non-nuclear or semi-nuclear powers is something that we would like to avoid. For many people this is the most alarming prospect of all.

★   ★   ★

Those who argue like this, point to the fact that proliferation has been much slower than was at one time feared. They say that nuclear disarmament by the existing nuclear weapon powers would not remove the danger of proliferation, which is in any case inherent in the nuclear energy programmes being pushed forward in many parts of the world. On the contrary, by underpinning global security, nuclear deterrence at superpower level reduces the incentive for regional proliferation and insures against its possible effects. It is local conditions which will in the end determine whether or not a particular state takes up the nuclear option. They tend to say that they do not expect the situation to deteriorate seriously. The United States and the Soviet Union have an identity of interest here, and the Non-Proliferation Treaty and the work of the International Atomic Energy Agency show what can be done by mutual consent.

Critics find this illogical and complacent. They are not convinced by the argument that nuclear weapons are good for those who happen to have them and bad for everyone else. They see a clear causal connection between current nuclear deterrent strategies and the inevitable spreading of nuclear weapons to other powers and groupings. They regard this prospect with alarm, and see the only remedy in an acceleration of the process begun with the Non-Proliferation Treaty within a context where the great powers are seen to be moving towards nuclear disarmament.

COMMENT:

This is a striking example of the way in which, once we are committed to a position, we are likely to interpret related situations in a way which is consistent with it. One side stresses how slow proliferation has been in the past; the other points to how likely it is to accelerate in the future. One cites the Non-Proliferation Treaty to show how the nuclear guarantee given by existing nuclear powers encourages non-proliferation; the other cites it to show how non-proliferation was made dependent upon general progress towards nuclear disarmament. This is a large, diverse, and complex subject, which is difficult to assess. It requires a technical mastery of the relationship between nuclear reactor capacity and weapons production, and a detailed knowledge of regional pressures towards proliferation and of international efforts to control them.

(ii) **Do multilateral arms control**   OR **Is 'arms control' an illusion which**
negotiations offer the best   **diverts attention from the only**
prospect for future stability?   **safe policy – nuclear**
                                             disarmament?

Those who argue like this see the role of arms control as being one of orches-
trating a perceived existing balance of forces, and expediting and underpinning political understanding. The underlying principles are those of
reciprocity and mutual self-interest. Looking ahead, they see the aim to be
one of stabilizing deterrence at reduced force levels, nuclear and non-nuclear.
They are, in general, hopeful that progress will be made, because of continuing
mutual fear of instability, recent improvements in verification technology, and
a new mood of economic realism on both sides. For example, among other
things, they would welcome fifty per cent cuts in strategic weapons, an INF
agreement, a mutual build-down of battlefield systems, and further constraints
on nuclear weapon testing. But, confident in the stability of deterrence, they
are usually not fearful of the consequences should this fail.

On the contrary, what alarms them more are some of the wilder interpretations that have been made of the Reykjavik summit. If Reykjavik proves to
have been part of a significant move forward in the direction which we have
just outlined, then they are prepared to give it cautious approval. But they do
not take the more extravagant rhetorical flourishes on either side seriously,
and are determined that rash impulses, played out in front of the world's
television cameras, should not jeopardize the solid basis of global security.
The laborious process of painstaking arms control negotiation in the end
achieves more than grandiose political gestures. And if Reykjavik is, indeed,
the beginning of a major shift away from Cold War confrontation, then it must
include the elimination of imbalances in chemical and conventional forces,
and the removal of the threat from the Soviet totalitarian system. Arms control
can only be one part of such a broad political settlement. It is, in the end,
policies that matter, not pieces of paper.

Critics are both less and more optimistic than this.

They are less optimistic, because they do not have confidence in nuclear deterrence in the first place, and have different ends in view. So, as we saw in A1(v), what they regard as forty years of failure in the past, does not encourage them to expect significant results from current or future arms control talks, unless the principles on which they are conducted are radically changed. This is followed up in B(vii).

But they are more optimistic about the prospects after Reykjavik. Many of them are prepared to take the programmes outlined by the Soviet General Secretary and the American President at face value. They welcome recognition by the leaders of the two superpowers that nuclear deterrence can no longer be seen to be the basis of world security. Reykjavik is the first clear sign that it is possible for international statesmanship at the highest level to break the conservative stranglehold of arms control bureaucrats and vested interests. The two leaders have recognized the overwhelming desire of peoples throughout the world that we should now move towards mutual accommodation, if not reconciliation between the power blocs and away from the nuclear arms race.

We should also remember that there are others who are critical of the desirability, let alone feasibility, of current arms control talks, but for different reasons and with different ends in view. They prefer unfettered unilateral adjustment to force-planning, and reject the whole process of bilateral and multilateral arms control as ultimately counter-productive.

COMMENT:

Here we reach the critical point in the search for a common programme. It may not seem that there is much room for compromise between two such radically different perspectives. But, in the short term, there seems to be agreement about the need for deep cuts in nuclear systems at all levels, and about further constraint on nuclear weapon testing and proliferation. In particular, it is possible that there is an approach to a consensus on moving towards the eventual elimination of fixed land-based strategic systems, and land-based INF and battlefield weapons in Europe. In the longer term, it may be possible to explore how much common ground there is in the idea of a 'minimum' or 'sufficient' nuclear force. Many who argue as on the left-hand side want to see a reduction in arsenals to the minimum level which preserves stability. Many who argue as on the right-hand side, are prepared to accept temporary, or semi-permanent, minimum nuclear forces held by the two superpowers. The trouble is likely to be that, in order to determine the size

and composition of a minimun nuclear force, we need to agree on what is to count as 'sufficient'. If the role is to include extended deterrence, then it is likely not to differ radically from what we have now. If the role is seen as being no more than a mutual guarantee against nuclear blackmail and insurance against cheating, then we may only be contemplating a handful of submarine-launched missiles on either side. The former will seem to be little improvement to some; the latter will seem dangerously destabilizing to others.

(B) WITHOUT NUCLEAR WEAPONS:

WOULD GLOBAL NUCLEAR DISARMAMENT MAKE THE WORLD SAFER?

(i) **If nuclear arsenals were dismantled would war between the great powers again become a rational option & therefore more likely?** OR **Would nuclear disarmament remove the incentive for nuclear preemption while not affecting the reluctance of the great powers to initiate a third world war?**

This argument is the complement of the argument in A1(i) that nuclear deterrence has kept the peace between the great powers. It is particularly used by those in the West who say that to remove nuclear weapons, while leaving Soviet non-nuclear force superiority, would be a recipe for disaster.

The response from those who argue as on the right is that the destructiveness of modern weaponry, non-nuclear as well as nuclear, means that war of any kind between the great powers can never again be a rational option in any case. The programme of global nuclear disarmament would, therefore, be part of a wider process of arms reduction and political meditation. It would itself profoundly alter the political climate for the better. The argument about the Soviet threat is met in ways which are examined in Section B.

COMMENT:

Throughout this section there is an implied reversal of roles. A number of those who were earlier reluctant to contemplate the possibility of the breakdown of deterrence are now pressing its likely consequences, and a number of those who were earlier pressing its consequences are now reluctant to contemplate its possibility.

(ii) Would a major conventional war   OR **Is conventional war, however**
be likely in itself to be as terrible   **terrible, preferable to nuclear war?**
as a limited nuclear war?

Here there is a warning that we should not allow ourselves to become obsessed
by the dangers of nuclear weapons, and forget how horrible modern conventional (not to mention biological and chemical) weapons would be likely to
make a non-nuclear war. This is a fundamental point for those who see the
essential role of nuclear weapons as deterring, not just the reciprocal use of
other nuclear weapons, but the use of all weapons.

As we have just seen, opponents do not deny that all forms of war would be horrible. Their premise is that current strategies make it highly likely that there will, sooner or later, be a nuclear exchange, and that, once that has happened, we will not be able to prevent its escalation to all-out nuclear war. Nuclear war would undoubtedly be more terrible than conventional war. Without nuclear weapons there will not be the same pressure to preempt, and the penalty of failure will no longer be annihilation.

COMMENT:

Both agree that war of all kinds must be avoided, but each accuses the other of making it more likely that it will break out.

(iii) **Because nuclear weapons cannot**   OR **As with nerve gases in the last**
      be uninvented would they not be   **war, would there be no incentive**
      bound to be used sooner or later   **to resort to capabilities which the**
      once war had broken out?   **other side had as well?**

For a number of people, the argument on the left is decisive in ruling out global nuclear disarmament, even as a desirable aim. The disproportionate advantage to be gained by possessing even one or two deliverable nuclear devices in those circumstances, would, they say, encourage secret manufacture, if only as an insurance against possible blackmail. This would in itself be highly unstable, and, in the event of war breaking out as envisaged in (i) and (ii), there would be a race to rebuild nuclear arsenals. So, ironically, global nuclear disarmament would make nuclear war more, not less, likely.

This is a scenario that is flatly rejected by those who argue as on the right. They turn the argument that nuclear weapons cannot be uninvented on its head. They say that it is precisely *because* nuclear weapons cannot be uninvented that war of any kind can no longer be a rational option for the great powers. We are in an entirely new situation now, and one which demands a new response from rational and responsible statesmen. What we must stop doing is deploying nuclear, chemical and biological weapons as part of traditional war-fighting strategies. And we must stop thinking that this will 'make the world safe for conventional weapons'. The destructiveness of modern conventional weapons and the perpetual possibility that, if war broke out, other types of weapon would reappear, makes all war between the great powers irrational.

COMMENT:

As the debate develops in this section, it becomes evident that, far from getting to grips with one another, the two groups of protagonists are moving further and further apart. Neither is prepared to argue on the other's terms.

**(iv) Is global nuclear disarmament   OR Is to argue that even multilateral
only feasible in a world in which   nuclear disarmament is not
war itself is no longer a   desirable to give up all hope of a
possibility?   rational world order?**

Here the philosophical disparity between the two sides is at its widest.

★ ★ ★

Those who argue like this appeal above all to realism. They say that the whole idea of global nuclear disarmament is imaginary. It just will not happen, no matter what the leaders of the two superpowers may say in their more irresponsible rhetorical moods. But it is also undesirable. It would be profoundly dangerous to eliminate nuclear arsenals in a world of predatory and highly armed nation states. So long as the causes of war and the means to wage war remain, so must the great deterrent against war. If it is true that the world is moving towards a situation in which war between the great powers is becoming more and more unthinkable, then this is largely a result of the continuing effectiveness of nuclear deterrence. Those who advocate global nuclear disarmament may be well-meaning, but their refusal to acknowledge political and military realities makes them dangerous. They must not be allowed to influence public policy.

But those who argue like this will not allow that a policy, which, in conditions of continuing political confrontation, purports to base security indefinitely on nuclear war-fighting strategies, deserves to be described as 'realism'. It is seen as manifest folly and irresponsibility – a refusal to acknowledge the realities of the nuclear age. The only rational course for world leaders to take is the one now recognized by the leaders of the two superpowers. Above all cultural, economic and political divisions, there is an over-arching community of inter-est–survival. This must be the top priority and long-term goal in all political and strategic planning, and in all bilateral and multilateral negotiations. Both the Soviet General Secretary and the American President have agreed that the mutual aim must be the elimination of weapons of mass destruction within a context where political tensions are reduced and war is recognized as no longer a rational option. The success of Reykjavik was the proclamation that this is the goal. The failure of Reykjavik was the demonstration that there is still a difference of opinion as to how we should get there. We must brush aside the failure and built on the success. There is no rational alternative.

COMMENT:

Here each side claims a monopoly of realism and rationality. Both aspire to a world in which global tensions are resolved by negotation and mutual accom-modation. Yet one advocates indefinite reliance on nuclear weapons, and the other swift progress towards their abandonment. That we share a common goal must make us hopeful that we will be able to reach it. That we disagree so profoundly about how to get there may begin to dispel much of that hope.

(v) Is peace only preserved when we   OR Do the years before 1914 show
     are seen to be prepared for war,   what happens when military
     as failure before 1939 and   planning and the arms race control
     success since 1945 show?   political choices?

This argument is persuasive to those who believe that appeasement of Hitler
in the 1930s encouraged the growth of Nazi power, whereas resolute contain-
ment of Soviet Russia and Communist China in the late 1940s and 1950s
tempered their expansionism. The parallel with 1914 is rejected on the
grounds that in many people's minds the aim of the build-up of arms then was
to fight war, whereas today the aim is to deter from war. No useful comparisons
of this kind can be made between the pre-nuclear and the nuclear age.

This argument convinces those who believe that current nuclear force dispositions have been shaped less by responsible strategic thinking than by the blind evolution of technology and the pressure of vested interest. The parallel with the 1930s is rejected on the grounds that Soviet Russia cannot be equated with Nazi Germany, and that deterrence strategies which may have been sound in the pre-nuclear age no longer make sense now.

COMMENT:

Rather as in A1(i), although there is a general acknowledgement that historical parallels of this kind should be treated with caution, proponents of alternative policies in many cases lean one way or the other. When they do, each tends to see the other as having chosen the paradigm which reinforces the case to which he was already committed anyway. On the one hand, we are told that, if we continue with current policy, we can prevent a repetition of the disasters of 1939, whereas, if we abandon it, we will be inviting them. On the other, we are told that, if we persist with current policy, we will be reenacting the mistakes of 1914, whereas, if we abandon it, we can avoid them. When each says that the pre-nuclear cannot be compared to the nuclear age, he is thinking mainly of the sense in which the other's paradigm does not apply. In short, we are told that we can learn important lessons from the past, but the lessons that we are told that we can learn are incompatible with one another.

B *NATO Policy*

WHICH IS THE MORE SERIOUS THREAT TO WESTERN PEACE AND SECURITY, SOVIET
EXPANSIONISM OR SUPERPOWER DOMINATION AND NUCLEAR RIVALRY?

(i) **Does the Soviet Union, together**   OR **Are NATO and WTO forces**
with her Warsaw Pact allies, enjoy   **relatively evenly matched?**
a strategically dangerous military
superiority in Europe?

Here we are dealing with non-nuclear forces.

★   ★   ★

The argument in this case is forthright. The claim that Warsaw Pact and
NATO non-nuclear forces are of equal strength is seen to be intellectually
dishonest. The situation is, indeed, a complicated one, which is difficult to
assess. There are areas in which NATO has certain advantages. It is also true
that Soviet strength has at times been exaggerated in the past – not least
because of the pathological secrecy with which Soviet military dispositions are
guarded. But no amount of statistical manipulation or special pleading can
disguise the fact that the Soviet Union enjoys a near-monopoly in chemical
weapons, and a vast preponderance in conventional forces, particularly along
certain sectors of the front. This is established clearly and unequivocally in the
most recent of the annual analyses of comparative force strengths published by
the International Institute for Strategic Studies (IISS). The Soviet Union's
numerical, organizational, logistical and geographical advantages cannot
reasonably be denied.

But the counter-case is equally forthright. When everything is taken into account, such as the overall economic and industrial capacity to wage war, the reliability of allies, and the significant number-advantage that an attacker needs in order to be confident of the likelihood of success, the two sides are seen to be of equal strength at conventional level. The statistics quoted in official sources are described as blatant selective manipulation. In those areas where there *is* a numerical advantage in favour of the Warsaw Pact, quantity is more than offset by quality, thanks, among other things, to the technological superiority enjoyed in almost every department by the West. And in any case, remaining shortfalls could be relatively easily made good, if NATO's obsessive reliance on nuclear deterrence did not sap the will to do it. The truth of the matter is that it is in the interest of NATO apologists to continue to exaggerate Soviet conventional strength, and they do so consistently, unashamedly, and outrageously. As the most recent IISS assessment shows, the two sides are effectively evenly matched.

COMMENT:

What are we to make of this astonishing discrepancy? It is the greatest single scandal in the nuclear weapons debate. There can be no doubt about the importance of establishing whether or not the Soviet Union enjoys a danger-ous non-nuclear military superiority in Europe. That she does is the major empirical premise upon which all the arguing represented on the left-hand side is based. That she does not is an essential element in the case of those who argue as on the right. Each has access to, and, indeed, quotes from, the same sources. Yet each accuses the other of misrepresentation and deception. Both pay lip-service to the idea that exact comparisons are difficult, but never-theless present the general public with confident and diametrically opposed conclusions. In a matter of such central public concern is one side investigat-ing the question with a proper objectivity and regard for the truth, whereas the other is guilty of deliberate and inexcusable distortion? Or is it that both are determined to see only what they want to find, in order to buttress convictions which are too habitual and too closely related to wider political commitment to be easily relinquished?

It is generally agreed that mutual acceptance of non-nuclear military

security must be an important part of any lasting settlement between the power blocs. But what hope is there of progress towards an improvement in the situation, if those in the West who are advocating such moves cannot begin to agree among themselves about what the situation is in the first place?

Confronted with demands from both sides that the facts should be faced, and a decision made accordingly, the voter can be forgiven for supposing that the single most useful contribution that could be made to the public debate would be for those on both sides who care more for truth than for party advantage to try to formulate a joint assessment of what the facts are. Those areas which can be empirically verified would then be mutually agreed, and those areas where there is legitimate scope for varied interpretation would simply be presented as such. But, in the absence of a joint enterprise of this kind, the voter is left with incompatible assertions of fact, between which there seems to be no means of discriminating, and upon which he is assured by both sides that a great deal of the arguing depends.

★   ★   ★

We should also note at this point that the debate as recorded in this section is conducted within Western terms. Soviet perspectives are not represented. This means that we have not raised the deep question – What are the relative merits and demerits of Socialist and Capitalist ways of organizing society, and how can such radically different systems come to a lasting settlement with one another? In political terms, this great issue underlies everything else that is written here, but, for that reason, it reaches beyond the scope of this book.

(ii) **Is the Soviet Union an**   OR **Is the Soviet Union an encircled**
     expansionist power which will   **and threatened power trying to**
     take advantage of unilateral   **keep up with Western technology**
     Western concessions and is only   **and likely to respond positively to**
     restrained and forced to accept arms   **unconditional offers of Western**
     control agreements by Western   **restraint within a general context**
     determination and strength?   **of detente?**

The argument here is that the Soviet Union remains the greatest threat to our peace and security. It is difficult to understand how this can be denied, in view of Soviet military strength and the nature of Soviet institutional ideology. Yet critics of nuclear deterrence will go to extraordinary lengths in trying to ignore this. They are the first to complain if they sense that there is the slightest infringement of domestic liberty in the West, and it is they who are most vociferous in criticizing the United States for 'eroding the sovereignty of her European allies'. Yet, for reasons which have little to do with the reality of international affairs, they choose to close their eyes to the manifestly totalitarian nature of the Soviet regime, and to the continuing brutality with which even moderate dissent is silenced within the Soviet Union and crushed in the Soviet satellite states. They seem not to recognize that the entire system is sustained only by the unscrupulous use of overwhelming force.

In view of this, it is not a question of whether or not Soviet leaders are planning a direct assault on the West. Soviet plans are, in any case, at the moment constrained by four decades of effective Western deterrence. It is simply that the only way to deal with a power like the Soviet Union is through a combination of pragmatic flexibility and strength. Experienced Sovietologists know that unilateral Western disarmament initiatives would be interpreted in the Kremlin as a weakening of Western determination, strengthening the aggressive elements within Soviet high command, and removing the incentive to search for bilateral agreements. Western disarray in the 1970s encouraged Soviet expansionism; Western resolve in the 1980s has been rewarded by the present mood of accommodation. Those who press for unconditional deep cuts in Western defences in the name of 'detente', 'security' and 'peace' are in fact urging policies which would bring tension, danger – and a far greater likelihood of war.

Here, both the assessment of the Soviet regime, and the analysis of how to respond to it, made opposite, are rejected.

More alarm is felt at the global policies of the USA than at those of the USSR, and the idea that the Soviet Union is bent upon aggression in a way that the Western allies are not, is discounted. To suppose this is to ignore the whole history and character of the Soviet experience, surrounded from the start by wealthier hostile powers, and bearing the brunt of the German attack in 1941. The Soviet Union sees itself as a beleaguered, rather than an expansionist power, struggling to keep up with Western technology, and increasingly preoccupied with the pressing need for internal reform. This has become particularly evident in recent months, as the older generation, whose thinking was shaped by their experiences in and before the last war, are replaced by younger leaders.

In these circumstances, Western belligerence will only provoke counter-antagonism, whereas restraint within a general atmosphere of detente will encourage mutual confidence and understanding. Soviet gestures in the direction of ending nuclear weapon testing, and drastically reducing nuclear stockpiles, are seen as genuine efforts towards accommodation, which should be reciprocated. The fear is that, if they are not, the reformist element within the Soviet leadership may be discredited, and an historic opportunity to end the cold war may be missed.

COMMENT:

The dispute here is difficult to resolve, not so much because it is too intractable, as because it is too indeterminate. Neither usually wants to press these arguments too far. For example, those who lean towards the left-hand view tend to agree that the Soviet Union is a conservative and cautious power; and those who lean towards the right-hand view above tend to agree that rapprochement must not mean a weakening of defence. But the breadth of the historical and political judgements involved, which allows for considerable overlap, can also conceal deep differences of attitude. The gulf between the person who interprets past Soviet refusal to negotiate reductions in chemical and conventional weapons as evidence that only toughness works, and the person who interprets Soviet offers made at and after Reykjavik as evidence of Soviet good intentions, may be a gulf of perception which spreads out to include the whole of politics.

(iii) **Is Soviet chemical and**   OR **Is NATO dependence on the early**
conventional preponderance such   **use of nuclear weapons**
that NATO must continue to be   **unnecessary and strategically**
able to threaten early use of   **suicidal?**
nuclear weapons?

As we have seen, the argument here is that, in view of Soviet non-nuclear preponderance, the West must continue to keep the nuclear option open as part of a credible flexible response strategy. The only alternatives are for the Soviet Union to reduce her non-nuclear forces, which she has shown no sign of doing; or for the West to build hers up to match them – a degree of militariz-ation which would not be tolerated within the Western democracies. Unless and until this non-nuclear imbalance is corrected, deterrence must include a nuclear component. But two points are stressed. First, the nuclear option is precisely that – an option. The idea is, of course, to hold a Soviet attack with non-nuclear forces for as long as possible, and, ideally, not to have to invoke it at all. A 'declaration of no first use' would be meaningless in this context. For example, a Soviet declaration to that effect means nothing, when Soviet nuclear forces are trained to preempt a suspected first strike from the West. Secondly, the whole point of keeping the nuclear option open is in order to *deter*. A declaration of no first use, if believed, would simply undermine deterrence. But the fundamental point here is that NATO is a purely defensive alliance, and has unequivocally made the only declaration which has any sig-nificance – that it will on no account initiate hostilities of any kind.

This logic is rejected by those who argue as on the right-hand side. For them, current NATO doctrine is self-defeating and incoherent. Present strategy plans for the early use of nuclear weapons, if, as is claimed would be likely, Soviet forces begin to prevail at non-nuclear level. This is profoundly danger-ous, because, as we have seen, it has led both sides to expose nuclear systems to all the hazards of local confrontation. It is also irrational. Far from serving to compensate for her supposed conventional inferiority, NATO's invoking of the nuclear option would in any case almost certainly, either compound her defeat, or lead to her own destruction. Since the enemy is similarly equipped, the use of battlefield nuclear weapons would result in the devastation of the areas in Western Europe being defended, while the more densely populated West would suffer more than the East if longer range systems became involved. In addition, if there is rough nuclear parity, and short of mutual annihilation, conventional strength is still likely in the end to remain decisive, so that NATO strategy fails in its prime objective. It is a mistake to assume that a European war would necessarily be a short one. Besides, plans for 'limited nuclear war' are only credible if both sides subscribe to them. But in this case the Soviet Union has all along made it clear that it does not recognize such a concept: any use of nuclear weapons would be likely to precipitate a general exchange. (We might also note that, whereas in (i), the stress in the argument on the left was on the overwhelming strength of Warsaw Pact con-ventional forces, here it is on how successful NATO might be in delaying the initiation of nuclear war.)

COMMENT:

Here we have the central confrontation in the whole of this area of the dis-agreement. It is on these grounds above all that we are being urged to support nuclear or non-nuclear defence policies. And yet, leaving aside the question of the relative strengths of non-nuclear forces which we have looked at in (i), the two sides can be said to agree about most of the substantial points that each is making. Those who support the argument on the left do not deny that the use of nuclear weapons might be mutually disastrous, and those who support the right-hand argument do not deny that NATO command does genuinely intend to prevent war. What divides them is the belief of those 'for' that mutual fear makes deployment safe and deterrence effective, and the belief of those 'against' that deployment is dangerous when the deterrent threat lacks credibility. This is a mis-match of perspectives with which we are already familiar.

(iv) **Does the growing size of the**   OR **Does the West initiate nearly all**
     Soviet nuclear arsenal threaten the   **phases of the nuclear arms race**
     delicate theatre and strategic   **and continue to enjoy a substantial**
     balance? Would Western failure to   **lead in most areas? Is the nuclear**
     match Soviet systems be   **'overkill' such that the West could**
     destabilizing?   **offer a nuclear 'freeze' or**
                                    unconditional cuts without risk?

Once again, the claim is, not that numbers of Soviet warheads need to be balanced quantitatively, but that qualitative improvements in the Soviet arsenal need to be matched. The argument is that at strategic level the Soviet Union took gross advantage of American restraint in the 1970s and initiated a massive qualitative and quantitative build-up, particularly of more accurate land-based systems, which were seen by the other side to threaten a possible first strike. And at intermediate level, among other things, a whole class of mobile, multiple-warhead longer-range systems (the SS20s), capable of reaching any target in Western Europe from the Soviet Union, threatened to overturn the theatre balance. The Soviets also enjoy a substantial numerical advantage in shorter range nuclear forces. Not to have gone some way towards matching these challenges would have gravely weakened deterrence, and reduced all incentive for bilateral and multilateral negotiation.

The scenario outlined above is flatly rejected here. The claim is that the West has initiated most phases of the nuclear arms race, has a significant (and, to the Soviet Union, alarming) lead in nearly all areas, and has all along enjoyed superiority in effective firepower at strategic and theatre levels – even before recent 'modernization' programmes were launched. At strategic level, Soviet ICBM deployment is more than matched by US predominance in SLBMs and bombers, and Soviet crude megatonnage is trumped by the larger numbers of US warheads and their far greater accuracy and sophistication. At theatre level, estimates for the arbitrarily defined Longer Range Intermediate Nuclear Forces (LRINF) include Soviet missiles deployed along the Chinese frontier, but disingenuously exclude submarine launched missiles and nuclear capable aircraft assigned to NATO, as well as shorter range missiles which can reach Eastern Europe, but not the Soviet Union. The Soviet Union, mortified by the discrepancy in power revealed during the Cuba missile crisis, has been trying to catch up with the West. It is highly destabilizing for the West to be pulling still further ahead now, using these fabricated figures as an excuse.

COMMENT:

This disagreement is a complement to that in B(i). Here again the reader is likely to be bemused by appeals on both sides to statistical fact, together with accusation and counter-accusation of transparent manipulation of it. It may also seem surprising that, whereas one claims that deterrence is stable but delicate, the other maintains that it is unstable but robust. Legitimate difficulties over problems of definition, when there is such geographical, operational and force-structure asymmetry between the two blocs, is compounded for the reader once again by partisan polemics.

(v) **Are NATO 'forward defence' and**   OR **Should NATO exploit her lead in**
  'deep strike' strategies essential   **'emerging technology' to explore**
  for effective deterrence?   **less provocative alternative**
                                              strategies?

'Forward defence', that is to say, roughly, the declared policy of holding the inner West German frontier, rather than being prepared to trade space for time, is more a prerequisite for West German cooperation than a strategy recommended by military analysis. There are a number of supplementary measures which could be taken were this not the case. The West Germans are not prepared to plan for a conventional war on German soil, and are reluctant to build elaborate defensive fortifications which might seem to make the division of Germany permanent.

But 'deep strike' is essential, in view of Soviet plans for the massing of successive waves of assault against chosen axes of attack. It cannot be called 'provocative' for the West to counter by threatening to strike at the follow-on forces. The Soviet Union will only be deterred if it knows that its own territory and that of its allies will not be immune in the resulting conflict. The so-called 'emerging technologies' of multiple-launch rockets, precision-guided systems, and so on, do, indeed, offer the prospect of strengthening NATO's non-nuclear forces, and reducing dependence on the likely early use of nuclear weapons – which is why a NATO initiative to exploit them was launched in 1982. But, in order to 'lower the nuclear threshold' in this way, we will again need to be able to use these weapons to strike at airfields and massing concentrations of armour deep in enemy territory. In any case, Emerging Technology is expensive and will take a long time to develop and deploy, and we must not forget that the Soviet Union is also engaged in a similar exercise. Nuclear weapons are still relatively cheap, and do not significantly inhibit a parallel strengthening of conventional defence. In short, it is the Soviet concentration on the massing of the kinds of heavy equipment needed for invasion which is 'aggressive', not NATO's plans for countering this threat in the only way it can.

NATO's reliance on the illusion of nuclear deterrence means that there is no incentive to plan for adequate non-nuclear defence. It is a counsel of despair. And yet the great wealth, manpower and technological superiority of the nations of the Western Alliance makes it unnecessary and absurd that NATO should still be clinging to this traditional mixture of belligerence and defeatism. There is simply no reason why the Eastern bloc's conventional threat, such as it is, should not be met by Western conventional forces. Particularly today, there are large numbers of possibilities to be exploited, which include a more effective use of reserve manpower, the construction of proper defensive fortifications, and the application of those advanced technologies in which the West holds such a commanding lead. The opportunity is there to be seized, as new technology threatens to make capital intensive systems, such as tanks, heavy aircraft and large surface ships, decreasingly cost-effective and vulnerable to cheaper precision-guided missiles and rockets, some of them handheld. It is disgraceful that NATO governments are doing so little in these directions, as a result of the inertia which habitual dependence upon nuclear deterrence has engendered. The heavily armed NATO dinosaur must be made to adapt, or it will carry all of us with it into extinction.

COMMENT:

Much of the arguing here is technical, and therefore difficult for those who are not experienced in current military strategy to assess. One side is accused of being short-sighted and inflexible, and the other of being ignorant and naive. Clearly, the scope that there is thought to be for the replacement of nuclear with non-nuclear options will depend upon a prior assessment of how great the non-nuclear threat from the Soviet bloc is. So the reader may interpret this part of the debate in the light of conclusions, which have perhaps already been drawn from earlier sections.

(vi) **Is it the presence of American**   OR **Is it domination by the two**
    front-line troops and the tying-in   **superpowers that poses the**
    of theatre nuclear forces to the   **greatest threat to European**
    American strategic deterrent that   **integrity? Would Europe be safer**
    guarantees W. European security?   **decoupled from the superpower**
    Should American policies   **nuclear confrontation? Should**
    therefore be supported?   **Europe be made a nuclear**
                                   weapon-free zone?

To those who support current policy, this argument is axiomatic. Western European security is in the end underpinned by the presence of American troops along a clearly defined frontier, and by the linkage between those troops and the undeniable and prohibitive power of the American strategic nuclear deterrent. Western Europe clearly has the resources to form itself into a potent deterrent force, and successive US administrations have been keen for the European contribution to the Alliance to be strengthened. But political divisions and a reluctance to devote further resources to defence makes significant change in this direction unlikely in the middle term, so that for the foreseeable future, the Atlantic Alliance remains essential to European security. Seen in this light, the anti-American feeling among many European radical nuclear disarmers is difficult to sympathize with. Clearly there cannot be an exact identity of interest between a number of smaller regional states, and one of the two greatest global powers. But it is an absurd travesty to suggest that the United States is as much of a 'threat to European integrity' as is the Soviet Union. Compare the fact that a freely elected British government can demand the removal of the few American bases in this country, with the situation in Eastern Europe. Radical nuclear disarmers often forget that it was Western European governments which implored the United States to base troops in Europe, and it is Western European governments which insist that American nuclear weapons should be based on European soil.

From this perspective, the argument presented opposite is an attempt to make the Yalta settlement permanent. Europe is to be for ever in thrall to the two superpowers and exposed to all the dangers of their global nuclear confrontation. The incredible concentration of weaponry, nuclear and non-nuclear, if it ever was necessary for European stability, is certainly not so now. On the contrary, it is a grave menace to it.

What is the remedy? There are essential short-term measures to be taken, and a clear long-term goal. Neither is remotely 'anti-American', and both are evidently in the interests of US defence policy. In the short term, the aim must be to clear nuclear weapons from the European mainland. Battlefield weapons should be removed from a corridor either side of the frontier, and longer range land-based systems should be swiftly phased out by mutual agreement, as already suggested by the superpowers. European governments should no longer ridiculously resist these moves. If both superpowers want to retain reserve second strike strategic nuclear forces, that will be something which cannot be determined within the European theatre. The longer term aim, of course, will be for Soviet troops to be withdrawn from Eastern Europe and US troops from Western Europe, a development which, once again, would be enthusiastically welcomed in the United States. What is certain is that no progress can be made in this direction if the brittle and inflexible intransigence expressed opposite is allowed to continue to dominate European councils. The proposals made here are no more than a pragmatic recognition of processes which are taking place anyway.

COMMENT:

Perhaps this partial mutual contradiction and partial mutual misunderstanding can be left to speak for itself. There is probably more in common between the two positions than either thinks, and what is not in common is largely made up of divergences which we have already considered elsewhere. In fact, this is an area in which there seems to be an almost continuous spectrum of opinion, including, towards the extremes, the attitudes of Western Europeans who are more hostile to the United States, and of Americans who are more indifferent to or resentful of Western Europe, than is suggested here.

(vii) **Would Western unilateral nuclear** OR **Are unilateral initiatives as part of**
disarmament invite Soviet **a general programme of nuclear**
blackmail? Are suggestions that **disarmament the only way to**
the West should take the lead in **reverse the arms race? Is talk of**
offering unilateral disarmament **'multilateral disarmament'**
initiatives the thin end of this **insincere in the mouths of those**
wedge? Do radical nuclear **who reject all suggestion of a**
disarmers consciously or **Comprehensive Test Ban Treaty,**
unconsciously serve Soviet **a Nuclear Freeze, a European**
interests and threaten to **Nuclear Weapon Free Zone, or a**
undermine Western defences? **declaration of No First Use?**

It is evident that complete and immediate nuclear disarmament in the face of
a determined nuclear-armed enemy would invite blackmail, which, if resisted,
would precipitate nuclear war, and, if not, would force surrender. The choice
in that case would indeed be to be 'either red or dead'. For this reason,
unilateralists usually choose to emphasize measures which initially stop short
of that. It is fashionable for them to deny that they are 'unilateralist' on the
grounds that they are only advocating 'unilateral' steps as part of some supposed general process of world-wide nuclear disarmament. But this is disingenuous. Either through ignorance, or through deliberate political calculation,
they tend to pass over the threat from totalitarian communism, and to reserve
their criticism for Western governments, especially that of the United States.
Radical nuclear disarmament pressure groups are almost all to be found in the
West. They would not be tolerated for a moment within the Eastern blocks.
And we have already seen the effect that this policy would have. It would
undermine Western cohesion and strength, and set back the whole process
of negotiated disarmament. Unconditional Western cuts would permanently
entrench Soviet advantage, and remove all incentive to negotiate nuclear and
non-nuclear force reductions. There *are* unilateral moves that the West can
make to advantage – such as the significant reduction in the numbers of battlefield weapons that is in any case now under way. But it is foolish to suggest
that what would in effect be a process of progressive unilateral nuclear disarmament can ever be central to prudent Western policy.

Here, the view opposite is seen to be nothing more than an argument for the indefinite perpetuation of the nuclear arms race. It is a transparent device adopted by those who have a vested interest in it. Every avenue which might lead to a reduction in tension or to a slowing down in the rate of escalation is blocked in advance on one pretext or another. It is entirely forgotten that escalation itself is made up of 'unconditional' or 'unilateral' moves, such as the American Strategic Defence Initiative, which will carry the arms race into space. Any suggestion that much more modest moves could be made in the opposite direction is met by the blanket charge that 'unilateral disarmament' will mean 'nuclear blackmail'. Four points can be made in refutation of this familiar and empty accusation. First, no one is suggesting unilateral Western nuclear disarmament. This is a deliberate exaggeration to divert attention away from what *is* being proposed. The only way ahead lies through both sides being prepared to offer and reciprocate a graduated series of unconditional initiatives in the direction of general nuclear disarmament, in order to break the vicious spiral of escalation embodied in the case presented opposite and build the mutual confidence needed for further progress. This was how important advances were made in the early 1960s after the Cuba Missile Crisis. The Soviet Union has recently made gestures of exactly this kind, such as the unilateral moratorium on nuclear weapons testing, and it is gross hypocrisy for those who argued against reciprocation at the same time to oppose Western initiatives on the grounds that the Soviet Union may not respond. Secondly, as we have seen, the size of current nuclear arsenals means that, even within terms of nuclear deterrent theory, large numbers of unconditional initiatives are possible without the slightest question of destabilization. Thirdly, there is no reason why both superpowers should not keep minimum nuclear forces during the process of build-down. And, finally, the whole idea of the nuclear blackmail of a non-nuclear by a nuclear power in any case lacks plausibility. It did not happen in Vietnam; it is not happening in Afghanistan. The accident at Chernobyl shows that an aggressor would be likely to suffer from his own aggression if he carried out his threat.

The fundamental problems are political, not military, and so must the sol-

utions be. But military, and particularly nuclear, confrontation, makes political accommodation almost impossible. The confidence-building gestures being proposed here are essential components in the process of reconciliation. Subsequent bilateral and multilateral agreements are also, of course, equally essential. But the latter can only be achieved within the context created by the former. Those who persistently oppose every conciliatory move on the grounds that it is a step towards 'unilateral disarmament', are wedded to the indefinite perpetuation of cold war antagonism between East and West, and are prepared to sacrifice future global security, if not survival, to it.

COMMENT:

This confrontation sums up the difficulties facing the reader in the debate. The disagreement has reached the point where opposite judgements are made about the same proposal, because each interprets it against a background of elaborate and incompatible prior argumentation. For example, what is described on the left-hand side as 'Western determination' and seen as an essential *cause* of current apparent progress towards arms control agreement, is described on the right-hand side as 'Western belligerence' and seen as the main *threat* to it. Each sees the other as undermining common and collective security. No one element can be singled out for separate consideration. What is at issue is a complex, made up of all the arguing that has gone on before. And the vocabularies that are used are themselves caught up in it. Each tries to resist the other's terminology. Those who want to refer to a 'nuclear arms race', or a 'military-industrial complex', or a 'nuclear war-fighting strategy', at the same time want to reject the concepts built into terms such as 'extended deterrence', 'nuclear umbrella', or 'arms control' – and vice versa. Are we talking about 'independent initiatives' or 'unilateral disarmament', about 'nuclear confrontation' or 'nuclear deterrence', about 'provocation' or 'defence'? So divergent have the two perspectives become by this stage, that neither of the protagonists can see substance, let alone force, in the other's case at all. If the other nevertheless persists with it, then it can only be for political reasons. We are no longer faced with arguments to be refuted, but with rationalizations to be set aside. The debate is on the verge of breaking down, as disagreement about issues degenerates towards a juxtaposition of mutually uncomplimentary judgements about people.

C *British Policy*

In Section 1 below we deal with Britain's independent nuclear forces. This means, above all, the four 'Polaris' submarines, which are committed to NATO, but also play an independent strategic role. In addition, there is a dual-capable theatre force of nine Tornado and two Buccaneer squadrons, which can deliver free-fall British nuclear bombs. Sea Harriers, and Sea-King and Lynx anti-submarine helicopters are also dual-capable.

Although the distinction is not as clear-cut as is suggested here, in Section 2, we move on to deal, first, with the British Army of the Rhine (BAOR) battlefield nuclear capability, including one Lance missile regiment and five regiments of guns able to fire American nuclear warheads under dual-key control (C2(i)). And, second, with the American nuclear weapon bases in this country – in particular, the Poseidon submarine base at Holy Loch, the F-III air bases at Upper Heyford and Lakenheath, and the ground-launched Cruise missile bases at Greenham Common and Molesworth (C2(ii)).

Apart from her nuclear contribution, Britain is usually seen to support NATO in three other ways: by securing the British home base, by garrisoning West Germany, and by protecting the sea-lanes of the Eastern Atlantic and the English Channel. Further commitments outside NATO include the defence of the Falkland Islands, and the maintenance of other Out-of-Area capabilities in general.

1 *The British Deterrent*

(i) **Is Britain's deterrent a weapon of   OR Would all possible uses of last resort which guarantees her   Britain's 'deterrent' be suicidal? Is sovereignty and independence and   its only effect to encourage protects her from nuclear   proliferation? blackmail?**

Those who argue like this usually say that Britain's involvement in nuclear weapon development and deployment can only realistically be debated against the background of Western defence policy, as we have just outlined it. Although, in the last resort, Britain retains undisputed sovereign control over her own independent nuclear deterrent forces, which can, as a result, be said to protect her against the possibility of nuclear blackmail, they are committed to the NATO alliance, and are disposed and targeted accordingly. The defence of Britain is inextricably tied up with the defence of the West, and it is senseless to try to consider Britain's role in isolation. Nevertheless, in a world in which, so far as can be seen, nuclear weapons will remain a reality for some powers and a perpetual possibility for others, well on into the next century, there is no doubt that Britain's possession of her own nuclear forces serves as an ultimate guarantee of her sovereign independence and freedom. That is why the British deterrent has always been strongly supported by a majority of the British people. It would be a pointless and foolish gesture to hand it away gratuitously.

The first thing that is stressed here is that, if Britain did not already have her own so-called 'independent' nuclear forces, she certainly would not be acquiring them now. Her original motives were less to do with considerations of strategy than with the instinct of a great imperial power to have whatever the other great powers had. The decision was taken by a tiny handful of men for reasons which today seem quaint. Since then, despite the transformation that there has been in global politics, in the nature of nuclear weaponry, and in our own position in the world, the process has been carried forward equally blindly and equally undemocratically by the kind of technological, institutional and psychological forces that we have described above. Official arguments in favour of the British deterrent are, therefore, little more than rationalization. They do not stand up to scrutiny.

For example, it can never be rational for Britain to use her strategic nuclear deterrent against the Soviet Union, and the idea of tactical or strategic nuclear weapons being used against other powers is equally irresponsible. It is virtually

impossible to imagine a scenario in which Britain on her own is faced with the threat of nuclear blackmail. Both the British and the French nuclear forces are nothing more than political symbols, expensive and dangerous expressions of ex-imperial delusions of grandeur. Militarily they are irrelevant to security. Moreover, being dependent in Britain's case upon US technology, they can hardly be called 'independent', and, if anything, serve further to erode our economic and political sovereignty, not 'guarantee' it. All that Britain's nuclear forces do internationally is to complicate superpower arms control negotiations, help to hold up measures such as a Comprehensive Test Ban Treaty, and contribute to the general proliferation of nuclear arsenals.

COMMENT:

Lurking behind this area of the dispute is, once again, the problematic relationship between 'deterrence' and 'use'. But, in general both sides agree that much of the argument here is based upon supposition. A number of those who support the left hand argument concede that a nuclear force of this kind might offer protection against nuclear blackmail in certain circumstances, and most of those who support the view expressed above agree that such an eventuality appears to be a very remote one. This part of the discussion is more to do with instinct than inference, and is, perhaps, less vulnerable to reasoned refutation as a result.

(ii) **Are British nuclear forces valuable** OR **Is the 'second centre of decision**
     to European allies because they   making' an illusion when there is
     provide a specifically European   no independent strategic role to be
     second centre of decision making?   played? Are European allies
     **   unenthusiastic about a parochial**
     **   British force likely to inhibit her**
     **   commitment to European**
     **   defence?**

We now look at the British deterrent from a European point of view.

★ ★ ★

Here we reach what is for many the main justification for the retention of
an independent British nuclear force. Does Britain's traditional investment in
independent nuclear forces, supported by every British government since the
war, contribute towards the greater security of the Alliance, or detract from
it? There can really only be one answer to this question, and that is the answer
unanimously given by our European and American allies. Not one of our
European partners wants us to give up our independent deterrent – not Italy,
nor West Germany, nor even France. It is seen to be a small, but significant,
increment to NATO's nuclear capabilities, and, above all, to be a *European-
controlled* force. This guards against the possibility of a Soviet perception
of American inhibition, and greatly strengthens the European pillar of the
Transatlantic Alliance. It also keeps open the option of future cooperation
with France, if it is thought that the evolution of Western European defence
should move in the direction of further integration. Certainly, British unilateral renunciation would mean that Western Europe would become even more
dependent upon the American nuclear deterrent, and would lose the possibility of greater independence and freedom of action.

From this perspective, the 'second centre of decision making' argument is seen as just one more official rationalization. The claim that without British nuclear forces the Soviet Union might think that the United States might be inhibited from defending Europe for fear of retaliation is regarded as an attempt to say that the Americans might be unreliable allies without offending them. Why should Britain be thought to be any more willing to sacrifice herself for her allies than is the United States? It seems unconvincing that the main justification for the existence of the small British deterrent should be the lack of credibility of the large American one. This just demonstrates once again the bankruptcy of nuclear deterrence theory.

The same applies to the concept of a 'European deterrent' – which suffers from the further drawback that it is in any case entirely unfeasible. European governments have not even been able to coordinate conventional weapon-building programmes, and there is no indication that things would be different with nuclear forces. Even if Anglo-French cooperation could be achieved, in what sense would this be a 'European' force? And how would the Soviet Union be likely to react if West Germany were implicated in the creation of a strengthened second Western deterrent? All of this is both unrealistic and dangerous. Britain's contribution to the Alliance is much better served by a significant strengthening of the conventional land, sea, and air forces upon which true security depends.

COMMENT:

The broad question behind these considerations is this – in which direction should Western European defence evolve? It seems to be generally agreed that we cannot expect the relationship with the United States to remain unchanged indefinitely. Sooner or later adjustments must be made. But what should the role of British nuclear forces be in this process? Those who argue as opposite tend either to think that we must continue to rely on the American nuclear guarantee until the threat from Soviet nuclear and non-nuclear forces is removed (we will call this, position A); or to envisage the possibility that the future unity and independence of Western Europe may require the creation of a European nuclear deterrent (we will call this, position B). For the former, British nuclear forces are a useful addition, for the latter, part of a possible

future substitute, for the US deterrent. Those who argue as above, however, reject the concept of a nuclear-armed Europe altogether. They see nuclear weapons, whether American, British, or French, as endangering, not enhancing, European security (we will call this, position C). From position A, the other two seem dangerously unrealistic and destabilizing; from position B, the other two seem in different ways to be betrayals of European integrity; from position C, the other two seem to do no more than compound the lunacy of past policy.

As presented here, these alternatives may have been overdrawn, but they are, nevertheless, representative.

(iii) **Does the US favour shared**   OR **Are US forces committed anyway**
     responsibility and do British   **and independent British initiatives**
     nuclear forces guarantee full US   **more likely to trigger Soviet**
     commitment to Europe and Soviet   **retaliation than US involvement?**
     recognition of it?

We now look at the British deterrent from a US point of view.

⋆   ⋆   ⋆

There are those who have suggested that Britain's independent use of her nuclear forces might involve the United States in an impending European war, which she would otherwise be reluctant to enter. This argument is rarely heard today, and will from now on be ignored.

The main suggestion here is that the United States is firmly in favour of Britain's independent deterrent, as can be seen by her continued willingness to contribute towards it. She welcomes the shared responsibility, and rightly fears that, no matter what may be claimed at the time, British nuclear renunciation will, in the end, be found to be part of a significant weakening in Britain's overall defence effort. Little of what is said by those most vociferous in support of renunciation can be seen to allay this fear. Transatlantic ties are more likely to be loosened by European weakness than by European strength. And European strength must include a nuclear component.

The idea that Britain's nuclear forces somehow help to tie the United States in to European defence is rejected. The United States is in Europe, because it is in her own interest to be there. Any independent British initiative would more probably trigger separate Soviet (or even American) retaliation than American involvement. Emphasis on the need for multiple decision-centres of this kind indicates a lack of cohesion within the Alliance, and, if anything, is likely to invite, rather than deter, Russian adventurism.

Most American commentators are seen as being relatively indifferent to a British deterrent, at most tolerating it out of loyalty to an old ally. If anything, it is regarded as an irritating anomoly in arms control negotiations with the Soviet Union.

COMMENT:

As presented here, there is general agreement about the importance of US commitment to the defence of Europe, but not about the role of the British nuclear deterrent in securing it. This is only regarded as critical by those who see nuclear deterrence as essential to European defence, and a European contribution as essential in persuading a number of Americans to continue to support full involvement.

In saying all this, what we have not done justice to is the view of those who do not want Transatlantic ties to be maintained at all, but would welcome the withdrawal of the US presence from Europe. This is not part of the policy of any of the three main political groupings in this country.

(iv) Is the cost of the British deterrent OR **Can Britain's nuclear forces only**
small in view of the vital defence   **be afforded at the expense of**
role it plays? Are alternatives   **conventional strength and of other**
likely to be more expensive?   **more important economic**
                                                priorities?

For some, the role of the British deterrent is vital to national security, so that the price must be paid whatever it is. The question of relative cost does not arise if the priority is absolute. France, for example, is prepared to pay much more than Britain for her nuclear independence, because she regards it as indispensable.

For others, the argument is that the percentage of the defence budget absorbed by the nuclear weapons programme (2.3 per cent of the defence budget in 1982–3) is not large enough to force difficult choices by precluding other major options, and that alternative measures would be decisively less effective and relatively more expensive. The claim that money saved would be spent on conventional arms is seen to be irrelevant. If these putative improvements are considered vital (which is hard to conceive, because they are marginal increments in already existing capacity), then the money could just as well come from areas less crucial than the British nuclear deterrent; if not, then we will be better off without them. Either way, the argument about cost is usually invoked disingenuously by those, who, given their head, would drastically reduce defence spending as a whole anyway. We are being asked to make an entirely false economy, which can only have the result of accelerating British industrial decline as the nuclear programme is wound down, and reducing long-term security.

Here the crux of the argument is that, against a background of mounting balance of payments constraints, Britain will only be able to afford the next generation of nuclear weapons at the expense of her broader and more important conventional commitments. It is pointed out that the overall cost of the nuclear weapons programme is much higher than officially estimated, when all the overheads are taken into account; that the Trident programme will raise this very substantially; and that, in any case, the defence budget is being severely cut back in real terms over the next few years. Britain already cannot afford all her present defence commitments. What is urgently needed is a proper review of defence priorities, which have not been adequately worked out. We have now reached the moment when we have to choose between major areas of commitment, and, in these circumstances, there can really only be one conclusion: the money being squandered on nuclear weapons, which make no significant contribution to our defence, should be reallocated within the traditional Armed Services, where it will generate far more benefit for the economy, and contribute far more substantially to our security.

COMMENT:

Once again, we have neglected the arguing of those who do not want defence spending to be maintained at its present level, but would prefer money saved by nuclear renunciation to be spent instead on industrial investment and social welfare.

So far as concerns the alternatives being offered here, the choice clearly depends upon how important the defence role of an independent deterrent is seen to be. If it is seen to have no importance, then any price would be too high; if an absolute importance, then no price would be too great. But, between these extremes, the reader is again faced with an area of the debate in which statistics and counter-statistics regularly confront one another. It does seem that we are moving into a period in which constraints on the defence budget will force difficult choices. But, whereas one side attributes this very largely to the mounting cost of the British nuclear deterrent, the other denies that this is central at all. So it is difficult to assess this question without at the same time assessing overall defence priorities.

(v) **Would unilateral British nuclear   OR Does the British deterrent**
disarmament have no effect on   encourage proliferation and do
other countries and only serve to   nothing to enhance British
weaken British influence and allow   prestige? Would British
France unchallenged ascendancy   disarmament within the context
in Europe?   outlined in B help to break the
**   nuclear log-jam?**

The idea that British unilateral nuclear disarmament might act as an example to the world and serve to 'break the nuclear log-jam' is seen to be misconceived. British forces are relatively too small to make a significant difference to the overall strategic balance between the superpowers (although Soviet leaders will make encouraging noises about phasing out equivalent systems in order to strengthen the disarmament lobby), while, so far as the rest of the world is concerned, British 'example' counts for much less than insular-minded unilateralists would like to think. As it is, Britain's possession of an independent deterrent reinforces her close relationship with the United States, and allows her considerable influence, as shown in the Camp David accords of December 1984. That France should be left as the only nuclear power in Europe is a prospect which may offend British pride, but, more importantly, is also regarded with dismay by our European allies – including France herself.

Within the general context of what has been argued earlier, a firm commitment to nuclear disarmament by Great Britain could at last help to throw the momentum of the arms race into reverse – particularly if the Soviet response confirmed the principle that build-down can be achieved by graduated reciprocation of unconditional initiatives. Pressure would then perhaps build for the United States to respond as well, and the nuclear weapon debate might be opened up in France. Above all, as the first post-nuclear power, British renunciation must, if anything, be a brake on proliferation, and would be likely to increase, rather than decrease, her international prestige and influence. As it is, her nuclear status as an American client does not enhance her standing in the world, nor even significantly affect her ability to modify the policies of her patron. If France wants to waste her money on what is nothing more than a political symbol, then let her.

COMMENT:

This is not at the moment considered to be a crucial area of the debate by any of the three main political groupings in this country. But there are others who find it central. Behind it could perhaps be said to lie different concepts of what Britain's future role in the world should be. There are those who would like to maintain the present position, including the 'special relationship' with the United States (A); there are those who would rather move more in the direction that France has taken within a stronger Europe (B); and there are those who find the vigorous internationalism of some of the Scandinavian countries a more inspiring model (C). As an ex-Imperial power and member of the Commonwealth, with a permanent seat in the Security Council, and close Transatlantic ties, Britain does not share the experience of a number of her European partners. She may be said to have found it harder to adjust to her dramatically changed status in the world. And all of this is connected to her economic difficulties, and to the deep divisions in her domestic political life. Visions of a future international role for Britain are not separate from ideas about how British society itself should evolve.

(vi) **Is investment in Trident the best** OR **Would commitment to Trident**
       way to continue to ensure   **exacerbate all the drawbacks listed**
       effective British strategic defence   **above?**
       into the 21st century?

Position A

If Britain wants to maintain an effective independent nuclear deterrent, then
there can be no doubt that Trident will be the best system for the quarter
century that begins in the 1990s, just as Polaris has been in the quarter century
before that. There just are no cheaper alternatives that can pose as credible a
deterrent threat. For example, submarine-launched Cruise missiles would be
less effective, because, among other things, the submarines would have to
move much nearer to the target in order to fire them, and would therefore be
easier to detect; and more expensive, because we would need many more of
them. Trident will provide protection at least until the year 2020. If we want
a deterrent, then we should have the best available. And it will still be a
minimum deterrent. It is not the intention to arm the submarines to full
warhead capacity.

Position B

Trident can and should be cancelled. It can be cancelled, because the costs of doing so are not yet prohibitive, and could in any case be mitigated in various ways. It should be cancelled for three main reasons. First, Trident would represent a huge leap in targeting potential over Polaris, encouraging further escalation and proliferation quite out of keeping with the concept of a minimum deterrent. Second, there are cheaper alternatives, which do not commit us to vast expenditure for years ahead at a time when the defence budget will in any case be coming under severe constraint. Other essential programmes will undoubtedly suffer if we persist with Trident. We can prolong the life of Polaris in order to give us time to make a proper review of options, and to see whether superpower negotiations are likely to lead to a build-down, as part of which, at a later stage, Britain can safely relinquish her nuclear capability altogether. Third, Trident means a permanent locking in to American technology, since the essential missile components will be built there. We should explore the possibility of cooperation with our European partners.

Position C

Trident should be cancelled as part of an immediate switch of emphasis within British defence policy, away from the whole illusion of nuclear deterrence, and towards a proper strengthening of conventional forces.

COMMENT:

'A' argues for the importance of indefinite nuclear deterrence with independence of use and operation; 'B' argues for temporary nuclear deterrence conditional upon international negotiation, with, if possible, independence of supply and support as well as use; 'C' argues that nuclear deterrence is a dangerous delusion. From the standpoint of A and B, C seems unrealistic and irresponsible; from that of B and C, A seems inflexible and misguided; from that of A and C, B seems to get the worst of both worlds. The choice confronting the reader is not an easy one to make.

2 *NATO Forces and US Bases*

(i) Must Britain continue to share OR **Should British obligations to**
responsibility for manning NATO **NATO be met by strengthening**
nuclear systems upon which her **conventional forces where**
security depends? Would refusal **necessary within an overall non-**
to do so fatally weaken the **nuclear strategy as recommended**
alliance? **in B?**

What would the effect be if a future British government unilaterally refused to man the nuclear systems currently deployed with BAOR and RAF (Germany)? Clearly, it would be profoundly damaging, and incompatible with continuing full membership of the NATO Alliance. It is disingenuous to pretend that we can carry through the logic of such policies, and at the same time reaffirm our commitment to NATO. The whole of NATO strategy has been, is, and for the foreseeable future will continue to be, based upon the complementary deterrent use of conventional and nuclear capabilities. The reasons why this must be so have already been given. It is not within the power of a British government to alter this through unilateral action. So, it is either British policy to accept NATO strategy, or to reject it. There is no half-way position. If NATO strategy is accepted, then the refusal to man nuclear delivery systems in Europe becomes a gratuitous political gesture. The burden of deterrence is shifted to allies, and Britain is prepared to reap the benefits of their effort without sharing the responsibility. If, on the other hand, NATO nuclear deterrent strategy is rejected, then it is evident that Britain can no longer claim to be a full member of an Alliance which is firmly committed to it. Either way, such unilateral renunciation would gravely damage the cohesion and strength of the Alliance, weakening particular sectors of the front, and making integrated command, where troops from one country serve under officers from another, almost impossible. It is not certain that the Alliance would survive.

The argument that there are smaller powers within the Alliance which do not man or host nuclear forces is irrelevant. They are not comparable to Britain. France, Italy, and West Germany, which are comparable, all contribute in their different ways to the nuclear defence of Europe.

The major premise here, of course, is that NATO's current nuclear deterrent policy is disastrous, and that the Allies could and should move decisively towards a proper non-nuclear defence. This, and only this, is in the long-term interest of all those whom the Alliance is there to protect. A further important premise, as we have seen, is that this transition can be effected safely. The rationale behind this has already been elaborated. So the question becomes: how should a member of an Alliance act, when it sees the Alliance itself as essential to communal security, but current policy as a grave and unnecessary danger to it? Clearly, the only rational option in these circumstances is for the member to do whatever lies within his sole competence safely to do, while continuing to contribute to it, and trying to persuade the other members to act accordingly. The claim that by doing this we shift the burden to others, and divide the Alliance, is empty. The 'burden' in this case is a militarily unusable and highly destabilizing capability, which endangers those it is meant to defend. If others choose to persist with it, that will be up to them. We will go on trying to dissuade them. And it is the nuclear deterrent policy which divides and weakens the Alliance already, not a renunciation of it. Already seven of the sixteen NATO countries refuse to have nuclear weapons on their soil, including Canada which took this step in 1978. The initiative towards sound non-nuclear defence is one which will be accompanied by full consultation, and, above all, by a major injection of resources into those components of Alliance strategy which *do* constitute a proper defence. A nation which continues to devote ninety-five per cent of its defence budget, and five per cent of its national income, to NATO cannot be accused of being half-hearted. In short, this is the only rational and responsible policy, and, far from being a dilution of effort and commitment, it is an emphatic reaffirmation of it.

COMMENT:

We have reached the heart of the matter. It is here that we can see most clearly that the controversy about the future direction of British defence policy presupposes what has gone before. It is only within the terms already set out in previous sections that the full significance of these alternatives can be appreciated. If nuclear weapons are essential to deterrence, and there are no stable· non-nuclear alternatives, then to relinquish the nuclear option is to weaken the Alliance and put the liberty and security of future generations at

risk (A). If nuclear weapons endanger rather than protect, and there are safer non-nuclear alternatives, then to persist with the nuclear pretence is to undermine proper defences and to take an inexcusable gamble with the lives of our children and grandchildren (C). And, between these two positions, there is a third (B), which is that, although it is true that current NATO nuclear strategies are dangerously flawed, so long as the Alliance as a whole is committed to them, and the Soviet Union has comparable nuclear capabilities, a member state, such as Britain, must continue to support them. Her proper response should, therefore, be to work energetically towards an overall shift of Alliance strategy towards non-nuclear defence, but in the meantime to play a full part in implementing current policy. She must on no account sow dissension within the Alliance.

We must also mention a fourth view, not subscribed to by any of the three main political groupings in this country, which is that Britain should withdraw from NATO at once, and join the non-aligned states.

It is, perhaps, underlining the obvious, to say that, whether policies A, B or C are seen to strengthen or weaken the Western Alliance, depends upon the context within which the policies are understood to be defined, what the nature of the Alliance is conceived to be, and where future security needs are thought to lie. In short, we cannot confidently assess these recommendations for British policy unless we have come to a conclusion about the broader regional and global judgements from which they are drawn. A major aim of the second part of this book is to make this possible.

(ii) Would the forced withdrawal of US nuclear bases from Britain make US defence of the West impossible? Is American interference in British affairs negligible?

OR **Do the large numbers of nuclear facilities yielded to the US erode British sovereignty? Would their removal do no more than restore a normal peacetime relationship?**

The forced removal of American nuclear weapons from Britain strikes many, who argue as on the left-hand side, as the most disastrous single action that could be taken, short of leaving the NATO Alliance altogether. The presence of American frontline troops in Europe, and the clear connection which the Soviet Union sees between those troops and the threat posed by the American strategic nuclear deterrent, are thought to be fundamental to continued Western European security. To jeopardize this is regarded as the height of irresponsibility. To remove American nuclear weapons from this country (and, by implication, to support their removal from other European countries as well), would be to deprive the American troops who are here to defend us of the protection that they clearly need in the face of Soviet nuclear capabilities. It would be a profound shock to the Western Alliance, and would send a signal to Moscow that NATO was beginning to break up. That this should be done by the country upon whom the Americans had thought that they could rely most, would make the shock all the greater. As the reverberations died away, those elements on the other side of the Atlantic, particularly in Congress, which favour isolationism, would be greatly strengthened. It is not at all certain that the Transatlantic Alliance would survive.

It is absurd to say that the American presence 'erodes our sovereignty'. It was the Europeans who asked for weapons such as Cruise to be based here. They cannot be used without the agreement of the British Prime Minister – as the Libyan raid showed. They expose America as much to British manipulation as vice versa. And the very fact that we can contemplate their forced removal demonstrates where sovereignty lies.

To those who argue like this, however, it seems clear that at the moment Britain is seen as little more than a large American aircraft carrier, and is targeted by the USSR accordingly. Mobile systems, such as Cruise, mean blanket targeting. Britain will inevitably fall an early victim in any global superpower confrontation, even if that confrontation has its origin in another part of the world. There can be no doubt that British independence in defence and foreign policy is severely restricted by current nuclear strategies – as the French understood a number of years ago. Even Britain's 'independent' deterrent is dependent upon the United States for missile technology, warhead materials, testing, navigational facilities and targeting information. And the idea that in a crisis a British veto on American use of her bases in this country will count for much is an illusion. The lameness with which American policy has been endorsed at every turn in recent years, even when most out of line with majority opinion in this country and in Europe, shows the debilitating effects of such tutelage.

In any case, the range and accuracy of modern weapons systems means that Britain is no longer needed as a forward base, even within the context of a nuclear deterrent strategy. (This applies to the airfields, and to the submarine base at Holy Loch. Cruise missiles have never been a necessary component of Western defence.) So the function of these weapons has become political, not military. There are many in the United States who recognize all of this, and the United States will certainly not give up her vital European interests just because she is asked to remove nuclear weapons from Britain. In fact, even with their removal, there will still be large numbers of American facilities left. So the proposed policy is not nearly as radical as that unilaterally imposed by France in 1967. This is not in any way an anti-American policy. It is an attempt to move towards a sound defensive strategy, which will be of long-term benefit, not only to Britain, but to her Allies as well.

COMMENT:

In this case, we are concerned, not only with the strategic implications of alternative policies, but also with their effect on politically significant opinion in the United States. It is striking that those whose arguments are in line with the argument on the left tend to maximize and those who take the argument expressed above, to minimize, the strategic and political implications of a forced withdrawal of American nuclear weapons from Britain. That is because,

unlike some other commentators, both agree about the importance of maintaining strong Transatlantic ties. The necessarily theoretical nature of the deterrent role attributed to nuclear weapons allows scope for disagreement about the former; and the diversity of American public life allows scope for disagreement about the latter. Perhaps not surprisingly, the assumption in each case is that, since the strategic arguments behind the particular policy are evidently rational, it must be the case that rational commentators in the United States will agree with them.

(iii) **Will Britain continue to be**   OR **Is Britain seen as an American**
      targeted by Soviet warheads   **aircraft carrier and targeted by the**
      whether or not she unilaterally   **USSR accordingly? Will Britain**
      disarms?   **fall an early victim in any**
                                                 superpower confrontation unless
                                                 bases are removed?

The idea that Britain can turn herself into a nuclear-free haven as a result of unilateral nuclear disarmament is dismissed summarily by those who argue like this. Apart from fallout and other effects of nuclear war on the continent of Europe, Britain's geographical position and resources mean that she will inevitably become involved, whether or not she remains within the NATO Alliance.

This argument has widespread popularity, although it is not emphasized by any of the main political groupings in this country. It is an instinctive feeling that we must at least escape the worst consequences of nuclear war, if we have nothing to do with nuclear weapons – particularly if we distance ourselves from the two armed camps which deploy them.

COMMENT:

The political parties probably shun the argument on this page, because none of them wants to be associated with the 'Little England' attitude, which it seems to imply. It is the same with locally declared 'nuclear weapon-free zones', which are also considered naïve and unrealistic. And yet the sense of outrage that millions of people should be targeted as a result of policies to which they do not subscribe is deep and widespread. Perhaps it can be given vent in no other way.

(iv) **Can non-nuclear defences only**   OR **In a nuclear-free Europe,**
     safely be afforded by countries   **decoupled from the superpower**
     prepared to shelter beneath the   **nuclear confrontation, would**
     American nuclear umbrella?   **Britain no more expect to depend**
                                                    upon the US 'umbrella' than any
                                                    other Western ally – or than
                                                    Eastern Europe upon the USSR?

If Britain unilaterally pulls out of NATO's deterrent strategy, by the logic inherent in such a move she must inevitably drift towards neutrality. This may seem an attractive option to some, and much play among unilateralists is made of the non-nuclear defences of countries like Sweden or Switzerland. But, in view of the realities of European power politics, this is an indulgence which is once again only safe so long as others are bearing the brunt of an effective defence. It means nothing to say that we will not shelter under the American nuclear umbrella. It is American front-line troops and the American second strike strategic nuclear force which continue to protect Western Europe. If Western Europe as a whole adopted such a policy, the entire region would automatically slide into the orbit of Soviet power and influence without a shot being fired. Either way, the effect of these policies must be to disrupt and weaken the West, causing dismay and incomprehension among our European allies, and understandable resentment in the United States, which, as we have said, is already bearing so much of the burden of the defence of Western Europe. Britain would not be able to turn herself into a sanctuary, immune from nuclear war. She would simply become an anomalous fellow-traveller, as in so many other areas of public life in recent years, preferring to indulge in insular illusion rather than to play her part in the real world.

The fundamental fact to be understood at the outset here is that there is no such thing as an American nuclear *'umbrella'* over Europe. The explanation has already been given. Ever since the Soviet Union gained a comparable strategic capability, it has been evident that there is no way in which an American president will immolate the United States by launching a nuclear attack on the Soviet Union in defence of Europe. 'Extended deterrence' is an entirely empty concept – as all informed commentators on both sides of the Iron Curtain know. All that mutually held strategic nuclear forces of this kind can do is to cancel one another out. If the United States and the Soviet Union choose to keep such forces, that is something which is not in our power in Europe to decide. But it is irrelevant to pretend that anyone outside the United States or the Soviet Union will be sheltering under anything. And that also disposes of the outmoded idea that we would be laying ourselves open to 'nuclear blackmail'. Enough has already been said about this in B(vii).

The truth of the matter, as all our earlier argument has shown, is that continuing reliance on the myth of nuclear deterrence undermines our defences, sows dissension within the Alliance, and carries us ever closer to the catastrophe of nuclear war. To call this a *'nuclear umbrella'* is a grotesque contradiction in terms.

COMMENT:

Behind the alternative policies being offered to the British electorate lie coherent, elaborate and powerful interpretations of past history, present circumstance, and future direction. With this final question, we see how an assessment of British policy must depend upon a judgement about the nature of global deterrence with which we began. And nothing shows us more clearly the paradoxical nature of the nuclear age than that what is described by one as the fundamental underpinning of the whole of global security, is described by the other as what threatens global security most. The potency of nuclear weapons is not in question, but almost everything else is – the lessons that we can learn from the past, the situation that we find ourselves in at the present, and the prospects that alternative policies open up for us in the future.

The Disagreement about Morality

In this analysis we do no more than touch on the deep problems associated with the morality of nuclear weapon deployment. Because our aim is to clarify, not complicate, we will assume distinctions, which fuller discussion would begin to call in question.

(i) **Is it morally right to pursue the policy least likely to cause human suffering? May this sometimes involve doing things which in other circumstances would be wrong?**   OR **Are there actions which are in themselves wrong no matter what the situation? Is the alternative to excuse almost any act of barbarism?**

For those who argue like this, the implied statement on the right-hand side is an attempt to apply the simple moral absolutes, which may be appropriate in private life, to the complexity of public affairs, where they are usually irrelevant. We can all think of examples, such as deliberate genocide, which are wrong in all conceivable circumstances. But these are not typical. Usually we find ourselves confronted with a choice between alternatives, none of which we would ideally have wanted. It is a question of weighing up which is the lesser or least of two or more evils. In short, we are faced with a moral dilemma. But those who take the opposite view do not seem to recognize this. They think that they somehow have access to a privileged position, from which they can make categorical judgements, and impose them on others. The consequences of doing this are often disastrous. No-one is more dangerous in public life than the naïve, self-proclaimed idealist.

For those who argue like this, the implied statement on the left-hand page opens the door to the kind of dehumanized computation, which has been regularly used to justify unspeakable barbarism. Consequentialism – the calculation of the value of likely consequence – is a useful tool, but it does not on its own yield moral conclusions. It does not tell us *why* we should prefer one course of action to another. All that we learn is what the quantifiable probabilites and relative costs will be. To argue as opposite is to collapse the moral into the prudential sphere. It is not to be speaking about morals at all.

COMMENT:

These alternatives are overdrawn. Most people are tempted to keep a foot in both camps. Nevertheless, when pressed, we may tend one way or the other, and this may turn out to mark a fundamental divide, not only between the ways in which different people look at different moral questions, but between different conceptions of what counts as 'moral' in the first place. We will return to this briefly at the end.

(ii) **In formulating policy should we weigh up the probability of success and the relative costs in terms of human suffering of alternative nuclear and non-nuclear strategies?**   OR **Is the only relevant point here that a nuclear exchange of almost any kind would in itself cause unimaginable suffering to largely civilian populations?**

This is an application of the general principles established in (i). It says that, when we are responsible for formulating public policy, we can work out what should be done (what is morally right) by weighing up, first, the probabilities of success, and, second, the relative benefits and costs, of alternative policies (what is sometimes called their 'expected value'). The kind of categorical statement implied on the right, even if true, is so far morally neutral. For example, the dropping of the atomic bombs on Hiroshima and Nagasaki was morally justified if it shortened the war and saved millions of lives in a way that no less costly action could have done – even though it harmed large numbers of innocent people.

In fact, those who argue in this way usually deny that what is implied on the right-hand side is true. They say that there are uses of nuclear weapons which do not 'cause unimaginable suffering to largely civilian populations'.

To those who argue like this, the reasoning at the left-hand side is incomprehensible. In the case of Hiroshima and Nagasaki, anyone with an awakened moral sense must see at once that these actions were in themselves wrong, no matter what the supposed alternatives may have been. The crucial point is that what is morally wrong is to *do* this. What we think that other people may or may not do as a result of our refusal to act immorally is not a reason for acting immorally. It will not turn an immoral act into a moral one.

So far as concerns the morality of the possible future use of nuclear weapons, the only relevant fact is that all such use will cause worse damage to civilian populations than did the Hiroshima and Nagasaki bombs.

COMMENT:

Here we have a remarkable disjunction. It is hard to see how the two sides relate to one another at all. In fact, this discontinuity is usually concealed, because neither is prepared to argue on the other's ground in the first place – in other words, each denies the other's factual premises. In the case of Hiroshima and Nagasaki, those who argue as on the right-hand side usually deny that the dropping of the atomic bombs was the only alternative to an invasion of Japan; in the case of the possible future use of nuclear weapons, those who support the view on the left-hand side usually deny that this necessarily implies unacceptable civilian casualties. But what is startling is what happens on the rare occasions when each *does* accept the other's premises – even if only for the sake of argument. In these circumstances, each discovers that the other seems to understand something different by 'dropping the bombs on Hiroshima and Nagasaki' and 'the future use of nuclear weapons'. For example, in the former case, in what sense are both pointing to the same thing, when one says '*that was an evil which had to be done in order to prevent a greater evil*', and the other says '*that is what can be seen to have been absolutely wrong in itself*'? If we say that all the *facts* are agreed, then what divides them? We are on the edge of a realization that we cannot explore further here. It is what lies at the heart of this disagreement.

(iii) **So far as concerns intention, need** OR **Is there no such thing as a fully**
      we look further than the fact that   **deployed weapons system which is**
      our sole aim in deploying nuclear   **a bluff, so that to deploy nuclear**
      weapons is to prevent their use?   **weapons is undoubtedly to intend**
                                        to use them in certain
                                          circumstances?

As we move away from a consideration of our use of nuclear weapons in war to a consideration of our intentions in deploying them as a deterrent, we add another level of complication to the debate.

★   ★   ★

Many of those who argue like this do not see that a conditional 'intention' to use nuclear weapons is implied in deterrence at all, or, insofar as it is, that this has central moral significance. Since the purpose of deterrence is to deter from war, our intention in deploying nuclear weapons is to defend liberty and preserve peace. This is eminently moral.

Those who insist that we must 'intend' what would happen if deterrence failed, should equally accept that they must 'intend' what would happen if immediate nuclear disarmament failed. If we would be morally responsible for a nuclear exchange, they would be morally responsible for loss of liberty and a Third World War. Their habitual refusal to accept this shows that they care more for, as they think, keeping their own hands clean, than for the fate of the millions who would be affected by their policies. This is a profoundly immoral attitude.

The case presented opposite seems outrageous from this position. It is an abdication of moral responsibility to refuse to recognize that the deployment of nuclear weapons involves a conditional willingness that they should be used. Apart from anything else, weapons crews are committed to carrying out orders to use them, and voters have approved a declared policy which says that those orders would be given. So long as there is the slightest chance that deterrence might fail, these murderous intentions are already complete. The likelihood of future outcomes does not affect the profound immorality of these present intentions. There is simply no parallel between this, and the risks admitted to be inherent in a policy of immediate nuclear disarmament. The former involves the conditional intention of an agent to act immorally; the latter involves a risk that others may act immorally. To allow the first because of the second is to say '*because the world is evil, I will do evil, too*'. It is precisely *that* that *is* evil.

COMMENT:

For many people, the alternatives presented here are too sharply drawn. For example, they may be persuaded by those who argue as on the left that at the moment nuclear deterrence carries fewer risks than nuclear disarmament, and by those who oppose them that it is nevertheless morally wrong to deploy nuclear weapons with a conditional willingness that they should be used. This is, as it were, to internalize the debate, and considerable anguish can be felt as a result. A number of church leaders in the West have responded like this. The attempt of some of them to drive a wedge between the threat implied in deterrence, and the intention to carry out that threat should deterrence fail, and of others to make a distinction between deployment and implied threat, have been controversial.

Returning to the two alternatives here, it may be worth pointing out that this is where the 'watershed' between an emphasis on 'deterrence' and an emphasis on 'use', which we first noted in the Disagreement about Rationality, again becomes critical. For those who argue as on the left-hand page, the more stable nuclear deterrence is thought to be, the less we need concern ourselves about the morality of what we intend to do should it fail. For those who argue as on the right-hand page, given the fact that there is even a possibility that it might fail, it is what we intend to do in those circumstances which rules out nuclear deterrence as immoral from the start. Probability affects morality for the former, but not for the latter.

But the main point in all this concerns the moral significance of intention. From the perspective of those who argue as on the right, it is the intentions of agents which make actions and policies moral or immoral. From the perspective of those who support the views expressed on the left, the intentions of agents are not what is important. What matters are beneficial or harmful consequences, and actions and policies are moral or immoral insofar as they maximize or minimize one or the other. This has often been seen to mark a fundamental polarity in human moral thinking. Insofar as it does, it is a divide across which it is difficult for either to understand the other.

(iv) **Are there possible uses of nuclear** OR **Is a conditional intention to cause**
weapons which are allowed by   indiscriminate and
Just War theory? Can there be a   disproportionate suffering of this
theory of Just Deterrence?   kind ruled out by Just War theory?

Here we sum up what has been worked out in (i) to (iii) and apply it to the
morality of nuclear deterrence.

★   ★   ★

We have seen in (ii) that there are possible uses of nuclear weapons, which
are no more ruled out by the principles of Just War, than are the uses of any
other weapons. We have seen in (iii) that an effective nuclear deterrent can be
based on the threat of such use. And in any case, as we have also seen in (iii),
the main moral justification of a nuclear deterrent policy is that it is more
likely to prevent this and similar suffering than is the alternative of nuclear
disarmament.

We have seen in (ii) that any likely use of nuclear weapons would in itself cause unacceptably indiscriminate and disproportionate suffering to civilian populations, and would in addition carry an intolerable risk of escalation to all-out nuclear war. We have seen in (iii) that nuclear deterrence necessarily involves a conditional willingness that nuclear weapons should be used in these ways. For this reason, there can be no theory of 'Just Deterrence'. To argue otherwise is to abrogate morality altogether.

COMMENT:

Whether or not readers are happy with the 'Just War' terminology, in which so much of this has been debated, the substantial question of whether it is moral to go on deploying nuclear weapons remains. We have seen enough now to realise that, if each accepts the other's factual premises, we reach a strange situation, which borders on mutual incomprehension. And it is how *that* relates to the actual deployment or non-deployment of nuclear weapons, which is the central question raised in this part of the book.

(v) **Is there no relevant connection**   OR **Is it a scandal that such huge**
     between the development and   **resources are devoted to the**
     deployment of nuclear weapons,   **development and deployment of**
     and world poverty and disease?   **nuclear weapons, and not to the**
                                                    alleviation of suffering?

From this perspective, because nuclear weapons successfully deter from world war, their deployment by the great powers clearly benefits mankind as a whole. There is simply no connection between this and world poverty and disease. Global nuclear disarmament would just add another threat to those that already hang over us.

For many of those who argue like this, because nuclear weapons endanger the lives of us all, their deployment by the great powers is an unpardonable scandal. What is wrong with nuclear weapon deployment is not the detail, as debated in the Disagreement about Rationality, but the whole picture. Nuclear weapons represent the logical terminus for everything that is most brutish and inhuman in the world. Instead of beginning by identifying ourselves with our fellow human beings and asking what our global priorities should be, nuclear weapon deployers start by projecting the image of a hated enemy, and then turn image into reality by militarizing and brutalizing the society that they claim to 'protect'. There can be no more callous disregard for mankind than is shown by those who unilaterally manufacture and target weapons which threaten the existence of millions in other parts of the world. Nuclear weapons represent the logic inherent in the domination of the North over the South, the rich over the poor, the white over the black, the male over the female. It is, perhaps, fitting that those who take the sword should perish with the sword, but why should all other living creatures be dragged into oblivion with them?

COMMENT:

The depth of emotion behind these positions – especially that outlined above – makes discussion almost impossible. For those who support the left-hand view, their opponents are illogical, hysterical, and silly. Conversely, those opponents find them crass, self-satisfied, and inhuman. When world-views as divergent as this are in conflict, it is hard to see that there is even enough in common for us to be able to describe it as 'disagreement'.

(vi) Does Christian teaching allow the OR **Does Christian teaching condemn**
deployment of nuclear weapons? **the deployment of nuclear**
weapons?

The fact that we have made no mention of Christian teaching before this
paragraph means that, for some readers, nothing that we have recorded so far
has been adequate to the issue we are considering, and that, if we want to
reach to the heart of the matter, we will have to re-run the whole debate in
Christian terms. Others would be happier for the question of Christian teaching to be left out altogether. Does this set of questions contain all the others,
or should it be treated as an optional extra? Clearly, the framework of questions
used here is not neutral in this respect. The question of Christian teaching has
been included as distinct from, but on an equal footing to, others. It is
presented as if it were possible, first to settle the main moral issues, and then
either to answer it or to ignore it. The framework of analysis has once again
broken down. And once again we will just note the fact and move on.

★   ★   ★

Here we will record two contrasted criticisms of the argument that Christian
teaching condemns nuclear weapon deployment as immoral.

First, the reader is reminded of the argument set out in full at the end of
the Argument about Morality in the Case in Favour of Continued Nuclear
Weapon Deployment (page 30). The two main points were, first, that the
official churches have not condemned such deployment. And, second, that in
a fallen world, Christian leaders have a duty to restrain the wicked and protect
the innocent. This is borne out in the whole tradition of Just War teaching in
the past, and Just Deterrent principles today. Central to the latter are the facts
that the purpose of nuclear weapon deployment is to prevent oppression and
to deter from war; that the deterrent threat does not involve a conditional
intention to transgress against the principles of proportion and discrimination;
that the likelihood of success is high; and that the likelihood that alternative,
non-nuclear, options would succeed is low. In these circumstances, the Christian magistrate is morally right to act in this way. Not to do so would be an
abdication of responsibility. Nuclear pacifism is no different to pacifism in
general in this respect.

Second, Christian teaching is, in essence, purely spiritual. Christ did not
concern Himself with public policy at all. It is not necessarily more Christian
to oppose a policy of nuclear weapon deployment than it is to defend it.
Neither of these is the proper business of the Christian in the first place. The
Christian should concern himself only with the things of the spirit, as did
Christ Himself. '*Render to Caesar the things that are Caesar's*'. Politics should
be left to the politicians.

In answer to the first argument:

Our Christian love of our neighbour is the love of a person for another person, in full awareness of what it is to be a person. To love our neighbour is for him to become as real to us in the eternal significance of his being as we are to ourselves, and for us to embrace his ultimate interests as our own. It is to love the Christ in him. The dehumanized quantitative language in which nuclear weapon use and deployment is described and defended is the opposite of this. It is to lose sight entirely of the reality of persons and to deal only with abstractions. For example, reference to 'exchanges', 'targeting', and so on, is a disgusting glossing over of the fact that what we are talking about is our readiness to murder people. No Christian can possibly have anything to do with this. Christian love is love of real persons, not expendable ciphers. Moreover, although our Christian love of our neighbour is usually expressed through action, it is in itself a disposition of our hearts and minds. An action of ours, which happens fortuitously to benefit our neighbour, is not as such a Christian action. A Christian action is one which is intended to benefit him – even if, in the event, it does not. Similarly, an action of ours, which happens to harm him, is not un-Christian, so long as, in doing it, we did not intend to harm him or know that he would be harmed. So it is strictly irrelevant how 'probable' it is that our nuclear weapons will, as it turns out, be used – as also our claim that, by deploying them, we hope to decrease that probability. What will or will not happen in the future will be the result of factors which we can neither foresee now, nor, in the end, control. What is of absolute significance for us as Christians is our present wickedness in having already acquiesced in the possibility of that use in our hearts. It is here that our transgression of the Second Commandment lies. The moment we admit that there is the slightest possibility, however small, that our nuclear weapons will be used, our wickedness is complete. As Christians we take full responsibility upon ourselves for our thoughts and for the actions that we know may spring from them. We do not attribute our moral or immoral intentions to 'society at large', or blame 'the wickedness of the age' for the evil that we do. Our nuclear arsenals did not just 'happen' to come about, as certain processes in nature may be said to have done. They have been manufactured, deployed, targeted and manned by us as individual persons, capable of discrimination and choice – and they are direct expressions of our will. If we had had nothing to do with the kind of thinking that produces them, they would not exist. They are manifestations of a deeply wicked disposition on our part, of our hatred for one another and readiness to use them against one another should certain circumstances arise. The Christian love of his neighbour is universal, total and absolute. It does

not admit of exception or degree. By His teaching and example, Christ revealed the transforming power of this love to us. In loving one another, we are loving Him. Nothing could be more grotesquely incompatible with this than the actions and intentions involved in nuclear weapon deployment. To try to argue otherwise is either deliberately to misrepresent Christian teaching, or to have no conception of what it is.

In answer to the second:

What is objectionable in nuclear weapon deployment – our present condoning of the destruction of innocent lives by our weapons in possible future circumstances – is not a political misjudgement, but a mortal sin. For example, it is blatant casuistry for Christians, who are directly involved in the nuclear weapons business, at the same time to pretend that their spiritual lives are 'above' politics. Whether they are politicians, civil servants, manufacturers, military commanders, members of weapons crews, it is they who are personally responsible for this whole grossly immoral and sinful enterprise. Nor can other Christians, who say that they are not directly involved, claim that as a result they are freed from having to condemn nuclear weapon deployment as un-Christian when the subject is raised. By admitting that it would be wrong for *us* to become involved in the nuclear weapons process, we have ipso facto said that it is wrong for others as well. Christian moral judgements are universal and binding. Christians must be prepared to witness against evil whatever form it takes and whenever it appears.

COMMENT:

The controversy about the application of Christian teaching to nuclear weapon deployment is deep and disquieting to many Christians. The whole debate, as we have surveyed it so far, is argued out in Christian terms. This can raise questions, not only about how Christian teaching applies, but also about what Christian teaching is. For instance, a number of Christians say that, as Christians, we would be morally justified in launching a retaliatory strategic nuclear second strike against targets in or near enemy centres of population if the enemy had attacked our cities first. To other Christians this kind of thinking is so monstrously incompatible with New Testament teaching that it calls in question how those who advocate such actions can be Christians at all. Although this is an extreme example, the tension between the two opposing arguments, which causes anguish to those who are pulled both ways, also creates great difficulties for Church leaders, who are trying to avoid scandal by accommodating these potent and apparently incompatible positions within official pronouncements. They tend to try to rise above the debate by saying that they respect what is being said on both sides, and to contain, if not resolve, it by emphasizing distinctions, such as those between deployment and threat, threat and conditional willingness that the weapons should be used, conditional willingness and conditional intention to use them, conditional intention and use itself. But, as is frequently the case in such circum-

stances, they are only able to do so by seeming to deny a number of the terms within which each is often argued. For example, on the one hand, they may prohibit almost all possible uses of nuclear weapons, and tolerate their continued deployment only as a temporary measure, while a process of global nuclear disarmament is being accomplished. On the other, existing practices may, in the meantime, be condoned in general, and the claim that full deployment of nuclear weapons necessarily implies a conditional willingness to use them may be denied. This leaves them open to criticism from both sides. Severe critics on one side say that it is well known that there is no prospect whatsoever of immediate global nuclear disarmament, so that it is naïve or disingenuous to pretend that there is. The Church must face up to the fact that it is morally right for Christian communities to continue to rely on effective nuclear deterrence, as generally understood by political and military leaders, for the foreseeable future. Critics on the other side condemn what they say is, in effect, an indefinite endorsement of the status quo. They are scornful of what they see as the pretence that it does not involve serious preparations for use and a readiness on the part of all those involved to give and obey orders to that effect. Critics on both sides tend to see official pronouncements of this kind as deliberate exercises in diplomatic ambiguity, rather than as considered formulations of traditional teaching. Nowhere else are the moral implications of nuclear weapon deployment debated with more thoroughness and intensity than within the Christian community. Such is the rack on which Church leaders are stretched. It is a measure of the honesty and seriousness with which the debate is conducted that it causes so many of them so much anguish.

A Note on the Relationship between the Disagreement about Rationality and the Disagreement about Morality

Does the argument about rationality tell us, morally, how we should act?	OR Does the argument about rationality show us the expected values of alternative policies without telling us which is morally right?

Two apparently different approaches will be considered together here. As we have seen, the first explicitly refutes the Moral Argument, on the right, on the grounds that preoccupation with ones own personal guilt is not appropriate to the search for the policy most likely to benefit the public at large. The second would prefer not to argue in moral terms at all. *'I'm not very good at morals. I would rather leave that to the theologians'*. What both approaches share is the conclusion that, whether or not we want to call this 'moral', the Argument about Rationality tells us which policy we should adopt. That is the crucial step which is rejected by the objectors.

Those who argue like this deny that they are immorally preoccupied with their own guilt at the expense of public welfare. They do not recognize a distinction between private and public morality of this kind. Morality is to do with our personal responsibility for our own actions and intentions. And it is vital that public life is not dehumanized by our losing sight of this. There have been too many examples of criminal acts carried out in the name of the 'public interest' by people who appeal to 'rational' calculations of overall 'benefit'. We must not allow ourselves to become cogs in that kind of machine. Morality is qualitative. It cannot be deduced from quantitative computations.

COMMENT:

It is of interest that almost all those who accept the views expressed on the left-hand page in the Argument about Rationality reject those shown on the right in the Argument about Morality, and that almost all those who support the views shown on the right in the Argument about Morality reject those on the left in the Argument about Rationality (the other 'crossover', for obvious reasons, is not so critical). That this is not necessarily so is shown by the few who accept both arguments and are faced by a moral dilemma in consequence. The fact that these are so few in number shows, perhaps, how reluctant we are to admit such tension into our own thinking. We have reached the point where the disagreement about the rationality and morality of nuclear weapon deployment begins to involve disagreement about the nature of rationality and morality itself. Distinctions invoked by both sides, such as that between 'fact' and 'value' begin to break down. For example, for those who support the right-hand view, the fact of the damage done by the Hiroshima and Nagasaki bombs *is* the moral point. It is what can be seen to have been morally inadmissible. To their opponents, the fact of the damage is in itself morally neutral. We have not yet begun to determine whether or not it should have been inflicted. Conversely, for supporters of the left-hand view, the fact of the different probabilities of various equal-value outcomes *is* the moral point. It is what decides which we should prefer. For those on the other side of the argument, the probabilities of the outcomes are morally neutral. We have not yet asked whether or not it would be morally legitimate in itself to bring any of those outcomes about.

It is in this and in similar ways that the disagreement about nuclear weapon

deployment is found to involve wider questions about our understanding of the situation we are in, and our thoughts concerning how we should behave, in general.

4

A Note on the Alternatives being Offered to the British Electorate in 1987-8

Each of the three main party groupings claims to be working towards the strengthening of the NATO Alliance, the reduction of tension between the power blocs of East and West, and the resolution of the great global scandals of poverty, disease and war. Each stresses the importance of consolidating Western European unity in equal partnership with the United States and of maintaining effective Western defences, while at the same time encouraging dialogue and exchange of all kinds with the Soviet bloc, in a search for the peaceful modus vivendi, which is widely recognized to be in the common interest of all.

But the disagreement begins when it comes to the question of how we are to achieve all this. As in most periods when political consensus is breaking down, the polarization of arguments is further widened by inter-party polemics. Party programmes are essentially composite platforms. But, since each is trying to present a distinct and uniquely appealing alternative to the electorate, differences between the policies tend to be mutually exaggerated, and rival positions caricatured. Each hopes in this way to identify its own policy uniquely in the public mind with those general principles, to which, as we have seen, nearly all subscribe.

The Labour Party

The Labour Party answers 'NO' to the Recommendation (LEFT), and 'YES' to all the proposals in Recommendation (RIGHT). These recommendations are repeated as an alternative on page 38. The rationale behind this programme can be found in policy documents, such as '*A Modern Britain in a Modern World*', published at the end of 1986. In general, it tends to endorse the arguments presented on the right-hand pages of our analysis.

Briefly, there are two main areas of emphasis, the first to do with NATO strategy and global politics, and the second to do with British defence priorities.

The background to the former is provided by a frontal assault on the dangers and delusions inherent in so-called 'nuclear deterrent' policies. The unusability of mutually deployed nuclear forces is pointed out and the concept of extended deterrence consequently rejected. The dangerous likely effects of time-urgent first-strike weapons and nuclear war-fighting strategies on crisis instability are stressed. The idea that there is a Soviet military advantage which cannot be matched at non-nuclear level is denied. NATO reliance on nuclear weapons is seen to do no more than inhibit a proper modernization of conventional forces and defensive strategies (described as 'defensive deterrence'). The leaders of the two superpowers are applauded for recognizing this, and their proposals for the elimination of strategic ballistic systems by 1996, and for the removal of all land-based theatre nuclear weapons from Europe (the zero-zero option) are welcomed. The Conservative Party is castigated for trying to block both possibilities, the former largely because this would threaten to sweep away the Trident option, upon which conservative paranoia is now fixated. Motivated largely by pressure from the military-economic-bureaucratic establishment, whose interests the Conservative Party represents, and by the outmoded delusions of grandeur to which so many Conservative politicians cling, the government is seen as having systematically turned its back on all the more progressive movements in the world. Britain has become a client of the United States, tied to it by nuclear apron-strings. Foreign aid has been effectively cut, the Commonwealth has been weakened by the refusal to take action against apartheid, and the opportunity to achieve an historic rapprochement between East and West, by responding to the overtures from the new reformist government in Moscow, is being squandered.

The charge that Labour Party policy will divide and weaken NATO is denied on the grounds that a majority of NATO members already reject a nuclear deterrent strategy anyway, and that the United States will come to understand that its true European interests will be not only safeguarded, but enhanced, as a result of Labour policy. A new agreement about the status of remaining US bases and facilities in Britain will re-establish the partnership as a relationship between equals. But the main thrust of this part of the argument is the accusation that it is a hypocritical Conservative government, which, while paying lip-service to the importance of maintaining defences, is in fact covertly undermining them, by its unpublicized reductions in the defence budget, and by its heavily increased spending on nuclear weapons. The resources now being unnecessarily poured into the 'defence' of the Falkland Islands, and into other out-of-area operations, should also be reduced, and procurement procedures tightened and rationalized, in order to get proper value for money from defence contracts. The money thus saved will enable a future Labour government to arrest and reverse this serious decline in the strength of Britain's conventional forces by air, land and sea. It is the Labour Party, and not the Conservative Party, which stands for sound defence.

The Conservative Party

The Conservative Party answers 'YES' to the Recommendation (LEFT), and 'NO' to all the proposals in Recommendation (RIGHT), except no. 7. The rationale behind this programme can be found in a number of government publications on defence and national security issues, such as the annual Statement on the Defence Estimates. In general, it tends to endorse the arguments presented upon the left-hand pages of our analysis.

The main claim is that the policy of strength and flexibility, deterrence and detente, which has successfully protected us for forty years, and has led to the present stability and mood of accommodation between East and West, must be maintained. In view of Soviet non-nuclear as well as nuclear military power, the threat of nuclear retaliation must remain integral to Western deterrent strategy. Significant progress towards nuclear disarmament can only safely be made as part of a broader settlement, which must include a build-down of Soviet chemical and conventional forces. And this in turn can only be done through mutual negotiation and reciprocal action. It is Western strength that induces the Soviet Union to engage in this process. Britain's independent nuclear deterrent, and support for NATO and US nuclear policies, are, therefore, important contributions to the strategy upon which her integrity and future security depends.

The two main Opposition Party charges are rejected. First, it is not true that the Conservative Party obstructs progressive movements. Leaving aside false accusations about Foreign Aid and the Commonwealth, this is to misunderstand the international situation. The Conservative Party welcomes all measures towards reconciliation and tension reduction, as, among other things, full support for the standing Conference on Security and Cooperation in Europe shows. The ultimate aim is, indeed, to reduce all armed forces on both sides of the Iron Curtain, non-nuclear as well as nuclear. But a number of the measures proposed by the Opposition Parties, far from facilitating this, would instead set it back. For example, proposals 10 to 20 in Recommendation (RIGHT) are one-sided, and therefore counter-productive, for the reasons already explained on the left-hand pages in earlier sections. A number of the 'global' proposals 1 to 9 sound attractive, but are either meaningless in practice (like No. 6, if applied to Europe), or too clumsily formulated (like No. 1, which would freeze the bad along with the good; and No. 3, which would at the same time prevent necessary modernization and improvement in safety). So far as concerns No. 5, the Conservative Party welcomes mutually agreed deep cuts, but warns against over-hasty moves which would upset the strategic balance prematurely. The way ahead is to tackle the chemical and conventional imbalance at the same time, because that is what underlies the need for extended nuclear deterrence.

The second Opposition Party charge, that conventional forces suffer as a result of Conservative Party policy, is rejected out of hand. This is seen as a transparent device for trying to draw attention away, in particular, from the catastrophic implications of Labour Party plans. Apart from the gratuitous irresponsibility of handing away Britain's own nuclear capability, the logic behind the policy is clearly unilateral nuclear disarmament for the West. The disastrous consequences of this are too familiar to need repeating. The fact that no other major Western Power will act as irresponsibly may protect us from these consequences, but only at the expense of the integrity of the Alliance. There is nothing whatsoever to be said for such a policy, either on prudential or on moral grounds. Since there can be no rational justification for it, it is seen to be little more than a sop to buy off domestic left-wing pressure. It is interpreted as a further stage in the capture of the Labour Party by its own extremists, which, in the eyes of all responsible people, must rule it out as a serious candidate for reliable government.

The Alliance Parties

The Alliance Parties answer 'NO' to the Recommendation (LEFT), and roughly, 'YES' to most of the Global proposals in Recommendation (RIGHT), but 'NO' to what they see as the radical unilateralist proposals 16-20.

The rationale behind their programme can be found in a number of individual policy documents produced by each party separately, as well as in formulations of recommended joint policy, such as the Defence and Disarmament report, published by the SDP-Liberal Alliance Commission in June 1986. The Alliance differs most radically from the Conservative Party on the global setting to British policy, and from the Labour Party on its specific immediate recommendations for it. We will deal with each in turn.

Although the reality of Soviet nuclear and non-nuclear power is seen to rule out precipitate unconditional measures, the Alliance Parties accept that NATO and WTO nuclear war-fighting strategies are irresponsible, and that NATO's dependence on the likely early use of nuclear weapons, in particular, is fundamentally and dangerously misguided. The removal of all land-based nuclear weapons from the European theatre must be a central aim of Western policy, and the greater accuracy of modern longer-range systems means that there is scope for bold moves in this direction. The Conservative Party's perpetuation of cold war paranoia, and clinging to the myth that there is a 'delicate' theatre nuclear balance in Europe, have seriously obstructed progress towards detente and a nuclear weapon build-down. It is disgraceful that the British Government should have so lamely endorsed American adventurism, and opposed every opportunity to secure an end to nuclear weapon testing, a nuclear weapon free corridor in central Europe, the zero-zero option for the removal of intermediate systems, and the elimination of ballistic systems by the superpowers. Instead, the British Government should be vigorously pressing for a whole range of arms-reduction and confidence-building measures, in a search for common security between East and West, and should be urging Western restraint in order to facilitate this.

But the search for common security through detente and restraint must go hand-in-hand with robust collective security within the Western Alliance. If Conservative Party policy jeopardizes the former, by failing to recognize that long-term security can only be achieved through cooperation, Labour Party policy jeopardizes the latter by failing to understand that Britain can only take a lead in working towards this goal through her membership of a strong and united Alliance. Both, in their different ways, are forms of escapism. What we have described as 'Position B' in $C_1(vi)$ and $C_2(i)$ sum up Alliance policy for Britain's independent nuclear forces, and for Britain's role within the wider NATO nuclear deterrent, respectively. The longer-term aim is for Britain to negotiate away her independent deterrent as part of a general East-West settlement, and for NATO to move away from dependence on the early use of nuclear weapons. Trident must be cancelled, and any money saved spent on strengthening conventional forces. This would all be part of the move towards common security. But Britain must on no account undermine collective security by pointlessly throwing away the possibility of contributing to European nuclear independence, or by unilaterally pulling out of Western defence commitments. The direction ahead should lie in strengthening links with European partners in order to build a more equal balance between the European and American pillars of the Western Alliance. The polarization of Conservative and Labour policies in recent years means that it is only the Alliance which points to the way in which Britain can take a lead in working towards greater global cooperation and security, through the closeness of her association with her European partners, and the strength of her friendship with the USA.

The Radical Alternative

This book is not long enough to offer an adequate analysis of the policies of smaller political groupings. But we should at least take note in general terms of a programme subscribed to by considerable numbers of people, and not reflected in any of the main party platforms.

There are three distinguishing elements in it. First, a rejection of Proposal 17 in Recommendation (RIGHT). Money saved by the renunciation of British nuclear weapon capabilities should not be spent on conventional defence. Indeed, defence spending as a whole should be substantially cut, and the resources transferred to domestic industrial and welfare enterprises, and to foreign aid. Second, Proposal 18 is also rejected. Britain should withdraw from NATO immediately, and join the other non-aligned countries which belong to neither armed camp. Third, Proposal 19 is expanded. Not only should American nuclear weapons be withdrawn from Britain, but the whole American military presence should be removed. Apart from anything else, facilities such as the Ballistic Missile early warning station at Fylingdales in Yorkshire, and the Submarine tracking station at Brawdy in Pembrokeshire, play a much more important role in US nuclear deterrent strategy than do F-111 airfields or Cruise Missile bases.

PART 2 ANSWERS

The sets of answers which follow are responses to the framework of questions established in Part I. Unless otherwise indicated, the method used has been to take the contributor through the questions orally, to type out the answers, and to send them to him or her to be checked and amended. Each is prefaced by a brief biographical note, and by an editorial comment to serve as a quick reference guide for readers who may be unfamiliar with particular names.

The numbered recommendations at the end of each set of answers refer to the twenty selected proposals under Recommendation (RIGHT), which are repeated in the Appendix to this part on pages 466–7. They are presented as a 'throwout' for easy reference. Those who say 'no' to all, or nearly all, of them, in general accept Recommendation (LEFT). In other words, they are recommending that current policies should be broadly maintained.

The Rt Hon The Lord Carrington

K.G., C.H., K.C.M.G., P.C.

Biographical Note

Lord Carrington has been Secretary-General of NATO since June 1984. Born in 1919, he won the Military Cross in the Second World War, first held Ministerial office as Parliamentary Secretary of State at the Ministry of Agriculture and Fisheries in 1951, and served as United Kingdom High Commissioner in Australia from 1956 to 1959. He then served successively as: First

Lord of the Admiralty 1959–63; Leader of the Opposition, House of Lords 1964–70, 1974–79; Secretary of State for Defence 1970–74; and Secretary of State for Energy 1974. He was Secretary of State for Foreign and Commonwealth Affairs from 1979 until his resignation in April 1982.

Editorial Comment

Communicated during the course of an informal interview in Brussels on July 14, 1986, this set of answers represents the response of an influential international statesman, who has held office of Ministerial rank almost continuously since the age of thirty-two. His familiarity with the working of national and international bureaucracies, and his wide experience in the conduct of public affairs, make him impatient of what he regards as unpractical theorizing of all kinds. In the conversational form of this interview, his exposition of the central perception that deterrence depends upon uncertainty is characteristically clear, forthright and direct. The reader may, perhaps, learn most from answers such as those to questions **A2(A)(iii)** and **B(iii)**, which, within this context, explicitly acknowledge the conceptual gulf separating those who believe in the efficacy of nuclear deterrence from those who do not, and explain why the latter fail to grasp the essential principle upon which collective security continues to depend.

LORD CARRINGTON

A. *Global Policy*

1. *The History of the Past Forty Years*

(i) *Has it been nuclear deterrence that has* OR *Has it mainly been other factors?*
kept the peace between the great powers
since 1945?

You can't prove it one way or the other – it's almost impossible to say that one or the other is true. But is it just coincidence that, since nuclear weapons have existed, there has been no serious quarrel in Europe, which before was so quarrelsome?

(ii) *Does mutual possession of an invulnerable* OR *Does the threat of strategic nuclear*
second strike strategic nuclear force prevent *retaliation, particularly against a similarly*
war? *armed enemy, lack credibility and invite*
sub-deterrent encroachment?

The two sets of questions are too clever. The real reason is much more simple. It's to do with the horror of nuclear weapons in everybody's minds. They deter from all major wars, because we are all so frightened of what might happen. It's as simple as that.

iii) *Have limited nuclear options at strategic and theatre levels enhanced deterrence by dramatically raising the threshold between peace and war?*   OR *Have most military planners from the start been aiming for nuclear war-fighting superiority? Has 'flexible response' dangerously lowered the threshold between conventional and nuclear war?*

If you believe, as I do, that the answer to the second question is as I have said that it is, then the answer to the third question is that it is better for people to be frightened of nuclear war all the way down the scale. It has to do with credibility. If you didn't have these options, people might be less frightened.

v) *Has the size and variety of the nuclear arsenals held by the superpowers stabilized deterrence?*   OR *Has the logic of nuclear confrontation and worst-case analysis generated a dangerous and strategically pointless superfluity of weapons systems?*

I don't hold either of these views. It seems to me that it's perfectly possible to have your nuclear deterrence at a much lower level than you have now. There's much too much, so get rid of what is not needed. We would probably all be happier if numbers were reduced. That is why we are currently negotiating for substantial reductions in the nuclear arsenals of both sides.

On the other hand, I don't believe that, because you've got too much, it necessarily makes life more dangerous. The capability to kill yourself eleven times over is superfluous, but not necessarily dangerous.

v) *Has the idea of nuclear balance between the superpowers been essential to stability and have arms-control negotiations helped to achieve it?*   OR *Have ideas of 'nuclear defence' and 'parity' proved illusory and is 'multilateral negotiation from strength' a contradiction in terms? Has 'arms-control' been just another name for the arms race?*

I don't agree with either of these alternatives. It seems to me that balance between the super powers has been achieved over a period of years, because the Russians have caught up. Beforehand you had just as good a deterrent from the Western point of view, because the Americans had an enormous superiority and were invulnerable. As they didn't intend to use their nuclear weapons in a first strike, but only if the Russians did anything disagreeable, you had a very reasonable nuclear deterrent. Now the Russians have caught up, so you have a nuclear balance. It's not a question of whether you want a nuclear balance.

As to the question of arms control, both sides have a different idea of balance. The role of arms control has been to codify two different perceptions and two different force structures. Within these parameters, I think that, apart from the fact that critics can make the case that numbers in certain areas have increased, they have overall established a framework that has been helpful.

(vi) *Has force-planning been controlled by strategic thinking?* OR *Has the self-reinforcing impetus of technology and vested interest dictated policies subsequently justified post hoc?*

Certainly not the latter, but not entirely the former either. It's a sort of grey area, isn't it? There undoubtedly are pressures from inventors and technologists and the military, but they are held in political check in the West and are on the whole under political control. There has been an overall discipline about force requirements, and so on, in NATO. It may be that the greater relative strength of the military within the Soviet Union and the large sums of money available, mean that there the momentum is held less closely under political restraint – I wouldn't know.

2. *The Prospect for the Future*

(A) WITH NUCLEAR WEAPONS

(i) *Does the threat of an enemy first strike remain inconceivable for the foreseeable future?* OR *Is there an increasing threat from accurate and time-urgent first-strike weapons?*

What you have to do here, I think, is separate two questions. If you are asking 'is there a greater technical capacity to effect a first strike?', then the arguments that there may be such a capacity are probably fairly convincing as far as they go – although that debate is full of uncertainties. But if you are asking 'is it more likely that someone is going to try this?', then you are in a completely different area, and I would have said definitely 'no'.

You cannot say that it is 'inconceivable' that someone might try this, because you never know what political developments there may be in any country – Mr Gorbachev might be unexpectedly replaced by a more extreme figure, perhaps slightly deranged, and believing that he has a first-strike weapon that can give him superiority. But this remains highly improbable.

(ii) *Are command, control, communication and intelligence facilities likely to remain secure?* OR *Does the amount of information to be processed, pressure of time and fear of preemption put command and control systems under intolerable strain and make inadvertent war more likely?*

Once again it can be argued that there are technological developments that could threaten the survivability of command, control and communications facilities. But I don't see any particular development making that happen. In any case, the more worried people get, the more careful they are going to be. And that, as I have said before, is in general a good thing.

As to inadvertent war, it remains, or should remain, a major objective of the arms control process to make this less likely. It has already done quite a lot in that direction.

ii) *If nevertheless there were a limited*   OR *Is the idea that nuclear war could be*
     nuclear exchange would it be likely to end   *limited once it had broken out a dangerous*
     hostilities swiftly?   *illusion?*

I find this sort of question absolutely impossible to answer. All I can do is give
you my view of deterrence. To begin with the Americans had an overwhelming
superiority. First of all, they were the only people who had nuclear weapons.
Then there was a period when they had the ability to wipe out the Soviet
Union and they were almost invulnerable. But now that you have got a balance,
the only thing that makes deterrence credible is uncertainty. Since you can
never get certainty, what you actually want is uncertainty. We are not going
to be the aggressors; but we want to leave in the mind of the Soviet Union a
real doubt as to what would happen if they were to attack us. That's why a
declaration of 'no first use' of nuclear weapons is a bad idea: it makes it easier
for the Kremlin to calculate the costs of military adventure.

So, from the point of view of nuclear deterrence, it's a good thing that there
is doubt as to whether a nuclear exchange be limited. The difficulty with these
sorts of things is that you are arguing on two levels. You are arguing first of
all about deterrence, and then those represented by the questions on the right
are arguing about what you would do if deterrence failed. And the two things
are not the same. The aim is to make it as difficult as possible for deterrence
to fail – to make it so difficult that deterrence doesn't fail.

v) *Do new generations of battlefield and*   OR *Do new battlefield and theatre weapons*
     theatre nuclear systems reinforce   *threaten a dangerous lowering of the*
     deterrence?   *nuclear threshold?*

It is not the modernization of theatre nuclear weapons that lowers the nuclear
threshold, but the weakening of conventional capabilities. If theatre nuclear
forces are modernized as part of a response to a qualitatively new threat,
then they reinforce deterrence. It is failure to meet that threat which would
undermine your deterrent abilities.

) *Does the Strategic Defence Initiative offer*   OR *Is the Strategic Defence Initiative simply*
     the hope of an effective defence against   *the most recent and destabilizing example*
     nuclear weapons?   *of the process outlined in 1?*

How on earth can we know this until we know what it can do? All we can do
at this stage is to speculate about the possible implications. For example, if
you had a system which you thought would work and you deployed it by
agreement with the Soviet Union, and at the same time substantially reduced
your offensive weapons, I think that everybody would say that that would be
stabilizing. But we can also imagine possibilities that would be destabilizing.
Both the Soviet Union and the United States are engaged in this area of
research, but none of us can know yet what the possibilities will be, so we
cannot answer these questions. Find out what you can do, and what the
consequences would be, before you make your decision whether or not to
carry on and deploy.

(vi) *Is the threat of 'horizontal' nuclear*   OR *Is continuing reliance on nuclear deterrence*
proliferation best met by a continuation   *by the great powers bound to accelerate the*
of past policies?   *process of proliferation and make nuclear*
                                                    war more likely?

I would rather not see further proliferation, but it is not what the great powers do along these lines that will be decisive. I suspect that what determines the attitude of, say, the Argentinians and Brazilians, or the Indians and Pakistanis, depends much more on Argentina/Brazil or India/Pakistan than on anything the great powers are doing. But the conference rhetoric is of course rather different. In this kind of forum, where the great powers may be trying to campaign against nuclear proliferation, it may be diplomatically helpful if they can say 'look, we are cutting down our arsenals' – but it's no more than that.

(vii) *Do multilateral arms-control negotiations*   OR *Is 'arms-control' an illusion which diverts*
offer the best prospect for future stability?   *attention from the only safe policy –*
                                                        nuclear disarmament?

I think that current bilateral and multilateral negotiations will produce worthwhile measures of disarmament.

The 'alternative school' appear to recommend unilateral concessions in the hope that the Soviet Union will reciprocate, but they never explain why this should happen, or what we should do if it doesn't.

Even if the Soviet Union did reciprocate, it would only be with the coin that they had offered in existing negotiations, and that would almost certainly be an unsatisfactory bargain from the Western point of view. It might well be that they would offer even less than this, and extremely unlikely that they would offer more.

Take the example of chemical weapons. The Americans did in effect unilaterally disarm for seventeen years, when they made it plain to the Russians that they were not going to produce more chemical weapons. Meanwhile, the Russians continued to maintain enormous stocks of 350,000 tons of these beastly things, and saw no reason to behave differently.

When you pin the critics down in private and say 'are you a unilateral disarmer?', many of them say 'no'. But they are reluctant to say so in public, or to explain what the alternatives are.

(B) WITHOUT NUCLEAR WEAPONS

(i) *If nuclear arsenals were dismantled*   OR *Would nuclear disarmament remove the*
would war between the great powers again   *incentive for nuclear preemption while not*
become a rational option and therefore   *affecting the reluctance of the great powers*
more likely?   *to initiate a third world war?*

If you believe, as I do, that nuclear deterrence has played a part in preventing a third world war, then to remove it is to increase the danger that there will be one. Without nuclear deterrence, you have a very large preponderance of conventional weapons and superiority for the Warsaw Pact over NATO. Whatever they may sometimes say, advocates of unilateral nuclear disarmament for the West are certainly not prepared to put more money into conventional weapons. Does that fill you with confidence?

(ii) *Would a major conventional war be*   OR *Is conventional war, however terrible,*
likely in itself to be as terrible as a limited   *preferable to nuclear war?*
nuclear war?

A major conventional war would, indeed, be appalling. I have fought in one. It was very nasty. The next would probably be worse.

(iii) *Because nuclear weapons cannot be*   OR *As with nerve gases in the last war, would*
uninvented would they not be bound to be   *there be no incentive to resort to*
used sooner or later once war had broken   *capabilities which the other side has as*
out?   *well?*

I don't know. This is all hypothetical, and it's not going to happen.

(iv) *Is global nuclear disarmament only*   OR *Is to argue that even multilateral nuclear*
feasible in a world where war itself is no   *disarmament is not desirable to give up all*
longer a possibility?   *hope of a rational world-order?*

Let's be practical about this. You are not going to get 'global nuclear disarmament'. What you may get is a very much lower level of weaponry, which would make everybody feel better, including me.

(v) *Is peace only preserved when we are seen*   OR *Do the years before 1914 show what*
to be prepared for war, as failure before   *happens when military planning and the*
1939 and success since 1945 show? Under   *arms race control political choices? Do*
likely future conditions would global   *present strategies make nuclear war almost*
nuclear disarmament make war, including   *inevitable under likely future conditions?*
nuclear war, more likely?   *Is global nuclear disarmament the only*
    rational policy?

The suggestion on the right that there is an arms race galloping out of control is wrong. But the other side isn't the whole answer either, because it's all too compressed.

B. *Nato Policy*

(i) *Does the Soviet Union, together with her*   OR *Are NATO and WTO forces relatively*
Warsaw Pact allies, enjoy a strategically   *evenly matched?*
dangerous military superiority in Europe?

This depends upon a number of factors. For example, which forces you count, which area, whether both sides mobilize at the same time and so on. Under the right circumstances we would hope to do reasonably well, but reinforcement would be a critical factor. However, all theorizing apart, let's just say that, whether you like it or not – and I don't – they have the capacity to do a great deal more than we can.

(ii) *Is the Soviet Union an expansionist power* OR *Is the Soviet Union an encircled and*
which will take advantage of unilateral   *threatened power trying to keep up with*
Western concessions and is only restrained   *Western technology and likely to respond*
and forced to accept arms-control   *positively to unconditional offers of*
agreements by Western determination and   *Western restraint within a general context*
strength?   *of detente?*

No one can say for certain what their intentions are. A simple analogy helps
to make the point: if there is an elephant in the next-door garden, you have a
fence to protect your flower beds. You do not spend a lot of time trying to
find out what the elephant's intentions are.

(iii) *Is Soviet chemical and conventional*   OR *Is NATO dependence on the early use of*
preponderance such that NATO must   *nuclear weapons unnecessary and*
continue to be able to threaten early use of   *strategically suicidal?*
nuclear weapons?

I have really already answered this, because we are back to the question of
uncertainty. But let me be clear, we do not threaten anything – all we say is
that we maintain the option to use nuclear weapons if and when necessary if
we are attacked.

And once again we are arguing on two levels. I am arguing from the point
of view of deterrence: making it clear to the elephant that he cannot be sure
what we would do if he trampled down the fence, in order to deter him and
keep him off the flower bed. Critics ask what would happen if deterrence
failed tomorrow morning. If I were to try to reassure them in the way they
want, I would be undermining the deterrent which is designed to prevent that
from happening.

(iv) *Does the growing size of the Soviet nuclear* OR *Does the West initiate nearly all phases of*
arsenal threaten the delicate theatre and   *the nuclear arms race and continue to enjoy*
strategic balance? Would Western failure   *a substantial lead in most areas? Is the*
to match Soviet systems be destabilizing?   *nuclear 'overkill' such that the West could*
*   offer a nuclear 'freeze' or unconditional*
*   cuts without risk?*

What is important here is the change in composition of Soviet nuclear forces,
not so much the growth in size. If there is a qualitative change on the other
side, you reassure people by adjusting accordingly, so that we are seen to have
the ability to respond. Although the SS20s in a way replaced the SS4s and
SS5s that were already there, they seemed to be a different kind of threat and
Europeans did find them that degree more terrifying. If the other side is
getting qualitatively stronger and you do nothing, for long enough, you undermine your deterrent abilities, so that in that sort of situation modernization
reinforces deterrence. And at the same time, by the way, you strengthen
Transatlantic linkage.

As to the idea of a 'freeze', I can't see why people are so keen on it. It seems
to me that it's much better to get reductions than to freeze the thing at the
wrong levels; and we would do much better to concentrate on reductions.

(v) *Are NATO 'forward defence' and 'deep*   OR *Should NATO exploit her lead in*
strike' strategies essential for effective   *'emerging technology' to explore less*
deterrence?   *provocative alternative strategies?*

I fail to see how people can use the term 'provocative' to describe our capabilities. It's idiotic to call it 'provocative' if you hit back when the other side starts a war. Everything we say and do points to a defensive strategy. Forward defence cannot be called provocative. It's just that West German territory is relatively small and understandably they don't want it sacrificed. If it were not for forward defence, our forces might look slightly different, but neither posture is provocative. And 'emerging technology' has nothing to do with it.

(vi) *Is it the presence of American front-line*   OR *Is it domination by the two super-powers*
troops and the tying-in of theatre nuclear   *that poses the greatest threat to European*
forces to the American strategic deterrent   *integrity? Would Europe be safer*
that guarantees W. European security?   *decoupled from the super-power nuclear*
Should American policies therefore be   *confrontation? Should Europe be made a*
supported?   *nuclear weapon-free zone?*

The left-hand side is right. The right-hand side is partly wrong, partly unrealistic. People tend to forget that an independent Western European defence could have serious and potentially dangerous consequences. A European defence force capable of defending itself against the Soviet Union would, among other things, mean Western Europe building up quite a large strategic nuclear force; and then the Soviet Union might see itself facing two very powerful, potential opponents and count them together and respond accordingly. So all you would be doing would be to build up an arms race.

If the Americans did decide to go home, you would probably find it very difficult to get the Europeans to take their own defence seriously. But the Americans have no intention of pulling out, not so much because they love us, but because it's in their own interest to stay. There are, of course, Americans who question this; and others who complain about how much they do to defend Europe. But that's not the whole story, because it is also their own interests they are defending.

As for a European nuclear weapon-free zone, it's all part of goodwill flabbiness. Whatever you might declare yourself to be, the Soviet Union would retain systems targeted on Western Europe. And if you are nevertheless prepared to believe Soviet assurances that they would not target you if you were a nuclear weapon-free zone, why not believe them when they say that they will never use their conventional weapons against you either? Why bother about defence at all? The idea of a European nuclear weapon-free zone is meaningless – except, of course, to those other countries who would be left shouldering the burden and responsibility for Western defence.

(vii) *Would Western unilateral nuclear*   OR *Are unilateral initiatives as part of a*
      disarmament invite Soviet blackmail? Are   *general programme of nuclear disarmament*
      suggestions that the West should take the   *the only way to reverse the arms race? Is*
      lead in offering unilateral disarmament   *talk of 'multilateral disarmament' insincere*
      initiatives the thin end of this wedge? Do   *in the mouths of those who reject all*
      radical nuclear disarmers consciously or   *suggestion of a Comprehensive Test Ban*
      unconsciously serve Soviet interests and   *Treaty, a Nuclear Freeze, a European*
      threaten to undermine Western defences?   *Nuclear Weapon-Free Zone, or a*
            declaration of No First Use?

Those who talk about radical Western unilateral disarmament concessions are
not talking about defence. They are talking about giving in – whatever they
may say. Some of these people may have ulterior political motives, but many
are well-intentioned people, whose main aim is to avoid war, but who do not
understand that the only way in which this can be done is through the kind
of deterrence that we have been discussing here.

C. *British Policy*

I. *The British Deterrent*

(i) *Is Britain's deterrent a weapon of last*   OR *Would all possible uses of Britain's*
      resort which guarantees her sovereignty and   *'deterrent' be suicidal? Is its only effect to*
      independence and protects her from nuclear   *encourage proliferation?*
      blackmail?

There are so many strands to this whole question that one can't just answer
'yes' or 'no'. I think that there's a very powerful feeling in Britain in favour
of keeping a British nuclear capability. Perhaps a greater number supportive
of our own deterrent than of American bases.

(ii) *Are British nuclear forces valuable to*   OR *Is the 'second centre of decision making' an*
      European allies because they provide a   *illusion when the weapons are dependent*
      specifically European second centre of   *upon the US and there is no independent*
      decision making?   *strategic role to be played? Are European*
            allies unenthusiastic about a parochial
            British force likely to inhibit her
            commitment to European defence?

Then there is the question of ensuring European defence in the longer term.
What would happen if in ten, fifteen or twenty years' time, the Americans
thought that we were no longer sufficiently interested in defending ourselves,
and decided to pull out of Europe? Where would that leave us? We need to
keep a European nuclear option open in case that eventuality is forced on us.
Other Western Europeans are in favour of the British nuclear force, incidentally.

(iii) *Does the US favour shared responsibility*   OR *Are US forces committed anyway and*
      and do British nuclear forces guarantee   *independent British initiatives more likely*
      full US commitment to Europe and Soviet   *to trigger Soviet retaliation than US*
      recognition of it?   *involvement?*

This is a factor that is usually neglected. The Americans actually like having the French and British nuclear deterrents, because to some extent it absolves them from having total responsibility for these things. Do you think that they are allowing us Trident because of our bright blue eyes? No. They want to feel that others are prepared to share the responsibility.

(iv) *Is the cost of the British deterrent small in view of the vital defence role it plays? Are alternatives likely to be more expensive?*   OR *Can Britain's nuclear forces only be afforded at the expense of conventional strength and of other more important economic priorities?*

It depends how much you're prepared to pay for your own national sovereign independence. If you are not prepared to pay, and want something else instead, that's your business. Although there is a lot of talk about cheaper alternatives, I very much doubt that there are any. Of course, it all depends how effective you want your deterrent to be.

(v) *Would unilateral British nuclear disarmament have no effect on other countries and only serve to weaken British influence and allow France unchallenged ascendancy in Europe?*   OR *Does the British deterrent encourage proliferation and do nothing to enhance British prestige? Would British disarmament within the context outlined in B help to break the nuclear log-jam?*

British unilateral nuclear disarmament would have virtually no effect on other countries who might be considering taking up the nuclear option. And it would have no effect on the Soviet Union, either. We are told that the Soviet Union is willing to reduce by the number we reduce by. What does this amount to? I suspect that it is really double counting. Suppose that the British reduce by a hundred and the Russians go down by a hundred. But the Russians then continue to insist on parity with the Americans in their negotiations with them, so that the hundred that have been 'sold' to us are double counted and are sold to the Americans as well. We would only get a real trade-off if the Americans and the Russians reach agreement and established parity first, and then the Russians were prepared to reduce by an extra hundred in response to a corresponding British reduction. That is not a very likely thing for the Russians to do.

In addition to this, we must ask whether it would be a good thing from a European point of view, if we were to give up a British nuclear capability. I think most of our Allies are happier if we and the French both share this particular burden.

vi) *Is investment in Trident the best way to continue to ensure effective British strategic defence into the 21st century?*   OR *Would commitment to Trident exacerbate all the drawbacks listed above?*

We need Trident for all of the reasons I have already given. Despite the cost, it is still relatively cheap for the job it will do.

2. *NATO Forces and US Bases*

(i) *Must Britain continue to share*   OR *Should British obligations to NATO be*
responsibility for manning NATO nuclear   *met by strengthening conventional forces*
systems upon which her security depends?   *where necessary within an overall non-*
Would refusal to do so fatally weaken the   *nuclear strategy as recommended in B?*
alliance?

Britain must indeed continue to share responsibility for her own defence. And this includes her involvement in manning nuclear systems in Germany, and so on.

(ii) *Would the forced withdrawal of US*   OR *Do the large numbers of nuclear facilities*
nuclear bases from Britain make US   *yielded to the US erode British*
defence of the West impossible? Is   *sovereignty? Would their removal do no*
American interference in British affairs   *more than restore a normal peacetime*
negligible?   *relationship?*

I think that the removal of American nuclear bases from Britain would do more than make the defence of the West much more difficult. It would put the Alliance under tremendous strain. If the Americans found that one of their major Allies had gone unilateral, then it would really call in question the whole basis upon which the Americans take part in this Alliance. It would also make life very difficult for the Germans, and others. I think it would have very serious implications indeed, for our security and for that of our allies.

Turning to the right-hand side, of course any alliance or association will make some difference to you, because you have to accommodate the views of other people. But there has certainly not been an 'erosion of British sovereignty'. The British Prime Minister could have said 'no' to the use of bases in Britain for the bombing of Libya. People often forget that it is just as likely (or unlikely) that we would drag the Americans into something, as that they would drag us in. It works both ways.

(iii) *Will Britain continue to be targeted by*   OR *Is Britain seen as an American aircraft*
Soviet warheads whether or not she   *carrier and targeted by the USSR*
disarms unilaterally?   *accordingly? Will Britain fall an early*
   victim in any superpower confrontation
   unless bases are removed?

What do you think? Of course Britain would go on being targeted. The idea that by going 'non-nuclear' you can turn yourself into a sanctuary in these circumstances is illusory. I just don't believe it.

(iv) *Can non-nuclear defences only safely be*   OR *In a nuclear-free Europe, decoupled from*
afforded by powers prepared to shelter   *the superpower nuclear confrontation,*
beneath the American strategic umbrella?   *would Britain no more expect to depend*
   upon the US 'umbrella' than any other
   Western ally – or than Eastern Europe
   upon the USSR?

I do indeed think that if you did this you would just be taking an easy ride. I agree with what is said on the left. As to the right-hand side – it's so silly, I have no further comment to make.

Moral Considerations

I am neither a theologian nor a philosopher, and I suspect that one would have to be both to do justice to the many questions in this section. Instead of addressing them one-by-one, let me try to say briefly how I look at the question as a whole.

As I see it, the main job of the Alliance is to prevent our countries from being attacked or effectively blackmailed by a militarily very strong and nuclear-armed power, whose own conception of morality is, to say the least, very different from our own. I am satisfied that this job could not be done without there being nuclear weapons also on the Western side.

Those who imply that it might be all right to have nuclear weapons, provided that we made it clear that we would never use them, are not solving the moral problem, but evading it: if your potential opponent were sure that you would never use them, they would be useless as a deterrent to aggression or as a counter to nuclear blackmail; if, on the other hand, you secretly hoped that he would remain uncertain as to whether or not you would use them, you would be making present allied strategy less clear – and I would say less effective – but morally no different.

The points to remember are that:

  (i) The purpose of our nuclear weapons is to deter war and counter nuclear blackmail;

 (ii) We have succeeded in doing both;

(iii) We shall never use any of our weapons unless we are attacked;

(iv) If deterrence failed, and we were attacked, it would be for our political leaders to decide whether or not to use nuclear weapons; and the moral considerations would of course weigh very heavily on their minds;

 (v) Meanwhile, we shall continue to do everything we can to reduce the number of nuclear weapons on both sides.

If nuclear weapons did not exist, or could be disinvented, we wouldn't have these difficult moral questions to answer. But, as things are, I think that our policy is morally justified; and I would certainly question a morality which appeared to suggest that we should leave a monopoly of nuclear weapons to the Soviet Union.

Recommendations

NOTE. The unqualified 'yes' and 'no' answers below represent the editor's reading of what Lord Carrington would say, if he had to reply in one word. It should be understood that Lord Carrington himself would no doubt have wanted to expand, and perhaps qualify, some of them.

1 No (see **B(iv)**).
2 No (see **A2**(A)(**v**)).
3 We are not at present in a position where a CTB could be signed with a sufficient degree of confidence in the verification regime, or of certainty about its implications for the credibility of our deterrent.
4 No (see **A2**(A)(**iii**)).
5 There should be deep, but not unconditional, cuts: this needs to be done by negotiation, and with effective provisions for verification (see **AI(iv)**).
6 No (see **B(vi)**).
7 Yes (see A2 (A)(**vi**)).
8 No (see **A2**(B)).
9 Does not apply.
10 No (see A2 (A)(**V**)).
11 No (see **A2**(A)(**iii**)).
12 No (see **B(vii)**).
13 No (see **C1**).
14 No (see **B(vi)**).
15 No (see **B(vi)**).
16 No (see **CI**).
17 Does not apply.
18 No (see **C2(i)**).
19 No (see **C2(i)** & (**ii**)).
20 Does not apply.

Field Marshal
Lord Carver

G.C.B., C.B.E., D.S.O., M.C.

Biographical Note

Born in 1915, Lord Carver won the D.S.O. and the Military Cross in the Second World War, at the end of which he was commanding the Fourth Armoured Brigade. Subsequently he served as Commander-in-Chief, Far East, between 1967 and 1969; G.O.C., Southern Command, between 1969 and 1971; Chief of General Staff between 1971 and 1973; and Chief of the Defence Staff between 1973 and 1976.

Among his other publications is *A Policy for Peace*, published by Faber and Faber in 1982, where a fuller exposition of his thinking can be found.

Editorial Comment

Communicated during an interview at his home in Hampshire on February 19th, 1986, this set of answers represents the response of an experienced man of action, who has held high military command for a number of years, and is well known for the radical nature of his thinking about military strategy. In the spirit of Clausewitz, Lord Carver goes back to first principles in his criticism of NATO 'flexible response' policies as they have evolved over the past twenty or thirty years, and suggests ways in which this could be remedied. His aim is to re-establish a sound basis to military thinking, so that the threat of force is once again clearly related to political purpose through a coherent strategy for its possible use. Lord Carver's criticisms of current policy, particularly evident here in sections **A1**, **A2(A)**, **B**, and **C1**, have been widely influential within the peace movements. Less popular in those quarters has been his defence of the principle of strategic nuclear deterrence, as expounded in sections **A2(B)**, and **C2**.

FIELD MARSHAL LORD CARVER

A *Global Policy*

1 *The History of the Past Forty Years*

(i) *Has it been nuclear deterrence that has*   OR *Has it mainly been other factors?*
kept the peace between the great powers
since 1945?

My answer is that it has not by any means been nuclear deterrence alone that has kept the peace between the great powers since 1945 – although that has been a very important factor.

(ii) *Does mutual possession of an invulnerable* OR *Does the threat of strategic nuclear*
second-strike strategic nuclear force prevent   *retaliation, particularly against a similarly*
war?   *armed enemy, lack credibility and invite*
  sub-deterrent encroachment?

Mutual possession of an invulnerable second-strike nuclear force is indeed important in preventing the use of nuclear weapons by either of the great nuclear powers, and also in helping to prevent major war between them, because of the inherent fear on both sides that a clash between their military forces could eventually lead to an exchange of nuclear weapons. That is why I do not want to see nuclear weapons abolished altogether.

But the essential link in all this is the physical presence of the conventional forces of the nuclear powers in the area. If there were no US airforce or army forces stationed in Europe, then, although the Soviet Union would still very seriously have to consider the risk of nuclear retaliation, she might nevertheless judge that limited action in, say, West Germany could be possible.

(iii) *Have limited nuclear options at strategic and theatre levels enhanced deterrence by dramatically raising the threshold between peace and war?*   OR *Have most military planners from the start been aiming for nuclear war-fighting superiority? Has 'flexible response' dangerously lowered the threshold between conventional and nuclear war?*

It is, as I have said, the physical presence of United States armed forces on the ground and in the air that is the important link – far more essential to my mind than the presence of American nuclear delivery systems in Europe.

In response to the statement on the left, I should say 'no': limited nuclear options at strategic and theatre levels have not enhanced deterrence since the time the Soviet Union has had the capacity to answer back at every level.

As to the statement on the right – yes, I do think that it is dangerous. Military planners have indeed been aiming for war-fighting superiority, whether in terms of pure counter-force nuclear weapons strategies or more general war-fighting strategies which include the use of nuclear weapons. This is bound to be so once you try to produce military arguments to justify the existence of these weapons. It's probably even more applicable to the Soviet Union than it is to the other side.

iv) *Has the size and variety of the nuclear arsenals held by the superpowers stabilized deterrence?*   OR *Has the logic of nuclear confrontation and worst-case analysis generated a dangerous and strategically pointless superfluity of weapons systems?*

The answer is that it is the constant *change* in the size and variety of nuclear arsenals that has tended to be destabilizing – although as a result of what has been done by both sides the situation is fairly stable at the moment. But, turning to the question on the right-hand side – yes, this has generated a dangerous and strategically pointless superfluity of weapons systems. Undoubtedly. Particularly in the field of counter-force systems. And the principal threat to stability that both sides see is the fear that their static land-based intercontinental ballistic missiles, on which they both rely heavily, could be preemptively destroyed by the other. That's the principal destabilizing element and it's the principal element in the escalation in the numbers of warheads.

v) *Has the idea of nuclear balance between the superpowers been essential to stability and have arms-control negotiations helped to achieve it?*   OR *Have ideas of 'nuclear defence' and 'parity' proved illusory and is 'multilateral negotiation from strength' a contradiction in terms? Has 'arms-control' been just another name for the arms race?*

If arms control is significant here – and it's something I'm beginning to doubt – then it is as part of the attempt to achieve the lowest possible level of strategic balance of forces. At the time of SALT I Henry Kissinger saw clearly (and I was arguing this with General Abrahamson[1] only yesterday over SDI) that, if both sides continued in the way they were going, they would have to devote more and more effort to their strategic nuclear systems, and the result would not in fact enhance the security of either. He realized that you have got to try to find something which is clearly in the self-interest of both sides to follow – as when the Russians and Americans agreed to control nuclear testing in order to prevent proliferation. He wanted to bring about a situation in which both sides recognized this, and in the first instance stopped where they were, and then agreed to move downwards, as it were, almost back to the 1945–1950 state of affairs.

Turning to the statement on the right, I wouldn't say that 'arms control' has just been 'another name for the arms race' – what I would say, though, is that as yet it has shown hardly any promise of limiting the numbers and variety of nuclear weapons. It has so far proved impossible to achieve what Kissinger wanted because of mutual mistrust. Some kind of balance at reduced levels depends on confidence on both sides that each is in fact attempting to pursue the target and not attempting to evade it – and that's very difficult to achieve. But it's not impossible.

(vi) *Has force-planning been controlled by*   OR *Has the self-reinforcing impetus of*
    strategic thinking?   *technology and vested interest dictated*
                                       policies subsequently justified post hoc?

I would have said that on balance, as Solly Zuckerman[2] has pointed out in a number of different articles, it has definitely been the impetus of technology and vested interest on both sides of the Iron Curtain dictating policies, which have then been justified afterwards.

2 *The Prospect for the Future*

(A) WITH NUCLEAR WEAPONS
  (i) *Does the threat of an enemy first strike*   OR *Is there an increasing threat from accurate*
     remain inconceivable for the foreseeable   *and time-urgent first-strike weapons?*
     future?

The threat of an enemy first strike is obviously not inconceivable, because, as long as both sides maintain weapons systems which are clearly designed for first strike, the threat remains. All counter-force systems are by definition first strike weapons, because there is no point in firing at the other side's weapons system after it has itself been fired. Therefore you must strike first. There is also no doubt that a combination of MIRVs and of greater accuracy makes the threat of a strike against a static land-based missile system more difficult to counter than it was before – although of course a solid fuel powered missile in a deep silo is more difficult to destroy.

---

1. Director of the Strategic Defence Initiative Office.
2. Former Chief Scientific Adviser to the Government, 1960–1966. See, for example, *Science Advisers, Scientific Advisers, and Nuclear Weapons* (1980).

Both the Soviet Union and the United States maintain that they would never be the first to make a strategic nuclear strike. But both at the same time argue that they must nevertheless retain that capability, in case they come to the conclusion that the other is about to do so – and if they do come to that conclusion, then they will have to strike first! So each is a reflection of the other. If they would only go for systems that were mobile or very difficult to detect, like long-range submarine ballistic missile systems, they would not have the problem.

(ii) *Are command, control, communication and* OR *Does the amount of information to be intelligence facilities likely to remain secure?* *processed, pressure of time and fear of preemption put command and control systems under intolerable strain and make inadvertent war more likely?*

Command and control systems are, on the contrary, likely to become more secure in future even than they are now, I think. In the days when you had liquid fuelled systems to get ready to fire and almost archaic communications networks which were extremely vulnerable, not only to electronic but also to physical counter-measures, there was a much greater danger of inadvertent war. But now, with the astonishing advances that there have been in microelectronics, seventy-five percent of your communications can be knocked out and the system will still work perfectly well.

By far the most important confidence-building measure that has ever been introduced, by the way, has been mutual acquiescence by each side in the ability of the other to observe activity from space – and the greatest possible danger would come if either threatened to do away with the other's observation satellites.

(iii) *If nevertheless there were a limited nuclear* OR *Is the idea that nuclear war could be exchange would it be likely to end hostilities swiftly?* *limited once it had broken out a dangerous illusion?*

There is absolutely no likelihood that a limited nuclear exchange would be likely to end hostilities swiftly. The one clear distinction that can be made in this whole field is that between the use and the non-use of nuclear weapons. Almost everybody, including people like Harold Brown[1] and others, agrees that once you have used nuclear weapons there is no knowing where it will lead – you just cannot calculate what the other side's reaction is going to be. Indeed, you can't even calculate what your own side's reaction is going to be.

(iv) *Do new generations of battlefield and* OR *Do new battlefield and theatre weapons theatre nuclear systems reinforce deterrence?* *threaten a dangerous lowering of the nuclear threshold?*

So far as concerns the question on the left, I can't see how new theatre systems make the slightest difference to deterrence. For example, the fact that the Pershing II has got a longer range than the Pershing I doesn't alter the characteristics of the system. The Soviet authorities are fussed because it is

---

1. US Secretary of Defense under President Carter, 1977–81.

now possible to reach the Soviet Union from Western Europe, but submarine-based missiles could do this before anyway. As for the Cruise missile, it worries the Soviet Union because, although it would not be difficult to devise a defence against it, this would be very expensive. But once again it doesn't make any difference to deterrence. I would like the Cruise missile restricted to non-nuclear warheads and used for all those missions other than very short range ones for which NATO now thinks it wants to employ manned aircraft. Half the problem for NATO over the past twenty years has been to find targets for its nuclear weapons!

So far as the right-hand side goes, it's things like enhanced radiation weapons, which everyone has almost forgotten about now, that would indeed lower the nuclear threshold and for that reason be very dangerous. It would increase the pressure from the military on the President to agree to the initial use of nuclear warheads.

(v) *Does the Strategic Defence Initiative offer* OR *Is the Strategic Defence Initiative simply*
    the hope of an effective defence against   *the most recent and destabilizing example*
    nuclear weapons?   *of the process outlined in 1?*

In response to these questions you have to consider what the aim of the Strategic Defence Initiative is and that has never been clear.

First there is the President's vision of making nuclear weapons obsolete, or, a little less ambitious, of defending the whole of the United States. The critical target here is said to be that ninety-five per cent of all warheads launched should be intercepted and destroyed: that is a very stringent test. In any case even five per cent of the present deliverable stock of Soviet warheads would do untold damage. And no-one is suggesting that anything like this will apply, say, to Europe.

Then we must consider whether a lower target is something worth getting involved in – for example, just the protection of the US delivery systems themselves. The sophisticated argument used here by the state department, the defence department, the arms control agency and everybody else who is involved, when they can agree among themselves, is to invoke Paul Nitze's[1] criteria: that SDI will enhance deterrence by making the system more survivable and therefore more stable, and will also make it more cost-effective than the alternative continuing escalation in offensive systems. This takes us right back to all the arguments why at the time of the ABM treaty the US, correctly in my opinion, decided not to go ahead with ABM systems. I challenged General Abrahamson with this yesterday. I asked him why he thought that there was going to be a totally different result from what the whole history of weapons development has shown, which is that the moment one side begins to improve its defence the other improves its offence, and so on. This is exactly the sort of situation that Henry Kissinger foresaw which impelled him into arms control talks. So I believe it's a wrong road to follow.

---

1. Chief United States arms negotiator for many years.

(vi) *Is the threat of 'horizontal' nuclear*   OR *Is continuing reliance on nuclear deterrence*
proliferation best met by a continuation of   *by the great powers bound to accelerate the*
past policies?   *process of proliferation and make nuclear*
war more likely?

I find this a difficult question to answer because, although I can't, in theory, see why mutual possession of nuclear weapons by, say, Iran and Iraq shouldn't prevent war between them, nevertheless I think that a world in which a great many people had nuclear weapons would be less safe. So I am in general against proliferation. But although there's a lot of talk to the effect that continuing reliance on nuclear deterrence by the great powers encourages proliferation, I don't think that decisions taken by countries like South Africa, Israel, South Korea, Argentina or anybody else to develop or not to develop a nuclear weapon is going to be determined by how many the Soviet Union, the United States, we, the French or the Chinese have; nor do I think that if we suddenly decided tomorrow to give up all our nuclear weapons it would make anybody else give them up.

(vii) *Do multilateral arms-control negotiations*   OR *Is 'arms-control' an illusion which diverts*
offer the best prospect for future stability?   *attention from the only safe policy –*
nuclear disarmament?

I fall back here on what Michael Howard never tires of saying which is that it is policies which matter, not arms control negotiations. It is the policy adopted by the West towards the Soviet Union and vice versa which is significant. If policies are sensible, you might get sensible answers in other fields. In particular it might be possible for each side to realize at last that it is in their mutual interest first of all to give up these wretched static land-based systems (the Russians will be particularly reluctant to do this), and secondly to do away with the battlefield systems which NATO has tended to pioneer. If we could get rid of these two we would be half way to solving the problem and eliminating the main areas of proliferation. But if both sides go on feeling that arms control negotiations are a threat and that the only way to conduct them is by negotiating from strength, then we might well be better off without them.

(B) WITHOUT NUCLEAR WEAPONS

(i) *If nuclear arsenals were dismantled would*   OR *Would nuclear disarmament remove the*
war between the great powers again   *incentive for nuclear preemption while not*
become a rational option and therefore   *affecting the reluctance of the great powers*
more likely?   *to initiate a third world war?*

I do not share the President's vision and I find it hypocritical of the British government to claim in successive White Papers that its aim is total and complete nuclear disarmament. My answer is, therefore, that, if nuclear arsenals were dismantled, war between major industrial nations would indeed appear to become a rational option again.

(ii) *Would a major conventional war be likely*   OR *Is conventional war, however terrible,*
in itself to be as terrible as a limited   *preferable to nuclear war?*
nuclear war?

Depending upon a number of factors a major conventional war in Europe, if it lasted any length of time, would create terrible destruction, but nothing comparable to a limited nuclear war.

(iii) *Because nuclear weapons cannot be*   OR *As with nerve gases in the last war, would*
uninvented would they not be bound to be   *there be no incentive to resort to*
used sooner or later once war had broken   *capabilities which the other side has as*
out?   *well?*

But the fact remains that even if through international agreement, nuclear weapons had somehow or other been eliminated, and some sort of international inspection had verified this (though I have no idea how), the moment hostilities did start it would not be long before they reappeared. Even schoolboys now know how to make them.

(iv) *Is global nuclear disarmament only*   OR *Is to argue that even multilateral nuclear*
feasible in a world where war itself is no   *disarmament is not desirable to give up all*
longer a possibility?   *hope of a rational world-order?*

On the right hand side – in a way this is what both the Soviet Union and the United States are professing that they want. So what's to stop it? It would certainly be far cheaper than the Strategic Defence Initiative! But the fact is that I can't imagine a world where war itself is no longer a possibility.

(v) *Is peace only preserved when we are seen*   OR *Do the years before 1914 show what*
to be prepared for war, as failure before   *happens when military planning and the*
1939 and success since 1945 show? Under   *arms race control political choices? Do*
likely future conditions would global   *present strategies make nuclear war almost*
nuclear disarmament make war, including   *inevitable under likely future conditions?*
nuclear war, more likely?   *Is global nuclear disarmament the only*
                                                  rational policy?

As I have said I do think that global nuclear disarmament would make war, including nuclear war, more likely. But the continuing proliferation of nuclear weapons systems is unnecessary and dangerous. The only rational policy would therefore be one in which, among other things, nuclear arsenals were reduced to the minimum strategic force needed for effective mutual deterrence – preferably in the form of long range submarine ballistic missile systems.

B. *NATO Policy*

(i) *Does the Soviet Union, together with her*   OR *Are NATO and WTO forces relatively*
Warsaw Pact allies, enjoy a strategically   *evenly matched?*
dangerous military superiority in Europe?

In terms of conventional arms within the European theatre the Soviet Union enjoys a considerable superiority in numbers of land forces and air forces but is inferior in naval forces. And there is no doubt that the Soviets can, as they did in the Second World War, develop the most enormous conventional military power. But the presence of United States ground and air forces in Europe, together with her undoubted capacity to inflict enormous damage on the Soviet Union, to my mind means that there is a stable strategic balance. Of course, if NATO's conventional forces became so weak that the Soviet Union thought that it could achieve a swift result and present the other side with a *fait accompli*, particularly if it didn't involve any direct hostilities against United States forces, well, then that might be another matter.

(ii) *Is the Soviet Union an expansionist power* OR *Is the Soviet Union an encircled and which will take advantage of unilateral threatened power trying to keep up with Western concessions and is only restrained Western technology and likely to respond and forced to accept arms-control positively to unconditional offers of agreements by Western determination and Western restraint within a general context strength? of detente?*

This is a very interesting question because, in territorial terms, I don't think that the Soviet Union's history shows it to be an expansionist power at all. What lies at the heart of the problem and makes the whole thing so difficult is that the Soviet Union believes in and propagates an ideological, cultural, political, social and economic theory of how society should be organized which is in total opposition to the capitalist democratic West. They, like us, would like to see as many countries as possible turn in their direction. But they have in many ways been more cautious than we have in setting about it – and extraordinarily unsuccessful too.

(iii) *Is Soviet chemical and conventional* OR *Is NATO dependence on the early use of preponderance such that NATO must nuclear weapons unnecessary and continue to be able to threaten early use of strategically suicidal? nuclear weapons?*

I don't think that the question of chemical weapons is so important. So far as redressing any conventional imbalance goes, reliance on the early use of nuclear weapons is simply no answer. The facts of the matter are that, if NATO initiated the use of nuclear weapons, it would suffer proportionately much more damage than the Warsaw Pact and its forces, so it would be cutting off its nose to spite its face.

(iv) *Does the growing size of the Soviet nuclear* OR *Does the West initiate nearly all phases of arsenal threaten the delicate theatre and the nuclear arms race and continue to enjoy strategic balance? Would Western failure a substantial lead in most areas? Is the to match Soviet systems be destabilizing? nuclear 'overkill' such that the West could offer a nuclear 'freeze' or unconditional cuts without risk?*

I don't think that the theatre balance matters at all. I don't go along with this constant German fear of decoupling – that if you don't have American nuclear delivery systems based on land in Europe then the Soviet Union might think that it could invade Western Europe without receiving anything nuclear in reply. A fraction of the present Soviet nuclear arsenal could wipe out the whole of Europe tomorrow, so that adding or subtracting a few warheads doesn't make the slightest difference. The number of SS20s that they have is completely irrelevant.

I'm against freezes, because you begin to argue about what you're going to freeze, and then you can't give anything up because you've frozen it. I favour unconditional cuts. That's the better way.

(v) *Are NATO 'forward defence' and 'deep*   OR *Should NATO exploit her lead in*
     strike' strategies essential for effective   *'emerging technology' to explore less*
     deterrence?   *provocative alternative strategies?*

The important thing about emerging technologies in terms of warheads, delivery systems and, above all, target acquisitioning is that it makes it much more possible for you to have a non-nuclear way of dealing with the other side's forces, particularly his threatened superiority in conventional weapons, than you had before – which is a very good thing. It could free you to a certain extent from overdependence on first use of nuclear weapons.

Forward defence on the other hand is forced on NATO for German political reasons. The Federal Republic is not prepared to sacrifice great stretches of land in order to play for time. If it wasn't for this, we would adopt a military posture in greater depth for good military reasons.

(vi) *Is it the presence of American front-line*   OR *Is it domination by the two super-powers*
      troops and the tying-in of theatre nuclear   *that poses the greatest threat to European*
      forces to the American strategic deterrent   *integrity? Would Europe be safer*
      that guarantees W. European security?   *decoupled from the super-power nuclear*
      Should American policies therefore be   *confrontation? Should Europe be made a*
      supported?   *nuclear weapon-free zone?*

I think that this is the heart of the matter. It is absolutely essential both that American troops remain in Europe and that the United States should maintain an effective strategic nuclear deterrent. But there's a great exaggeration of the need for a whole series of steps in the nuclear ladder. Since NATO would suffer more than the other side, the question is raised whether we need theatre nuclear forces at all. To my mind the only valid function of theatre nuclear forces now is to make it absolutely clear to the Soviet Union that it could not itself employ nuclear weapons in Europe with impunity. It is a retaliatory and not a first use function.

But it makes no sense to talk about 'decoupling' Europe from the super-power nuclear confrontation, or to recommend a nuclear weapon-free zone, when the Soviet Union will retain any number of means of delivering nuclear weapons which don't depend upon what you call theatre nuclear systems.

(vii) *Would Western unilateral nuclear disarmament invite Soviet blackmail? Are suggestions that the West should take the lead in offering unilateral disarmament initiatives the thin end of this wedge? Do radical nuclear disarmers consciously or unconsciously serve Soviet interests and threaten to undermine Western defences?*

OR *Are unilateral initiatives as part of a general programme of nuclear disarmament the only way to reverse the arms race? Is talk of 'multilateral disarmament' insincere in the mouths of those who reject all suggestion of a Comprehensive Test Ban Treaty, a Nuclear Freeze, a European Nuclear Weapon-Free Zone, or a declaration of No First Use?*

Unilateral initiatives are not the only way to reverse the arms race, but I do think that they are probabaly the best way. If we have decided in Western Europe that we don't need certain systems, it is probably much better for us to say, as we have done in certain cases, that we are going to give them up and hope that the other side would do the same, but that we are not going to get involved in an argument about reciprocity or verifiability. Of course, this would not necessarily mean that the other side would give up theirs straight away – although it might persuade them that it wasn't worth their while developing successor systems.

So far as the questions on the left-hand side go, if for example we and the French were to decide to give up our nuclear weapons tomorrow, it wouldn't make the slightest difference to what the Soviet Union did, as long as we were prepared to go on manning NATO delivery systems with American nuclear warheads. If, on the other hand, all the European members of NATO were to turn to the US and say that they would no longer go on manning these systems, that *would* be a shattering blow to NATO, would make it more likely that the Americans would wash their hands of Europe, and, in the event, would indeed lay Europe open to Soviet blackmail.

C *British Policy*

1 *The British Deterrent*

(i) *Is Britain's deterrent a weapon of last resort which guarantees her sovereignty and independence and protects her from nuclear blackmail?*

OR *Would all possible uses of Britain's 'deterrent' be suicidal? Is its only effect to encourage proliferation?*

The left-hand side represents an instinctive response that has been there from the start. If all else fails, we can stand on our own feet. It's what Margaret Thatcher and Heseltine have said and is sometimes heard running around the Ministry of Defence. But it doesn't make sense, and in any case is not an argument you can put forward in front of your allies, because it implies that you have let Europe be overrun without doing anything about it with your nuclear weapons.

(ii) *Are British nuclear forces valuable to
European allies because they provide a
specifically European second centre of
decision making?*

OR *Is the 'second centre of decision making' an
illusion when the weapons are dependent
upon the US and there is no independent
strategic role to be played? Are European
allies unenthusiastic about a parochial
British force likely to inhibit her
commitment to European defence?*

This is the theory put forward by the government in its official paper 'The
Future of the British Strategic Deterrent' when Francis Pym was Minister of
Defence. It's exactly the opposite of the 'last resort' argument, because it
implies, absurdly, that even though the Russians might think that the Americans would hesitate to use nuclear weapons for fear of retaliation against their
cities, they would believe that the British would be happy to sacrifice their
cities for the sake of Europe. British independent nuclear forces are of no
value to European allies, and this 'second centre' argument implies mistrust
of the Americans.

(iii) *Does the US favour shared responsibility
and do British nuclear forces guarantee
full US commitment to Europe and Soviet
recognition of it?*

OR *Are US forces committed anyway and
independent British initiatives more likely
to trigger Soviet retaliation than US
involvement?*

British nuclear forces guarantee nothing. The only thing the American like
about it is that there are other people besides themselves who can share the
odium of having these weapons. They are also afraid that an anti-nuclear
movement in this country could affect them.

(iv) *Is the cost of the British deterrent small in
view of the vital defence role it plays? Are
alternatives likely to be more expensive?*

OR *Can Britain's nuclear forces only be
afforded at the expense of conventional
strength and of other more important
economic priorities?*

In answer to the left-hand side: since I don't believe that it playes a vital
defence rôle at all, you don't need an 'alternative'. Turning to the right-hand
side: it's bound to be at the expense of conventional strength – as long as the
money set aside is to be spent on defence as it should be.

(v) *Would unilateral British nuclear
disarmament have no effect on other
countries and only serve to weaken British
influence and allow France unchallenged
ascendancy in Europe?*

OR *Does the British deterrent encourage
proliferation and do nothing to enhance
British prestige? Would British
disarmament within the context outlined in
B help to break the nuclear log-jam?*

I think that I have already answered this. I don't believe that whether or not
Britain keeps an independent nuclear force makes much difference to anybody
else. If the French want to waste their money on these things let them.

(vi) *Is investment in Trident the best way to*   OR *Would commitment to Trident exacerbate*
continue to ensure effective British strategic   *all the drawbacks listed above?*
defence into the 21st century?

It is the cohesion, self-confidence and general strength of NATO that is essential for British strategic defence, not an independent nuclear force. On the other hand, if you *did* think that an independent nuclear force was important, then there can be little doubt that Trident is the best answer. David Owen's recommendation of alternatives is just equivocation. My only argument against Trident is that it's a waste of money.

2 *NATO Forces and US Bases*

(i) *Must Britain continue to share*   OR *Should British obligations to NATO be*
responsibility for manning NATO nuclear   *met by strengthening conventional forces*
systems upon which her security depends?   *where necessary within an overall non-*
Would refusal to do so fatally weaken the   *nuclear strategy as recommended in B?*
alliance?

I would certainly say 'yes' to the left-hand side.

(ii) *Would the forced withdrawal of US*   OR *Do the large numbers of nuclear facilities*
nuclear bases from Britain make US   *yielded to the US erode British*
defence of the West impossible? Is   *sovereignty? Would their removal do no*
American interference in British affairs   *more than restore a normal peacetime*
negligible?   *relationship?*

What really matters is what the Germans do – they're the people who really matter – although of course the forced removal of American nuclear bases from Britain would be an extremely serious blow to NATO. If we were neutral, US defence of the West would still be physically possible, but politically this would threaten the total break-up of NATO.

As for American interference in British affairs – I should say that as far as defence is concerned it's negligible, but it appears that in economic affairs it's quite considerable!

(iii) *Will Britain continue to be targeted by*   OR *Is Britain seen as an American aircraft*
Soviet warheads whether or not she   *carrier and targeted by the USSR*
disarms unilaterally?   *accordingly? Will Britain fall an early*
      victim in any superpower confrontation
      unless bases are removed?

Because Soviet nuclear delivery systems are primarily targeted against American nuclear delivery systems in Europe, we are less likely to be targeted if we don't have American nuclear delivery bases in this country. This is one of the arguments for having them at sea. I can't see the argument for having these things on land. It's a question of persuading the Germans of this.

(iv) *Can non-nuclear defences only safely be*   OR *In a nuclear-free Europe, decoupled from*
afforded by powers prepared to shelter   *the superpower nuclear confrontation,*
beneath the American strategic umbrella?   *would Britain no more expect to depend*
upon the US 'umbrella' than any other
Western ally – or than Eastern Europe
upon the USSR?

Ideally we would have American ground troops in Europe and then sub-marine-based nuclear forces. It is perfectly possible to have a valid theatre nuclear weapons system under the aegis of the Supreme Allied Commander Europe (SACEUR) that is based at sea. All theatre systems should be totally detached from the land, airforce and navy organizations and held under very tight separate control by the Supreme Allied Commanders. This would get Margaret Thatcher off the hook – there would be no land-based nuclear delivery systems and British nuclear forces would be assigned to NATO, which is what we have always said is their primary purpose. I would drop the independent strategic side to it. But in the meantime Britain must be prepared to man NATO nuclear delivery systems.

Moral Considerations

(i) *Is it morally right to pursue the policy least*   OR *Are there actions which are in themselves*
likely to cause human suffering? May this   *wrong no matter what the situation? Is the*
sometimes involve doing things which in   *alternative to excuse almost any act of*
other circumstances would be wrong?   *barbarism?*

(ii) *In formulating policy should we weigh up*   OR *Is the only relevant point here that a*
the probability of success and the relative   *nuclear exchange of almost any kind*
costs in terms of human suffering of   *would in itself cause unimaginable*
alternative nuclear and non-nuclear   *suffering to largely civilian populations?*
strategies?

I'm not very good on morals, but taking the right-hand side first, I think that there are actions which are wrong in themselves – shooting a man in cold blood when he's helpless is a thing which is wrong no matter what the situation. There is no doubt that a nuclear exchange would cause terrible suffering to civilian populations and I think that Mgr O'Brien made an important point when he said to me once that, although it may in certain circumstances be moral to kill someone in order to prevent him from killing your wife, it is not moral to kill him in revenge afterwards – so a retaliatory second strike would be morally wrong. But all of life is a matter of very difficult judgement – usually between two conflicting evils, not between right and wrong.

(iii) *So far as concerns intention, need we look*   OR *Is there no such thing as a fully deployed*
no further than the fact that our sole aim in *weapons system which is a bluff? Is to*
deploying nuclear weapons is to prevent   *deploy nuclear weapons to intend to use*
their use?   *them in certain circumstances?*

This is very difficult. Our response must be at any rate to try to reduce the thing so that the smallest possible number are employed. But there is no doubt that to deploy and man these systems is to be prepared to use them in certain circumstances.

(iv) *Are there possible uses of nuclear weapons* OR *Is a conditional intention to cause which are allowed by Just War theory, for indiscriminate and disproportionate example the bombing of Hiroshima and suffering of this kind, whether admonitory, Nagasaki in order to prevent worse preemptive or retaliatory, ruled out by Just suffering? Can there be a theory of Just War theory? Was it wrong to bomb Deterrence? Hiroshima and Nagasaki in 1945?*

What was wrong in the cases of Hiroshima and Nagasaki was to drop the bombs on cities. But at the time it was greeted with relief and didn't seem to be so different to other things that had been going on.

But the fact remains that now, particularly with the introduction of the fusion weapon, there is absolutely no means of ensuring what what you have started off is going to remain at that level.

Question: So there are circumstances in which you could be morally justified in using your presumably retaliatory submarine-based nuclear force?

Answer: I think that's frightfully difficult.

Question: But, if you can't use it, don't you get to the stage where you ask what the point of it is?

Answer: Yes you do. The whole thing begins to unravel.

(v) *Is there no relevant connection between the* OR *Is it a scandal that such huge resources are development and deployment of nuclear devoted to the development and deployment weapons and world poverty and disease? of nuclear weapons and not to the alleviation of suffering?*

This has nothing to do with it. Don't tell me for one moment that the money being spent by any of the nations on their nuclear weapons systems would be used for alleviating suffering in this way – except possibly in their own country.

(vi) *Does Christian teaching allow the* OR *Does Christian teaching condemn the deployment of nuclear weapons? deployment of nuclear weapons?*

Christian teaching condemns all killing. So that finishes that one.

Recommendations

1 No (See **B(iv)**).
2 Yes (See **A2** (A) **(ii)** & **(v)**).
3 Not 'at once', because of the need to go on testing to make warheads safer and cleaner. But, as part of a general agreement on the reduction of warheads, 'yes'.
4 Yes. But, if counter-force systems are retained, this will not prevent their preemptive use when it is thought that the other side is about to strike (See **A2(A)(i)** & **B(iii)** & **B(vi)**).

5 Yes (See **AI(iv)** & **AI(v)** & **A2**(A)(**vii**)).

6 So far as concerns Europe – No (See **B(vi)**).

7 Yes (See **A2**(A)(**vi**)).

8 No (See **AI(ii)** & **A2**(B)).

9 This should be a permanent arrangement (See **A2**(B)).

10 Yes (See **A2**(A)(**v**)).

11 See 4.

12 Unconditional cuts, Yes; a freeze, No (See **B(iv)**).

13 Yes (See esp. **CI(v)** & **C2(iv)**).

14 No (See **B(vi)**).

15 See 6.

16 Yes. Alternatively, assign it to NATO in its entirety, and drop the independent strategic side to it (See **C2(iv)**).

17 Yes (See **CI(iv)**).

18 No (See **C2(i)**).

19 No (See **C2(i)** & **C2(ii)**).

20 Does not apply.

Group Captain Leonard Cheshire

V.C., O.M., D.S.O., D.F.C.

Biographical Note

Group Captain Cheshire is well known for two main reasons. First, because he was awarded the Victoria Cross for bravery after one hundred operations as a bomber pilot in the Second World War. Second, because of the work he has since done in founding homes for the sick and disabled. Beginning with the conversion of his own house into the first Cheshire Home soon after the war, the enterprise has progressed to the point where there are now seventy-five Cheshire Homes in the United Kingdom and a further 147 in forty-five other countries throughout the world. There are also twenty Family Support Services in England, offering part-time help to elderly and handicapped people and to families with a handicapped member living in their own homes.

As the official British observer, Leonard Cheshire witnessed the dropping of the atomic bomb on Nagasaki in 1945. His book, *The Light of Many Suns*, published by Methuen in 1985, describes that experience and explains the effect that it has had upon his own attitude to nuclear deterrence.

Editorial Comment

The answers recorded here were given in an interview on 24th June 1986 in Maunsel Street, the London headquarters of the Cheshire Foundation. They represent the conclusions of someone who has been concerned with the problems of just defence in the nuclear age for over forty years. Two features may strike the reader in particular. The first is the idea, proposed in the answers to **A2**(A)(**vii**) and **B**(**vii**), that what is needed is not so much a reduction in certain classes of nuclear weapons, as a drastic and, if necessary, unilateral reduction in conventional forces. This is an approach which has not been given proper emphasis elsewhere in the book. It may be seen to carry through to its logical conclusion the conviction that the mutual possession of flexible and invulnerable second-strike nuclear forces in itself deters from war. The second is the fearless way in which Leonard Cheshire defends the use of nuclear weapons in 1945, and their deployment today, on moral grounds.

GROUP CAPTAIN LEONARD CHESHIRE

A *Global Policy*

1 *The History of Past Forty Years*

(i) *Has it been nuclear deterrence that has*   OR *Has it mainly been other factors?*
kept the peace between the great powers
since 1945?

It has mainly been nuclear deterrence.

(ii) *Does mutual possession of an invulnerable* OR *Does the threat of strategic nuclear*
second-strike strategic nuclear force prevent   *retaliation, particularly against a similarly*
war?   *armed enemy, lack credibility and invite*
                                                     sub-deterrent encroachment?

Mutual possession of an invulnerable second-strike nuclear force does prevent war. I don't agree with the right-hand side.

(iii) *Have limited nuclear options at strategic and theatre levels enhanced deterrence by dramatically raising the threshold between peace and war?* OR *Have most military planners from the start been aiming for nuclear war-fighting superiority? Has 'flexible response' dangerously lowered the threshold between conventional and nuclear war?*

I think that these limited nuclear options do enhance deterrence, because, if the only option that you had was a full strategic strike, this would be totally incredible. I don't agree with what is suggested on the right, because the really vital threshold is the one between no war at all and nuclear war. I suppose that it is true that military planners in the East and in the West have at heart been aiming for nuclear war-fighting superiority – it's only human to do that if you are a military planner. In fact, I think that this is unattainable, but nevertheless I do agree that there is a danger here. This way of thinking should be changed.

(iv) *Has the size and variety of the nuclear arsenals held by the superpowers stabilized deterrence?* OR *Has the logic of nuclear confrontation and worst-case analysis generated a dangerous and strategically pointless superfluity of weapons systems?*

I would like to see as minimal a deterrence as is effective and credible, and I think that there are types of nuclear weapons that we would be better without. In particular, I would like to do away with all battlefield nuclear weapons. There is a different logic to the battlefield nuclear weapon and to the strategic nuclear weapon. The battlefield nuclear weapon is aimed at striking the attacker's army; the strategic nuclear weapon is aimed at destroying his country. So the latter deters in an absolute sense, but the former only in a relative sense. Moreover, since you also have the intermediate range between the two, which is partly battlefield because it is situated there, but also partly strategic because it is aimed at your homeland, there is a confusion of logic, which, I think, inhibits the arms control process.

(v) *Has the idea of nuclear balance between the superpowers been essential to stability and have arms-control negotiations helped to achieve it?* OR *Have ideas of 'nuclear defence' and 'parity' proved illusory and is 'multilateral negotiation from strength' a contradiction in terms? Has 'arms-control' been just another name for the arms race?*

I think that the idea of nuclear balance is essential for stability. But I don't know the extent to which the arms control negotiations have helped or hindered it. That requires specialized knowledge which I do not have.

(vi) *Has force-planning been controlled by strategic thinking?* OR *Has the self-reinforcing impetus of technology and vested interest dictated policies subsequently justified post hoc?*

I am certainly afraid of the inevitable struggle on both sides to harness technology to their advantage, and of the vested interests that are aroused as a result. Military planners are cast in a mould that they cannot escape from. But

I do think that there is also a strong effort to control force-planning by strategic thinking.

2 *The Prospect for the Future*

(A) WITH NUCLEAR WEAPONS

(i) *Does the threat of an enemy first strike*   OR *Is there an increasing threat from accurate*
remain inconceivable for the foreseeable   *and time-urgent first-strike weapons?*
future?

I cannot believe that either side will think that it has got a first-strike capability. You would have to have a one hundred per cent certainty of eliminating all the enemy systems – you could not even afford a ninety per cent certainty. I just cannot believe it. And in any case, if this were threatened, you would know that the other side would resort to launch-on-warning. He would have to.

(ii) *Are command, control, communication and* OR *Does the amount of information to be*
intelligence facilities likely to remain   *processed, pressure of time and fear of*
secure?   *preemption put command and control*
                                                      systems under intolerable strain and make
                                                      inadvertent war more likely?

I don't think that inadvertent war is likely, because both sides have a common vested interest in preventing it. But I think that there is a great need to make certain that command, control and communication facilities are secure. I think that there is a danger here – but not a danger of a degree that is likely to lead to war.

(iii) *If nevertheless there were a limited nuclear* OR *Is the idea that nuclear war could be*
exchange would it be likely to end   *limited once it had broken out a dangerous*
hostilities swiftly?   *illusion?*

I simply do not know. I don't think that anyone can know, because it has never happened. On the one hand, as I think Olof Palme[1] put it, the dynamics of interaction might be so powerful that neither side could prevent escalation. On the other, the shock might be so great that hostilities would rapidly cease. I simply cannot believe that the superpowers would knowingly destroy one another. Above all, governments want to stay in power, and escalation would mean that they would not. It doesn't make sense. So I think that there is a strong case for believing that, even if some accident were to happen, both sides would do everything that they could to stop it rather than to carry on.

(iv) *Do new generations of battlefield and*   OR *Do new battlefield and theatre weapons*
theatre nuclear systems reinforce   *threaten a dangerous lowering of the*
deterrence?   *nuclear threshold?*

I don't like new generations of battlefield systems, but I do see a need to update theatre systems – but only on the grounds that they are obsolete. I

---

1. Chairman of the Independent Commission on Disarmament and Security Issues, and Prime Minister of Sweden until his assassination in 1986.

can't make a judgement on particular systems, such as Pershing II and Cruise, because I do not have the knowledge.

(v) *Does the Strategic Defence Initiative offer* OR *Is the Strategic Defence Initiative simply the hope of an effective defence against the most recent and destabilizing example nuclear weapons? of the process outlined in 1?*

There are persuasive arguments on both sides here. I do not believe that it can offer a blanket defence. When you see what accidents there have been to what were supposed to be well-proved enterprises like the Challenger space shuttle and the Chernobyl reactor, you cannot believe that a complicated system such as SDI, which can never be tested, has a hope of being one hundred per cent reliable. It could be destabilizing, because it could cause the enemy to think that you were going for a first strike capability. On the other hand, I'm quite certain that the Russians are proceeding with one, too.

vi) *Is the threat of 'horizontal' nuclear* OR *Is continuing reliance on nuclear deterrence proliferation best met by a continuation of by the great powers bound to accelerate the past policies? process of proliferation and make nuclear war more likely?*

As I have said, I see no alternative to our continuing to rely on nuclear deterrence at great power level. And I think that the danger of 'horizontal' proliferation can be met. In the first place, a Gadaffi would only have short-range delivery systems, so that whatever he did could only be local. But, above all, if something like that were to happen, then I am sure that Russia and America would combine swiftly to stop them. So I don't think that the danger is as great as the public thinks that it is.

vii) *Do multilateral arms-control negotiations* OR *Is 'arms-control' an illusion which diverts offer the best prospect for future stability? attention from the only safe policy – nuclear disarmament?*

I do not think that we should lose faith in the multilateral arms control process. But I would propose something that is not usually recommended. First of all, in view of the terrible consequences that there would be were war of any kind to break out in Europe between the great powers, each side should say that war between the superpowers is a crime against humanity, whether conventional or nuclear. Either way, it's a crime against humanity. We totally renounce it. We declare before the world that we'll never even contemplate it. If that is so, then the present levels of armament in Europe, both nuclear and conventional, are excessive. They should be drastically reduced. But what form should these reductions take? It seems to me that, contrary to what most disarmers say, it is conventional forces that are least necessary and that pose the greatest risks. The most likely way for a nuclear war to break out is a conventional entanglement that begins to escalate. Most disarmers say that we should abolish nuclear deterrence and instead provide a secure conventional defence in Europe. But no-one has ever succeeded in doing this before. I just do not believe that you can be so clever that you can thwart anything that the opposition may think up. So surely the correct thing to do is to do it the other way round: it is to dismantle, or virtually to dismantle, conventional defences in Europe – everything that could be aggressive at the conventional level – and merely aim to keep a policing force to maintain internal order (and conventional forces outside Europe for other security problems). And then, in the common interest of both sides, each should keep the insurance of a nuclear deterrent. Even Bruce Kent agrees that nuclear war between the superpowers is not a rational option – they will never deliberately fight each other with nuclear weapons. So in this way we would keep the deterrent effect of nuclear weapons, while getting rid of all the other incentives to war. We would have a safe world between superpowers.

The main argument that is invoked against this proposal is that it would not be credible. I will meet this objection in my answer to **B(vii)**.

(B) WITHOUT NUCLEAR WEAPONS

(i) *If nuclear arsenals were dismantled would* OR *Would nuclear disarmament remove the war between the great powers again become a rational option and therefore more likely?* *incentive for nuclear preemption while not affecting the reluctance of the great powers to initiate a third world war?*

Well, global nuclear disarmament obviously would make war between the great powers a rational option again. It was always a rational option before, because you could think that you could achieve a limited objective and stop. Conventional weapons don't threaten the destruction of your homeland. They only threaten the defeat of your armies. There is a total difference between conventional and nuclear weapons.

(ii) *Would a major conventional war be likely* OR *Is conventional war, however terrible, in itself to be as terrible as a limited preferable to nuclear war?* *nuclear war?*

Conventional war is, of course, preferable to nuclear war. But conventional war would in itself be so terrible that our goal must be the prevention of both.

(iii) *Because nuclear weapons cannot be* OR *As with nerve gases in the last war, would uninvented would they not be bound to be there be no incentive to resort to used sooner or later once war had broken capabilities which the other side has as out?* *well?*

Yes, I do think that, if a conventional war broke out, nuclear weapons would be bound to be used sooner or later. Both sides would think that the other was getting a nuclear capability, there would be a frantic struggle on both sides to regain the capability, and there would be none of the balanced restraints that we have at the moment. So we would be in a worse position than we are in now.

(iv) *Is global nuclear disarmament only feasible in a world where war itself is no longer a possibility?*   OR *Is to argue that even multilateral nuclear disarmament is not desirable to give up all hope of a rational world-order?*

The left-hand side is correct.

(v) *Is peace only preserved when we are seen to be prepared for war, as failure before 1939 and success since 1945 show? Under likely future conditions would global nuclear disarmament make war, including nuclear war, more likely?*   OR *Do the years before 1914 show what happens when military planning and the arms race control political choices? Do present strategies make nuclear war almost inevitable under likely future conditions? Is global nuclear disarmament the only rational policy?*

There is a difference between the situation as it was in the years before 1914, and the situation today. Before 1914, war was a normal option of state policy. Now it can no longer be. So, although the situation today is more like the 1930's, nuclear weapons have so altered things that no historical analogy really applies. We have hardly yet understood the extent to which things have been altered.

B *NATO Policy*

(i) *Does the Soviet Union, together with her Warsaw Pact allies, enjoy a strategically dangerous military superiority in Europe?*   OR *Are NATO and WTO forces relatively evenly matched?*

I do think that the Soviet Union enjoys a dangerous military superiority in Europe. It's not just a question of comparing numbers of divisions and so on. All sorts of other factors come into it, particularly geographical. The Soviet front line has the whole weight of the Soviet Union behind it, whereas we have to cope with 3000 miles of Atlantic. I don't in fact believe that the Soviet Union wants to launch a frontal assault. But, if they were to do so with the determination with which they fought in World War 2, we couldn't stop them. Western Europe could never withstand a Soviet conventional attack. We might hold it up for a month or so – but I doubt even that.

(ii) *Is the Soviet Union an expansionist power which will take advantage of unilateral Western concessions and is only restrained and forced to accept arms-control agreements by Western determination and strength?*   OR *Is the Soviet Union an encircled and threatened power trying to keep up with Western technology and likely to respond positively to unconditional offers of Western restraint within a general context of detente?*

I rather think that both are partly true. Nobody can deny that Marxism-Leninism is an expansionist ideology. It has always preached world revolution. We are doing the leadership a discredit if we say that it no longer believes in that. So the régime is expansionist. But that does not mean that they want to use military force openly against the West to achieve that expansion, because they clearly recognize the dangers involved. And the Russian people, as distinct from the régime, have never been as imperialistic as, say, the Germans or the British. Above all, historically, they have been terrified of invasion and obsessed by the fear of war being fought on their territory. That is why they acquired those buffer states at the end of World War 2. Nothing is ever black or white in these cases.

(iii) *Is Soviet chemical and conventional preponderance such that NATO must continue to be able to threaten early use of nuclear weapons?* OR *Is NATO dependence on the early use of nuclear weapons unnecessary and strategically suicidal?*

Well, I think that for deterrent reasons it is necessary for NATO to keep open the option of the early use of nuclear weapons – although, if it came to it, it could well be suicidal. That is why I have suggested that we should work towards conventional disarmament.

(iv) *Does the growing size of the Soviet nuclear arsenal threaten the delicate theatre and strategic balance? Would Western failure to match Soviet systems be destabilizing?* OR *Does the West initiate nearly all phases of the nuclear arms race and continue to enjoy a substantial lead in most areas? Is the nuclear 'overkill' such that the West could offer a nuclear 'freeze' or unconditional cuts without risk?*

I do not think that we need to match the Soviet Union number for number, and no doubt some unilateral cuts could be made safely. But anything that threatens to impair the mutual second strike capability is destabilizing and dangerous. I fear that a freeze would do that, particularly as the Soviet Union has recently installed a new generation of missiles which the West has not matched.

(v) *Are NATO 'forward defence' and 'deep strike' strategies essential for effective deterrence?* OR *Should NATO exploit her lead in 'emerging technology' to explore less provocative alternative strategies?*

As I have already indicated, I do not like these strategies. But I don't think that 'emerging technology' helps at all. The remedy must lie in the direction of my main proposal: the dismantling of conventional forces in Europe.

(vi) *Is it the presence of American front-line troops and the tying-in of theatre nuclear forces to the American strategic deterrent that guarantees W. European security? Should American policies therefore be supported?* OR *Is it domination by the two super-powers that poses the greatest threat to European integrity? Would Europe be safer decoupled from the super-power nuclear confrontation? Should Europe be made a nuclear weapon-free zone?*

At the moment, if Western Europe were decoupled from the United States, she would have no defence at all – or practically no defence. Similarly, to make Europe a nuclear weapon-free zone would be to have given in. Since I do not believe that the superpowers are likely to become involved in a serious confrontation so long as nuclear deterrence is secure, I do not see that as a great danger. That is the situation as I see it today.

But, if there were a major reduction in the vast NATO conventional forces, as suggested in my answer to **A2**(A)(**vii**), and the resources thus released were put into a second strike, flexible, nuclear capability, then I think that Western Europe would have the ability to inflict unacceptable damage on the Soviet Union, and this therefore would act as a credible deterrent. In those circumstances, Western Europe would no longer need to rely on the Americans.

(vii) *Would Western unilateral nuclear disarmament invite Soviet blackmail? Are suggestions that the West should take the lead in offering unilateral disarmament initiatives the thin end of this wedge? Do radical nuclear disarmers consciously or unconsciously serve Soviet interests and threaten to undermine Western defences?*

OR *Are unilateral initiatives as part of a general programme of nuclear disarmament the only way to reverse the arms race? Is talk of 'multilateral disarmament' insincere in the mouths of those who reject all suggestion of a Comprehensive Test Ban Treaty, a Nuclear Freeze, a European Nuclear Weapon-Free Zone, or a declaration of No First Use?*

I agree with the right-hand side to the extent that Gorbachev and Reagan are both being insincere when they say that they want complete nuclear disarmament. It is an unattainable goal, and, for the foreseeable future, an undesirable one. I am also sure that there are some unilateral steps that we could take which would not be dangerous – although I don't know whether they would have much effect. I'm not in the arms control business. But, on the whole, what is implied on the left-hand side is more realistic. I would be inclined to think that the Russian leadership understands force better than anything else. It's force that keeps the system going. From what I have seen in Poland, I'm inclined to think that force is the language that they understand. So, if we are tough but fair, we will probably get the best results.

Now I must meet the main criticism of my proposal that conventional forces should be virtually dismantled in Europe. It is said that, in view of Soviet inertia, if not belligerence, a significant reduction in Western conventional capabilities would undermine the credibility of nuclear deterrence. It is not credible that, if the Soviet Union occupied West Berlin tomorrow, America would respond with a nuclear strike. There are two things to be said. First, I am not suggesting a return to an 'all-or-nothing' policy of massive retaliation. I propose that we keep a graduated nuclear capability that does not include battlefield nuclear weapons, but does include intermediate nuclear weapons – preferably located under the sea, so that nobody can say 'our bases are threatened'. Secondly, it will be up to us to make this graduated deterrent credible. We must define precisely what we mean by aggression, even if it takes us five years to work that definition out, and then we must say 'if you put even one foot over the border, our response will be nuclear. It will not necessarily be total, but perhaps a warning shot across the bows. Enough to show you that we mean it. And you do the same on your side.' The argument that such a threat would not be credible works both ways. Why would the Soviet Union risk its own destruction for the sake of West Berlin?

But in order to achieve all this, we have to recognize that nuclear weapons have permanently altered the situation. We have to think in a new way. When I came back from Nagasaki in 1945, I wrote a report in which I said that nuclear weapons were from now onwards the decisive weapons in war, that rockets would replace bombers as the main delivery vehicles, and that this called for revolutionary thinking that in turn called for young minds. That was my conclusion then, and that is my conclusion now. At the moment we are still incapable of thinking in these new ways. Traditional habits of thought are too strong. But I'm sure that this is the direction we must move in. And I'm determined to fight for it.

C *British Policy*

1 *The British Deterrent*

(i) *Is Britain's deterrent a weapon of last*   OR *Would all possible uses of Britain's*
resort which guarantees her sovereignty and   *'deterrent' be suicidal? Is its only effect to*
independence and protects her from nuclear   *encourage proliferation?*
blackmail?

Obviously Britain can't 'go it alone' against the Soviet Union. That would make no sense at all. Britain is part of NATO. So I would be happy to see the British deterrent go, as long as it would be replaced by an American one.

(ii) *Are British nuclear forces valuable to*   OR *Is the 'second centre of decision making' an*
European allies because they provide a   *illusion when the weapons are dependent*
specifically European second centre of   *upon the US and there is no independent*
decision making?   *strategic role to be played? Are European*
   allies unenthusiastic about a parochial
   British force likely to inhibit her
   commitment to European defence?

I think that there is a case for saying that an independent British deterrent enhances deterrence in general, and that the value of a second centre of decision-making of this kind is that it creates another area of uncertainty for the Soviet Union. But I do not think that this is a critical point. In the last resort it is only the American deterrent that deters. My fear would be that, if we got rid of the British deterrent, the next thing to go would be the American – and then we would be defenceless.

(iii) *Does the US favour shared responsibility*   OR *Are US forces committed anyway and*
and do British nuclear forces guarantee   *independent British initiatives more likely*
full US commitment to Europe and Soviet   *to trigger Soviet retaliation than US*
recognition of it?   *involvement?*

The linkage with the United States is essential, but I do not think that independent British nuclear forces are necessary for this. We could accept American nuclear forces in their place.

(iv) *Is the cost of the British deterrent small in*   OR *Can Britain's nuclear forces only be*
view of the vital defence role it plays? Are   *afforded at the expense of conventional*
alternatives likely to be more expensive?   *strength and of other more important*
   economic priorities?

I don't believe that conventional forces give us proper strategic protection. The cost of Britain's independent nuclear force may be small compared with the cost of suggested replacements, but there can be no effective conventional replacement for a nuclear deterrent.

(v) *Would unilateral British nuclear disarmament have no effect on other countries and only serve to weaken British influence and allow France unchallenged ascendancy in Europe?*   OR *Does the British deterrent encourage proliferation and do nothing to enhance British prestige? Would British disarmament within the context outlined in B help to break the nuclear log-jam?*

I don't know that our prestige matters much, and I'm not sure how much influence our possession of an independent nuclear force gives us with, say, the United States. I certainly don't mind France having a nuclear capability and Britain not. The only thing that matters is the cohesion of NATO. So long as we and other Western European countries are committed to NATO and to its nuclear policies, then Europe is safe.

vi) *Is investment in Trident the best way to continue to ensure effective British strategic defence into the 21st century?*   OR *Would commitment to Trident exacerbate all the drawbacks listed above?*

I don't know. I always refrain from making a judgement on a given weapon-system.

2 *NATO Forces and US Bases*

(i) *Must Britain continue to share responsibility for manning NATO nuclear systems upon which her security depends? Would refusal to do so fatally weaken the alliance?*   OR *Should British obligations to NATO be met by strengthening conventional forces where necessary within an overall non-nuclear strategy as recommended in B?*

I totally disagree with the idea that NATO should adopt a non-nuclear policy, for reasons which I will give later. I think that the more we involve ourselves in the overall NATO nuclear policy and its systems the better. It makes the deterrent more credible.

ii) *Would the forced withdrawal of US nuclear bases from Britain make US defence of the West impossible? Is American interference in British affairs negligible?*   OR *Do the large numbers of nuclear facilities yielded to the US erode British sovereignty? Would their removal do no more than restore a normal peacetime relationship?*

Apart from the qualification made in my answer to **B(vi)**, I think that the US nuclear bases are essential. The suggestion that the United States might be tempted to fight a war on European soil while herself remaining unharmed is nonsensical. A war on this scale would be bound to affect everyone. Nor do I think that we have yielded our sovereignty by having these bases.

(iii) *Will Britain continue to be targeted by*   OR *Is Britain seen as an American aircraft*
Soviet warheads whether or not she   *carrier and targeted by the USSR*
disarms unilaterally?   *accordingly? Will Britain fall an early*
                                              victim in any superpower confrontation
                                              unless bases are removed?

I don't like the argument on the right. It says, if there's going to be a war, let someone else be hit and not us. In any case, if the disarmers are arguing that we should compensate by increasing our conventional forces, then this seems hardly likely to make us less of a target.

(iv) *Can non-nuclear defences only safely be*   OR *In a nuclear-free Europe, decoupled from*
afforded by powers prepared to shelter   *the superpower nuclear confrontation,*
beneath the American strategic umbrella?   *would Britain no more expect to depend*
                                              upon the US 'umbrella' than any other
                                              Western ally – or than Eastern Europe
                                              upon the USSR?

If it were true a non-nuclear defence could be effective against a nuclear aggressor, those on the right-hand side would be right. But it is not true. I simply cannot understand the premise of people like Bruce Kent. You may be able to upgrade your conventional defence to the point where you can hold an aggressor on the battlefield, perhaps even though he is using battlefield nuclear weapons. But the moment he invokes strategic missiles targeted on your cities, it no longer matters what is going on on the battlefield – you go under. I cannot understand how a rational person can think that conventional defences could ever be effective against the threat of a strategic nuclear attack.

Moral Considerations

(i) *Is it morally right to pursue the policy least* OR *Are there actions which are in themselves*
likely to cause human suffering? May this   *wrong no matter what the situation? Is the*
sometimes involve doing things which in   *alternative to excuse almost any act of*
other circumstances would be wrong?   *barbarism?*

(ii) *In formulating policy should we weigh up*   OR *Is the only relevant point here that a*
the probability of success and the relative   *nuclear exchange of almost any kind*
costs in terms of human suffering of   *would in itself cause unimaginable*
alternative nuclear and non-nuclear   *suffering to largely civilian populations?*
strategies?

Although it may be true in the absolute that certain actions are wrong, when you come to apply them to the concrete reality of war, you may have to try to choose the lesser of two evils. Take World War 2, which is the only war I know. In that war roughly two civilians died for every military – thirty-five million civilians and twenty million military – something like that. Now, isn't that totally wrong? So the moral objections that nuclear disarmers raise against nuclear war, I also raise against conventional war between major powers in a modern context. My argument is that we have passed that threshold of history beyond which war between major powers is no longer morally permissible. The question which should concern moralists here is – how can we prevent this happening again?

(iii) *So far as concerns intention, need we look*   OR *Is there no such thing as a fully deployed*
no further than the fact that our sole aim in   *weapons system which is a bluff? Is to*
deploying nuclear weapons is to prevent   *deploy nuclear weapons to intend to use*
their use?   *them in certain circumstances?*

Now we come to the question of intention. And the second stage of the argument is this: assuming that it is nuclear deterrence that prevents all forms of war between major powers, and this is your sole intention in deploying nuclear weapons, how can it be morally wrong to do so? First of all, I don't believe that the intention of those who deploy the deterrent is to use it. Both the Russians and the Americans who deploy it are convinced that, by deploying it, they can make its use impossible. And, secondly, how can it be right to permit the horror of conventional war by removing nuclear deterrence, simply because of the supposed immorality of the intentions of those who are deploying the deterrent? This seems to me to be an extraordinary position. It is this argument from conditional intention that carries most Christian moralists, but they just haven't thought it out.

(iv) *Are there possible uses of nuclear weapons*   OR *Is a conditional intention to cause*
which are allowed by Just War theory, for   *indiscriminate and disproportionate*
example the bombing of Hiroshima and   *suffering of this kind, whether admonitory,*
Nagasaki in order to prevent worse   *preemptive or retaliatory, ruled out by Just*
suffering? Can there be a theory of Just   *War theory? Was it wrong to bomb*
Deterrence?   *Hiroshima and Nagasaki in 1945?*

I hold that it was not wrong to bomb Hiroshima and Nagasaki. And the reason why I say that is that the only forseeable alternative was the all-out invasion of Japan. Given the Japanese military mind at the time, that would have involved a fight to the last man, total war across the whole of Japan, in which, not hundreds of thousands, but millions would have died. Now, what do those who disapprove of the dropping of the bombs say when I challenge them with this? Pax Christi[1] tell me that a full-scale invasion would have been wrong, too. They say that we should have used a blockade. But a blockade inevitably causes terrible suffering, particularly to the innocent. As the blockade tightens, the armed forces have to keep the food and medical supplies for those who can fight. In Leningrad 800,000 civilians died through blockade, and they died worse deaths than those in Hiroshima and Nagasaki – lingering deaths, frozen, without food, without medical supplies. It's unimaginable. According to these moralists, if we had imposed such a blockade against Japan, we would not have been to blame for the fact that civilians were hit worst, because we would not have made that choice. But this is Pharisaical. It is part of a rather hypocritical search for our own purity by pretending to shift the

---

1. International Catholic Movement for Peace.

blame to the defenders. When I put that to Bruce Kent, he said that a blockade would also have been wrong. In other words, there was nothing that we could have done to the Japanese. We would have had to have given in.

And the same thing applies to those who say that we are not allowed even the conditional intention to use nuclear weapons which they say is implied in deterrence. If the only alternative to nuclear deterrence is that there will be a greater likelihood of conventional war, then it is hypocritical of those who want to abandon nuclear deterrence to say that they would not share moral responsibility for that war. To say this is again to be more concerned with your own moral purity than with the effect of your policy.

(v) *Is there no relevant connection between the development and deployment of nuclear weapons and world poverty and disease?* OR *Is it a scandal that such huge resources are devoted to the development and deployment of nuclear weapons and not to the alleviation of suffering?*

Although there is obviously a certain truth in the argument on the right, it is in general dishonest. We spend as much money on alcohol as we do on defence – why not say 'cut back on your alcohol'? And I'm sure that any money saved would not go to the poor. It would go on better roads, or lower taxes, or the Trade Unions would ask for higher wages. What is lacking is the will to help the poor.

(vi) *Does Christian teaching allow the deployment of nuclear weapons?* OR *Does Christian teaching condemn the deployment of nuclear weapons?*

I would say that Christian teaching regrets that there is a need for nuclear deterrence, but, in the circumstances, allows it. When it was a question of the Just War theory, the Church longed to abolish war. But it could not do so, and therefore had to make the best of the sinful situation that we are in. Bruce Kent says that the Roman Catholic Church does not allow the continuing deployment of nuclear weapons. But it does. None of the bishops' conferences have forbidden the deployment of nuclear weapons. The American bishops, who have actually written the most profound document of all[1] on the morality of war, have got into a muddle over it. They seem to condemn all use of nuclear weapons, but then leave an ambiguity as to whether they mean all use or not. If they do mean that all use is inadmissible, then they should have forbidden deployment, too. They try to say *'you may deploy them, so long as you state that they will never be used'*. But in that case, how do they deter? The answer that is given is that they will still deter, because the enemy won't know that you mean it. Well, that is a deliberate deception. You are living a lie. And how they can justify that morally I don't know. That is not Christian. It isn't straight dealing. How is he going to believe anything else you say?

---

1. The Challenge of God's Peace, May 3, 1983.

Recommendations

1 No (See **B(iv)**).
2 Not on research programmes (See **A2(A)(v)**).
3 I don't know.
4 I question its usefulness, because I doubt whether it's really going to be believed by the other side. It sounds good, but I don't think it's significant (See **B(iii)**).
5 Yes. And in some cases unconditional (See **A1(iv)**).
6 I don't think that a European nuclear weapon-free zone would enhance security. I think it would do exactly the opposite. Anyway, you cannot guarantee that weapons won't drop on Europe just because you have declared it nuclear free (See **B(vi)**).
7 I don't know.
8 No (See **A2(B)**).
9 The idea of a 'minimum' or 'sufficient' nuclear deterrent is a good one. But not as a stage on the way to swift nuclear disarmament as CND wants. It should be a permanent arrangement. CND have shifted their ground here.
10 I don't see why we shouldn't, as long as it's research. I like any advance in technology. It might be put to civilian use.
11 No. See 4.
12 (a) Yes.
(b) No – keep them, especially if they are sea-based. Although then they are not so accurate. That's the snag.
13 On balance, I would like to keep them. But, as long as there are American replacements, I don't make too much of this.
14 No, she certainly should not. But see the qualification in **B(vi)**.
15 No. See 6.
16 No, but this is not crucial (See **CI**).
17 I am very much against this. I think that it's dangerous (See **A2(A)(vii)** & **B(vii)**).
18 No (See **C2(i)**).
19 No (See **C2(i)** & **C2(ii)**).
20 Does not apply.

The Rt. Hon.
Denzil Davies

P.C., M.P.

Biographical Note

Born in 1938, Denzil Davies was Bacon scholar at Gray's Inn, and then a teaching fellow at the University of Chicago, before becoming Labour Member of Parliament for Llanelli in 1970. He was Minister of State at Her Majesty's Treasury between 1975 and 1979. Since then he has been Opposition Spokesman on Foreign Affairs, 1979-1981, Opposition Spokesman on Defence, 1981-1983, and, from 1983, Chief Opposition Spokesman on Defence and Disarmament.

Editorial Comment

These answers were communicated in an interview in the House of Commons on December 4, 1986. Their political importance for the reader is that they offer the full rationale behind current Labour Party policy. As Denzil Davies points out at the beginning of Section C on British Policy, what the Labour Party proposes for Britain can only be understood against the background of earlier answers. Because nuclear weapons are rationally unusable (**A2(B)(ii)**, **B(iii)**), they do not deter (**A1(ii)**), but, on the contrary, are likely to convert political crisis into catastrophe (**A1(iii)**, **A2 (B)(v)**). Continued Western dependence upon them means that proper non-nuclear defences are neglected. This is unnecessary (**B(i)** and **B(ii)**). Britain's renunciation of her own nuclear weapons will enable her to maintain effective defences which will otherwise be seriously weakened (**C1(iv)**). The proposed move towards non-nuclear defence within NATO (**C2(i)**, **C2(ii)**) must be seen against the background of the answers to questions **B(iii)**, **B(iv)**, **B(v)**, and **B(vi)**, which justify it. Finally, it is the important answers to questions **A2(A)(vii)** and **B(vii)** which support the argument in **C2(iv)**, and provide the overall context within which the proposed British policy is set.

THE RT HON DENZIL DAVIES MP

A *Global Policy*

1 *The History of the Past Forty Years*

(i) *Has it been nuclear deterrence that has kept the peace between the great powers since 1945?*   OR *Has it mainly been other factors?*

Without going into details, I think that, whatever the situation just after the Second World War when the Americans had a nuclear monopoly, in recent years it has mainly been other factors.

(ii) *Does mutual possession of an invulnerable second-strike strategic nuclear force prevent war?*   OR *Does the threat of strategic nuclear retaliation, particularly against a similarly armed enemy, lack credibility and invite sub-deterrent encroachment?*

As I say, it may have been the case when only one side had an invulnerable and effective nuclear force that this prevented war, but it certainly cannot be the case when both have. For example, the main reason why President Reagan says that he is proposing his Strategic Defence Initiative is because he cannot see how he can defend America with 11,000 warheads, when the Russians have got 11,000 warheads pointing at America. And that, in particular, is why 'extended deterrence' cannot work. There is no American 'nuclear umbrella' over Europe – as people like Henry Kissinger are right to point out to us. There can't be. No American president will authorize the use of American strategic nuclear forces in the defence of Europe, when the inevitable result would be the destruction of America.

Have limited nuclear options at strategic and theatre levels enhanced deterrence by dramatically raising the threshold between peace and war? OR *Have most military planners from the start been aiming for nuclear war-fighting superiority? Has 'flexible response' dangerously lowered the threshold between conventional and nuclear war?*

The suggestion on the left-hand side is entirely wrong. In fact, the opposite is the case. It is a mistake to think that the danger is of some kind of Blitzkrieg war, in which one side deliberately decides to launch an all-out attack on the other. Much the greater danger is that a period of heightened political tension will spill over into war, and then the fact that we have scattered battlefield and theatre nuclear weapons throughout Europe will make it much more likely that this will quickly degenerate into nuclear war.

Has the size and variety of the nuclear arsenals held by the superpowers stabilized deterrence? OR *Has the logic of nuclear confrontation and worst-case analysis generated a dangerous and strategically pointless superfluity of weapons systems?*

In general I don't think that piling strategic weapons on strategic weapons makes much difference. I wouldn't have thought that the danger was greater with 11,000 warheads than it is with 5000. I'll concede this argument to the Richard Perles[1] of this world. The main dangers lie in the types of weapon deployed, and in the effect which larger numbers – particularly of battlefield and theatre nuclear weapons – have in making command and control more difficult.

Has the idea of nuclear balance between the superpowers been essential to stability and have arms-control negotiations helped to achieve it? OR *Have ideas of 'nuclear defence' and 'parity' proved illusory and is 'multilateral negotiation from strength' a contradiction in terms? Has 'arms-control' been just another name for the arms race?*

The idea of balance seems reassuring, but in a situation of mutual suspicion and partial ignorance of what the other side has got, it breaks down. There is no agreement about what you count, or how you count it, or what the overall situation is. So, when one side reaches a point where it thinks that there is a balance, the other gets worried and thinks that it is behind. That is what has been happening repeatedly since 1962. It has gone in spurts. At the time of the Cuba missile crisis, the Russians had 300 missiles, and the Americans had 5000. So the Russians then did a great spurt, and the Americans thought that they had been overtaken. Then the Americans did a spurt to try to catch up again. And so it goes on.

---

1. US Assistant Secretary of Defense until March 1987.

Arms control has had a very limited success. It has not stopped new technology, but has perhaps done something to limit the application of some of the technology already developed. One trouble is that particular systems are justified as 'bargaining chips' on the grounds that this will force the other side to negotiate. But then, when it comes to it, they are not given up, and only stimulate further expansion on the other side. So there are more and more 'bargaining chips' and no bargains. But arms control negotiations do serve as a forum for discussion, so, to that extent, we should not be against them.

(vi) *Has force-planning been controlled by*   OR *Has the self-reinforcing impetus of*
     strategic thinking?   *technology and vested interest dictated*
                                          policies subsequently justified post hoc?

I agree very strongly with what is written on the right-hand side. Those who have done step-by-step analyses of the life-history of particular nuclear weapons systems, find that the starting point is an equation somewhere. Then, when the technological possibility of a new weapon has been established, people start to devise reasons for having it. Most of the arguing in post hoc rationalization.

2 *The Prospect for the Future*

(A) WITH NUCLEAR WEAPONS
 (i) *Does the threat of an enemy first strike*   OR *Is there an increasing threat from accurate*
    remain inconceivable for the foreseeable   *and time-urgent first-strike weapons?*
    future?

First strike is in the eye of the beholder. For example, although the Americans say that Star Wars is to be a purely defensive system, the Russians are convinced that it is part of an evolving first strike strategy. There is considerable mutual fear that new systems of all kinds will give the other such an advantage. Once again, we are not talking so much of a sudden deliberate surprise attack, as of what is likely to happen in a time of acute political crisis.

(ii) *Are command, control, communication and* OR *Does the amount of information to be*
    intelligence facilities likely to remain   *processed, pressure of time and fear of*
    secure?   *preemption put command and control*
                                       systems under intolerable strain and make
                                       inadvertent war more likely?

Of course we should be alarmed about the threat to command and control systems. In the kind of situation which we have been describing, they are likely to become increasingly vulnerable and therefore increasingly unreliable.

(iii) *If nevertheless there were a limited nuclear* OR *Is the idea that nuclear war could be*
     exchange would it be likely to end   *limited once it had broken out a dangerous*
     hostilities swiftly?   *illusion?*

Frankly, I don't think that I can answer this question. I certainly don't subscribe to the idea that it makes any sense at all to plan in terms of 'limited nuclear war' – whatever that's supposed to mean. I don't subscribe to NATO or Warsaw Pact nuclear war-fighting strategies. But whether, if there were an initial exchange, it would escalate to all-out nuclear war, or lead both sides to terminate hostilities quickly, I just don't know.

(iv) *Do new generations of battlefield and theatre nuclear systems reinforce deterrence?* OR *Do new battlefield and theatre weapons threaten a dangerous lowering of the nuclear threshold?*

I have answered this. I think that new generations of battlefield and theatre nuclear weapons, deployed as part of NATO and Warsaw Pact war-fighting strategies, are indeed highly dangerous.

(v) *Does the Strategic Defence Initiative offer the hope of an effective defence against nuclear weapons?* OR *Is the Strategic Defence Initiative simply the most recent and destabilizing example of the process outlined in 1?*

As nearly all commentators agree, Star Wars is very unlikely to give us a totally effective defence against ballistic nuclear weapons. And it is also flawed in the sense that the technology developed as part of it would provide us with ingenious and dangerous offensive systems as well. The distinction between offence and defence here is illusory. In the meantime, it clearly is destabilizing, both because the Russians inevitably see it as part of a threatened first strike capability, and because it jeopardizes past arms control agreements, such as the ABM treaty, and blocks future ones, as we saw at Reykjavik.

But we must not ignore the thinking behind it. President Reagan no longer believes in the nuclear umbrella, which is why he is trying to substitute another one for it. His speech of September 23, 1983, challenges the whole strategic assumption of the past forty years – the M.A.D. world, if you like. He is quite rightly groping towards an alternative.

vi) *Is the threat of 'horizontal' nuclear proliferation best met by a continuation of past policies?* OR *Is continuing reliance on nuclear deterrence by the great powers bound to accelerate the process of proliferation and make nuclear war more likely?*

I don't know whether the fact that the great powers have got nuclear weapons makes it more likely that other countries will want to have them, or whether, if the great powers were to give them up, other countries would then not want to have them. I don't know. But I suspect that each country which has the technology will decide independently in terms of its own interests. But those who say that nuclear weapons have kept the peace for forty years in Europe, certainly should not argue against exporting them, say, to the Middle East. Both the Iraqis and the Iranians should be given them. That is the logic of it. They can't have it both ways.

(vii) *Do multilateral arms-control negotiations   OR   Is 'arms-control' an illusion which diverts
offer the best prospect for future stability?*   *attention from the only safe policy –
                                                        nuclear disarmament?*

As we look ahead, what is important from a global perspective is what happened at Reykjavik. I don't think that things will be the same again. In the
past, arms control has done little more than regulate the nuclear arms race,
because the assumption behind it has been that the two superpowers would
continue to rely on nuclear deterrence indefinitely. But this has now changed.
There has been a challenge to the system. And the challenge has come from
the leaders of the two greatest powers. I think that we must recognize that
both Mr Gorbachev and Mr Reagan are genuine in their desire to rid the world
of nuclear weapons. Both understand that we cannot go on as we have in the
past. They feel that, without nuclear weapons, the East and the West can live
together and avoid war. Reagan is genuine, if misguided, about Star Wars.
And Gorbachev is genuine in proposing that we eliminate nuclear weapons by
the end of the century. I don't think that he is saying this just to divide Western
Europe from America, or just because he cannot afford to take up the Star
Wars challenge – counter-measures are likely to be far cheaper than Star Wars
itself. No. Reykjavik has established the global context within which all of us,
including Britain, should now be moving. It is depressing to see the way in
which it is Western Europe which is dragging its feet. Mrs Thatcher is horrified at the prospect of Reykjavik, because it takes away the justification for
her nuclear defence policies.

(B)   WITHOUT NUCLEAR WEAPONS

(i) *If nuclear arsenals were dismantled would   OR   Would nuclear disarmament remove the
war between the great powers again   incentive for nuclear preemption while not
become a rational option and therefore   affecting the reluctance of the great powers
more likely?*   to initiate a third world war?*

Well, once again it is a question of what you believe. Those who think that
there is no such thing as conventional deterrence, and that there is only such
a thing as nuclear deterrence, will never be convinced. If you believe that it is
only nuclear deterrence that prevents war, then you will be terrified of losing
it. But, as I have said, I do not believe this. On the contrary, I believe that
much greater dangers lie in continuing to base defence on irrational and
unstable nuclear strategies.

(ii) *Would a major conventional war be likely   OR   Is conventional war, however terrible,
in itself to be as terrible as a limited   preferable to nuclear war?*
nuclear war?*

Yes. The implication on the left-hand side is familiar. 'If you are proposing
to get rid of nuclear forces and to increase conventional forces, what's the
difference?' The difference, I think, is pretty basic. Its a difference in the very
nature of the conflict. We don't need to go as far as imagining a major

exchange, and the possibility of a 'nuclear winter', to realize this. In a conventional war, with modern weaponry, large numbers of civilians would undoubtedly be killed on both sides, and moral questions, comparable to those associated with the bombing of Dresden in the last war, would be raised. A conventional war would, of course, be terrible. But a nuclear exchange would, in addition, involve radiation and fallout. The accident at Chernobyl has brought home to us how people living hundreds of miles away from the battle zone would be affected. Countries which had nothing to do with the war would suffer. Crops would be blighted, livestock would die, and the contamination might last for generations. There is a clear difference in quality between the two.

(iii) *Because nuclear weapons cannot be uninvented would they not be bound to be used sooner or later once war had broken out?* OR *As with nerve gases in the last war, would there be no incentive to resort to capabilities which the other side has as well?*

This phrase sounds good, but means nothing. 'Nuclear weapons cannot be uninvented'. Of course we cannot abolish science. Nothing that we do can affect the fact that $e = mc^2$. But we are talking about turning the equations into technology, and that is something that we can and must control. We can make it much more difficult to do this, and we can build political systems which remove most of the incentive to do so.

iv) *Is global nuclear disarmament only feasible in a world where war itself is no longer a possibility?* OR *Is to argue that even multilateral nuclear disarmament is not desirable to give up all hope of a rational world-order?*

We are really talking about bilateral nuclear disarmament, aren't we? In the past, people like Mrs Thatcher have said that they are in favour of 'multilateral nuclear disarmament'. But now they have been flushed out. The moment the two world leaders seem to be on the verge of achieving this, Mrs Thatcher has to come out into the open and admit that she is not in favour of bilateral or multilateral nuclear disarmament after all. She wants perpetual nuclear deterrence. To argue as she does is, indeed, to give up all hope of a rational world order.

v) *Is peace only preserved when we are seen to be prepared for war, as failure before 1939 and success since 1945 show? Under likely future conditions would global nuclear disarmament make war, including nuclear war, more likely?* OR *Do the years before 1914 show what happens when military planning and the arms race control political choices? Do present strategies make nuclear war almost inevitable under likely future conditions? Is global nuclear disarmament the only rational policy?*

The trouble is that people are always trying to fight the last war. They cling onto what they are used to. In this case, the people who believe in perpetual nuclear deterrence are saying '*We must do what we did not do in the 1930s. We must stop the Russians from starting a Third World War by going on building up more and more nuclear weapons.'* In fact, Britain and France had very powerful military forces in the 1930s, and, in any case, Soviet Russia today cannot usefully be compared to NAZI Germany then. But, if we are going to make historical comparisons, a closer parallel would be with the years before 1914 – the two armed alliances, the building up of more and more powerful arsenals, the elaboration of war-fighting strategies, the prospect of a confrontation being triggered by some incident in central Europe, or even further afield. And today, as we have seen, the nature and disposition of new generations of nuclear weapons makes it more and more likely that, in those circumstances, the situation would rapidly escalate to nuclear war.

b *NATO policy*

(i) *Does the Soviet Union, together with her*   OR *Are NATO and WTO forces relatively*
Warsaw Pact allies, enjoy a strategically   *evenly matched?*
dangerous military superiority in Europe?

This is a crucial area. People are still being fed the idea that the Warsaw Pact enjoys a four to one advantage in conventional forces over NATO. In introducing a programme on defence on television recently, David Dimbleby repeated it. It was an extraordinary statement to make, and he should have done his research properly. It is true that the Russians have more tanks, and the Warsaw Pact can be said to have local superiority along certain sectors of the Central Front. But, if you look at the totality of forces, which is what matters, then both sides are probably evenly matched. It is not just a question of numbers either, but of an overall capacity to wage war. This includes industrial and technological capabilities, the reliability of your Allies, and so on. And an attacker needs decisive superiority if he is to be confident of success in a frontal assault. When everything is weighed up together, it is probably true to say that the two sides are relatively evenly matched. Continued talk of a four to one Warsaw Pact advantage must be shown up for what it is – a gross, and often deliberate, distortion of the facts.

(ii) *Is the Soviet Union an expansionist power* OR *Is the Soviet Union an encircled and*
which will take advantage of unilateral   *threatened power trying to keep up with*
Western concessions and is only restrained   *Western technology and likely to respond*
and forced to accept arms-control   *positively to unconditional offers of*
agreements by Western determination and   *Western restraint within a general context*
strength?   *of detente?*

I think that, as they stand, both of the alternatives here are rather exaggerated. I do not believe that the Soviet Union is an expansionist power, which wants to drive West or South. But the Russians are equally paranoid about the West. We have no intention of attacking them, either. So mutual paranoia feeds on itself. The danger is that wars don't just start because one side deliberately decides to attack the other, but often as a result of mutual suspicion, fear, and misunderstanding. This is what must be dispelled. And it can only be done by restraint on both sides, and a readiness to believe that the other's offers are genuinely made with a view to reducing tension and building confidence.

A number of Mr Gorbachev's recent proposals should be welcomed in this spirit. We should recognize that significant changes have been taking place in Russia. We often forget that Russia has been through a terrible dark age. There was the appalling suffering of the First World War, the upheaval of the Revolution, the ruthlessness with which Stalin drove through industrialization in the 1930s, the trauma of the Second World War, the post-war period of Stalinist purges, the débacle of Cuba when Khruschev overreached himself and the military realized how far behind they were in the arms race, the consequent build-up of arms under Brezhnev as the Russians tried to catch up. And now they are coming out of it. Gorbachev represents a new generation, no longer conditioned by the revolutionary and immediate post-revolutionary experience. We have a real opportunity to put the past behind us and to move slowly out of the Cold War era. The West should respond with flexibility and not react with suspicion to everything that Mr Gorbachev proposes. Funnily enough, a number of people within the Reagan administration, such as George Schultz, realize this in a way that people in our government in Britain do not. Mrs Thatcher, for example, refuses to let go of her habitual hostility, because she has a vested interest in the perpetuation of the enemy threat.

(iii) *Is Soviet chemical and conventional*   OR *Is NATO dependence on the early use of*
preponderance such that NATO must   *nuclear weapons unnecessary and*
continue to be able to threaten early use of   *strategically suicidal?*
nuclear weapons?

We have already seen why NATO's dependence on nuclear weapons is militarily unnecessary. It is also strategically suicidal. We can't use our nuclear weapons without causing far more damage to our own side, and risking indiscriminate, if not universal, catastrophe. So what is the point of having them? As it is, all that they do is to make it more and more likely that a future political crisis will precipitate nuclear war. I am not a military historian or a military expert, but increasing numbers of those who are now recognize this. Like all other areas of policy, military strategy must evolve and change with circumstances. It is quite possible that the strategy was all right twenty years ago. It may or may not have been. But there is no doubt that today it is unnecessary, irrational and dangerous. Just as in the years leading up to 1940 the French generals showed themselves to be incapable of recognizing that circumstances had changed, so there is a great danger that we are in the process of doing the same now. We keep thinking that the danger that we face is of a Second World War Blitzkrieg, and fail to realize that an unpremeditated collapse into war, triggered by political crisis, and precipitated by nuclear war-fighting strategies, is a far more serious threat. The policy must be changed.

One of the troubles here has been the traditional refusal of the Federal Republic of Germany even to contemplate the possibility of a war being fought on her territory. As a result, she has tried to convince herself that with nuclear weapons this will not happen. So, paradoxically, she continues to support a strategy which is far more likely in the event to destroy her. It is a major objective of British Labour Party policy to persuade NATO allies to shift towards a proper non-nuclear defence strategy.

(iv) *Does the growing size of the Soviet nuclear* OR *Does the West initiate nearly all phases of arsenal threaten the delicate theatre and the nuclear arms race and continue to enjoy strategic balance? Would Western failure a substantial lead in most areas? Is the to match Soviet systems be destabilizing? nuclear 'overkill' such that the West could offer a nuclear 'freeze' or unconditional cuts without risk?*

The important point to be made here is that, even within the terms of nuclear deterrence theories, there is ample room for both NATO and the Warsaw Pact to begin to shift towards non-nuclear defence, without having at every stage to become enmeshed in intricate multilateral bargaining. This is *not* to advocate 'unilateral nuclear disarmament'. It is to decide the overall strategy that is in our own best interest, and then to move towards it in whatever way seems prudent and safe at the time.

A further point to be made here is that even Americans like Richard Perle, who want to keep a nuclear deterrent, agree that with modern technology there is no need to persist with land-based nuclear systems in Europe. Once again, it has been Western European governments which have foolishly insisted on this, largely for political reasons. Militarily these weapons are a liability, serving only to ensure enemy targeting. NATO is already cutting down her battlefield nuclear arsenal in Europe. She can also safely begin to remove her land-based theatre systems too.

(v) *Are NATO 'forward defence' and 'deep* OR *Should NATO exploit her lead in strike' strategies essential for effective 'emerging technology' to explore less deterrence? provocative alternative strategies?*

It is important to understand that NATO's dependence on nuclear weapons is part and parcel of her continuing commitment to forward defence. It is largely because West Germany does not want to accept the logic of in-depth defences, and insists on the holding of the frontier at all costs, that NATO has had to fall back on the nuclear deterrent threat. For the same reason, 'deep strike', the engagement of the enemy follow-on forces, instead of being mainly concerned with their destruction once they have crossed the frontier, has to involve apparent plans for offensives deep into enemy territory. So a second major objective of Labour Party policy will be to persuade NATO Allies to accept military reality, and supplement the present *in*flexible response with a proper flexible mix of defence options. There are large numbers of possibilities, which are being widely studied by military planners at the moment. We don't need to commit ourselves to the fate of the Spartans at Thermopylae.

(vi) *Is it the presence of American front-line troops and the tying-in of theatre nuclear forces to the American strategic deterrent that guarantees W. European security? Should American policies therefore be supported?*

OR *Is it domination by the two super-powers that poses the greatest threat to European integrity? Would Europe be safer decoupled from the super-power nuclear confrontation? Should Europe be made a nuclear weapon-free zone?*

These alternatives are too extreme. The main reason why American troops are in Europe is to defend the interests of the United States. This is just as it should be. It is in the American interest that Western Europe should not be dominated by the rival superpower. But that does not mean that Western Europeans have supinely to support every American policy. We should certainly try to develop greater European awareness, so that there can be a more equal discussion of priorities within the Alliance. The Americans have always said that they would welcome this. Indeed, I feel rather sorry for them. First of all, Chancellor Schmidt says that he desperately wants American Cruise and Pershing missiles in Europe, because he no longer believes in the strategic umbrella. Then, when they are installed, the Americans are blamed for putting them there. Then the Americans negotiate with the Russians to get rid of them, and General Rogers and Mrs Thatcher rush off to Washington to persuade them not to. Western European governments should be supporting any moves which seem likely to lead to the negotiated removal of these weapons. As can be seen, it is quite wrong to call this an 'anti-American' policy.

But it doesn't mean anything to say that Europe should be 'decoupled' from the superpower confrontation. Apart from anything else, Russia is in Europe.

(vii) *Would Western unilateral nuclear disarmament invite Soviet blackmail? Are suggestions that the West should take the lead in offering unilateral disarmament initiatives the thin end of this wedge? Do radical nuclear disarmers consciously or unconsciously serve Soviet interests and threaten to undermine Western defences?*

OR *Are unilateral initiatives as part of a general programme of nuclear disarmament the only way to reverse the arms race? Is talk of 'multilateral disarmament' insincere in the mouths of those who reject all suggestion of a Comprehensive Test Ban Treaty, a Nuclear Freeze, a European Nuclear Weapon-Free Zone, or a declaration of No First Use?*

I repeat. The Labour Party does not advocate unilateral nuclear disarmament. That is something that opponents like to accuse us of, because then they can simply say that we would be exposing the West to Soviet nuclear blackmail, and do not have to argue out the implications of their own policies any further. But nuclear blackmail does not come into it. What we are working towards is a proper strengthening of NATO defences, so that we no longer have to rely on the increasingly dangerous illusion of extended nuclear deterrence. This would, of course, be part of a broader negotiated settlement within the terms already roughly laid out by the President of the United States and the General Secretary of the Soviet Communist Party. It is essential that we set this up straight away as a long-term policy objective, and move towards it as far and as fast as we safely can. Some of this can be done independently; some will require bilateral or multilateral agreement. At no point is there any question of laying ourselves open to Soviet nuclear blackmail. I have already explained why land-based battlefield and theatre nuclear systems can be built down with less risk than was involved in building them up in the first place. And it is hypocritical of those who oppose Mr Reagan's declared desire to rid the world of nuclear weapons, and argue against an acceptance of Mr Gorbachev's offer to negotiate nuclear weapons away by the year 2000, at the same time to say that we cannot move towards the elimination of nuclear weapons from Europe because we would then be laying ourselves open to Soviet nuclear blackmail. The elimination of defence policies based on irresponsible nuclear war-fighting strategies is recognized to be an urgent mutual priority for both East and West. There is only one rational middle-term function for nuclear weapons, and that is as minimum forces to be held by both superpowers during the period of adjustment, in order to allay fears on both sides that the other might be tempted to cheat.

By saying that the British Labour Party is irresponsible because it is advocating unilateral nuclear disarmament, opponents like to imply that they are responsibly advocating multilateral nuclear disarmament. This is not the case. As their reaction to Reykjavik has shown, they are not nuclear disarmers at all, but advocates of indefinite reliance on nuclear deterrence and on defence based on nuclear war-fighting strategies. The British Labour Party advocates independent, bilateral, and multilateral moves towards long-term political stability and non-nuclear defence. It is those Western European governments which continue to cling to outmoded and increasingly dangerous nuclear deterrent policies, and are prepared, as a result, to jeopardize joint progress by the superpowers towards a non-nuclear world, which are guilty of short-sightedness and irresponsibility.

C *British Policy*

British policy must be seen against the background that we have just outlined. A lot of the misunderstanding of Labour Party policy comes from failing to do this.

If you like, we could say that there are, roughly, three interrelated areas of British interest and influence. First, there are those things that are within the sovereign competence of a British government to do, in what are thought to be the best interests of Britain. These are the independent actions which the Labour Party is proposing. But this can only be understood within the context of Britain's membership of the NATO Alliance. This is the second of the circles of influence. Here Britain is not sovereign. We have influence and can work towards a strategy which we think is in the best interest of the Alliance as a whole. But we may not be able to persuade all our Allies. Finally, there is the global circle, where our influence on, say, arms control negotiations between America and Russia is pretty limited. But at least we need not be obstructive. At least the policies that we propose can be seen to contribute to what is in the best long-term interest of us all. At least we can push forward the debate that was begun at Reykjavik. It is depressing that, whereas in America the debate is being carried on energetically, not only by Democrats like Senator Nunn, but also by members of the administration, like George Schultz, Richard Perle, and the President himself, in this country there is almost no debate at all.

1 *The British Deterrent*

(i) *Is Britain's deterrent a weapon of last resort which guarantees her sovereignty and independence and protects her from nuclear blackmail?*   OR *Would all possible uses of Britain's 'deterrent' be suicidal? Is its only effect to encourage proliferation?*

Britain's so-called 'independent deterrent' is not a 'weapon of last resort', because it cannot be used. And the idea that it can protect us against nuclear blackmail is fanciful. An imagined scenario in which we successfully stand out alone against the Soviet Union, is, to put it mildly, unconvincing. And to say that the supposed enemy is some other, as yet non-nuclear, power, is to argue for the indiscriminate spread of nuclear weapons.

(ii) *Are British nuclear forces valuable to European allies because they provide a specifically European second centre of decision making?*   OR *Is the 'second centre of decision making' an illusion when the weapons are dependent upon the US and there is no independent strategic role to be played? Are European allies unenthusiastic about a parochial British force likely to inhibit her commitment to European defence?*

What the argument on the left-hand side is really saying here is that we no longer believe in the American umbrella. We no longer believe in extended deterrence. And the proposed remedy simply compounds this. Are we to believe that, if the Americans with their 11,000 warheads will be reluctant to use them for fear of retaliation, Britain, with 200, will not? The same is true of a 'European nuclear force'. Apart from being a political impossibility, it would also heighten tension and increase instability – Anglo-French cooperation would have to be extended to include the West Germans.

(iii) *Does the US favour shared responsibility and do British nuclear forces guarantee full US commitment to Europe and Soviet recognition of it?*   OR *Are US forces committed anyway and independent British initiatives more likely to trigger Soviet retaliation than US involvement?*

There is no overall 'American view' by the nature of the way in which American government works. But most Americans probably see the British deterrent as a bit of a nuisance, which just complicates arms talks. On the other hand, if we want to go on indulging this delusion of grandeur, they are prepared to let us do so. It makes no material difference to our relationship with America whether we do or do not.

(iv) *Is the cost of the British deterrent small in*   OR *Can Britain's nuclear forces only be*
view of the vital defence role it plays? Are   *afforded at the expense of conventional*
alternatives likely to be more expensive?   *strength and of other more important*
                                                          economic priorities?

First of all, it does not play a 'vital defence role'. But the important point here
is that the money for, say, Trident, comes out of money that would otherwise
go into non-nuclear defence. Future constraints on the defence budget mean
that conventional forces will undoubtedly suffer if we carry through the proposed 'modernization' of our nuclear forces.

Nor is it true that the economy benefits more from investment in nuclear
than in non-nuclear programmes. With Trident, for example, we may employ
a few whizz-kids with PhDs in physics at Aldermaston building warheads,
but the really difficult bit – the missiles – is made by the Americans. Technologically and industrially, investment in conventional forces would benefit us
more.

(v) *Would unilateral British nuclear*   OR *Does the British deterrent encourage*
disarmament have no effect on other   *proliferation and do nothing to enhance*
countries and only serve to weaken British   *British prestige? Would British*
influence and allow France unchallenged   *disarmament within the context outlined in*
ascendancy in Europe?   *B help to break the nuclear log-jam?*

Our so-called independent deterrent gives us virtually no influence at all, even
with the Americans. America is a super-power and will act according to its
own interests.

As for the French nuclear forces, they are just as much of an illusion as
ours. And, when you talk to them about it, you find that they are just as much
at sixes and sevens as we are. What are they going to do with them? Bomb
Russia? Bomb Germany?

On the other hand, I do not subscribe to the idea that Britain's giving up
of her nuclear weapons would influence the Soviet Union, or other as yet
semi-nuclear or non-nuclear powers. You can't negotiate effectively with a
superpower when you are not in that league. And why should other powers
be particularly interested in what Britain does? It's a hang-over from empire
to think that they will be. As I have said earlier, the reason for Britain to give
up nuclear weapons is because it is in her own strategic interest to do so.

(vi) *Is investment in Trident the best way to*   OR *Would commitment to Trident exacerbate*
continue to ensure effective British strategic   *all the drawbacks listed above?*
defence into the 21st century?

I have already answered this.

2 *Nato Forces and US Bases*

(i) *Must Britain continue to share*   OR *Should British obligations to NATO be*
responsibility for manning NATO nuclear   *met by strengthening conventional forces*
systems upon which her security depends?   *where necessary within an overall non-*
Would refusal to do so fatally weaken the   *nuclear strategy as recommended in B?*
alliance?

This is where we begin to enter the second circle of influence, which I was mentioning earlier. The fundamental point here is that, for reasons already explained, our security does not depend on NATO's nuclear policies. Neither the West Germans, nor the 55,000 British troops in Germany, are going to be too happy if nuclear bombs are dropped on their heads by F-111s. These weapons have no credible military use. That is why the Labour Party will work towards non-nuclear defence for NATO, and will substantially increase Britain's conventional contribution.

But the question being asked here is, given the fact that we do not control overall NATO strategy, can a non-nuclear Britain continue to be a member of an Alliance which, wrongly in our opinion, still commits itself to a nuclear war-fighting strategy? And the answer is, of course, yes. There are a number of countries already in NATO which are non-nuclear, such as Denmark. And it is an insult to them to say that, if we go non-nuclear, we will be 'reduced' to their status. As for the argument that in that case we will be shifting the burden to, say, West Germany, well, it will be up to the West Germans to decide whether they do or do not want to go on with suicidal and dangerous nuclear deterrent policies. We will be trying to persaude them that they do not.

(ii) *Would the forced withdrawal of US nuclear bases from Britain make US defence of the West impossible? Is American interference in British affairs negligible?*   OR *Do the large numbers of nuclear facilities yielded to the US erode British sovereignty? Would their removal do no more than restore a normal peacetime relationship?*

And the same applies to American bases. The withdrawal of American nuclear weapons from Britain will not affect defence very much at all. They are not integral to defence in the first place – even within terms of American strategic nuclear deterrence. America will keep her bases and all her other facilities. None of her ships will be barred from visiting our ports, even if they are nuclear capable. As I have said, American troops are in Europe, quite rightly, for the main purpose of defending American interests. It is also in our interest that they should remain here. So neither they nor we will jeopardize our mutual interest by making more of this than is in fact the case.

(iii) *Will Britain continue to be targeted by Soviet warheads whether or not she disarms unilaterally?*   OR *Is Britain seen as an American aircraft carrier and targeted by the USSR accordingly? Will Britain fall an early victim in any superpower confrontation unless bases are removed?*

This is not for me a decisive issue. It is probably true that we are more of a target with the missiles here, because there is more of a temptation to take them out. But it is silly to suppose that an island twenty miles from the mainland will not be involved if a war started on the continent.

(iv) *Can non-nuclear defences only safely be afforded by powers prepared to shelter beneath the American strategic umbrella?*   OR   *In a nuclear-free Europe, decoupled from the superpower nuclear confrontation, would Britain no more expect to depend upon the US 'umbrella' than any other Western ally – or than Eastern Europe upon the USSR?*

Now we reach the third circle of influence. It is out of our power to dictate whether Russia or America go on with their nuclear deterrent policies. We hope that they will be moving away from them. If they do not, there is nothing that we will be able to do about it. But this cannot be called 'sheltering under the American nuclear umbrella', because, as we have seen, there is no such thing. There may have been an umbrella when the Americans had a nuclear monopoly, but there certainly isn't now. Helmut Schmidt does not believe in it. Henry Kissinger does not believe in it. And President Reagan does not believe in it.

Moral Considerations

(i) *Is it morally right to pursue the policy least likely to cause human suffering? May this sometimes involve doing things which in other circumstances would be wrong?*   OR   *Are there actions which are in themselves wrong no matter what the situation? Is the alternative to excuse almost any act of barbarism?*

(ii) *In formulating policy should we weigh up the probability of success and the relative costs in terms of human suffering of alternative nuclear and non-nuclear strategies?*   OR   *Is the only relevant point here that a nuclear exchange of almost any kind would in itself cause unimaginable suffering to largely civilian populations?*

(iii) *So far as concerns intention, need we look no further than the fact that our sole aim in deploying nuclear weapons is to prevent their use?*   OR   *Is there no such thing as a fully deployed weapons system which is a bluff? Is to deploy nuclear weapons to intend to use them in certain circumstances?*

(iv) *Are there possible uses of nuclear weapons which are allowed by Just War theory, for example the bombing of Hiroshima and Nagasaki in order to prevent worse suffering? Can there be a theory of Just Deterrence?*   OR   *Is a conditional intention to cause indiscriminate and disproportionate suffering of this kind, whether admonitory, preemptive or retaliatory, ruled out by Just War theory? Was it wrong to bomb Hiroshima and Nagasaki in 1945?*

All weapons can be used immorally, and a lot has been written in an attempt to define this. But, as I have said, nuclear weapons are different, because I just do not think that there can be a moral use of them. I believe that the American catholic bishops came to the same conclusion.[1] And, if the use is immoral, then the threat to use them is immoral. It is immoral to deploy them.

---

1. In the pastoral letter, *The Challenge of Peace*, May 1983.

(v) *Is there no relevant connection between the*   OR   *Is it a scandal that such huge resources are*
development and deployment of nuclear   *devoted to the development and deployment*
weapons and world poverty and disease?   *of nuclear weapons and not to the*
                                                alleviation of suffering?

I think that, in general, it is morally wrong that we are spending so much on armaments, and so little on constructive economic and social programmes. But I do not think that this is peculiar to nuclear weapons. I can't see that there is a special link here which does not apply to other weapons as well.

(vi) *Does Christian teaching allow the*   OR   *Does Christian teaching condemn the*
deployment of nuclear weapons?   *deployment of nuclear weapons?*

I have said that it is immoral to deploy nuclear weapons. So I suppose that, if Christian teaching coincides with morality here, it, too, must condemn their deployment. And the same might apply to other religions. I just don't know.

Recommendations

1 Yes.
2 Yes (See **A2(A)(v)**).
3 Yes.
4 Yes (See **B(iii)**).
5 Yes (See **A2(A)(vii)**).
6 I don't think that this would mean much.
7 Yes.
8 If it were possible, yes. But it seems too optimistic.
9 Let us say that both sides had negotiated 90 per cent reductions, then I would not object to their saying that they wanted to keep 10 per cent in order to see how it went.
10 Yes.
11 Yes (See **B(iii)**).
12 Yes (See **B(iv)** & **B(vii)**).
13 Yes (See **C1(v)**).
14 This would be part of 12, part of a NATO agreement (See **B(iv)** & **B(vii)**).
15 See 6.
16 Yes (See **C1**).
17 Yes (See **C1(iv)**).
18 Yes (See **C2(i)**).
19 Yes (See **C2(i)** & **(C2(ii)**)).
20 Britain will not leave NATO, even if she fails to persuade her Allies to adopt her preferred policies. She will simply keep on trying.

Dr. John Finnis

Biographical Note

Born in 1940 and educated in Australia, John Finnis came to Oxford in 1962 as a Rhodes scholar, and has been a fellow of University College and a lecturer and reader in law at the university since 1966–7. He has been a barrister at Gray's Inn since 1972, an adviser on constitutional matters to Australian state governments and to the UK House of Commons, and a member of English,

British and Irish Catholic Bishop's committees on bio-ethical and nuclear issues.

Among a large number of books and articles on legal, jurisprudential, moral, theological and philosophical subjects, special mention should be made of *Nuclear Deterrence, Morality and Realism,* written in collaboration with Joseph M. Boyle Jr. and Germain Grisez, to be published in April 1987 by the Clarendon Press. In it, readers will find a more detailed working out of the ideas which are presented in brief here.

Editorial Comment

These answers were communicated in an interview on October 30, 1986, in University College, Oxford. What may impress the reader most in these pages is the uncompromising way in which Dr Finnis accepts both the prudential arguments in favour of a policy of continuing nuclear deterrence, and the moral arguments against. (The kernel of the moral case can be found under *Moral Considerations* in the answers to questions **(iii)** and **(iv)**.) This is very unusual. Although it seems that many people are drawn in these two directions, it is rare for them both to be followed through as consistently as this. Usually we avoid what we see as the threat of internal inconsistency by saying that nuclear deterrence is *either* both prudentially wise and morally right, *or* both prudentially unwise and morally wrong. The remarkable results of not doing this, but of following the tension through to the end, can be seen in the two paragraphs at the beginning of the final set of *Recommendations.*

DR JOHN FINNIS

Global Policy

I *The History of the Past Forty Years*

(i) *Has it been nuclear deterrence that has*   OR *Has it mainly been other factors?*
   kept the peace between the great powers
   since 1945?

I think probably mainly nuclear deterrence.

(ii) *Does mutual possession of an invulnerable*   OR *Does the threat of strategic nuclear*
    second-strike strategic nuclear force prevent   *retaliation, particularly against a similarly*
    war?   *armed enemy, lack credibility and invite*
                                                        sub-deterrent encroachment?

Mutual possession of an invulnerable second strike nuclear force has, I think, been the main factor that has so far kept the peace at great power level. It has not, of course, prevented all wars, and it's also true that it is not altogether stable. But it's pretty stable.

(iii) *Have limited nuclear options at strategic*   OR *Have most military planners from the start*
and theatre levels enhanced deterrence by   *been aiming for nuclear war-fighting*
dramatically raising the threshold between   *superiority? Has 'flexible response'*
peace and war?   *dangerously lowered the threshold between*
                                                    conventional and nuclear war?

I don't think that these are really true alternatives. If you are going to have an
effective deterrent – especially an extended deterrent – then you need limited
nuclear options, because the threat simply to escalate from nothing to all-out
strategic exchange is less credible than the threat to do it by stages with time
for everyone to opt out of the battle. And in order to mount this threat, you
must plan for war-fighting – which means in a sense planning for superiority
in at least some aspects or phases of the potential battle. But, as I say, this
enhances *deterrence*.

The extent to which this is dangerous has, I think, not so much to do
with lowering the threshold between conventional and nuclear war, as with
generating a system of immense complexity, which under certain conditions
could become unstable – especially under conditions of alert.

(iv) *Has the size and variety of the nuclear*   OR *Has the logic of nuclear confrontation and*
arsenals held by the superpowers stabilized   *worst-case analysis generated a dangerous*
deterrence?   *and strategically pointless superfluity of*
                                                 weapons systems?

Again I say 'yes' to both sides. If we could somehow unravel the whole inter-
superpower setup and start again, then clearly we would not choose to have
so many. In that sense there is a superfluity of weapons systems. And I don't
think that anyone, except for polemical purposes, would want to deny that
size (which involves complexity) can be dangerous. But no one has been in
charge of the whole 'system'. Each has been faced by varying threats from the
other side, and in these circumstances the size of the arsenals does not seem
to be strategically pointless – especially if your aim is to defend an extended
alliance. Almost everyone who has tried to manage Western deterrence policy
has been tempted by the attractive idea of a much reduced, 'minimum' deterrent – but all of them have in the end decided that it is too dangerous. I
think that within these terms of reference their reasoning has been essentially
correct.

(v) *Has the idea of nuclear balance between*   OR *Have ideas of 'nuclear defence' and*
the superpowers been essential to stability   *'parity' proved illusory and is 'multilateral*
and have arms-control negotiations helped   *negotiation from strength' a contradiction*
to achieve it?   *in terms? Has 'arms-control' been just*
                                                 another name for the arms race?

'Parity' is not a proper synonym for 'balance here'. 'Parity' suggests crude and
unhelpful ideas of numerical equality, whereas 'balance' – meaning that each
sort of threat that one side can pose is properly checked by some kind of
counter-check – is, I think, essential to deterrent stability.

As to whether arms control negotiations have helped to achieve it – I'm rather agnostic. There are quite strong arguments which suggest that arms control negotiations have in some cases been destabilizing in their actual, not intended, effects. For example, SALT I may be seen to have encouraged a great explosion in warhead technology. But one gets into very refined assessments when one tries to sort all this out.

(vi) *Has force-planning been controlled by strategic thinking?*   OR *Has the self-reinforcing impetus of technology and vested interest dictated policies subsequently justified post hoc?*

I think that, at the most basic level, strategic thinking has been decisive – elementary thoughts such as these: we need a deterrent, we need an extended deterrent, we need a graduated response, limited options, etc. But many of the details have been controlled by what you are calling 'the self-reinforcing impetus of technology and vested interest' and so on.

2 *The Prospect for the Future*

(A) WITH NUCLEAR WEAPONS
(i) *Does the threat of an enemy first strike remain inconceivable for the foreseeable future?*   OR *Is there an increasing threat from accurate and time-urgent first-strike weapons?*

I think that a unilaterally determined first strike, out of the blue, from 'ungenerated' force postures to hot war in twenty-four hours, is extremely unlikely. It is a very uninviting prospect for anyone to undertake. On the other hand, against a background of political or military confrontation, the possibility that one side may think that it has to 'go first' under conditions of great stress arising out of mutually 'ratcheted' alerts is far from negligible. And the existence of increasingly accurate offensive weapons makes that all the more possible.

(ii) *Are command, control, communication and intelligence facilities likely to remain secure?*   OR *Does the amount of information to be processed, pressure of time and fear of preemption put command and control systems under intolerable strain and make inadvertent war more likely?*

This is a very complicated matter, and, when you look at the literature, you find that there are powerful considerations on each side. The trouble is that you can never tell what the ultimate pay-off will be. *Vulnerable* command and control facilities may be dangerous; on the other hand they may make a first strike *less* inviting to the enemy, in so far as it is clear that their destruction will trigger their side's whole system. Again, under certain conditions the amount of information which electronic systems make available to decision-makers will help them to avoid error, but under conditions of alert, the flood of information may make error more possible. Errors are possible out of ignorance, but they are also possible out of a superfluity of information.

(iii) *If nevertheless there were a limited nuclear* OR *Is the idea that nuclear war could be*
exchange would it be likely to end   *limited once it had broken out a dangerous*
hostilities swiftly?   *illusion?*

Nobody knows. There would probably be tremendous pressure to end hostilities swiftly and on almost any terms. On the other hand there would be tremendous pressure to plunge on in the hope of salvaging something from the wreckage. Nobody knows.

(iv) *Do new generations of battlefield and*   OR *Do new battlefield and theatre weapons*
theatre nuclear systems reinforce   *threaten a dangerous lowering of the*
deterrence?   *nuclear threshold?*

In many cases they clearly reinforce deterrence. But they also lower the nuclear threshold. These are not alternatives. As to detailed questions about whether Pershing and Cruise were necessary to balance SS20s, I do not feel competent to make a judgement. It is not something that I have thought worthwhile to investigate very carefully.

(v) *Does the Strategic Defence Initiative offer* OR *Is the Strategic Defence Initiative simply*
the hope of an effective defence against   *the most recent and destabilizing example*
nuclear weapons?   *of the process outlined in 1?*

I think that the Strategic Defence Initiative is partly the product of morally inspired hopes that we can somehow simply levitate out of the appalling quagmire, which everyone recognizes that we are in. And, indeed, if we could create the system which the planners envisage *overnight*, and share it with the other side, then that might well be an immense change for the better. But there is no prospect of this, and the process of getting there would be very dangerous, because it would look to the other side as if we were aiming to disarm him, particularly since the Reagan administration has made it clear that it intends to keep its offensive capability right through the process. Admiral Poindexter's remark the other day, that he could not see how anyone could object to SDI because it is purely defensive, is alarming, if he meant it seriously; it is blind to the inevitable *strategic* assessment the Soviets will make (or else supposes that his audience is blind to that). In the meantime, the threat of SDI *may* have helped to bring the Soviet Union back to the negotiating table. But bringing someone to the bargaining table is not the same as striking a bargain, and SDI may well play a major role in preventing that. Many influential American politicians support SDI only as a bargaining chip, but the administration seems to deny that it is one.

(vi) *Is the threat of 'horizontal' nuclear*   OR *Is continuing reliance on nuclear deterrence*
proliferation best met by a continuation of   *by the great powers bound to accelerate the*
past policies?   *process of proliferation and make nuclear*
                                                 war more likely?

There *may* be certain causal links between the size of the arsenals held by the established nuclear weapons powers and the proliferation of nuclear weapons to other powers, but I think that they are tenuous. If the great powers were to give up nuclear deterrence altogether, that might make a big difference. But I don't think that relatively small reductions have much effect.

(vii) *Do multilateral arms-control negotiations* OR *Is 'arms-control' an illusion which diverts*
offer the best prospect for future stability?   *attention from the only safe policy –*
                                                     nuclear disarmament?

I have no lively anticipation that the current talks will yield anything much at all. I don't think that there is much prospect in general of gaining stability or disarmament measures from multilateral negotiation. Each responsible person involved in these processes must think how much better it would be if we could do the same essential job of deterring the other side with much less expenditure of resources and many fewer of the risks that come from huge complexity and 'overkill'. The apparently dramatic offers made on either side are partly a genuine attempt to levitate out of the quagmire. But no one is in full command of any of these giant political systems, and, among other things, neither can trust the other not to cheat or take advantage of the opportunities that bargaining opens up. Neither is willing to take the chance involved in an acceptance which measures up to an offer, or an offer which is likely to meet acceptance. Nevertheless, a world in which people are still talking to one another in this sort of way seems better than one in which they simply turn their backs on one another.

(B) WITHOUT NUCLEAR WEAPONS

(i) *If nuclear arsenals were dismantled would* OR *Would nuclear disarmament remove the*
war between the great powers again   *incentive for nuclear preemption while not*
become a rational option and therefore   *affecting the reluctance of the great powers*
more likely?   *to initiate a third world war?*

I think that war would become significantly more likely. At the very least, I think that the kind of brinkmanship which typically generates wars would become much more attractive as an option – and this would be more likely to result in a major war.

(ii) *Would a major conventional war be likely* OR *Is conventional war, however terrible,*
in itself to be as terrible as a limited   *preferable to nuclear war?*
nuclear war?

If one could imagine a major conventional war that did not in fact escalate into a nuclear war, it would probably be as frightful as certain forms of very limited nuclear war; but it would not be as terrible as the sort of nuclear war that is currently being planned for.

(iii) *Because nuclear weapons cannot be* OR *As with nerve gases in the last war, would*
uninvented would they not be bound to be   *there be no incentive to resort to*
used sooner or later once war had broken   *capabilities which the other side has as*
out?   *well?*

I am sure that nuclear weapons would reappear, given enough time to reconstruct them.

(iv) *Is global nuclear disarmament only*   OR *Is to argue that even multilateral nuclear*
feasible in a world where war itself is no   *disarmament is not desirable to give up all*
longer a possibility?   *hope of a rational world-order?*

What the previous question has demonstrated is that global nuclear disarmament is very risky. It carries all sorts of appalling possible consequences. In that sense it is 'undesirable'. But we should not leap from there to the conclusion that therefore we must prefer the alternative; the alternative in this case is the present sort of nuclear confrontation, which is in itself 'undesirable' and also carries other appalling risks. So, which is the least undesirable? This is the bottom line consideration and is an entirely different question. As I will be arguing later, it is folly to think that you can compute the probabilities against the values at stake, in other words the anticipated consequences, and arrive at a sum which will enable you to say *'therefore this option is the more desirable'*. The sum cannot be done. So all we can say here is that the anticipated consequences of global nuclear disarmament are in many respects extremely uninviting.

(v) *Is peace only preserved when we are seen*   OR *Do the years before 1914 show what*
to be prepared for war, as failure before   *happens when military planning and the*
1939 and success since 1945 show? Under   *arms race control political choices? Do*
likely future conditions would global   *present strategies make nuclear war almost*
nuclear disarmament make war, including   *inevitable under likely future conditions?*
nuclear war, more likely?   *Is global nuclear disarmament the only*
                                                      rational policy?

They are both true, aren't they? That's all one can say.

B *NATO Policy*

(i) *Does the Soviet Union, together with her*   OR *Are NATO and WTO forces relatively*
Warsaw Pact allies, enjoy a strategically   *evenly matched?*
dangerous military superiority in Europe?

This is once again not something that I have given much attention to, but, if I am forced to answer, I will say – yes, the Soviet Union and her allies have a dangerous conventional military superiority in Europe.

ii) *Is the Soviet Union an expansionist power*   OR *Is the Soviet Union an encircled and*
which will take advantage of unilateral   *threatened power trying to keep up with*
Western concessions and is only restrained   *Western technology and likely to respond*
and forced to accept arms-control   *positively to unconditional offers of*
agreements by Western determination and   *Western restraint within a general context*
strength?   *of detente?*

I think that there are two big questions being run together here. One is: given mutual nuclear deterrence, what are the factors that are operating on the Soviet Union? The other is: what would be likely to happen if we unilaterally gave up our nuclear deterrent, leaving them with a nuclear capability, or if both sides gave up their nuclear deterrents?

In answer to the first, I would say that the Soviet Union that exists today has from the start been constrained by Western strength and has in many ways been transformed as a result.

In answer to the second, it seems likely that Western unilateralism might encourage an intrinsic expansionism, which springs from, among other things, Soviet ideology. Mutual nuclear disarmament would have unpredictable consequences. As I have said, it might lead to dangerous confrontations between East and West, and therefore make war more likely – although the situation would be so different to the one that exists today that it's very hard to say. Who was being expansionist might not in every case be clear. The Soviet Union has an ideology which authorizes and encourages unilateral expansionism, without excluding any means. The West has far-flung interests, which it is prepared to defend or attain by the use of military power, for example in the Middle East. It has an ideology which encourages expansion-ism, if not by any means, then by means which include military pressure of a kind that can lead to confrontations and war.

(iii) *Is Soviet chemical and conventional preponderance such that NATO must continue to be able to threaten early use of nuclear weapons?*   OR *Is NATO dependence on the early use of nuclear weapons unnecessary and strategically suicidal?*

For NATO to use her nuclear weapons might well be strategically suicidal. On the other hand, it would seem to me to be dangerous if she were not able to threaten to make early use of them.

(iv) *Does the growing size of the Soviet nuclear arsenal threaten the delicate theatre and strategic balance? Would Western failure to match Soviet systems be destabilizing?*   OR *Does the West initiate nearly all phases of the nuclear arms race and continue to enjoy a substantial lead in most areas? Is the nuclear 'overkill' such that the West could offer a nuclear 'freeze' or unconditional cuts without risk?*

As I have said earlier, this is not a matter which I have tried to investigate very closely, and I am not prepared to conclude that NATO's policy is illegitimate or mistaken.

(v) *Are NATO 'forward defence' and 'deep strike' strategies essential for effective deterrence?*   OR *Should NATO exploit her lead in 'emerging technology' to explore less provocative alternative strategies?*

There is much to be said for exploring less dangerous alternative strategies. But exploring is one thing and finding is another.

(vi) *Is it the presence of American front-line troops and the tying-in of theatre nuclear forces to the American strategic deterrent that guarantees W. European security? Should American policies therefore be supported?*   OR *Is it domination by the two super-powers that poses the greatest threat to European integrity? Would Europe be safer decoupled from the super-power nuclear confrontation? Should Europe be made a nuclear weapon-free zone?*

In a sense it is possible to agree with both sides here. Given the fact that we need American support, we had better keep them in the front line and tie in our defences to their nuclear capability. This is certainly a very substantial guarantee of Western European security. On the other hand, if everything went wrong and we were dragged into a military superpower clash, that would probably be the end of Europe. There is much that is attractive about the idea of Western European neutrality. But there would be immense costs – and we would be in danger of falling a prey to one of the two superpowers – the less attractive of the two!

vii) *Would Western unilateral nuclear disarmament invite Soviet blackmail? Are suggestions that the West should take the lead in offering unilateral disarmament initiatives the thin end of this wedge? Do radical nuclear disarmers consciously or unconsciously serve Soviet interests and threaten to undermine Western defences?*

OR *Are unilateral initiatives as part of a general programme of nuclear disarmament the only way to reverse the arms race? Is talk of 'multilateral disarmament' insincere in the mouths of those who reject all suggestion of a Comprehensive Test Ban Treaty, a Nuclear Freeze, a European Nuclear Weapon-Free Zone, or a declaration of No First Use?*

Let me take these questions one by one, starting on the left. Would Western unilateral disarmament invite Soviet blackmail? Yes, undoubtedly. Would unilateral initiatives be the thin end of this wedge? Not necessarily, unless they were intended to be. The bottom line of nuclear deterrence is so far away from particular unilateral disarmament initiatives, and in the end it's the bottom line that matters most. Do radical disarmers serve Soviet interests? My reading of much of the radical disarmament literature is – yes, many of them do. A number are unrealistic about the nature of Soviet power and unconsciously serve Soviet interests. Some of them, I suspect, do so consciously. Turning to the right-hand side, I do think that unilateral initiatives of this kind are the only way to reverse the arms race. They are a risky way, and might not succeed in reversing it. But they are probably the only way, and I think that we should be prepared to take some risks. Finally, I do not think that multilateral disarmers who reject those policies are necessarily insincere – although some probably are.

C British Policy

I The British Deterrent

(i) *Is Britain's deterrent a weapon of last resort which guarantees her sovereignty and independence and protects her from nuclear blackmail?*

OR *Would all possible uses of Britain's 'deterrent' be suicidal? Is its only effect to encourage proliferation?*

I do think that all probable uses would be likely to be suicidal. But it does not follow from that this the British deterrent does not protect Britain from many forms of nuclear blackmail.

(ii) *Are British nuclear forces valuable to European allies because they provide a specifically European second centre of decision making?*   OR *Is the 'second centre of decision making' an illusion when the weapons are dependent upon the US and there is no independent strategic role to be played? Are European allies unenthusiastic about a parochial British force likely to inhibit her commitment to European defence?*

I think that it is largely a rationalization to say that one of the main reasons why Britain retains an independent deterrent is to contribute to a second centre of decision-making in Europe. That is not why we have it. It may be the case that in fact others in Europe welcome it as a second centre and think that it usefully complicates Soviet calculations – but this is not in itself a sufficient reason for keeping it.

(iii) *Does the US favour shared responsibility and do British nuclear forces guarantee full US commitment to Europe and Soviet recognition of it?*   OR *Are US forces committed anyway and independent British initiatives more likely to trigger Soviet retaliation than US involvement?*

Although the considerations on either side here are reasonable, I think that for most people they are peripheral. The deep consideration is the one in number (i).

(iv) *Is the cost of the British deterrent small in view of the vital defence role it plays? Are alternatives likely to be more expensive?*   OR *Can Britain's nuclear forces only be afforded at the expense of conventional strength and of other more important economic priorities?*

The saving would not be all that great. It would not buy much in the way of conventional strength. This again is not a decisive argument.

(v) *Would unilateral British nuclear disarmament have no effect on other countries and only serve to weaken British influence and allow France unchallenged ascendancy in Europe?*   OR *Does the British deterrent encourage proliferation and do nothing to enhance British prestige? Would British disarmament within the context outlined in B help to break the nuclear log-jam?*

I think that this is also marginal. We might lose a certain amount of influence with the United States. I don't think that the fact that France would be left as the only European nuclear power makes much difference one way or the other – although there are refined calculations that it might encourage the Germans to go nuclear, which would be dangerous. On the other side, I do not believe that it would help to break the nuclear log-jam or influence other powers to go non-nuclear.

(vi) *Is investment in Trident the best way to continue to ensure effective British strategic defence into the 21st century?*   OR *Would commitment to Trident exacerbate all the drawbacks listed above?*

I haven't any special reason to question the political-economic-strategic calculations made or expounded by Michael Quinlan.[1] (See footnote page 229.)

2 NATO Forces and US Bases

(i) *Must Britain continue to share*   OR *Should British obligations to NATO be*
responsibility for manning NATO nuclear   *met by strengthening conventional forces*
systems upon which her security depends?   *where necessary within an overall non-*
Would refusal to do so fatally weaken the   *nuclear strategy as recommended in B?*
alliance?

All talk about working towards 'an overall non-nuclear strategy' in NATO is just fantasy. And the belief that one somehow improves one's moral position by getting rid of one's own weapons, while retaining one's place within an alliance whose whole policy involves 'flexible response' based on nuclear deterrence, seems to to me largely illusory. Of course we have a moral obligation to get rid of our own weapons, and therefore we should get rid of them. So far I agree with Labour Party policy. But we should also get out of an alliance whose fundamental strategy is nuclear.

(ii) *Would the forced withdrawal of US*   OR *Do the large numbers of nuclear facilities*
nuclear bases from Britain make US   *yielded to the US erode British*
defence of the West impossible? Is   *sovereignty? Would their removal do no*
American interference in British affairs   *more than restore a normal peacetime*
negligible?   *relationship?*

For the same reason we should also get rid of American nuclear bases. It is clearly the case that it would weaken Western defences, but we must do it on moral grounds.

(iii) *Will Britain continue to be targeted by*   OR *Is Britain seen as an American aircraft*
Soviet warheads whether or not she   *carrier and targeted by the USSR*
disarms unilaterally?   *accordingly? Will Britain fall an early*
    victim in any superpower confrontation
    unless bases are removed?

If we got rid of our own nuclear weapons, got out of the Alliance and removed American nuclear bases – in other words, if we became effectively neutral – I don't see any special reason why the Soviet Union would want to target us for actual massive nuclear attack. I just do not believe the story that everyone is under direct *nuclear* threat, no matter what their stance in the world.

(iv) *Can non-nuclear defences only safely be*   OR *In a nuclear-free Europe, decoupled from*
afforded by powers prepared to shelter   *the superpower nuclear confrontation,*
beneath the American strategic umbrella?   *would Britain no more expect to depend*
    upon the US 'umbrella' than any other
    Western ally – or than Eastern Europe
    upon the USSR?

Perhaps in those circumstances, no matter what Neil Kinnock may say, we would still be effectively under the American umbrella. But that would be up to the Americans.

---

1. Sir Michael Quinlan, Deputy Under-Secretary of State at the Ministry of Defence 1977–1981, now Permanent Secretary at the Department of Employment.

Moral Considerations

(i) *Is it morally right to pursue the policy least* OR *Are there actions which are in themselves*
likely to cause human suffering? May this   wrong no matter what the situation? Is the
sometimes involve doing things which in   alternative to excuse almost any act of
other circumstances would be wrong?   barbarism?

I say 'yes' to the right-hand side.

As to the left, there are two sources of confusion to be dispelled. First, it is
an illusion to assume that we will be in a situation in which all our options are
morally wrong, so that we are simply having to choose between moral evils.
There has been no demonstration that we are in such a position, nor do I
believe that such a demonstration of a true *moral* dilemma is even conceivable.

Secondly, it is a fundamental mistake to think that we can weigh up greater
and lesser risks, and greater and lesser quantities of human suffering, measure
them against one another, and thereby reach a morally significant conclusion.
Goods, harms, risks, probabilities, and so on, are factors which pull in different directions and cannot be measured against one another. They are incommensurable.

(ii) *In formulating policy should we weigh up* OR *Is the only relevant point here that a*
the probability of success and the relative   nuclear exchange of almost any kind
costs in terms of human suffering of   would in itself cause unimaginable
alternative nuclear and non-nuclear   suffering to largely civilian populations?
strategies?

Taking the statement implied on the left, we now apply this to the question
of alternative nuclear and non-nuclear strategies. In making our moral choice,
we must of course be aware of the probability of success and attend to the
relative costs of alternative policies. In this sense morality has a great deal to
do with consequences. It's better not to go in blind, and to have as full a
picture as possible of the resulting scenarios that we will be likely to finish up
with if we choose in different ways. But this working out of the different
scenarios will not in itself constitute or determine our moral judgement and
choice. As I say, the relevant factors are in the end incommensurable, so that
we cannot just feed in the data, turn the handle, and then expect to find out
in this consequentialist way how we should act morally. For example, here we
are faced with an impressive case for unilateral nuclear disarmament, based
on the fear of the holocaust and the likelihood that this will come about if we
carry on indefinitely as we are going now. And also with an impressive case
for continuing to rely on nuclear deterrence, based at any given time on the
quite low risk of the holocaust and the preservation of the immense goods of
Western civilization against the dangers of being unjustly taken over. These,
let us say, are the two alternative scenarios that our assessments picture for
us. But there simply is no calculation that will show which is the more rational
or moral of the two choices. In order to discover that, we do not rely on
mechanical computation, but on all sorts of commitments that we have made

in our earlier moral lives. We go for the option that is most continuous with the commitments that we have made, and the vocation that we as individuals and as a community have responded to, provided that that option does not violate a moral absolute, or involve choosing (intending) something 'in itself wrong', as you have put it.

(iii) *So far as concerns intention, need we look* OR *Is there no such thing as a fully deployed no further than the fact that our sole aim in weapons system which is a bluff? Is to deploying nuclear weapons is to prevent deploy nuclear weapons to intend to use their use? them in certain circumstances?*

Well, I think that what is suggested on the left is often advanced as a way out of an otherwise uncomfortable position, especially by Christian moralists. They want to retain the deterrent, but recognize that it would be utterly immoral to use it and see that it seems to be geared up for use if need be. So they try to turn it into a sort of bluff. But I am afraid they are mistaken. It isn't a bluff, nor could it be a bluff. Even if, as is logically possible, but exceedingly unlikely, all the weapons operators were bluffing, so that on the day when the orders went out no buttons were pressed, even so it is logically impossible for the policy as a whole to be a bluff, and there are many people who participate in the policy who cannot be bluffing. Let me take this by stages. The policy does not announce itself as a bluff. It declares itself to be the policy of having the capability of wiping out cities in tit-for-tat city swaps and/or in *final* retaliation, and of having the *will* to use that capability. That policy is reiterated every year by the United States, and occasionally by the United Kingdom and France. 'We have the capability and the will' is the threat. So the *policy itself* is not to bluff, and cannot be to bluff. And it is that policy that you and I are invited to subscribe to or detach ourselves from. So when we vote for it, for example, in Parliament or in Congress or at the polls, *we* cannot be bluffing. We may be hoping that other people are bluffing, but we cannot ourselves be bluffing in the part we play as voters. Similarly, nor can people who build nuclear weapons or send nuclear submarines out, which are then out of their control. They are simply *doing their bit* for a policy which is not one of bluff; in other words, when we vote for the policy, we say 'yes' to the announced intention to use. Our motive, of course, is to prevent situations arising in which we might 'have to' execute our threats of use. Non-use is our hope; preservation of peace with freedom is our motive. But our intention is to have the weapons, and, so the policy says, to use them if we have to. Reagan's and Thatcher's innermost intentions are irrelevant to the moral choice that we are asked to make *now*. No one is asked to subscribe to Reagan's and Thatcher's innermost intentions. We are only asked to subscribe to the policy, which does not alter whenever Reagan or Thatcher secretly alter their innermost intentions.

(As to the idea that we might keep our weapons, but change our announced policy and say that we will never use them – the policy would be almost unintelligible. As announced it would have virtually no deterrent capability. And if, in order to give it deterrent capability, we continued to deploy and update our forces, our total policy could only seem to be one of keeping our options open, which once again is a kind or policy of use – a conditional intention or at least *willingness* to use).

(iv) *Are there possible uses of nuclear weapons*   OR *Is a conditional intention to cause*
which are allowed by Just War theory, for   *indiscriminate and disproportionate*
example the bombing of Hiroshima and   *suffering of this kind, whether admonitory,*
Nagasaki in order to prevent worse   *preemptive or retaliatory, ruled out by Just*
suffering? Can there be a theory of Just   *War theory? Was it wrong to bomb*
Deterrence?   *Hiroshima and Nagasaki in 1945?*

Those who say that if deterrence failed there are certain morally legitimate uses of nuclear weapons, may be imagining restricted strikes against missile fields or fleets at sea and so on. But this is to abstract from the necessities of a total military strategy. It is not sane to threaten to use nuclear weapons unless this is backed up by one or both of the following two threats. First, the threat to make tit-for-tat attacks on the other side's cities if he has made an attack on your cities. You must threaten to *city-swap*, lest your cities be simply taken out one by one until you are blackmailed into surrender. Secondly, and I think that this is probably the more basic, you must say '*if you make an all-out nuclear attack on us and we are wiped out and have lost everything, you will regret it, because we will wipe you out*'. This is the threat of *final retaliation*. There cannot be a coherent or effective nuclear deterrent strategy, within a context where both sides have nuclear weapons, which does not rely wholly or partly on one or both of these two threats. Since neither the threat of city-swapping, nor the threat of final retaliation, can conceivably be reconciled with 'Just War Theory', no nuclear deterrent strategy can be, either. But I prefer not to talk about 'Just War', let alone 'Theory'. We are talking about an absolute norm of common and Christian morality: You must not intend to kill innocents (here, non-combatants).

As to Hiroshima and Nagasaki, the dropping of the two atomic bombs on those cities was indeed morally wrong. In fact, as one can plainly see from the records of those who made the decision, neither the motive nor the intention was to attack military targets. The intention was simply to cause maximum damage in largely civilian areas in order to shock the Japanese out of the war – which it did. Even if Leonard Cheshire is right, and this was the only way in which the war could have been ended short of a much more costly invasion of Japan, it was still clearly morally wrong and should certainly not have been done.

(v) *Is there no relevant connection between the*   OR *Is it a scandal that such huge resources are*
development and deployment of nuclear   *devoted to the development and deployment*
weapons and world poverty and disease?   *of nuclear weapons and not to the*
                                                    alleviation of suffering?

In a way both alternatives are mistaken. Nuclear weapons are one of the cheapest components in our defence, so it is wrong just to point the finger at them. On the other hand, the enormous expense involved in the huge enterprise of defending ourselves against the Soviet Union undoubtedly does contribute to the suffering of the poorest of the poor – and the costs of the Soviet's own efforts even more so.

(vi) *Does Christian teaching allow the deployment of nuclear weapons?*   OR *Does Christian teaching condemn the deployment of nuclear weapons?*

Because, as we have seen, the deployment of nuclear weapons is only rational within a strategic framework which includes the threat and capability to city-swap and carry out final retaliation, Christian doctrine requires us to condemn their deployment. If it was not for these two threats, it does not seem to me that Christian teaching would necessarily condemn either the use or deployment of nuclear weapons any more than it condemns the use or deployment of other weapons. What is mistaken is the attempt made by many of the churches in their official pronouncements to suggest that the systems are or can become purely counter-military, or that they can become a bluff. On inspection, both of these suggestions are clearly unrealistic. The facts have not been fully attended to. Quite often, of course, governments deliberately try to draw a veil of obscurity over these facts. (The British are more mealy-mouthed than the French over this.) So people need to engage in a bit of strategic analysis to uncover them. Once the facts are established the application of Christian doctrine becomes clear enough. The minimum that the churches ought to say is this: '*If our nuclear deterrent system involves either or both of the two threats to city-swap and carry out final retaliation, then it cannot be morally justified, even if it preserves peace and justice and lives which could not otherwise be preserved.*' That would be sufficient. It would then be up to Christians as men of the world to judge what the facts about our threats actually are.

Recommendations

As you can see, broadly speaking I agree on prudential grounds with those who defend current policies. But these policies turn out on analysis to be clearly and irrevocably immoral. So what should be done? I have two types of recommendation to make. If I had my way, we would give up our nuclear weapons immediately and unconditionally. We would give them up very fast, because we are bound to renounce the deterrent policy *immediately*, and because the process of more leisurely dismantling would be dangerous – the Soviets would have such an incentive to prevent us backsliding on our resolve to give them up. So that is my basic recommendation.

But now I am faced with your list of possible courses of action in a world where my basic proposal is not going to be accepted. So what I say is this. Don't mix morals with strategy. If you are determined to go on being immoral by keeping some form of nuclear deterrent, then at least make the damn thing safe. This may well involve you in updating it, complexifying it, enhancing it. In fact, I think that one should be prepared to take some risks in order to get rid of some of the more dangerous features of the present system. But don't let us kid ourselves that by doing this we are making it more morally satisfactory – except in the sense that it is always morally right to reduce risks.

1 I think that there is a case for a freeze, although it is not conclusive.
2 If we could be sure that the other side was also doing the same, this would be good (See **A2** (A) (**v**)).
3 This does not seem to me to be critical, but, given appropriate verification, yes.
4 A declaration of No First Use might be quite dangerous in the European theatre.
5 Up to a certain depth this would be safe and desirable. Beyond that it becomes actually destabilizing (See **A1(iv)**).
6 That would be nice.
7 So would this.
8 As I have said, despite the great risks involved in universal nuclear disarmament, we are clearly under an obligation to do anything that would get rid of our threats of city-swapping and final retaliation. But there is no such thing as a 'process of universal nuclear disarmament' and *no one* can bring such a process into being by his own decision. It's an illusory question (See **A2(B)(iv)**).
9 A minimum deterrent could be dangerous, particularly if one of the powers was at the same time committed to extended deterrence (See **A1(iv)**).
10 This depends upon a number of contingencies, such as whether the Russians are in it themselves, whether the Americans make this a prerequisite for their continuing to uphold the NATO Alliance, and so on.
11 See 4.
12 I am undecided. I would not favour unconditional cuts for the sake of it, but certain unconditional measures might help to break the log-jam.
13 Yes.
14 No. The withdrawal should be immediate.
15 See 6.
16 Yes.
17 I have no strong views (See **C1(iv)**).
18 This is unrealistic. Britain should immediately get out of an alliance whose fundamental strategy is nuclear (See **C2(i)**).
19 Britain should also get rid of American nuclear bases (See **C2(ii)**).
20 See 18.

Professor
Lawrence Freedman

Biographical Note

Born in 1948, Lawrence Freedman was a Research Fellow at Nuffield College, Oxford between 1974 and 1975, at the International Institute for Strategic Studies between 1975 and 1976, and at the Royal Institute of International Affairs between 1976 and 1978. From 1978 to 1982 he was Head of Policy Studies at the Royal Institute of International Affairs, and since 1982 has been Professor of War Studies at King's College, London.

Among a large number of books and articles, special mention can be made of *Britain and Nuclear Weapons* (1980), and *The Evolution of Nuclear Strategy* (1981).

Editorial Comment

This set of answers was given during the course of an interview in King's College, London, on August 14, 1986. Perhaps what may strike the reader most is Professor Freedman's insistence throughout that these are nearly all highly complex issues to which there are no clear-cut or simple answers. The question of nuclear weapons is only part of a much broader set of problems (A2(A)vii), nuclear deterrence theory itself is deeply ambiguous (AIiii), and there are no simple remedies (Biv). This applies as much to sweeping official claims, such as those made on behalf of the American Strategic Defence Initiative (A2(A)v), as to the proposals of the more radical critics of current policy (Bvii). The result is that, seen from these polarized positions, Professor Freedman's is an influential, but ambivalent, voice.

PROFESSOR LAWRENCE FREEDMAN

A *Global Policy*

1 *The History of the Past Forty Years*

(i) *Has it been nuclear deterrence that has*   OR *Has it mainly been other factors?*
kept the peace between the great powers
since 1945?

I think that, if nuclear weapons had not existed, war between the great powers might have been more likely – but by no means inevitable. As it is, fear of nuclear war has probably been an important restraining factor at key moments – perhaps more important in the first twenty years after the Second World War, when the international system was still settling down, than recently. For example, in the absence of such a threat, it is possible to imagine a Soviet seizure of West Berlin, or the temptation for America to have intervened in Hungary in 1956.

(ii) *Does mutual possession of an invulnerable*   OR *Does the threat of strategic nuclear*
second-strike strategic nuclear force prevent   *retaliation, particularly against a similarly*
war?   *armed enemy, lack credibility and invite*
sub-deterrent encroachment?

An enemy's possession of an invulnerable second strike strategic nuclear force means that there are profound disincentives to launching a first strike should a war seem imminent. In theory, mutual possession does introduce a degree of neutralization, which perhaps ought to invite things lower down the spectrum. But this has not happened, largely, I think, because of the fear that somewhere or other nuclear weapons could get used, and this might then escalate.

(iii) *Have limited nuclear options at strategic and theatre levels enhanced deterrence by dramatically raising the threshold between peace and war?*   OR *Have most military planners from the start been aiming for nuclear war-fighting superiority? Has 'flexible response' dangerously lowered the threshold between conventional and nuclear war?*

To begin with, flexible response does not necessarily mean limited nuclear options. By and large it was introduced with conventional options in mind. Nor were the limited nuclear options that were envisaged necessarily of a war-fighting sort. They were, if anything, thought of more as a signal to indicate the terrible things that might happen if the aggression continued.

Having said that, there does seem to be a problem here. I think that the existence of such a diversity of nuclear weapons around the place, and such a variety of ideas about how they may be employed, does increase the possibility that they could be used. But this is all part of deterrence. Clearly, the paradox of deterrence is that it is reinforced to the extent that you think that nuclear weapons can be used – but, the more that you think that you can use them, the lower the threshold of their use and the more dangerous the situation seems to be. So there is always a balance to be struck. My own view on this is that it is not that the use of nuclear weapons has in fact become more likely, but that even a very small percentage chance that they may be used is in itself deterring.

I do not think that military planners have in general been aiming for war-fighting superiority. They do tend to believe that they need to have things to do should deterrence fail, but very few think seriously in terms of the possibility of achieving a meaningful victory in a nuclear war. I don't think most European planners believe for a moment that you can fight a nuclear war along conventional lines.

(iv) *Has the size and variety of the nuclear arsenals held by the superpowers stabilized deterrence?*   OR *Has the logic of nuclear confrontation and worst-case analysis generated a dangerous and strategically pointless superfluity of weapons systems?*

Well, again there is a tension here. There are arguments both ways. On the one hand, you can say that large and complicated arsenals reinforce deterrence by increasing apparent risk. On the other hand, when you spread the arsenals too wide, command and control problems may arise, which could be dangerous. I do think that a lot of the systems we have at the moment are unnecessary. So there is superfluity. But that does not necessarily mean that they are dangerous. I do not think that 'overkill' is necessarily more dangerous than 'kill'. In fact 'kill' may even be more dangerous, because the calculations may then become rather delicate and you may get it wrong.

I do not, by the way, think that 'worse case analysis' has in general been a determining factor here. It has been an element, but cannot be said to have driven the process.

(v) *Has the idea of nuclear balance between* OR *Have ideas of 'nuclear defence' and*
the superpowers been essential to stability   *'parity' proved illusory and is 'multilateral*
and have arms-control negotiations helped   *negotiation from strength' a contradiction*
to achieve it?   *in terms? Has 'arms-control' been just*
                                                                         another name for the arms race?

These are very complex relations. The idea of parity has at times seemed to be a suitable and generally acceptable objective for arms control negotiations, but has often in practise turned out to be rather elusive. There have been successes, such as the ABM treaty, which, I think, has been a stabilizing force. But you can also argue that the idea of parity in arms control negotiations has encouraged imitation, force-matching, and so on. It's difficult to assess this, because we are dealing with a complex process, and you can't prove that the same sorts of thing wouldn't have been happening anyway.

Much the same applies to the idea of 'Negotiation from strength'. By and large it is probably the case that using 'bargaining chips' in order to negotiate from strength leaves you with the strength of the chips rather than negotiations. But this is hard to judge. For example, if, as some see as possible, we get an INF agreement this year, it would in part be a vindication of the idea that in some cases you can successfully bargain from strength. But it all depends. The threat of a developed ABM system by the United States has undoubtedly had an effect as a bargaining chip, whereas I don't think that other things, like MX,[1] have. This is one of those arguments that is not a general rule, but on occasion may apply.

(vi) *Has force-planning been controlled by*   OR *Has the self-reinforcing impetus of*
strategic thinking?   *technology and vested interest dictated*
                                                                         policies subsequently justified post hoc?

A bit of each. For example, you can't say that SDI has been technologically created, because the technology is not yet there. It is a strategic idea. And what is written on the right-hand side here is a way of describing things which aren't quite as sinister and stark as that. On the other hand, there are certain imperatives within an organization towards continuity, towards following traditional patterns, towards doing things the way they've always been done. And this had been a very powerful factor. Then, after that, I think that it is an interaction between technology and strategic thinking.

---

1. 'Missile Experimental', now known as 'Peacekeeper', the main United States ICBM development for the late 1980s and 1990s.

2 *The Prospect for the Future*

(A) WITH NUCLEAR WEAPONS

(i) *Does the threat of an enemy first strike*   OR *Is there an increasing threat from accurate*
remain inconceivable for the foreseeable   *and time-urgent first-strike weapons?*
future?

I am definitely with those who believe that it's inconceivable.

(ii) *Are command, control, communication and* OR *Does the amount of information to be*
intelligence facilities likely to remain   *processed, pressure of time and fear of*
secure?   *preemption put command and control*
                                           systems under intolerable strain and make
                                           inadvertent war more likely?

No systems of this kind can be absolutely secure. There will always be vulner-
abilities. And our command and control systems, like any others, would be at
risk if there were a major crisis deteriorating towards war. There would be
intolerable strain in an intolerable situation. As in any conflict, if the commanders panic, then all sorts of things could happen. But in different circumstances it could also be dangerous if they are not properly alarmed when they
should be. You can't be dogmatic. Nevertheless, this is certainly an important
issue that requires looking at.

(iii) *If nevertheless there were a limited nuclear* OR *Is the idea that nuclear war could be*
exchange would it be likely to end   *limited once it had broken out a dangerous*
hostilities swiftly?   *illusion?*

The answer is that we cannot be sure what would happen. It might be stopped,
or it might escalate. If it came to it, we could be grateful that we had options
that gave us hope of limiting the conflict. But we would be very unwise to
work on the assumption that we can control matters, because that might well
prove to be a dangerous illusion.

(iv) *Do new generations of battlefield and*   OR *Do new battlefield and theatre weapons*
theatre nuclear systems reinforce   *threaten a dangerous lowering of the*
deterrence?   *nuclear threshold?*

The two are not contradictory. Reinforcing deterrence often requires a lowering of the nuclear threshold. But I would distinguish between the longer-range
and the short-range systems. Systems like Cruise and Pershing II have, by
and large, been helpful and positive in their influence on Soviet calculations
– in particular, by denying them the thought that they could maintain Soviet
territory as a sanctuary in war. But I have less time for battlefield systems,
which on the whole probably do just lower the nuclear threshold without
significantly reinforcing deterrence.

(v) *Does the Strategic Defence Initiative offer* OR *Is the Strategic Defence Initiative simply*
the hope of an effective defence against   *the most recent and destabilizing example*
nuclear weapons?   *of the process outlined in 1?*

The answer is quite easy. No. It does not offer the prospect of a defence against nuclear weapons, nor is it likely to affect deterrence. The whole thing is based on illusions and on faulty strategic judgement. It is little more than a cobbled together series of research programmes that have been going on anyway, and in ten years time will be seen as little more than a footnote. It will be interesting to talk about it in a nostalgic sort of way. That's all.

(vi) *Is the threat of 'horizontal' nuclear proliferation best met by a continuation of past policies?*   OR *Is continuing reliance on nuclear deterrence by the great powers bound to accelerate the process of proliferation and make nuclear war more likely?*

It's hard to show that any given potential proliferator is likely to be particularly influenced by, say, whether or not Britain stays in the nuclear business. And, so far as concerns the superpowers, a convincing case can be made the other way. You can say that by diminishing the superpower's nuclear guarantee to their allies you are creating incentives for proliferation. To some extent the Chinese thought that they needed nuclear weapons themselves, because they no longer believed in the Russian guarantee in the late 1950s. The French felt the same about the Americans. Similar influences can be said to be operating today with countries like Taiwan, South Korea, or, to a certain extent, Israel. By and large, the incentives for proliferation are found within the security environment of the potential proliferators, and that is where policy has to operate. Overall, I do think that proliferation must be seen as a danger, and there are things that could be done to tighten up current policies. But the process has been much slower than was at one time anticipated, and this is not at the moment a disaster area.

(vii) *Do multilateral arms-control negotiations offer the best prospect for future stability?*   OR *Is 'arms-control' an illusion which diverts attention from the only safe policy – nuclear disarmament?*

It depends what you think are the main sources of instability. The trouble with so much of the debate is that it tends to be too narrow. There is too much exclusive emphasis on nuclear weapons, and not enough on the broader political factors, such as East-West relations in general, which are the ones that make the nuclear arsenals stabilizing or destabilizing, and give the stimulus. Nuclear weapons are important in international politics, but so are conventional weapons. They are important in East-West relations, but differences go well beyond that. So there may be a relationship between arms control negotiations and political stability, but it is a tenuous one. The best that arms control can do is consolidate an existing stability, not create one. The fundamental sources of stability and instability are political, and that is what needs to be worked at.

Turning to the right-hand side, it again depends what we are talking about. Is it going to mean total nuclear disarmament? Is it going to be partial? If partial, are you sure that you will be in a safer relationship as a result? Is it really the case that less means safer? There are a lot of obvious questions to be asked here. There is certainly plenty of waste and surplus capacity that we can do without. But you could have a degree of disarmament that made very little difference one way or the other. Or doing without it might have important political consequences that are difficult to foresee. Again, the idea of a 'minimum deterrent' is not straight-forward either. By what criteria do we judge this? By numbers? By missions? Will the calculations become more delicate, and the situation therefore less stable, as a result? Are we to keep graded options? How will this affect the guarantee that the United States has been asked to provide for Europe? The lower the 'minimum', the more questions will be raised in Western Europe. It may challenge the credibility of extended deterrence. And so on.

So I don't see any of these measures as panaceas. The overall situation is extremely complicated, and the problem of nuclear weapons is only a part of it.

(B) WITHOUT NUCLEAR WEAPONS

(i) *If nuclear arsenals were dismantled would*   OR *Would nuclear disarmament remove the*
war between the great powers again   *incentive for nuclear preemption while not*
become a rational option and therefore   *affecting the reluctance of the great powers*
more likely?   *to initiate a third world war?*

Yes. Possibly. You would have removed one of the inhibitions against war. I'm not as convinced as are some others that, if we abandoned the nuclear deterrent, there would be war in Central Europe. I don't think that the conventional situation in itself provides incentives to war. But there might well be a greater likelihood of US-Soviet skirmishing on the peripheries.

(ii) *Would a major conventional war be likely*   OR *Is conventional war, however terrible,*
in itself to be as terrible as a limited   *preferable to nuclear war?*
nuclear war?

It depends how limited the nuclear war was. Obviously more people were killed by firebombing and so on at the end of the Second World War than in Hiroshima and Nagasaki – which counts as a kind of limited nuclear war. Major conventional war would be terrible. Let's leave it at that.

iii) *Because nuclear weapons cannot be*   OR *As with nerve gases in the last war, would*
uninvented would they not be bound to be   *there be no incentive to resort to*
used sooner or later once war had broken   *capabilities which the other side has as*
out?   *well?*

I think this is probably true. If it happened, nuclear weapons would probably be used anyway. There would be the likelihood that, during the course of a prolonged land war, both sides would be getting nuclear arsenals together. Even the assumption in the mid-to late-1940s when the Baruch Plan[1] was being talked about, was that that's what would happen. (See footnote on page 242.)

(iv) *Is global nuclear disarmament only*   OR *Is to argue that even multilateral nuclear*
feasible in a world where war itself is no   *disarmament is not desirable to give up all*
longer a possibility?   *hope of a rational world-order?*

I think that what Reagan and Gorbachev say about wanting complete nuclear
disarmament is an illusion. I don't think that politicians should peddle
illusions. I don't think you will ever get rid of the thing. You will never get
rid of war itself. All you can do is to marginalize them both, so that they
become less and less important in international affairs. That may indeed be a
worthwhile object, but it requires a different set of policies from the almost
exclusive concern with reducing nuclear weapons stocks, which seems to pre-
occupy some people. Nuclear arsenals will be with us indefinitely. We live in
the nuclear age.

(v) *Is peace only preserved when we are seen*   OR *Do the years before 1914 show what*
to be prepared for war, as failure before   *happens when military planning and the*
1939 and success since 1945 show? Under   *arms race control political choices? Do*
likely future conditions would global   *present strategies make nuclear war almost*
nuclear disarmament make war, including   *inevitable under likely future conditions?*
nuclear war, more likely?   *Is global nuclear disarmament the only*
                                                   rational policy?

I think that analogies like this are very dangerous. The situation now is different to the situation as it was in either 1914 or 1939. And often the analogy is
in any case based on a misapprehension of what was going on at the time.
There are things to be learnt from those occasions, but I don't think they are
necessarily the simple lessons that we are sometimes told that we should learn.
Study history, but don't draw too many simple analogies from it.

B *NATO Policy*

(i) *Does the Soviet Union, together with her*   OR *Are NATO and WTO forces relatively*
Warsaw Pact allies, enjoy a strategically   *evenly matched?*
dangerous military superiority in Europe?

This is very important. I'm probably somewhere in between. The Soviet
Union has taken conventional capabilities very seriously indeed and has
impressive armed forces. They are well trained and well positioned, and they
have thought about mobilization strategies and so on. On the other hand, I
think that NATO could probably cope with the Warsaw Pact better than
NATO leaders normally suggest. I am sure that Soviet Commanders do not
feel that they have reached a point of overwhelming war-fighting superiority.
They themselves are well aware of key weaknesses that could be readily
exploited. But I would not say that the two sides are 'evenly matched'. That
would be putting it too strongly. Apart from anything else, they are not trying
to do the same sort of thing.

---

1. A plan presented by Bernard Baruch on behalf of the United States Government to the first
meeting of the Atomic Energy Commission in 1946. It proposed the handing over of all potential
nuclear war-making activities to international control and the destruction of existing stocks of
weapons. It was rejected by the Soviet Union because it would perpetuate the advantages held
by the United States.

(ii) *Is the Soviet Union an expansionist power*   OR   *Is the Soviet Union an encircled and*
which will take advantage of unilateral   *threatened power trying to keep up with*
Western concessions and is only restrained   *Western technology and likely to respond*
and forced to accept arms-control   *positively to unconditional offers of*
agreements by Western determination and   *Western restraint within a general context*
strength?   *of detente?*

Although there are elements of truth in it, I do not think that conventional Western wisdom about the Soviet Union's being a simple 'expansionist power' is very helpful. The searing experiences of the last war should not be forgotten. The Soviet Union is conducting a diplomacy in which it is looking for reassurances as much as it is making threats. But the two alternatives offered here are not mutually exclusive. Encircled and threatened powers have often been expansionist in the past – that's how we got our empire! I think that the Soviet Union went into Afghanistan because it felt encircled and threatened. So its very weaknesses can make it quite dangerous. Part of the problem here is that one of its weaknesses is ideological, which, living in the way we do, we cannot help but inflame. So the West needs a tactful diplomacy, sensitive to time and occasion, which is realistic and flexible. It does not need grand gestures and ostentatious symbols, which are in any case a bad way of conducting international relations.

(iii) *Is Soviet chemical and conventional*   OR *Is NATO dependence on the early use of*
preponderance such that NATO must   *nuclear weapons unnecessary and*
continue to be able to threaten early use of   *strategically suicidal?*
nuclear weapons?

If it came to it, NATO's use of nuclear weapons probably would be suicidal. So I would prefer it if, in force planning, there were a presumption on our part that we would not use nuclear weapons first. This raises quite large issues, given the symbolism of what has been said so often in the past. But there are things that we could do in this direction, such as reduce the number of battlefield nuclear systems and instead give more thought to equivalents on the conventional side.

But I am against a declaration of No First Use, first, because I don't think that it would be believable. And, secondly, because of the effect on deterrence. If we were actually moving into a crisis, I think that a lot of the people who are now clamouring for such a declaration would be begging for it to be ignored. If Western leaders said '*we will not use nuclear weapons first*' and Soviet leaders said '*nor will we, so let's have war,*' there would be widespread alarm.

(iv) *Does the growing size of the Soviet nuclear* OR *Does the West initiate nearly all phases of*
arsenal threaten the delicate theatre and   *the nuclear arms race and continue to enjoy*
strategic balance? Would Western failure   *a substantial lead in most areas? Is the*
to match Soviet systems be destabilizing?   *nuclear 'overkill' such that the West could*
*   offer a nuclear 'freeze' or unconditional*
*   cuts without risk?*

I don't think that the balance is particularly delicate. One of the problems here is that we are dealing with elements of political perception, which in some cases can make the situation seem potentially unstable. But, by and large, we probably have enough options already not to have to match everything that the Soviets are doing. Turning to the right-hand side, it's true that the West has initiated many of the phases of the nuclear arms race, but this is by no means overwhelmingly true. The first ABM system was Soviet deployed, the first anti-satellite system was Soviet deployed, the first ICBM tests were Soviet. It's not true in all areas.

I think that the trouble with the freeze is that it would freeze the bad along with the good. It's a bit indiscriminate. It's a simple idea, but not easy to do – there are enormous negotiating problems. I don't think that it would be disastrous if there were a freeze, though. As with many of these suggestions, I'm relatively indifferent to them, because I think that they are oversold.

I feel much the same about the idea of unconditional Western cuts. There have been unconditional Western cuts, for example to certain battlefield systems, but they do not seem to have made much of an impression. It was just sensible from our own point of view – we didn't need them. Once again, this is an instrument that we might consider using in certain circumstances. At the right time it can sometimes work. But you have to know what you are doing. It's not a cure-all.

(v) *Are NATO 'forward defence' and 'deep* OR *Should NATO exploit her lead in*
strike' strategies essential for effective   *'emerging technology' to explore less*
deterrence?   *provocative alternative strategies?*

'Forward defence' simply means defending the inner German border. This may not be sound militarily, because it is a very difficult thing to do, but it has to be done in order to satisfy the West Germans. It can hardly be said to be destabilizing. As for 'deep strike', in essence it hardly counts as a new strategy (although FoFA[1] partly does, I suppose). We have had it for years in terms just of interdiction capabilities.[2] If you don't interdict, then basically what you are saying is that the Warsaw Pact forces' logistical problems are eased dramatically. In any case, interdiction of this kind is not the same as an offensive capability. To create a full invasion force you need, not just aircraft to reach Soviet territory, etc., but masses of troops, a huge logistical back-up, and so on.

---

1. Follow-on Forces Attack. The strategy of countering an enemy assault by attacking his follow-on forces.
2. The ability to deny an enemy immunity in his build-up of attacking forces.

Some alternative strategies are quite interesting and are worth looking at. Greater use of militias, greater use of fortifications, and so on, seem to me to be admirable in many ways. But only as supplements to, not replacements of, current defences. You would still have to have an effective airforce, for example. 'Emerging technology' works in all sorts of ways, not just in favour of defence.

vi) *Is it the presence of American front-line troops and the tying-in of theatre nuclear forces to the American strategic deterrent that guarantees W. European security? Should American policies therefore be supported?*   OR *Is it domination by the two super-powers that poses the greatest threat to European integrity? Would Europe be safer decoupled from the super-power nuclear confrontation? Should Europe be made a nuclear weapon-free zone?*

I think that Western Europe could move further in the direction of becoming more self-reliant and independent, but our security still basically depends upon our links with the Americans. Some people may not like American policy in Libya or the Middle East or Central America, but this should not cloud their judgement of what we need in Europe. We should remember why we were desperate for the Americans to come and help us twice this century. And how, before Russian and American power sobered us up, we were not exactly one big happy family. Although political conditions seem to be improving now, we will need our close links with America for the forseeable future. It is possible to imagine an effective alliance with the United States without the presence of large numbers of American troops in Europe. But they have been here for a long time now and have become symbols. The political consequences of trying to do something different could be very destabilizing. It could be seen as a comment on the durability of the Alliance.

A European nuclear weapon-free zone is little more than a slogan. It doesn't mean much. If the Soviet Union is not included, there is no such weapon-free zone. If the Soviet Union is included, then so must the United States be, and we are no longer just talking about Europe. The idea collapses.

vii) *Would Western unilateral nuclear disarmament invite Soviet blackmail? Are suggestions that the West should take the lead in offering unilateral disarmament initiatives the thin end of this wedge? Do radical nuclear disarmers consciously or unconsciously serve Soviet interests and threaten to undermine Western defences?*   OR *Are unilateral initiatives as part of a general programme of nuclear disarmament the only way to reverse the arms race? Is talk of 'multilateral disarmament' insincere in the mouths of those who reject all suggestion of a Comprehensive Test Ban Treaty, a Nuclear Freeze, a European Nuclear Weapon-Free Zone, or a declaration of No First Use?*

The trouble with a number of those who argue as on the right is that they see an arms race which needs to be reversed. Unfortunately, it's not as simple as this. I don't think that there is an arms race involved here in the first place. There is competition in certain areas, but arms decisions are not just determined by what the other side is doing. There are all sorts of factors at work. That's why it's so difficult to reverse the process by unilateral, bilateral or multilateral measures – there isn't any simple thing *to* reverse. It's not like making two runners turn round and run in the opposite direction, or playing a film backwards. Too much emphasis is placed on unilateral initiatives. We have all taken unilateral initiatives of one sort or another – we have cut our navies unilaterally, for example. The results have not been spectacular.

But, turning to the left, I don't think that it is useful to characterize unilateralists as serving Soviet interests. The Soviet Union often does not like them any more than NATO does. Members of END (European Nuclear Disarmament), for example, want to dismantle the Warsaw Pact as well as NATO, together with the Soviet system in Eastern Europe, a thought which the Soviet Union finds very alarming indeed.

There are no simple remedies. Some people, members of CND but not just them, do not like to talk in terms of complexities, and get very irritated when someone comes along who does not agree with them and does not just repeat word-for-word the latest government White Paper or Daily Telegraph leader. Unilateral measures may at times be helpful, but at others they may have little effect or even be counter-productive. It depends upon the circumstances.

C *British Policy*

1 *The British Deterrent*

(i) *Is Britain's deterrent a weapon of last*   OR *Would all possible uses of Britain's*
resort which guarantees her sovereignty and   *'deterrent' be suicidal? Is its only effect to*
independence and protects her from nuclear   *encourage proliferation?*
blackmail?

Any *use* of Britain's deterrent against, say, the Soviet Union would be likely to be suicidal. But that is the problem with nuclear deterrence theory in general. The question is: are there possible circumstances in which our possession of nuclear weapons would mean that the Soviet Union was more likely to lay off us? The answer is probably 'yes'. But the circumstances are unlikely and it's a marginal argument. And I wouldn't say that Britain's deterrent guarantees anything – certainly not sovereignty and independence, which can be eroded by things like economic weakness.

(ii) *Are British nuclear forces valuable to*   OR *Is the 'second centre of decision making' an*
European allies because they provide a   *illusion when the weapons are dependent*
specifically European second centre of   *upon the US and there is no independent*
decision making?   *strategic role to be played? Are European*
                                                    allies unenthusiastic about a parochial
                                                    British force likely to inhibit her
                                                    commitment to European defence?

For a variety of political reasons, not necessarily to do with deterrence, a number of Europeans are surprisingly enthusiastic about us as a nuclear power. I think that some European governments see it as a means of providing a European input into Alliance nuclear decision-making – and to some extent as a balance to the French. So far as concerns deterrence, the argument about Soviet perceptions is largely a rationalization of an underlying uncertainty about the long-term reliability of the American nuclear guarantee. If it came to it, I am not convinced that an Anglo-French or European nuclear force would be an effective alternative. In any case, at the moment, within the context of NATO strategy, this is only marginal as an argument for the retention of a British nuclear force.

(iii) *Does the US favour shared responsibility* OR *Are US forces committed anyway and and do British nuclear forces guarantee independent British initiatives more likely full US commitment to Europe and Soviet to trigger Soviet retaliation than US recognition of it? involvement?*

I think that this is once again marginal. I find the Americans rather muddled as to why we should keep our deterrent. If they think hard about it, they tend to conclude that in itself it is a bit of a waste of time and money. But they think that, because it's psychologically important to us, it's politically significant to them. They fear that, if we relinquish the nuclear option, we will no longer take ourselves seriously as a military power.

(iv) *Is the cost of the British deterrent small in* OR *Can Britain's nuclear forces only be view of the vital defence role it plays? Are afforded at the expense of conventional alternatives likely to be more expensive? strength and of other more important economic priorities?*

I think that too much has been made of the question whether we can 'afford' our independent nuclear force. As an opportunity-cost the price is not outrageous, if you think that we need it. If you don't think that we need it, then even five million pounds is too much. As it stands, alternatives are now likely to be as expensive, or even more expensive – depending again, of course, on what you think is necessary. And getting out of the nuclear business is unlikely to ease the pressure on other defence areas for more than a year or two. This is a relevant factor, but not a decisive one.

(v) *Would unilateral British nuclear* OR *Does the British deterrent encourage disarmament have no effect on other proliferation and do nothing to enhance countries and only serve to weaken British British prestige? Would British influence and allow France unchallenged disarmament within the context outlined in ascendancy in Europe? B help to break the nuclear log-jam?*

Britain's nuclear capabilities do give her influence in certain areas. We must not exaggerate this, but there is more to it than is recognized by the people who say that it's all just delusions of grandeur. But there are many other forms of influence – a number of which we have not got!

If we were to decide to give up our nuclear deterrent, we should certainly try to gain as much from it as we could. We might be able to do good work along Ghandian lines in some quarters. But again it would be unwise to expect too much.

(vi) *Is investment in Trident the best way to*   OR *Would commitment to Trident exacerbate*
continue to ensure effective British strategic   *all the drawbacks listed above?*
defence into the 21st century?

In terms of hardware, I do think that investment in Trident is the best way to
continue current policies. To the extent that the deterrent is partly seen as an
insurance against American withdrawal, there might have been a case for
looking at more national ways of doing it, but they would have been more
expensive. And now, assuming that you are committed to having a deterrent,
it's hard to think that there is a more cost-effective way of doing it. David
Owen's alternatives might have made a lot of sense when he was Foreign
Secretary, or in the early 1980s but, by the time the next election is over,
billions will already have been spent. We might as well go on with it.

2 *NATO Forces and US Bases*

(i) *Must Britain continue to share*   OR *Should British obligations to NATO be*
responsibility for manning NATO nuclear   *met by strengthening conventional forces*
systems upon which her security depends?   *where necessary within an overall non-*
Would refusal to do so fatally weaken the   *nuclear strategy as recommended in B?*
alliance?

All my inclinations are against dual-capable and battlefield systems. I would
have fewer of them. Britain could work towards this within a NATO context
without major disruption, so long as she did not make a great song and dance
about it. But I don't see what would be gained by Britain's making great
gestures here.

(ii) *Would the forced withdrawal of US*   OR *Do the large numbers of nuclear facilities*
nuclear bases from Britain make US   *yielded to the US erode British*
defence of the West impossible? Is   *sovereignty? Would their removal do no*
American interference in British affairs   *more than restore a normal peacetime*
negligible?   *relationship?*

Yes I think that it would be absolutely disastrous. It would be the most disastrous thing that a British government could do in this whole area. The effect
on the Americans would be electric. The arguments that would be used to
defend such a policy would be extremely offensive to the US Administration
and to Congress. I just don't think that you can expel the Americans and then
expect them to defend us. It is our own security that would suffer.

Do these bases erode British sovereignty? No more than, say, our membership of the EEC. It's a cost you pay. We always have the option of getting rid
of them – which is not one that, for example, the Czechs have in their relationship with the Soviet Union.

(iii) *Will Britain continue to be targeted by*   OR *Is Britain seen as an American aircraft*
Soviet warheads whether or not she   *carrier and targeted by the USSR*
disarms unilaterally?   *accordingly? Will Britain fall an early*
  victim in any superpower confrontation
  unless bases are removed?

If you asked the Norwegians or the Danes or the Dutch whether they thought that Soviet weapons were targeted on them, they would tell you that they did. When you live in a strategically awkward part of the world, as we do, you are a creature of your geographical position.

(iv) *Can non-nuclear defences only safely be* OR *In a nuclear-free Europe, decoupled from afforded by powers prepared to shelter the superpower nuclear confrontation, beneath the American strategic umbrella? would Britain no more expect to depend upon the US 'umbrella' than any other Western ally – or than Eastern Europe upon the USSR?*

If the American nuclear umbrella were removed suddenly and dramatically, I do not think that many of us would feel particularly secure. A great many questions would be asked, most notably in West Germany. I don't think that we would like the alternatives. I certainly would not feel more secure in those circumstances.

Moral considerations

(i) *Is it morally right to pursue the policy least* OR *Are there actions which are in themselves likely to cause human suffering? May this wrong no matter what the situation? Is the sometimes involve doing things which in alternative to excuse almost any act of other circumstances would be wrong? barbarism?*

I tend towards the left-hand side. Not being a clever philosopher, there are some actions for which I can barely imagine a possible moral justification. But, by and large, I am a consequentialist, I suppose.

ii) *In formulating policy should we weigh up* OR *Is the only relevant point here that a the probability of success and the relative nuclear exchange of almost any kind costs in terms of human suffering of would in itself cause unimaginable alternative nuclear and non-nuclear suffering to largely civilian populations? strategies?*

We are living in the nuclear age. We cannot escape having to work out our policies in terms of the possibility of nuclear war. There is often a jump in the argument of those on the right-hand side in your analysis. They seem to assume that there is somehow a policy readily at hand, which will free us from the obligation of having to think about the possible deaths of large numbers of civilians. There isn't. If their main preoccupation is with the fact that, as long as they themselves don't have nuclear weapons, they will not personally be responsible for using them, then I do not find this particularly uplifting.

ii) *So far as concerns intention, need we look* OR *Is there no such thing as a fully deployed no further than the fact that our sole aim in weapons system which is a bluff? Is to deploying nuclear weapons is to prevent deploy nuclear weapons to intend to use their use? them in certain circumstances?*

This is very difficult. It's unfortunate that the choice is so often presented in these terms, because I don't think that either answer is entirely satisfactory. To take the left-hand side first, it is true that one can become insensitive to the implications of what one is doing. And, if you leave certain tools lying around, then you have to accept that someone may pick them up and use them. But deterrence in a way depends upon that possibility. Turning to the right-hand side, it would possibly have been better had nuclear weapons never been invented. But here we are with them; historically they have become an integral part of international relations. So we have to think what the consequences of abandoning them would be. It is irresponsible not to do so. We cannot just concern ourselves with our own conditional intentions. And as to those intentions themselves – well, no one is actually dying at the moment, and that must make a difference. The disincentives against using these weapons are substantial, and we can do a lot to make sure that decisions to use them would not be taken frivolously. And those disincentives themselves are in the end based on the possibility of use. There is no escape from this.

So it is a moral dilemma. I can't see it as anything other than that. But it is one that is not of my creation.

(iv) *Are there possible uses of nuclear weapons* OR *Is a conditional intention to cause*
which are allowed by Just War theory, for *indiscriminate and disproportionate*
example the bombing of Hiroshima and *suffering of this kind, whether admonitory,*
Nagasaki in order to prevent worse *preemptive or retaliatory, ruled out by Just*
suffering? Can there be a theory of Just *War theory? Was it wrong to bomb*
Deterrence? *Hiroshima and Nagasaki in 1945?*

You can only judge the bombing of Hiroshima and Nagasaki in the context of its time. As horrible things had been happening, moral restraints had already been reduced. It wasn't worse than other things that had been going on. I think that it's true that those taking the decision believed in all good faith that they were preventing something worse from happening. There are even a number of Japanese who will accept this now. Historical evidence is not so conclusive here. But that is not the point. At the time they had reason to believe that the alternative was going to be a full-scale invasion of Japan. It may not have been the right decision, but I don't think we can say that it was irretrievably immoral.

Although I am myself not very happy with Just War theory – people adopt various criteria rather uncritically and do not ask themselves about their relative weighting and so on – I think that there can be a sort of theory of Just Deterrence.

(v) *Is there no relevant connection between the* OR *Is it a scandal that such huge resources are*
development and deployment of nuclear *devoted to the development and deployment*
weapons and world poverty and disease? *of nuclear weapons and not to the*
alleviation of suffering?

There are a number of answers to the implied claim on the right. First, money is not just being spent on weapons. Second, nuclear weapons cost a fraction of what is spent on conventional weapons. It is possible that cutting back on the former may mean spending more on the latter. Third, we cannot assume that any money saved would in fact be spent in the ways suggested. Finally, one of the main causes of Third World misery is, not weapons spending as such, but war. That's what you must work to prevent. And sometimes expenditure on weapons prevents war.

(vi) *Does Christian teaching allow the*   OR *Does Christian teaching condemn the*
     deployment of nuclear weapons?   *deployment of nuclear weapons?*

I am not a Christian. Pass.

Recommendations

The simple 'yes' and 'no' answers below are on their own misleading. They should be understood to be qualified by the references that accompany them.

1 No (See **B(iv)**).
2 As already explained, I dislike the Strategic Defence Initiative (See **A2**(A)(**v**)). It is based on illusions. But I have no objection to current research programmes being continued. And I don't believe that a moratorium on either anti-satellite or strategic defence programmes would be either verifiable or useful – how do you distinguish this research from other, legitimate, areas? Questions of testing and deployment are much more important.
3 A comprehensive Test Ban Treaty is, in general, a laudable objective. But I think that it is a good idea whose time is past. It would have been very influential two-and-a-half decades ago, when it was first mooted. It would not make a lot of difference now. It might have certain beneficial effects, but not, I think, the decisive influence that some people claim.
4 No (See **B(iii)**).
5 In certain areas cuts would be beneficial, and in general there is an unnecessary superfluity of weapons systems. But there are important caveats (See **A1(iv)**, **A2**(A)(**iv**) & **A2**(A)(**vii**)).
6 So far as concerns Europe, no (See **B(vi)**).
7 Yes, but not too much should be expected of it (See **A2**(A)(**vi**)).
8 No (See **A2(B)**).
9 Does not apply. For minimum deterrence see **A2**(A)(**vii**).
10 There are problems with participating in SDI which I don't think need to be elevated to matters of principle. The question is whether it is possible to maintain an honest and consistent long-term perspective on the issues raised by SDI. It would be a shame if the Allies allowed themselves to be dragged into breaking the ABM Treaty simply in order to get American contracts.
11 No (see **B(iii)**).

12 Too much emphasis is placed on the significance of unilateral initiatives (See **B(iv)** & **B(vii)**). In general, at the moment **a** is desirable as an objective for the West, but **b** is not (See **A2**(A)(**iv**)).

13 No (See 16).

14 No.

15 No (See **B(vi)**).

16 No. I have always found the arguments for and against an independent nuclear force marginal. I suppose that when forced to the crunch, I would be reluctant to see us completely out of the nuclear business, partly as it is a question of continuity, partly because I do think that there are arguments for a European capability of some sort to avoid excessive dependence on the United States.

17 Does not apply (See **CI(iv)**).

18 No (See **C2(i)**).

19 No (See **C2(i)** & **C2(ii)**).

20 Does not apply.

The Reverend
Richard Harries

Biographical Note

Born in 1936, Richard Harries served as a Lieutenant in the Royal Corps of Signals between 1955 and 1958, and was then ordained as a priest in the Church of England. After some years in a curacy in Hampshire, he moved on to become the vicar of All Saints, Fulham, between 1972 and 1981. Since then he has been Dean of King's College, London, and has just been appointed Bishop of Oxford. Richard Harries is well-known as a broadcaster, and has written and contributed to a number of books on Christian prayer, and on the ways in which Christian teaching relates to contemporary life. Of particular

253

relevance here is *Christianity and War in a Nuclear Age*, published in 1986 by A. R. Mowbray & Co., where a fuller exposition of Dr Harries' ideas can be found.

Editorial Comment

These answers were given in an interview in Dr Harries' rooms in King's College, London, on December 11, 1986. They represent the thinking of an influential Christian commentator. Of special interest here are the answers under *Moral Considerations*, in which Dr Harries offers a carefully reasoned defence of the morality of continued nuclear weapon deployment, summed up in the answer to question (**iv**). Prudential considerations reached earlier about the high probability that nuclear deterrence will succeed, and that nuclear disarmament will not (**A2**(A) and **A2**(B)), are seen to have a critical bearing on the moral outcome. But Dr Harries takes the question of intention equally seriously, and only allows that continued deployment is morally justi-fied, because an effective deterrent threat can be made which does not involve a conditional intention to inflict unacceptable direct damage on non-combatant populations.

THE REVD. RICHARD HARRIES

Global Policy

1 *The History of the Past Forty Years*

(i) *Has it been nuclear deterrence that has*   OR *Has it mainly been other factors?*
kept the peace between the great powers
since 1945?

Yes, I do think that it has been nuclear deterrence that has kept the peace.

(ii) *Does mutual possession of an invulnerable* OR *Does the threat of strategic nuclear*
second-strike strategic nuclear force prevent   *retaliation, particularly against a similarly*
war?   *armed enemy, lack credibility and invite*
    sub-deterrent encroachment?

I think that mutual possession of such a force does prevent major war between the superpowers. But I also agree with the right-hand side that it invites what you nicely call 'sub-deterrent encroachment'. Under the nuclear umbrella all sorts of things have gone on in other parts of the world. And in Europe the crushing of resistance in Hungary and Czechoslovakia, for example, was accepted by the West for fear of nuclear retaliation. But it has certainly pre-vented a major war.

(iii) *Have limited nuclear options at strategic*   OR *Have most military planners from the start*
and theatre levels enhanced deterrence by   *been aiming for nuclear war-fighting*
dramatically raising the threshold between   *superiority? Has 'flexible response'*
peace and war?   *dangerously lowered the threshold between*
conventional and nuclear war?

To make deterrence credible, you must have some kind of flexible response.
You cannot go straight from the failure of conventional forces to the threat of
a full strategic exchange. There must be a range of options. So I would agree
with the left-hand side here.

(iv) *Has the size and variety of the nuclear*   OR *Has the logic of nuclear confrontation and*
arsenals held by the superpowers stabilized   *worst-case analysis generated a dangerous*
deterrence?   *and strategically pointless superfluity of*
weapons systems?

To the extent that they are needed for flexible response, the size and variety
of nuclear arsenals stabilizes deterrence. But at the moment they are clearly
unnecessarily large, and should be cut. I would like to see a reduction to a
minimum deterrent on both sides.

(v) *Has the idea of nuclear balance between*   OR *Have ideas of 'nuclear defence' and*
the superpowers been essential to stability   *'parity' proved illusory and is 'multilateral*
and have arms-control negotiations helped   *negotiation from strength' a contradiction*
to achieve it?   *in terms? Has 'arms-control' been just*
another name for the arms race?

I do believe in the theory of balance. That is what mutual nuclear deterrence
is based on. But there has been a great deal of propaganda on both sides about
who has been 'ahead' in the so-called 'arms race'. A agree with Laurence
Martin[1] that there has been loose talk about an 'arms race', when all that has
been happening has been legitimate modernization in a number of cases.

(vi) *Has force-planning been controlled by*   OR *Has the self-reinforcing impetus of*
strategic thinking?   *technology and vested interest dictated*
policies subsequently justified post hoc?

I do take the threat of the 'military-industrial complex' seriously. There has
been a momentum behind a number of undesirable weapons developments,
which strict strategic thinking should have kept under tighter control. Many
people would say now that MIRVing weapons was a mistake. And the enormous investment in Star Wars technology carries similar dangers. But, overall,
there has been more strategic purpose behind the main developments than is
suggested on the right-hand side.

---

1. Professor of War Studies, King's College, London, 1968–1977. Now Vice-Chancellor of the
University of Newcastle.

2 *The Prospect for the Future*

(A) WITH NUCLEAR WEAPONS
 (i) *Does the threat of an enemy first strike*   OR *Is there an increasing threat from accurate*
     remain inconceivable for the foreseeable   *and time-urgent first-strike weapons?*
     future?

The fact that both sides have an invulnerable strategic nuclear second-strike
force is fundamental for me. So long as second-strike forces are secure, deterrence is stable. We have got that at the moment, and I do not see that anything
seriously threatens it. Apart from anything else, submarines are virtually
invulnerable, and are likely to remain so.

(ii) *Are command, control, communication and* OR *Does the amount of information to be*
     intelligence facilities likely to remain   *processed, pressure of time and fear of*
     secure?   *preemption put command and control*
                                                          systems under intolerable strain and make
                                                          inadvertent war more likely?

But I think that there are real worries in this area. Too much attention has
been paid to a comparison between force structures, and not enough to what
I would call 'crisis management'. We must take much more care to ensure
that wars do not break out by accident, or by a misreading of signals and so
on, and to make provision for bringing hostilities to an end as rapidly as
possible should deterrence fail. I do not have the impression that at the
moment command, control, communications and intelligence facilities are
adequate in these respects.

(iii) *If nevertheless there were a limited nuclear* OR *Is the idea that nuclear war could be*
      exchange would it be likely to end   *limited once it had broken out a dangerous*
      hostilities swiftly?   *illusion?*

If deterrence failed, the risk of escalation would, of course, be great. It must
be taken with the utmost seriousness. But I would reject the idea on the right-
hand side that escalation would be automatic. There is an alternative scenario.
We must hope that leaders on both sides would act in the common interest
and prevent it. It is dangerous for people to think that there are only two
alternatives: successful deterrence or all-out nuclear war.

(iv) *Do new generations of battlefield and*   OR *Do new battlefield and theatre weapons*
     theatre nuclear systems reinforce   *threaten a dangerous lowering of the*
     deterrence?   *nuclear threshold?*

It depends which system we are talking about here. In this country the fuss
has mainly been about Cruise, but it seems to me that it is Pershing II which
is seen by the Soviet Union to pose the serious first-strike threat. The missiles
are so accurate and the flight-time is so short that this must make the other
side nervous and tempt them to act first. So it would have been better had
Pershing II not been deployed.

(v) *Does the Strategic Defence Initiative offer* OR *Is the Strategic Defence Initiative simply*
the hope of an effective defence against   *the most recent and destabilizing example*
nuclear weapons?   *of the process outlined in 1?*

I do not favour the Strategic Defence Initiative. First of all it will not work.
But in itself it is also destabilizing. The side that thought that it was behind
on strategic defence would have to develop enormous numbers of offensive
weapons in order to penetrate the system. This could lead to another round
of the arms race. The impetus behind Strategic Defence is destabilizing.

(vi) *Is the threat of 'horizontal' nuclear*   OR *Is continuing reliance on nuclear deterrence*
proliferation best met by a continuation of   *by the great powers bound to accelerate the*
past policies?   *process of proliferation and make nuclear*
                                                  war more likely?

Here again there is a perfectly proper and serious worry. But proliferation has
been much slower than people at one time predicted. The fact that so many
countries that could have developed nuclear weapons have not done so, shows
that it is generally recognized that they only have a very limited usefulness.
Although major arms reductions by the superpowers would reinforce the will
not to develop systems in other countries, I think that this is marginal. The
power of example on the international stage is only limited.

(vii) *Do multilateral arms-control negotiations*   OR *Is 'arms-control' an illusion which diverts*
offer the best prospect for future stability?   *attention from the only safe policy –*
                                                    nuclear disarmament?

First of all, I am a supporter of arms control, even if the achievements are
limited. It does help to keep the balance stable. But I would distinguish arms
control from arms reduction, and, in the wake of Reykjavik, I think that we
can now look for real reductions, not just control.

(B) WITHOUT NUCLEAR WEAPONS

(i) *If nuclear arsenals were dismantled would*   OR *Would nuclear disarmament remove the*
war between the great powers again   *incentive for nuclear preemption while not*
become a rational option and therefore   *affecting the reluctance of the great powers*
more likely?   *to initiate a third world war?*

Here I agree with the left-hand side.

(ii) *Would a major conventional war be likely*   OR *Is conventional war, however terrible,*
in itself to be as terrible as a limited   *preferable to nuclear war?*
nuclear war?

It is a mistake to become so obsessed with the idea of eliminating nuclear
weapons that we forgot how terrible a conventional war would be. The reason
for keeping nuclear weapons is to prevent all war between the major powers.

(iii) *Because nuclear weapons cannot be uninvented would they not be bound to be used sooner or later once war had broken out?*   OR *As with nerve gases in the last war, would there be no incentive to resort to capabilities which the other side has as well?*

I agree with the left-hand side.

(iv) *Is global nuclear disarmament only feasible in a world where war itself is no longer a possibility?*   OR *Is to argue that even multilateral nuclear disarmament is not desirable to give up all hope of a rational world-order?*

So long as there is a danger of war, we need nuclear weapons. I would have welcomed an agreement of the kind proposed at Reykjavik, in which minimum forces were kept on both sides as a continuing deterrent. And, in order to make extended deterrence effective, a wide range of targeting possibilities is needed. I do not myself believe that it must include tactical nuclear weapons, nor indeed land-based INF weapons – although others disagree. But we must never get to the stage where people can think that it would be in their interest to go to war.

(v) *Is peace only preserved when we are seen to be prepared for war, as failure before 1939 and success since 1945 show? Under likely future conditions would global nuclear disarmament make war, including nuclear war, more likely?*   OR *Do the years before 1914 show what happens when military planning and the arms race control political choices? Do present strategies make nuclear war almost inevitable under likely future conditions? Is global nuclear disarmament the only rational policy?*

I agree with historians like Michael Howard who say that the 1914–18 War was not just caused by an arms race. Other factors were much more crucial. And today what matters is mutual recognition of proper spheres of influence, and stable alliances. The comparison with the years before 1914 is a false one.

B NATO Policy

(i) *Does the Soviet Union, together with her Warsaw Pact allies, enjoy a strategically dangerous military superiority in Europe?*   OR *Are NATO and WTO forces relatively evenly matched?*

The Soviet Union does enjoy conventional military superiority at the moment, although I believe that it is not as great a superiority as a number of people think. I also believe that modern precision-guided weaponry could redress the balance still further. I am not an expert on all this, but that would be my reading of it.

(ii) *Is the Soviet Union an expansionist power which will take advantage of unilateral Western concessions and is only restrained and forced to accept arms-control agreements by Western determination and strength?*   OR *Is the Soviet Union an encircled and threatened power trying to keep up with Western technology and likely to respond positively to unconditional offers of Western restraint within a general context of detente?*

All medium-to-large powers are potentially expansionist. This need not be because they are particularly malevolent, but because they feel vulnerable and want to keep their borders secure. In order to do this, they are as likely as not to be inching those borders out. This is especially the case with the Soviet Union, which has long and often ill-defined frontiers, and feels that it needs buffer states to be secure. It is determined that past history should not repeat itself. It also still officially subscribes to Marxist-Leninist ideology, which is indeed expansionist, but this has been tempered over the years, so that now the Soviet Union is a rather conservative and cautious power.

(iii) *Is Soviet chemical and conventional preponderance such that NATO must continue to be able to threaten early use of nuclear weapons?* OR *Is NATO dependence on the early use of nuclear weapons unnecessary and strategically suicidal?*

In view of Soviet non-nuclear strength, it is right that for the time being NATO keeps open the early use of nuclear weapons as a possibility. It may be true that the weapons could not in fact be used – apart from anything else, the Soviet Union lets it be known that there could be no limited use, and that early use by the West would bring massive retaliation. But the threat of that use is important in order to underpin deterrence. It is a stalemate. And NATO's nuclear weapons help to keep it that way.

(iv) *Does the growing size of the Soviet nuclear arsenal threaten the delicate theatre and strategic balance? Would Western failure to match Soviet systems be destabilizing?* OR *Does the West initiate nearly all phases of the nuclear arms race and continue to enjoy a substantial lead in most areas? Is the nuclear 'overkill' such that the West could offer a nuclear 'freeze' or unconditional cuts without risk?*

I do not think that deterrence is 'delicate', in the sense that each side has to match the other side's nuclear forces in detail. All that is needed is the generally recognized ability to inflict unacceptable damage if attacked first. Deterrence is robust enough to allow the West to make unconditional reductions in some areas without risk.

(v) *Are NATO 'forward defence' and 'deep strike' strategies essential for effective deterrence?* OR *Should NATO exploit her lead in 'emerging technology' to explore less provocative alternative strategies?*

I am very much in favour of the development of Emerging Technology in order to scale down the relative advantage enjoyed by the Soviet Union in non-nuclear force strength, and to enable NATO to reduce reliance on the likely early use of nuclear weapons. But I do not see it as an alternative to FoFA (Follow-on Forces Attack). The two go together. FoFA needs to be argued on its own merits, as the most effective defensive strategy, or not, as the case may be.

(vi) *Is it the presence of American front-line troops and the tying-in of theatre nuclear forces to the American strategic deterrent that guarantees W. European security? Should American policies therefore be supported?*

OR *Is it domination by the two super-powers that poses the greatest threat to European integrity? Would Europe be safer decoupled from the super-power nuclear confrontation? Should Europe be made a nuclear weapon-free zone?*

I agree with what is written on the left-hand side. Obviously there will eventually come a time when these American troops are no longer stationed in Europe. But that probably lies many decades ahead, when the world will be very different to what it is now. A rapid decoupling at the present stage would be very destabilizing.

(vii) *Would Western unilateral nuclear disarmament invite Soviet blackmail? Are suggestions that the West should take the lead in offering unilateral disarmament initiatives the thin end of this wedge? Do radical nuclear disarmers consciously or unconsciously serve Soviet interests and threaten to undermine Western defences?*

OR *Are unilateral initiatives as part of a general programme of nuclear disarmament the only way to reverse the arms race? Is talk of 'multilateral disarmament' insincere in the mouths of those who reject all suggestion of a Comprehensive Test Ban Treaty, a Nuclear Freeze, a European Nuclear Weapon-Free Zone, or a declaration of No First Use?*

Well, as I say, I think that there are certain steps that can be taken unilaterally by either side without fundamentally destabilizing the system. But what is needed is overall bilateral or multilateral agreement, such as seemed to be within reach at Reykjavik. As it is, I just reaffirm my view that deterrence is fundamentally stable. Many of those in the Peace Movement play on people's fears that it is unstable. I think that this is quite untrue.

C *British Policy*

1 *The British Deterrent*

(i) *Is Britain's deterrent a weapon of last resort which guarantees her sovereignty and independence and protects her from nuclear blackmail?*

OR *Would all possible uses of Britain's 'deterrent' be suicidal? Is its only effect to encourage proliferation?*

I agree with those who say that, if Britain did not already have an independent deterrent, she would not now be acquiring one. But, in a world of notorious uncertainty, where we do not know what power configurations there may be in future, since we already have a deterrent, I think that on balance we should keep it. But I do not feel nearly as strongly about this as I do about the importance of nuclear deterrence as a whole, and about Britain's role in supporting it.

(ii) *Are British nuclear forces valuable to European allies because they provide a specifically European second centre of decision making?*

OR *Is the 'second centre of decision making' an illusion when the weapons are dependent upon the US and there is no independent strategic role to be played? Are European allies unenthusiastic about a parochial British force likely to inhibit her commitment to European defence?*

This seems to me to be one of the main reasons for Britain to retain a nuclear capability. If the Americans did begin to pull out of Europe, Europe would need to have an independent deterrent to which Britain would need to contribute.

(iii) *Does the US favour shared responsibility and do British nuclear forces guarantee full US commitment to Europe and Soviet recognition of it?*

OR *Are US forces committed anyway and independent British initiatives more likely to trigger Soviet retaliation than US involvement?*

There is also something in this – that the Americans welcome shared responsibility, and fear that British nuclear disarmament would be part of a general weakening of commitment to defence.

(iv) *Is the cost of the British deterrent small in view of the vital defence role it plays? Are alternatives likely to be more expensive?*

OR *Can Britain's nuclear forces only be afforded at the expense of conventional strength and of other more important economic priorities?*

Here I would agree with the left-hand side.

(v) *Would unilateral British nuclear disarmament have no effect on other countries and only serve to weaken British influence and allow France unchallenged ascendancy in Europe?*

OR *Does the British deterrent encourage proliferation and do nothing to enhance British prestige? Would British disarmament within the context outlined in B help to break the nuclear log-jam?*

I would not lay very much stress on this. I do not really think that Britain's possession of independent nuclear forces significantly increases her influence, even with the Americans.

(vi) *Is investment in Trident the best way to continue to ensure effective British strategic defence into the 21st century?*

OR *Would commitment to Trident exacerbate all the drawbacks listed above?*

I am not a conservative, but I would support Trident on the grounds that, if we are to retain an independent deterrent, then it should be the best available. I have been largely persuaded of this by Neil Cameron, the former principal of King's College, who was a keen advocate of Trident.

2 NATO Forces and US Bases

(i) *Must Britain continue to share*   OR *Should British obligations to NATO be*
responsibility for manning NATO nuclear   *met by strengthening conventional forces*
systems upon which her security depends?   *where necessary within an overall non-*
Would refusal to do so fatally weaken the   *nuclear strategy as recommended in B?*
alliance?

I am entirely in agreement with what is written on the left-hand side.

(ii) *Would the forced withdrawal of US*   OR *Do the large numbers of nuclear facilities*
nuclear bases from Britain make US   *yielded to the US erode British*
defence of the West impossible? Is   *sovereignty? Would their removal do no*
American interference in British affairs *more than restore a normal peacetime*
negligible?   *relationship?*

Here I would certainly say that, if we are to have a nuclear deterrent system,
largely operated by the Americans, then we must support them. Not to do so
would undoubtedly seriously weaken NATO. As I say, I feel more strongly
about this than I do about the need for an independent British force.

I do not think that the existence of American nuclear bases in this country
significantly erodes our sovereignty.

(iii) *Will Britain continue to be targeted by* OR *Is Britain seen as an American aircraft*
Soviet warheads whether or not she   *carrier and targeted by the USSR*
disarms unilaterally?   *accordingly? Will Britain fall an early*
                              victim in any superpower confrontation
                              unless bases are removed?

Given our geographical position and importance within the Western Alliance,
there is no prospect of our being able to turn ourselves into a nuclear-free
sanctuary.

(iv) *Can non-nuclear defences only safely be* OR *In a nuclear-free Europe, decoupled from*
afforded by powers prepared to shelter   *the superpower nuclear confrontation,*
beneath the American strategic umbrella? *would Britain no more expect to depend*
                              upon the US 'umbrella' than any other
                              Western ally – or than Eastern Europe
                              upon the USSR?

It means nothing to say that we do not want to shelter under the American
umbrella. The umbrella is there and it continues to protect us. We *are* sheltering under it, and therefore we should help to hold the handle.

Moral Considerations

(i) *Is it morally right to pursue the policy least* OR *Are there actions which are in themselves*
likely to cause human suffering? May this   *wrong no matter what the situation? Is the*
sometimes involve doing things which in   *alternative to excuse almost any act of*
other circumstances would be wrong?   *barbarism?*

My own view is that there are certain actions which are morally wrong under all conceivable circumstances. For example, it can never be right to launch a deliberate and direct attack against millions of non-combatants. But in public life the choices that face us are not usually as clear-cut as this. We normally have to decide between evils. If we are fighting a war, whatever we do will result in the loss of civilian life. Even an attack on purely military targets will cause some civilian deaths. So, in these circumstances, other things being equal, it must be morally right to pursue the policy which we think will cause least human suffering. The important distinction here is between directly intending non-combatant casualties, and acting in such a way that non-combatant casualties are an unintended (but foreseen) consequence of our action. The former is morally illegitimate; the latter may be morally allowed, if it really is the lesser of two evils.

(ii) *In formulating policy should we weigh up* OR *Is the only relevant point here that a*
the probability of success and the relative *nuclear exchange of almost any kind*
costs in terms of human suffering of *would in itself cause unimaginable*
alternative nuclear and non-nuclear *suffering to largely civilian populations?*
strategies?

When we turn to the question of nuclear weapons, the same applies. If the statement on the right were true, if the only use of nuclear weapons was a general exchange in which hundreds of millions died, then this could never be morally justified. But this is not the only scenario that we can envisage. Although the use of any nuclear weapon would almost certainly cause terrible collateral suffering, and would also carry the risk of escalation, there can well be a restricted employment of nuclear weapons against military targets, which would not cause more overall damage than conventional weapons in the war taken as a whole. So the statement on the right-hand side is misleading.

Given the caveat against directly attacking non-combatant populations already made, I tend to agree with the statement on the left. Particularly important here is the point about the probability of success. Again, if I did not think that nuclear deterrence is fundamentally stable, I might take a very different view. But, as things are, I think that it is stable, so it is unlikely that nuclear or conventional weapons will be used by the great powers against one another at all. Insofar as that is so, the question of relative costs does not arise.

(iii) *So far as concerns intention, need we look* OR *Is there no such thing as a fully deployed*
no further than the fact that our sole aim in *weapons system which is a bluff? Is to*
deploying nuclear weapons is to prevent *deploy nuclear weapons to intend to use*
their use? *them in certain circumstances?*

But here I agree with the statement on the right. Although it is true that our overall purpose or intention is to make sure that these weapons are never used, in order that this might be so we have to deploy them, and to retain the option of using them. The targeting policy necessary to make deterrence effective is not a bluff. Nor will it do to suggest, as does Anthony Kenny, for example, that we could deploy our nuclear weapons, but publicly declare that we will never use them. This would put servicemen into an impossible situation. They are trained to use these weapons, and have to assume that they might be called upon to fire them. If they were at the same time told that there were no circumstances in which it would be moral to do so, their position would become untenable. The statement on the left-hand side is correct so far as concerns our overall intention, but, as pointed out on the right, we must also face the moral implications of the fact that deterrence involves a conditional intention to use our weapons should it fail.

(iv) *Are there possible uses of nuclear weapons* OR *Is a conditional intention to cause*
which are allowed by Just War theory, for   *indiscriminate and disproportionate*
example the bombing of Hiroshima and   *suffering of this kind, whether admonitory,*
Nagasaki in order to prevent worse   *preemptive or retaliatory, ruled out by Just*
suffering? Can there be a theory of Just   *War theory? Was it wrong to bomb*
Deterrence?   *Hiroshima and Nagasaki in 1945?*

To sum up, two considerations in particular lead me to think that there can be a Theory of Just Deterrence. First, the probability of success seems to be so high, that it is very unlikely that it will ever come to use in the first place. But, second, we are nevertheless right to take seriously the question: what if deterrence were to fail? Here it is important that there are possible morally justifiable uses of nuclear weapons, the threat of which is sufficient to make deterrence effective. These two, largely non-moral considerations – the probability of success and the possibility of restricted use – underlie my conclusion. If I thought that either or both were not true, then I might well conclude that it is immoral to deploy nuclear weapons. To that extent, although the moral principles themselves are not affected, particular moral judgements are dependent upon prudential considerations.

The question of whether the dropping of the atomic bombs on Hiroshima and Nagasaki was morally justified depends upon whether they were seen as military targets. A case can be made out on grounds of proportionality, if, as Leonard Cheshire argues, the alternative was an invasion of Japan with the likelihood of over twelve million deaths. But, on grounds of discrimination, it depends upon whether a direct attack was made on non-combatants. So far as I understand it, Hiroshima and Nagasaki were not intended as military targets, but the aim was to deliver as great a psychological shock as possible to the Japanese war leaders. In that case, these actions cannot be encompassed within Just War theory, and must be judged to have been immoral.

(v) *Is there no relevant connection between the* OR *Is it a scandal that such huge resources are*
development and deployment of nuclear   *devoted to the development and deployment*
weapons and world poverty and disease?   *of nuclear weapons and not to the*
                                               alleviation of suffering?

In terms of the world in which we live, I do not accept the connection made on the right-hand side. It is not only, or even mainly, nuclear weapons which tie up all these resources. Nor is it an 'either/or'. If nuclear weapons prevent world war, then the poor will suffer along with the rich if we get rid of them.

But, judged by the absolute standards of the Kingdom of God, it certainly is a scandal. It is part of the whole scandal of human existence. Although in worldly terms it is essential for even the most underdeveloped societies to maintain armed forces, and they would suffer if they did not, in heavenly terms it is quite wrong. Nuclear weapons carry the same ambivalence, as do so many other features of our life on earth.

(vi) *Does Christian teaching allow the deployment of nuclear weapons?*   OR *Does Christian teaching condemn the deployment of nuclear weapons?*

For the reasons already given, Christian teaching does allow the continued development and deployment of nuclear weapons. It allows this in the same way that it allows many other things necessary for the right ordering of our society. We live in a fallen world, and, in those circumstances, the churches have always taught that force or constraint are needed to protect the innocent from the criminal elements within society, and malevolent enemies without. The whole of society depends to a greater or lesser measure on the use of constraint, and it's just illusion to pretend that it does not. Indeed, Christian authorities have a positive duty to perform these functions, and proper defence against external enemies is one of them. But they must be performed in a spirit of Christian love. We must never lose sight of the deeper purpose behind our actions. This has always been central to the Christian tradition of the Just War.

But, of course, in the Augustinian City of God, none of these things would be so.

Recommendations

1 No. This is a meaningless concept.
2 Yes (See **A2(A)(v)**).
3 I know the arguments against a Comprehensive Test Ban Treaty, but I would support it, at any rate for a period, as an important sign of sincerity. I am, in fact, more worried about French tests in the Pacific than I am about the underground tests.
4 No (See **B(iii)**).
5 Yes (See **A1(iv)** & **A2(A)(vii)**).
6 They do not mean much.
7 Yes (See **A2(A)(vi)**)
8 No (See **A2(B)**).
9 Yes (See **A1(iv)** & **B(iv)**).
10 Yes.
11 No (See **B(iii)**).
12 Not a unilateral freeze. There is room for cutting down dual-capable,

battlefield and land-based INF systems, but not right down unless the Soviets reciprocate (See **B(iv)**).

13 No.
14 No.
15 No. See 6.
16 No (See **C1**).
17 Does not apply.
18 No (See **C2(i)**).
19 No (See **C2(i)** & **C2(ii)**).
20 Does not apply.

Professor
Sir Michael Howard

C.B.E., M.C.

Biographical Note

Sir Michael Howard is Regius Professor of Modern History in the University of Oxford. Born in 1922, he served with the British Army in Italy between 1943 and 1945 and was awarded the Military Cross. He was Professor of War Studies at London University between 1963 and 1968, Fellow in Higher

Defence Studies at All Soul's, Oxford, between 1968 and 1977, and held the
Chichele Chair of the History of War at Oxford between 1977 and 1980.

Sir Michael was for many years Vice-Chairman of the Royal Institute of
International Affairs, and is Vice-President of the International Institute for
Strategic Studies, on whose Council he has served since its foundation in
1958. He is also a Vice-President of the Royal United Services Institute, the
Historical Association, and the Council on Christian Approaches to Defence
and Disarmament. He is a member of the Foreign Secretary's Advisory Panel
on Disarmament and Arms Control.

Among his many books and articles, special mention may be made of *War
in European History* (1976), and *The Causes of Wars* (1983).

Editorial Comment

These answers were communicated in Sir Michael's rooms in Oriel College,
Oxford, on May 28 and November 10, 1986. Apart from the careful moral
justification of continued nuclear weapon deployment at the end, perhaps of
special interest here is Sir Michael's refusal, as an historian, to accept either
of the analogies offered in question **A2(B)(v)**; his defence of the principles
behind current NATO strategy, but criticism of the unnecessary degree of
dependence upon the likely early use of nuclear weapons, in the answers to
questions **B(i)**, **B(iii)** and **B(v)**; and his review of policy options for Britain and
recommendation of 'burden-sharing' in the answer to question **C2(iv)**. The
answer to question **A2(B)(iv)** offers a cautiously optimistic assessment of the
direction in which we seem to be heading.

SIR MICHAEL HOWARD

A *Global Policy*

1 *The History of the Past Forty Years*

(i) *Has it been nuclear deterrence that has*   OR *Has it mainly been other factors?*
kept the peace between the great powers
since 1945?

I would say that nuclear deterrence has been one factor among many, and that
it is impossible to give it weight as against the other factors.

(ii) *Does mutual possession of an invulnerable* OR *Does the threat of strategic nuclear*
second-strike strategic nuclear force prevent   *retaliation, particularly against a similarly*
war?   *armed enemy, lack credibility and invite*
                                                     sub-deterrent encroachment?

I would say that it is a powerful disincentive to anybody initiating a war, either
conventional or nuclear. It does pose a terrifying risk, which, so far, no major
power has been inclined to take. I don't think that it lacks credibility – if it

did, then it is probable that by this time somebody would have started a major war, which they have not. The question of whether it invites sub-deterrent encroachment is really a different question altogether. Indeed, if it has credibility, then it is *likely* to do so.

<table>
<tr><td>(iii)</td><td>Have limited nuclear options at strategic and theatre levels enhanced deterrence by dramatically raising the threshold between peace and war?</td><td>OR</td><td>Have most military planners from the start been aiming for nuclear war-fighting superiority? Has 'flexible response' dangerously lowered the threshold between conventional and nuclear war?</td></tr>
</table>

I think that one has to answer this in terms of different time-frames. Initially, Western military planners assumed war-fighting superiority, and deployed theatre nuclear weapons on that assumption. With the creation of nuclear parity at theatre level, the original assumptions cease to be valid, and the question then does arise as to how far the purposes for which they were originally deployed still apply. What they are now meant to do is to make it clear that a war, which begins conventionally, might well end in a nuclear fashion, and thereby increase the deterrent to conventional attack. In my view they still do that. The fact that there is now parity of nuclear weapons at every level does not, in itself, erode the credibility of a nuclear response.

<table>
<tr><td>(iv)</td><td>Has the size and variety of the nuclear arsenals held by the superpowers stabilized deterrence?</td><td>OR</td><td>Has the logic of nuclear confrontation and worst-case analysis generated a dangerous and strategically pointless superfluity of weapons systems?</td></tr>
</table>

Well, frankly, I think that both are true. I think that to some extent a spectrum of nuclear weapons does stabilize deterrence, but I think that, nonetheless, the worst-case analysis and the logic of the thing have created a ludicous superfluity of weapons systems. One could undertake a rigorous degree of pruning, without destabilizing the situation.

<table>
<tr><td>(v)</td><td>Has the idea of nuclear balance between the superpowers been essential to stability and have arms-control negotiations helped to achieve it?</td><td>OR</td><td>Have ideas of 'nuclear defence' and 'parity' proved illusory and is 'multilateral negotiation from strength' a contradiction in terms? Has 'arms-control' been just another name for the arms race?</td></tr>
</table>

The alternate answer on the right contains so many issues, which are not necessarily directly related to one another, that it is very difficult to give a succinct response to it. I think that the whole concept of balance is an illusory one. It is the wrong concept to have in mind. The concept that one has to think about is stability. And stability is not provided by equivalent numbers of weapons, which is what 'balance' suggests. It is provided by the assurance that, however many weapons the other side has, one is still going to be able effectively to deter him from their use by the credibility of one's own nuclear response. And that is not a function of the number of weapons which one has. I think that it is an illusion on the part of hard-line strategists, as well as arms-controllers and disarmers, to think that there is such a relationship. I think that the concept of each power being able to preserve an effective nuclear response *is* essential to stability. I wouldn't say that arms control negotiations have helped to achieve it. But, insofar as arms control negotiations do aim at ensuring that stability, they are not utterly fruitless.

(vi) *Has force-planning been controlled by*   OR *Has the self-reinforcing impetus of*
strategic thinking?   *technology and vested interest dictated*
                                                                             policies subsequently justified post hoc?

Much more the latter than the former. Strategic thinking has not been completely irrelevant to force planning. But I do think that bureaucratic interests and inertia have, as historically they always have, played a far larger part in determining what force structures will be. All too often strategic justification is devised post hoc – or simply produced out of files in order to justify something which has been decided upon for other reasons.

2 *The Prospect for the Future*

(A) WITH NUCLEAR WEAPONS
  (i) *Does the threat of an enemy first strike*   OR *Is there an increasing threat from accurate*
remain inconceivable for the foreseeable   *and time-urgent first-strike weapons?*
future?

When someone says that something is inconceivable, he is talking about our capacity to conceive things, not about the subject under discussion. What we are talking about here is the degree of probability. In my view, the threat of an enemy first strike remains highly improbable. It has to be admitted that the greater accuracy of new weapons-systems may marginally increase the probability, by placing the survivability of land-based missiles that much more in doubt. This does, unfortunately, mean that there is likely to be more safety in redundancy than in reduction – which I wish was not the case. But, even so, the probability of the Soviet Union's being able effectively to eliminate the whole of the American land-based nuclear retaliatory force is so remote, that I really think that it's foolish to postulate it as a basis for planning. And, in addition, so long as the sea-launch ballistic missiles are there, they will still constitute an extremely effective second-strike force and a credible deterrent.

(ii) *Are command, control, communication and* OR *Does the amount of information to be*
intelligence facilities likely to remain   *processed, pressure of time and fear of*
secure?   *preemption put command and control*
                                                                                systems under intolerable strain and make
                                                                                inadvertent war more likely?

Here, on the other hand, I would plump for the latter answer without any hesitation at all. Everything that I have read confirms my worries about the capacity of either side to be able to function effectively in these respects under crisis.

(iii) *If nevertheless there were a limited nuclear* OR *Is the idea that nuclear war could be*
exchange would it be likely to end   *limited once it had broken out a dangerous*
hostilities swiftly?   *illusion?*

I think that this is an unanswerable question. In a sense, the whole concept
of flexible response does assume the possibility of a limited nuclear exchange.
And this cannot be dismissed as impossible. But the whole thing is a question
of unassessable probabilities.

(iv) *Do new generations of battlefield and*   OR *Do new battlefield and theatre weapons*
theatre nuclear systems reinforce   *threaten a dangerous lowering of the*
deterrence?   *nuclear threshold?*

I don't think that the deployment of recent theatre nuclear systems has made
much difference. It has neither enhanced, nor eroded deterrence. There were
ample resources for immediate retaliation anyway, quite sufficient to deter the
Soviet Union from using her SS20s in a nuclear first strike against NATO
command and control systems. What is far more significant than this, although
rarely stressed, is a capacity for an effective first strike with purely conventional warheads. That would, indeed, made conventional defence that much
more difficult.

(v) *Does the Strategic Defence Initiative offer* OR *Is the Strategic Defence Initiative simply*
the hope of an effective defence against   *the most recent and destabilizing example*
nuclear weapons?   *of the process outlined in 1?*

The Strategic Defence Initiative means one of two things. It either means the
maximalist objective, as outlined by President Reagan, of rendering nuclear
weapons impotent and obsolete, by making it impossible for them to get
through; or the minimalist objective, which is for developing more effective
point-defence systems for retaliatory forces. Insofar as it does the latter, I
don't think that it is necessarily destabilizing, because it probably provides
a rather necessary technological counter to the increasing penetrability and
accuracy of missiles. Insofar as it promises to do the former, however, aiming
at an absolutely secure blanket defence, then I'm afraid that I think that it
would be destabilizing. In fact, nothing that I have seen indicates to me that
this is likely to be achieved. But what is worrying is the way in which the
President and the Administration of the United States seem to think that it is
achievable. This in itself is highly destabilizing.

(vi) *Is the threat of 'horizontal' nuclear*   OR *Is continuing reliance on nuclear deterrence*
proliferation best met by a continuation of   *by the great powers bound to accelerate the*
past policies?   *process of proliferation and make nuclear*
    war more likely?

'Horizontal' and 'vertical' proliferation are linked, but not in the way that is
generally understood. I don't subscribe to the 'Swedish' doctrine, that the
example of the great powers affects what the potential nuclear powers decide
to do. The latter will determine their policy in accordance with what they

perceive their neighbours and rivals doing within their own regional sub-systems. They will calculate the cost-benefit of diverting the very considerable resources necessary for developing any kind of credible nuclear system away from the other things they may want to do. Where there is a link is in the technical development of nuclear weapons, which occurs as an inevitable result of the armament process engaged in by the great powers. But I don't have the technological knowledge to know whether this is likely to make the development of nuclear weapons easier and cheaper. If it does, then that will in itself make 'horizontal' proliferation more likely.

(vii) *Do multilateral arms-control negotiations* OR *Is 'arms-control' an illusion which diverts*
offer the best prospect for future stability? *attention from the only safe policy –*
nuclear disarmament?

I am not particularly optimistic about current arms control talks achieving anything more than a stabilization of the status quo. But I do not see that there is a better alternative. I do not distinguish between arms control and nuclear disarmament, as suggested on the right. I have yet to be convinced that unilateral disarmament initiatives would be any way of 'breaking the log-jam'. Like democracy, arms control is the worst system – except for all the others!

(B) WITHOUT NUCLEAR WEAPONS

(i) *If nuclear arsenals were dismantled would* OR *Would nuclear disarmament remove the*
war between the great powers again *incentive for nuclear preemption while not*
become a rational option and therefore *affecting the reluctance of the great powers*
more likely? *to initiate a third world war?*

Major war did not first become a possibility when nuclear weapons were invented, and therefore the suggestion that the abolition of nuclear weapons would eliminate the causes of war is, if I may say so, a very irrational and ignorant one. So conventional war would then again become an option.

(ii) *Would a major conventional war be likely* OR *Is conventional war, however terrible,*
in itself to be as terrible as a limited *preferable to nuclear war?*
nuclear war?

I think that the answer is that a major conventional war would be less terrible than a limited nuclear war, but would lead to the possibility of a nuclear war nonetheless. You would get the worst of both worlds.

(iii) *Because nuclear weapons cannot be* OR *As with nerve gases in the last war, would*
uninvented would they not be bound to be *there be no incentive to resort to*
used sooner or later once war had broken *capabilities which the other side has as*
out? *well?*

Although you may have abolished your nuclear weapons, you have not abolished your capacity to make them, so, once conventional war has broken out, both sides are likely to race in order to produce them. The abolition of nuclear weapons would in this way only lead to their reintroduction.

(iv) *Is global nuclear disarmament only*   OR *Is to argue that even multilateral nuclear*
feasible in a world where war itself is no   *disarmament is not desirable to give up all*
longer a possibility?   *hope of a rational world-order?*

By a 'rational world order' some people mean a kind of world government in which war has simply become civil war. But we are likely to go on with a framework of nation-states for the foreseeable future. This means, I'm afraid, a framework of armaments. No doubt this is very inadequate as a way of ordering the world, but there is reason to believe that we are going to be able to go on incrementally improving it. I think that we are. In the end, I would optimistically and ideally see an incremental change-over from a system which depends upon national armaments, to one which relies on mutual agreement. Armaments would become purely symbolic – rather like the palace guard. But, in the meantime, during the whole of this (presumably long) process, it will be necessary to maintain nuclear deterrent forces.

(v) *Is peace only preserved when we are seen*   OR *Do the years before 1914 show what*
to be prepared for war, as failure before   *happens when military planning and the*
1939 and success since 1945 show? Under   *arms race control political choices? Do*
likely future conditions would global   *present strategies make nuclear war almost*
nuclear disarmament make war, including   *inevitable under likely future conditions?*
nuclear war, more likely?   *Is global nuclear disarmament the only*
   rational policy?

I'm not happy with either of these analogies. It's totally illusory to do what A. J. P. Taylor does, and say that the great armaments before 1914 were seen as deterrents, and they failed. They weren't seen as deterrents. They were seen as means of fighting a war to which many people looked forward, and which many people thought that they could win. The view that 1914 was simply a terrible accident is one which I, and a great many other historians, simply do not believe in at all. The analogy falls down.

And the same is true of the 1939 analogy, I think. That happened, basically, because Hitler saw conventional war as an effective instrument of policy, which was going to enable him to gain his objectives at minimal cost. He miscalculated. The great thing about the existence of nuclear weapons is that it is very unlikely that anybody is going to believe that war is an effective instrument of policy in the same kind of way.

3 NATO Policy

1) *Does the Soviet Union, together with her*   OR *Are NATO and WTO forces relatively*
Warsaw Pact allies, enjoy a strategically   *evenly matched?*
dangerous military superiority in Europe?

Well, the way I would put it is that I would far rather be commanding the Soviet armed forces than commanding NATO armed forces. It's not so much a question of trading tank against tank, or aircraft against aircraft. To do a bean-count in this way is to overlook what is far more important – the structural weaknesses in NATO. It is the fact that the Soviet armed forces are under one single command, speak one single language, and conform to one single strategy, that is significant. And it's the sheer lack of coordination of NATO forces, the different degrees of training, the failures of communication between them, which worry me in the event of a war. All of this could be improved dramatically without any substantial increase in the actual number of armaments.

(ii) *Is the Soviet Union an expansionist power* OR *Is the Soviet Union an encircled and* *which will take advantage of unilateral* *threatened power trying to keep up with* *Western concessions and is only restrained* *Western technology and likely to respond* *and forced to accept arms-control* *positively to unconditional offers of* *agreements by Western determination and* *Western restraint within a general context* *strength?* *of detente?*

I think that it is true that the Soviet Union is essentially a defensively-oriented power. It certainly does see itself threatened by Western technology, and by Western ideology. Even if the technological conflict and the conflict over Eastern Europe were eroded, there will still remain a fundamental ideological hostility and lack of understanding, which is going to keep the Soviet Union profoundly suspicious.

But the Soviet Union sees its best security in extending its perimeter when it can. It is not a naive power, and is quite capable of exploiting naivety in the West. It will exploit divisions between allies, and weaken us in every way that it possibly can. So, should we make unconditional offers? Should we allow ourselves to be weakened? Will it in fact lead to a greater degree of mutual understanding? I'm afraid that I still believe that it's better to try to preserve coherence and firmness in the Western Alliance, when dealing with the Soviet Union.

(iii) *Is Soviet chemical and conventional* OR *Is NATO dependence on the early use of* *preponderance such that NATO must* *nuclear weapons unnecessary and* *continue to be able to threaten early use of* *strategically suicidal?* *nuclear weapons?*

I believe that we should have a force structure that enables us to fight success-fully with conventional weapons for the longest possible time, and in this way delay the introduction of nuclear weapons to the last possible moment. The Soviet Union needs to perceive that, even if we don't use our nuclear weapons, she will still suffer very heavy losses. But to abandon the possibility of the use of nuclear weapons is virtually to hand the game to the Soviet union, who might then be prepared to accept heavy conventional losses in the belief that she would eventually prevail. So I would wish to retain the nuclear option in Western strategy, but to make it an option for late use, rather than for early use.

It is true that, if it ever came to a major theatre nuclear exchange, then – *finis* Europa, East and West. So the use of nuclear weapons would be intended only to show that one had reached a point of such despair, that one was prepared to gamble on the possibility of a limited nuclear war, rather than admit total defeat. It is not a decision that I would wish to have to take.

(iv) *Does the growing size of the Soviet nuclear* OR *Does the West initiate nearly all phases of*
arsenal threaten the delicate theatre and   the nuclear arms race and continue to enjoy
strategic balance? Would Western failure   a substantial lead in most areas? Is the
to match Soviet systems be destabilizing?   nuclear 'overkill' such that the West could
*   offer a nuclear 'freeze' or unconditional*
*   cuts without risk?*

I think that the balance is not delicate at all. I also think that it's true that the West initiates nearly all phases of the nuclear arms race. On the other hand, the Soviet Union is very good at catching up and overhauling us, and I do not think that it's true that the West 'enjoys a substantial lead in most areas'. In those areas in which we do enjoy a lead the Soviet Union is hot on our heels.

The problem with a 'freeze' is choosing the moment when you can have a freeze, when neither side feels that it is at a disadvantage. So far nobody has found the precise point to do that.

As for 'unconditional cuts', we come up against the problem of what might be called the 'arms control game', in which there are protests that we should not give anything away without a quid pro quo. This is an argument that I simply don't buy. If you don't need the weapons, why have them? We are beginning, very reluctantly, to say that we have got far more theatre nuclear weapons than we need – and have, in fact, unconditionally abolished 2000 of the 6000 or so that we had.

v) *Are NATO 'forward defence' and 'deep*   OR *Should NATO exploit her lead in*
strike' strategies essential for effective   'emerging technology' to explore less
deterrence?   *provocative alternative strategies?*

There are two points to be made here. The first is that, if we stand purely on the defensive, the war will be fought on our territory – or, rather, West Germany territory. The second is rather more axiomatic. As Clausewitz has said, all defence must involve the concept of some kind of counter-strike. Just to sit there and allow oneself to be subjected to enemy blows is not defence at all. I have yet to see a convincing 'alternative strategy', which would hold out the prospect of eventually being able to destroy the weight of attack, which Soviet forces can bring against us – including their command of the air. Relatively untrained reservists, manning local point-defences, for example, simply would not be able to stand up to the sustained intensity of Soviet pressure. And the idea that 'emerging technology' will necessarily favour defence over attack is illusory.

So the military concept that the way to stop a Soviet attack is to absorb as much of it as you can in your front line, and then launch attacks against their lines of communication to prevent the follow-on forces from coming on, seems to me to be sound strategy and sound deterrence. Nor does it seem to me to be particularly provocative. So I don't have a problem about that.

(vi) *Is it the presence of American front-line troops and the tying-in of theatre nuclear forces to the American strategic deterrent that guarantees W. European security? Should American policies therefore be supported?*

OR *Is it domination by the two super-powers that poses the greatest threat to European integrity? Would Europe be safer decoupled from the super-power nuclear confrontation? Should Europe be made a nuclear weapon-free zone?*

About this I say two things. First, neutrality. It takes three to make a neutral. To declare that you are neutral or nuclear-free means nothing, unless the two belligerents are prepared to agree that you are. Neutrality is the privilege of certain geographically favoured areas. But an area like Western Europe, which is on the direct line between the two main belligerents, cannot possibly be regarded as neutral by them if the balloon were to go up. In these circumstances, the Soviet Union would either occupy Western Europe, or demand such guarantees as virtually to erode our sovereignty. And we could not prevent the use of nuclear weapons against us, or the seizure of parts of our territory as bases for nuclear weapons.

Secondly, I think that the idea that there can be a safe 'no-man's land' of this kind would in any case by a recipe for disaster. A large 'neutral' zone would be a constant prey for subversion by both sides, as each tried to support those within the area who they thought were inclined in their direction. There would be the perpetual danger of conflict and instability within every European country. It is the clarity of the distinction of the frontier, where there can be no doubt whatever where the border lies, that is the best security for peace in Europe and for peace in the world.

The presence of American front-line troops, and the tying-in of Western defences to the American stratetic nuclear deterrent, are fundamental in making it quite clear to the Soviet Union that their frontier stops at the Iron Curtain, and that there is a powerful alliance, which is going to make any use of military force as a means of attaining political objectives highly counterproductive.

(vii) *Would Western unilateral nuclear disarmament invite Soviet blackmail? Are suggestions that the West should take the lead in offering unilateral disarmament initiatives the thin end of this wedge? Do radical nuclear disarmers consciously or unconsciously serve Soviet interests and threaten to undermine Western defences?*

OR *Are unilateral initiatives as part of a general programme of nuclear disarmament the only way to reverse the arms race? Is talk of 'multilateral disarmament' insincere in the mouths of those who reject all suggestion of a Comprehensive Test Ban Treaty, a Nuclear Freeze, a European Nuclear Weapon-Free Zone, or a declaration of No First Use?*

In response to the questions on the left, I do not myself believe that radical nuclear disarmers consciously serve Soviet interest. But the divisiveness of their proposals, sincere as they are, does provide for a kind of incoherence in Western policy, which the Soviet Union naturally exploits. That is, I'm afraid, what happens in pluralistic democracies, and one has got to put up with it.

Turning to the questions on the right, I agree that, when Gorbachev or

Reagan say that their aim is to abolish nuclear weapons, they are being insincere. Both, fundamentally, wish to preserve their nuclear deterrents. And it's high time they came out and said so. It's also true that, if the United States were prepared to make certain unilateral initiatives, of a kind that could generally be seen not to erode her own security, but might be reassuring to the Soviet Union (and I believe that this might be possible), then this would be all to the good. But it is the United States, not Western Europe, which is significant here. And the rejection of a Comprehensive Test Ban Treaty, a Nuclear Freeze, a European Nuclear Weapon Free Zone, a Declaration of No First Use, and so on, is made on the perfectly practical grounds that they could be counter-productive.

C British Policy

1 The British Deterrent

(i) *Is Britain's deterrent a weapon of last resort which guarantees her sovereignty and independence and protects her from nuclear blackmail?*   OR *Would all possible uses of Britain's 'deterrent' be suicidal? Is its only effect to encourage proliferation?*

Within the context of a conflict with the Soviet Union, in which we were not members of an alliance, I cannot see our deterrent being credible. But in the world as it may develop in the 21st century, the Soviet Union may not be the only nuclear power with which we may be in conflict. I do find the argument, that, if the Argentines had had nuclear weapons, we might have had major problems in the recent war, quite persuasive. For that reason I think that there is a lot to be said for remaining in the nuclear game without necessarily thinking of maintaining credibility against the Soviet Union.

ii) *Are British nuclear forces valuable to European allies because they provide a specifically European second centre of decision making?*   OR *Is the 'second centre of decision making' an illusion when the weapons are dependent upon the US and there is no independent strategic role to be played? Are European allies unenthusiastic about a parochial British force likely to inhibit her commitment to European defence?*

In the past the 'second centre of decision-making' argument has not been very convincing, and our European allies, and in particular the West Germans, have not been enthusiastic about our possession of our nuclear weapons. But, as there comes to be increasing fear of decoupling from the United States, then the value of there being nuclear decision-makers on this side of the Atlantic does, I think, become more apparent to our continental allies. I also think that it is arguable that one does not so much need a second centre for decision-making if the United States is the first centre, but that, if the alternative is for Paris to be the only centre, then many of us would feel safer if there were another one as well.

(iii) *Does the US favour shared responsibility* OR *Are US forces committed anyway and*
and do British nuclear forces guarantee *independent British initiatives more likely*
full US commitment to Europe and Soviet *to trigger Soviet retaliation than US*
recognition of it? *involvement?*

I do think that the United States forces are committed anyway. The reason why they are prepared to help us to produce Trident is not because they think that this will in itself significantly strengthen the Western alliance, but because they fear that our giving up of our independent nuclear forces would be seen to be a weakening of our will to defend ourselves and our allies. But, in general, their defence decision-makers regard the British independent deterrent as more of an embarrassment than anything else.

(iv) *Is the cost of the British deterrent small in* OR *Can Britain's nuclear forces only be*
view of the vital defence role it plays? Are *afforded at the expense of conventional*
alternatives likely to be more expensive? *strength and of other more important*
economic priorities?

All I would say here is that nuclear weapons are still very cheap compared with conventional forces.

(v) *Would unilateral British nuclear* OR *Does the British deterrent encourage*
disarmament have no effect on other *proliferation and do nothing to enhance*
countries and only serve to weaken British *British prestige? Would British*
influence and allow France unchallenged *disarmament within the context outlined in*
ascendancy in Europe? *B help to break the nuclear log-jam?*

The idea that British unilateral nuclear disarmament would have any effect on other powers seems to me to be a sort of colonialist attitude – an assumption that Britain still provides moral leadership in the world. I do not believe that the Indians, or the Israelis, or the Pakistanis, or any of the other near nuclear powers, would be in the least interested in what Britain does or does not do.

What I think that it would do would be to weaken British influence on decision-makers in the United States. Unless it was accompanied by a really spectacular increase in our conventional capabilities, it would simply be taken as evidence that our will to defend ourselves was being eroded.

(vi) *Is investment in Trident the best way to* OR *Would commitment to Trident exacerbate*
continue to ensure effective British strategic *all the drawbacks listed above?*
defence into the 21st century?

I don't agree with the implication behind the question on the right. I don't think that commitment to Trident makes any difference in those respects. But nor do I accept that it is the only or best way to continue to ensure effective strategic defence. A capacity to explode a very small number of warheads on Soviet soil is a very effective deterrent, as the recent events at Chernobyl indicate. It is certainly not necessary for us to be able to penetrate the defences of Moscow and destroy Soviet headquarters, or to eliminate sixty Soviet cities. This is grotesque overkill. Arguments in favour of Trident along these lines are not valid.

2 *NATO Forces and US Bases*

(i) *Must Britain continue to share responsibility for manning NATO nuclear systems upon which her security depends? Would refusal to do so fatally weaken the alliance?*   OR *Should British obligations to NATO be met by strengthening conventional forces where necessary within an overall non-nuclear strategy as recommended in B?*

I think that, if we accept the overall NATO strategy, then we have got an obligation to do whatever is considered necessary within the alliance to play our part in upholding it. There are understandable reasons why neither Norway nor Denmark wish to have nuclear weapons on their soil, because they are part of a sort of Baltic balance, whose nuances have got to be taken into account. We have no excuses of that kind. Either we are full members of the Alliance, playing a full part in it by whatever is regarded as effective burden-sharing, or we are not. I really don't see a sort of half-way house.

(ii) *Would the forced withdrawal of US nuclear bases from Britain make US defence of the West impossible? Is American interference in British affairs negligible?*   OR *Do the large numbers of nuclear facilities yielded to the US erode British sovereignty? Would their removal do no more than restore a normal peacetime relationship?*

The withdrawal of US bases from Britain would, clearly, not make the defence of the West impossible. But they are there for a strategic purpose, and their removal would therefore create difficulties. What it would do, it seems to me, is unnecessarily to create major complications within the Western Alliance, and to that extent destabilize what I think is still a relatively stable relationship between the East and the West. The presence of these bases on our soil is to some extent an erosion of sovereignty, but it is arguable that this is a price which one has to pay for being part of any larger kind of community, whether it is the EEC or NATO or anything else.

(iii) *Will Britain continue to be targeted by Soviet warheads whether or not she disarms unilaterally?*   OR *Is Britain seen as an American aircraft carrier and targeted by the USSR accordingly? Will Britain fall an early victim in any superpower confrontation unless bases are removed?*

In a conflict between the Alliance, as it is at present, and the Soviet Union, there are a large number of legitimate military targets for the Soviet Union in Britain, apart from any nuclear bases and facilities – for example, places like Portsmouth, or Harwich, from which our reinforcements could sail or on which our Fleet is based. If we tried to remove ourselves from the Alliance, or to declare some sort of neutrality, then both the United States and the Soviet Union might feel that they would have to occupy us or deny occupation to the other.

So I see no safety whatever in trying to subtract ourselves from the equation.

(iv) *Can non-nuclear defences only safely be*   OR *In a nuclear-free Europe, decoupled from*
afforded by powers prepared to shelter   *the superpower nuclear confrontation,*
beneath the American strategic umbrella?   *would Britain no more expect to depend*
upon the US 'umbrella' than any other
Western ally – or than Eastern Europe
upon the USSR?

There are a number of different possibilities here. We have already rejected the possibility of a totally non-nuclear and neutral Europe. Then there is the possibility that Britain could opt out of the alliance, irrespective of what else is done in Europe. Britain would lose all capacity to influence the policy of those still in the Alliance, the Alliance would be severely weakened, and this would be likely to produce a very much more unstable situation than the one we have at present.

A third possibility we have also already dealt with – that we remain a member of the Alliance, but tell the United States to remove their nuclear bases from our soil. So we are left with a fourth possibility, which in many ways I favour. It is one of burden-sharing, in which we leave strategic nuclear forces to the United States, and ourselves concentrate on non-nuclear forces on a simple cost-effective bases. We would continue to provide nuclear facilities for the United States and to be members of an alliance, whose strategy is based fundamentally on American strategic nuclear retaliatory capability.

Moral Considerations

(i) *Is it morally right to pursue the policy least* OR *Are there actions which are in themselves*
likely to cause human suffering? May this   *wrong no matter what the situation? Is the*
sometimes involve doing things which in   *alternative to excuse almost any act of*
other circumstances would be wrong?   *barbarism?*

I think that there is a false apposition in the statement on the right. An action is 'in itself' morally neutral. What makes it moral or immoral is motive and consequence. The infliction of pain as an act of sadism is morally wrong; the same action carried out as a judicious punishment is not morally wrong, and may be morally desirable. Then there are notorious grey areas. Is it morally wrong to inflict pain in order to eliminate injustice? This will depend upon the circumstances. If you have an IRA prisoner, and know that he has set a time-bomb to go off in Oxford Street, is it not right to inflict great pain on him in order to find out where it is before it is too late? But in these cases you have to be certain. The more difficult it is to see the moral justification for an action, the more certain you need to be that there is a good moral reason for doing it. You could probably work out some sort of matrix for this. So, in these general terms, I would agree that, if your intention is to maximize human welfare and minimize human suffering, you will sometimes be morally right to do things which in other circumstances would be morally wrong.

(ii) *In formulating policy should we weigh up* OR *Is the only relevant point here that a*
the probability of success and the relative *nuclear exchange of almost any kind*
costs in terms of human suffering of *would in itself cause unimaginable*
alternative nuclear and non-nuclear *suffering to largely civilian populations?*
strategies?

Now we apply this to nuclear weapons deployment and use. There are, in fact, two separate, but related, issues here. There is, first of all, the question of whether there are particular limited uses of nuclear weapons that could in certain circumstances be morally justified. Second, there is the question of how great the risk would be that the limited action would escalate towards an all-out nuclear exchange. When the only nuclear weapons were very large and very dirty, the situation was simpler. But now, thanks to the confounded scientists, one does have a very wide range of nuclear weapons, some of which do no more damage than so-called 'conventional' weapons. I think that it is very necessary to keep these two issues separated out, because it is all too often said that the use of nuclear weapons is automatically an annihilating strategy. It is not. The statement on the right is incorrect, and, if I may say so, patently incorrect.

(iii) *So far as concerns intention, need we look* OR *Is there no such thing as a fully deployed*
no further than the fact that our sole aim in *weapons system which is a bluff? Is to*
deploying nuclear weapons is to prevent *deploy nuclear weapons to intend to use*
their use? *them in certain circumstances?*

This is a central issue. As far as I remember, the American Catholic bishops[1] say that it is morally all right to deploy nuclear weapons, as long as you don't intend to use them. This seems to me to be the weak point in their letter. To deploy nuclear weapons without intending to use them is self-contradictory. You do not develop Polaris submarines and train people to man them, if you *know* that, when it comes to the point, you are not going to use them. There may be a reasonable doubt as to whether you will. There will always be a chance that you will not. But the effectiveness of deterrence cannot be separated from the possibility that you will use your weapons. Deterrent forces cannot be a bluff. To that extent, the statement on the right is correct. And there is another weakness in the statement on the left. Given NATO strategy at the moment, the function of nuclear weapons is not simply to prevent the use of nuclear weapons by the other side. We do retain the option of first use – unfortunately.

(iv) *Are there possible uses of nuclear weapons* OR *Is a conditional intention to cause*
which are allowed by Just War theory, for *indiscriminate and disproportionate*
example the bombing of Hiroshima and *suffering of this kind, whether admonitory,*
Nagasaki in order to prevent worse *preemptive or retaliatory, ruled out by Just*
suffering? Can there be a theory of Just *War theory? Was it wrong to bomb*
Deterrence? *Hiroshima and Nagasaki in 1945?*

The right-hand side has already been dismantled. There are possible uses of

---

1. In the Pastoral letter, *The Challenge of Peace* (1983).

nuclear weapons, which in certain circumstances could be moral justified in the same way that the use of conventional weapons would be. For example, the destruction of a comparatively isolated military target in, say, the Kola peninsula, which would be likely to pre-empt a Soviet attack and prevent worse damage, while not carrying with it a high risk of escalation. And, if there are possible uses of nuclear weapons which do fit in with the principle of proportionality of Just War theory, then Just Deterrence is possible, too.

As to the question of Hiroshima and Nagasaki, there are two issues here. Given the perceptions and the state of knowledge of the time, was it a reasonable, and not immoral, decision to take? And, secondly, with hindsight, knowing what we do now, would we have done the same? Let us set the second question on one side. We now think that it would not have been necessary to invade Japan, because they were in any case on the verge of economic collapse. So for that reason we may say that the dropping of the bombs was unnecessary. But at the time this was not known. It was genuinely thought that, if the bombs were not dropped, the Japanese would go on fighting. Moreover, we must remember the ethics of the period. The destruction of Hiroshima and Nagasaki by single bombs was surely no more morally reprehensible than the destruction of Tokyo with rather higher casualties by fire-raids carried out by larger numbers of planes. It is the difference between being killed by a single bullet and a shot-gun. The question of radiation after-effects was not thought through as fully as it should have been, although the whole thing is still an open issue. So the question of the morality of the destruction of Hiroshima and Nagasaki is part of a wider question of the morality of area bombing in general. Would it have been better had Strategic Air Command used fire-bombs to burn every Japenese city, one after the other, with comparable casualties?

(v) *Is there no relevant connection between the*   OR *Is it a scandal that such huge resources are*
development and deployment of nuclear   *devoted to the development and deployment*
weapons and world poverty and disease?   *of nuclear weapons and not to the*
                                                 alleviation of suffering?

If we could be sure that a peaceful order would be preserved without the deployment of nuclear weapons, then we should dismantle them and devote the proceeds to the alleviation of suffering. But I have argued that this is not the case. We must continue with the search for a way of preserving the structure of order at far less cost, but must on no account put that structure at risk in the process. More relevant to this is the question of armaments in general, both the sale of arms to the Third World, and the over-investment by Third World states in military affairs and resources which they ought to be devoting to the welfare of their people and the infrastructure of their economiies. If there is any scandal about the failure to relieve suffering, it is about the general self-indulgence of the rich North and West. We could help to relieve suffering by paying rather more income tax, and by drinking and smoking less.

(vi) *Does Christian teaching allow the*   OR *Does Christian teaching condemn the*
deployment of nuclear weapons?   *deployment of nuclear weapons?*

If what I have said is valid, then Christian teaching does not condemn the deployment of nuclear weapons. But it does rather depend upon what you mean by 'Christian teaching'. I find that Roman Catholics tend to see Christian teaching as being an area of discourse which has been going on ever since the time of the early fathers. It is an attempt to define these issues in the light of what we know, or think we know, about God's providence, as applied to the development of humanity and human kind. And there is no single Christian dogma here. Christian teaching provides parameters, a framework, within which one takes decisions. Then there is the Protestant ethic, which does tend to try to draw clear and specific conclusions from Gospel teaching about what we should or should not do. It is Protestents, on the whole, who press for black-and-white judgements. I am more of a Catholic by temperament, and, I suppose, by upbringing. I look to the church for a framework of guidance, within which I and other people can decide what is the best thing to do under the circumstances. Official teaching does not rule out nuclear weapon deployment. It is not happy with it. But there is a great deal in a sinful world about which one is not happy.

Recommendations

1 No (see **B(iv)**).
2 I favour a moratorium on anti-satellite programmes. A general moratorium of Strategic Defence Programmes would be nice, but, since it would be impossible to monitor and there would be constant reciprocal accusations that it was being breached, I think that this would create far more tensions than it would resolve (see **A2(A)(v)**).
3 No. I see no point in it. I don't think that it would make the world any safer.
4 No (see **B(iii)**).
5 I would like to feel that each side would scrutinize its nuclear arsenals and decide what it could dispose of. But cuts do not necessarily produce greater stability, and could produce greater instability (see **A1(i)**, and 9 below).
6 Not in Europe (see **B(vi)**).
7 It would be nice if those powers, which have not yet signed, would do so. But tell that to the Indians. I don't see much point in this sort of declaration.
8 No, not in a context where we are still likely to have endemic war (see **A2(B)**).
9 By definition, a 'sufficient' force would be stable, because each side would decide what was 'sufficient'. I suspect that for this reason it would not do much to change the situation. On the other hand, if nuclear arsenals were reduced to the level where a first strike again began to look like a feasible

possibility, this would produce greater instability. To that extent, a degree of redundancy enhances stability.

10 No. I think that we have done the right thing. We have used our influence with the Americans to persuade them to give a satisfactory definition of what is involved. First, that the objective is to enhance deterrence, not get away from it; second, that this is at present just a research programme in order to keep us abreast of the Soviet Union; third, that there will be careful consultation within the Alliance and with the Soviet Union, if and when the question of deployment is raised. This is a good example of Britain, as a member of the Alliance and a nuclear power, being able to influence policy.

11 No. See 4.

12 No. (See **B(iv)**).

13 No. (See **C1(ii)**).

14 No.

15 No. (See **B(vi)**).

16 No. (See **C1**).

17 Does not apply.

18 Britain should remain in NATO, but not press for a non-nuclear strategy. Perhaps there could be more cost-effective burden-sharing, in which strategic nuclear defence was left to the United States and we concentrated on strengthening non-nuclear forces (See **C2(iv)**).

19 No. (See **C2(i)** & **C2(ii)**).

20 Does not apply.

Rebecca Johnson

Biographical Note

Rebecca Johnson has lived and worked at the Greenham Common Women's Peace Camp since August 9, 1982. She has been imprisoned many times for her non-violent resistance to male violence, bases, bunkers, and nuclear war preparations. Prison has increased her determination to use her life working for peace, freedom and justice, with love.

Editorial Comment

This set of answers was recorded at an interview in Marlborough on November 11, 1986. Rebecca Johnson is the only woman whose views are included in this book. For her this is a highly significant fact, as can be seen from the wording of the biographical note, and, above all, from the penultimate paragraph of her response to the *Moral Considerations* at the end. Equally important, and linked to it, is her rejection of the rational and dispassionate terms within which this issue is usually debated, and her insistence that, both from the point of view of those responsible for the implementation of public policy, and from the point of view of those who may be affected by it, this is a matter that can only be properly responded to in a directly personal and emotional way. In her answers to the questions in section **A2**(B), and in *Moral Considerations*, she may be speaking for a considerable number of people not represented elsewhere in this book.

REBECCA JOHNSON

A *Global Policy*

1 *The History of the Past Forty Years*

(i) *Has it been nuclear deterrence that has*   OR *Has it mainly been other factors?*
kept the peace between the great powers
since 1945?

There has not really been peace between the great powers in the last forty years. They have been trying to increase their spheres of influence and fight out their ideological conflicts by supporting and equipping other groupings. To say that it is nuclear weapons that have kept the peace is as ludicrous to say that it was mustard gas that kept the peace in the years after 1918. We could see the conditions that were leading to the Second World War then, and we can see them now – mutual mistrust, constructed paranoia about the enemy, weapons build-up. The problem is that today we have nuclear weapons, so we cannot allow the naivety that was possible between 1919 and 1939 to prevail now. The Second World War followed from the conflicts unresolved and created at the end of the First World War. If we continue with the naive view of a balance of terror in the world, then the Third World War, the nuclear war, is going to follow on from the military conflicts that we are seeing now.

(ii) *Does mutual possession of an invulnerable*   OR *Does the threat of strategic nuclear*
second-strike strategic nuclear force prevent   *retaliation, particularly against a similarly*
war?   *armed enemy, lack credibility and invite*
                                                     sub-deterrent encroachment?

Nuclear deterrence theory is strategically incoherent. Mutual Assured Destruction just displaces the fighting for a time in the way that I have described. But the scientists and military strategists are not satisfied with this, and in the 1960s they started to refine nuclear weapons so that they could be used to fight a war. The trouble is that there are all sorts of factors involved in wars. War is not just about military power – it's about political and economic competition. And these tensions and rivalries have not been resolved. So the incentive to war remains, and, the military mind being what it is, strategists could not be satisfied with stasis.

(iii) *Have limited nuclear options at strategic* OR *Have most military planners from the start*
and theatre levels enhanced deterrence by *been aiming for nuclear war-fighting*
dramatically raising the threshold between *superiority? Has 'flexible response'*
peace and war? *dangerously lowered the threshold between*
conventional and nuclear war?

The result of this has been the introduction of tactical battlefield nuclear weapons and so on, which have narrowed the gap between conventional and nuclear war, and changed our perceptions, so that now we are planning for limited nuclear war. All of this, of course, increases the likelihood that there will be such a war, and it won't be limited.

(iv) *Has the size and variety of the nuclear* OR *Has the logic of nuclear confrontation and*
arsenals held by the superpowers stabilized *worst-case analysis generated a dangerous*
deterrence? *and strategically pointless superfluity of*
weapons systems?

The size and variety of nuclear arsenals is part of the military perception that war can be fought with nuclear weapons. It is also very dangerous, because this vast number of weapons all have to be tested, stored, based, modernized – and this increases the possibility of accidental use or misuse, as well as radioactive pollution and contamination in places like the Pacific, where the Islanders have been victims of our 'Nuclear Peace' for forty years.

(v) *Has the idea of nuclear balance between* OR *Have ideas of 'nuclear defence' and*
the superpowers been essential to stability *'parity' proved illusory and is 'multilateral*
and have arms-control negotiations helped *negotiation from strength' a contradiction*
to achieve it? *in terms? Has 'arms-control' been just*
another name for the arms race?

The right-hand side is correct. I think that each side does aim for superiority. But, even if the planners in the Pentagon or the Kremlin are aware of exactly what the weapons levels are on each side, it is usually in their interest in terms of domestic political control to put out different stories to their people. If their aim is to build up military arsenals, they say that the other side has more; if their aim is to reassure their own people, they say that their own defences are strong. But I get impatient with having to go through all the arguments about balance and deterrence, when that is not where the important changes have to happen.

(vi) *Has force-planning been controlled by*   OR *Has the self-reinforcing impetus of*
     strategic thinking?   *technology and vested interest dictated*
                                                     policies subsequently justified post hoc?

I agree with the right-hand side. I think we have seen this very clearly with
Star Wars. Reagan is clinging to Star Wars, because he has already sold a
number of the contracts for research and development, and because he knows
that Republican party votes are going to depend in certain key areas on the
industry that is now already gearing up to investment in the programme. It
doesn't matter that the concept of Star Wars is a military nonsense, as long as
somebody is making money out of it. With things like Cruise and Pershing,
though, it was rather different. The military planners wanted a system that
was difficult to detect, could fly below the level of radar, and be launched
from various platforms, which Cruise can do; and be swift and accurate, like
Pershing. Military planning and industrial enterprise are hand-in-glove. Huge
profits are made from keeping us in fear. So much money and power become
vested in the arms industry and trade, the spiralling replacement of each new
technology and system. It would take a brave government to expose the waste,
risk the wrath of the warmongers, and try to rechannel the research and
resources into socially useful areas.

2 *The Prospect for the Future*

(A) WITH NUCLEAR WEAPONS
 (i) *Does the threat of an enemy first strike*   OR *Is there an increasing threat from accurate*
     remain inconceivable for the foreseeable   *and time-urgent first-strike weapons?*
     future?

The left-hand side is nonsense. The United States has always refused to give
an undertaking of 'no first use', and now France has reversed her earlier policy
and is wanting to develop a military arsenal which will make first- and second-
strike feasible. The dangers are, first, of accidental firing, because wrong
signals are sent through the computer, or there is a wrong interpretation of
them on the ground. And, second, the new first-strike weapons increase the
strain of bluff. In a situation of tension, with both sides jockeying for position,
throwing out propaganda both to the other side and to their own public,
watching one another, both afraid that the other will strike first and take out
command centres and weapons in their silos, in these circumstances the stakes
have become very high. All it needs is a failure of nerve in the game of bluff.
This is a very real and likely scenario with the weapons now being deployed.

(ii) *Are command, control, communication and* OR *Does the amount of information to be*
     intelligence facilities likely to remain   *processed, pressure of time and fear of*
     secure?   *preemption put command and control*
                                                       systems under intolerable strain and make
                                                       inadvertent war more likely?

Yes. The right-hand side follows on from this. I just do not think that the information is secure. I have lived at Greenham for four years, and I have been appalled at how stupid, naive, misinformed, disinformed, and confused these military officers, these people who are supposed to be defending us, really are. Their security is inadequate, it is very easy to get highly sensitive top secret information from them, and some of them do not seem to be able to interpret their own sources of information. I am terrified that peace is in the hands both of fallible communication systems and of badly-educated and ill-informed military personnel.

(iii) *If nevertheless there were a limited nuclear*   OR   *Is the idea that nuclear war could be*
      exchange would it be likely to end   *limited once it had broken out a dangerous*
      hostilities swiftly?   *illusion?*

I just do not think that we can risk it. My own impression, having seen the way in which the officers in charge of the Cruise convoy panic when faced with a few women standing in the road, is that if there was any kind of exchange it would very quickly escalate. They would try to get all their weapons out as quickly as possible, and probably not even programme them correctly. But any nuclear exchange would be so unimaginably horrifying that we cannot risk it. We have to prevent the possibility.

(iv) *Do new generations of battlefield and*   OR   *Do new battlefield and theatre weapons*
      theatre nuclear systems reinforce   *threaten a dangerous lowering of the*
      deterrence?   *nuclear threshold?*

They lower the threshold. Any honest military strategist will admit that. Their purpose is to take us out of Mutually Assured Destruction, and to make nuclear war thinkable and plannable. Take Cruise. It is supposed to be taken out on dispersal and hidden among the civilian population, and then fired secretly. But we know quite well that Soviet satellites can pick this up, so at a time of tension we will be depending on Soviet military planners to get the equation right and act with restraint. First we are told that the Soviet Union is evil, vicious and untrustworthy; then we place the lives of everyone living within a hundred-mile radius of Greenham at the mercy of the humanity and good sense of Soviet commanders. In April of this year, for example, Cruise went on an unscheduled exercise a few days before the Libyan bombing. In fact, it is stated in the Geneva and Hague Conventions that, just as you should not make civilians the indiscriminate object of your bombing, so you should not hide your weapons systems among the civilian populations. In order to neutralize Cruise, the Soviet Union would have to obliterate a large part of southern Britain. Of course they lower the threshold.

(v) *Does the Strategic Defence Initiative offer*   OR   *Is the Strategic Defence Initiative simply*
     the hope of an effective defence against   *the most recent and destabilizing example*
     nuclear weapons?   *of the process outlined in 1?*

The Strategic Defence Initiative is very destabilizing. And it's dishonest. If the scientists, technologists and many of the military are doubtful if it can work, why are they telling us that it will? They tell us that it will prevent missiles leaving the Soviet Union; that it will be a shield over the United States; Thatcher tries to pretend that it will be a shield over the West as a whole. This is all nonsense. If it were possible to give ninety-five percent protection to, say, Washington or New York, that would just mean that a rational attack would swamp the shield so that even five percent would be enough to annihilate the city. And behind all this is a more sinister implication. Once Congress has been conned into funding all the advanced electronic and laser research, at a certain point the Pentagon may be able to say '*we have done even better. We can now use this technology to control and immobilize whole populations without having to launch a nuclear attack*'. And, of course, they will be able to do this to their own domestic population, policing urban unrest brought about by the distortion of the economy and diversion of resources into the whole arms programme and away from education, jobs, social programmes to alleviate poverty, overcrowding and other social evils.

(vi) *Is the threat of 'horizontal' nuclear*   OR *Is continuing reliance on nuclear deterrence*
proliferation best met by a continuation of   *by the great powers bound to accelerate the*
past policies?   *process of proliferation and make nuclear*
                                                      war more likely?

If nuclear deterrence works, then we should be spreading it to as many countries as possible. Then we would all be safe! But, of course, the superpowers and Britain know that this is nonsense, and that there is no such thing as deterrence. That's why they are all terrified of proliferation. But there is also the desire to keep these weapons in the hands of the rich, predominantly white, north, because this perpetuates their dominance. It is a form of racial superiority.

Proliferation is indeed encouraged by the dependence of the great powers on nuclear deterrence. That is one of the main reasons why Britain should give up her independent deterrent. And she must do it quickly to have an effect. Once some of these other countries have them – tempted by the idea that their possession will bring them power, recognition and respect – it will be too late. We will have a whole other set of problems and instabilities.

(vii) *Do multilateral arms-control negotiations*   OR *Is 'arms-control' an illusion which diverts*
offer the best prospect for future stability?   *attention from the only safe policy –*
                                                       nuclear disarmament?

I would agree with the right-hand side. Anyone with a sense of history, looking back at the so-called forty years of multilateral arms control negotiations, has to be blind or stupid to argue that this is an effective way to reduce tension or cut back on arms. Although I welcome any attempt to reduce the vast nuclear arsenals, I am not hopeful about the present talks, because I don't think that this is where the problems lie. It is a mistake to separate defence and arms policies from broader foreign policies. They put all their arguing into haggling over numbers and quantities of explosive power, instead of getting to grips with the fundamental disagreements and conflicts of ideology, of spheres of influence, of resources.

(B) WITHOUT NUCLEAR WEAPONS

I would like to approach all this in a different way. I do not want to be pushed into the alternatives that the questions in the left-hand column assume. The question that I would like to ask is this: Can the Earth and the nations on it survive a nuclear war of any kind? And my answer would be 'no'. As the Thatcherites are always so keen to tell us, we cannot disinvent nuclear weapons. So war of any kind is no longer a rational option available to anyone. Since we cannot disinvent these weapons of mass destruction, we have to start working out other kinds of policies and means of resolving the problems that war has traditionally been used to resolve – conflicts of belief, territory, resource. In the past, each war has created the next. But with nuclear weapons we cannot afford the next. When wars were fought between small armies and were localized, most of the people who fought and died were soldiers. But in the Second World War forty-five percent of the people who died were civilian, and a lot of those were women and children. It makes me very angry when we have Armistice Day and they lay wreaths at the foot of monuments commemorating the heroic soldiers, and forget that those soldiers were at the same time killing millions of civilians. In any future war that number will be greatly increased.

We can no longer fight wars to protect homes and families. The rational objectives of human life are survival, an increase in the quality and health of life, the creation of a future for our children and grandchildren. In planning for the possibility of war of any kind, we are not making use of the qualities that made human beings fit to survive, our qualities of thought and mind and intelligence. We have to start creating the moral and political structures which will enable our species to survive. War of any kind in a nuclear age will not enable our species to survive. So we have got to discount that as a rational option for all time. We must not allow the evolutionary suicidals to destroy and poison the Earth, the waters, the very air we breath for all time.

So I have my eyes firmly fixed on the only possibility for the future – although there's a part of me that does not hold out much hope for it, because too many peoply are moral cowards, or are short-sighted and won't make the radical changes that are an urgent necessity.

But my feet are, of course, in the quicksand of the present. Multilateral nuclear disarmament is a little island, a tussock of grass, and conventional disarmament is a tussock a bit further on. We have to take those first very difficult, very sticky, very courageous steps of unilateral nuclear disarmament in order to get ourselves out of the quicksand to the first tussock. That first step of unilateralism could make the programme of multilateral disarmament possible. Then we have to manage our lives and our personal, political and international relations so as to recognize the pointlessness of all the conventional hardware that clogs the seas and land. That will take time and courage, but, if we hesitate now to reach for the first tussock, the quicksand will suck us deeper down and we will die.

B *NATO Policy*

The West's policies threaten our own peace and security, and that of many countries, far more than Soviet activities.

(i) *Does the Soviet Union, together with her*   OR *Are NATO and WTO forces relatively*
Warsaw Pact allies, enjoy a strategically   *evenly matched?*
dangerous military superiority in Europe?

There's a huge part of me that doesn't care too much who thinks they're superior. It's all the numbers game. But there probably is a rough parity in conventional forces. As we said before, when it suits their purposes to make us feel that we don't have as much as the other side, then they argue that way. When they are trying to reassure us, then, almost in the same breath, they argue the other way. Governments are liars. And, in any case, I don't think that this is where the problem lies.

(ii) *Is the Soviet Union an expansionist power* OR *Is the Soviet Union an encircled and*
which will take advantage of unilateral   *threatened power trying to keep up with*
Western concessions and is only restrained   *Western technology and likely to respond*
and forced to accept arms-control   *positively to unconditional offers of*
agreements by Western determination and   *Western restraint within a general context*
strength?   *of detente?*

The present situation has been created out of the aftermath of the Second World War. The twenty-two million deaths that the Soviet Union suffered in that war made her determined to reassure her people that this would never happen again. So Europe was divided up into two 'spheres of influence' – Russian and American. To criticize the Soviet Union for going into Hungary or Afghanistan, while ignoring the much greater expansionism of the United States in the same period, is rank hypocrisy. I would tend to agree with the right-hand side here. The Soviet Union is an encircled power, standing at bay, surrounded by forces which are hostile and are putting out increasingly violent rhetoric about how evil the Soviet system is. The West deliberately aims to destabilize the Soviet Union, forcing the diversion of resources away from autonomous national consolidation, and towards military build-up, so that in the end internal discontent boils over. This is the kind of paranoia and projection which has always created the emotional climate for war. It carries with it very great dangers, because, like an animal at bay, an encircled country can attack out of fear. So the essential task is to get rid of these buffer zones and spheres of influence, to emancipate ourselves from virulent propaganda which depicts the other side in dehumanized terms, and finally to break the mould set at the end of the Second World War.

(iii) *Is Soviet chemical and conventional*   OR *Is NATO dependence on the early use of*
preponderance such that NATO must   *nuclear weapons unnecessary and*
continue to be able to threaten early use of   *strategically suicidal?*
nuclear weapons?

Any use of nuclear weapons would be suicidal. So the threat of early use is
not credible. The same applies to all modern weapons of mass destruction –
biological and chemical, as well as nuclear. (The US claims not to store chemical weapons – but they do in the Welford bomb base, where I have seen the
storage facilities.) There cannot be such a thing as 'deterrence'. NATO's
dependence upon the early use of nuclear weapons is irrational and inexcusably
irresponsible. Chemical and biological weapons are as dangerous and uncontrollable as nuclear weapons in that they could get out of hand and spread, to
cause death and injury far beyond the battlefield or blinkered intentions of the
military users.

(iv) *Does the growing size of the Soviet nuclear*   OR *Does the West initiate nearly all phases of*
arsenal threaten the delicate theatre and   *the nuclear arms race and continue to enjoy*
strategic balance? Would Western failure   *a substantial lead in most areas? Is the*
to match Soviet systems be destabilizing?   *nuclear 'overkill' such that the West could*
                                         offer a nuclear 'freeze' or unconditional
                                         cuts without risk?

The right-hand side is probably true. But the very way in which these questions are framed one again brings out the incoherence of the so-called strategy
of nuclear deterrence. To invoke the Soviet threat and then say '*the Soviets
are increasing their forces and therefore so must we*' is exactly the fallacy that
creates the arms race. It is each side saying this that is carrying us to the
precipice. There is such overwhelming overkill that either side could freeze
without risk. They won't, because then they would have to admit the stupidity
of this expensive exercise in macho sizing, and also because decades of the
arms race means that industry is dependent upon the development of ever-
newer weapons-systems with built-in obsolence and spiralling demand.

(v) *Are NATO 'forward defence' and 'deep*   OR *Should NATO exploit her lead in*
strike' strategies essential for effective   *'emerging technology' to explore less*
deterrence?   *provocative alternative strategies?*

This is entirely irrelevant. The problem is artificial in the first place – the
Soviet threat has been created in order to legitimize arms programmes and
justify the control of domestic populations in the West – so the search for
'alternative strategies' is a diversion from what we should really be concerned
with.

(vi) *Is it the presence of American front-line troops and the tying-in of theatre nuclear forces to the American strategic deterrent that guarantees W. European security? Should American policies therefore be supported?*

OR *Is it domination by the two super-powers that poses the greatest threat to European integrity? Would Europe be safer decoupled from the super-power nuclear confrontation? Should Europe be made a nuclear weapon-free zone?*

I am not anti-American. I was brought up there when I was young and I love many things about America and American people. But I would agree that the major threat which faces us, both as a nation, and as members of the human race in general, is the continuing escalation of the superpower confrontation, fuelled principally by United States' sabre-rattling.

And the danger does not just lie in the outbreak of war, but in the steady and surreptitious erosion of democracy that the increasing militarization of Europe is bringing about. It allows governments to implement policies which take away our freedoms – the Public Order Act, the Police and Criminal Evidence Bill. This turns legitimate dissent and protest, which is what democracy should be about, into what is described as a treacherous disruption of public life. Health and social service programmes are being dismantled because so many resources are being poured into the bottomless pit of arms-spending. Europe should indeed be a nuclear weapon-free zone, and the NATO and Warsaw Pact alliances should be dissolved. Western European countries should contribute towards this by moving towards a policy of non-alignment. True defence in the nuclear age can only lie in the mutual respect and interaction of non-aligned countries.

(vii) *Would Western unilateral nuclear disarmament invite Soviet blackmail? Are suggestions that the West should take the lead in offering unilateral disarmament initiatives the thin end of this wedge? Do radical nuclear disarmers consciously or unconsciously serve Soviet interests and threaten to undermine Western defences?*

OR *Are unilateral initiatives as part of a general programme of nuclear disarmament the only way to reverse the arms race? Is talk of 'multilateral disarmament' insincere in the mouths of those who reject all suggestion of a Comprehensive Test Ban Treaty, a Nuclear Freeze, a European Nuclear Weapon-Free Zone, or a declaration of No First Use?*

This is like the people who say, '*I would love to see the view from the top of that mountain, but I am certainly not going to put one foot in front of the other in order to get there.*' Or it's like the twins, who never emerged from the womb, because each was saying '*after you*'. I see unilateral initiatives as part of that first crucial step. They certainly don't stand on their own. It would be ludicrous to think that they did. They are the first step in a broader programme. As we have seen, the only alternative is increasing escalation and the baying hounds of the military-industrial complex wanting more and more arms to be built up.

The trouble with the left-hand side is self-fulfilling expectations. If you expect that the Soviet Union will not reciprocate genuinely, then you create the conditions in which they cannot. They have, in fact, taken some significant first steps – making a pledge of no first use, declaring a unilateral test moratorium, offering bold initiatives at Reykjavik. But in each case we turn round and say, '*What are they doing that for? I don't trust them. They must have ulterior motives.*' So we have created the conditions in which that whole system of negotiations cannot succeed.

C *British Policy*

I *The British Deterrent*

(i) *Is Britain's deterrent a weapon of last resort which guarantees her sovereignty and independence and protects her from nuclear blackmail?*   OR *Would all possible uses of Britain's 'deterrent' be suicidal? Is its only effect to encourage proliferation?*

I welcome the Labour Party's recognition of the fallacy at the heart of Britain's possession of nuclear weapons. Our 'nuclear deterrent' can never be used. It does not protect us. We do not have a realistic defence strategy if it is based upon nuclear weapons. These illusory arguments need to be shown up for what they are.

(ii) *Are British nuclear forces valuable to European allies because they provide a specifically European second centre of decision making?*   OR *Is the 'second centre of decision making' an illusion when the weapons are dependent upon the US and there is no independent strategic role to be played? Are European allies unenthusiastic about a parochial British force likely to inhibit her commitment to European defence?*

The argument on the left-hand side is simply another rationalization. It is empty and entirely lacks credibility.

(iii) *Does the US favour shared responsibility and do British nuclear forces guarantee full US commitment to Europe and Soviet recognition of it?*   OR *Are US forces committed anyway and independent British initiatives more likely to trigger Soviet retaliation than US involvement?*

I have already answered this. I do not want the United States 'fully committed to the defence of Europe' when the cost is our liberty and independence. They tie us into attacks and alliances which are not necessarily in Europe's best interest. They consider that 'defending Europe' from threats, that they have helped to create, gives them the right to interfere with domestic internal politics. I wish they'd spend more time seeing to the interests and needs of the disadvantaged millions in their own country. I fear that the 'special relationship' means that our big American cousin covers his fist with a soft velvet glove. But, if we show too much independence and initiative in determining our own best defence policies, the glove will be thrown aside, and we'll feel the brutal iron fist experienced by Chileans, Nicaraguans and others. Many Americans are also deeply distressed by their Administration's warmongering.

(iv) *Is the cost of the British deterrent small in*   OR *Can Britain's nuclear forces only be*
view of the vital defence role it plays? Are   *afforded at the expense of conventional*
alternatives likely to be more expensive?   *strength and of other more important*
                                                      economic priorities?

Nuclear weapons do not play a 'vital defence role'. They simply help to perpetuate the militarization of Europe and the progressive erosion of our democracy. I want to see the resources now being spent on armaments in this country instead being spent on constructive long-term public programmes such as education and health. The effort should go, not into more nuclear or conventional arms, but into investment in combatting racism, in understanding and respecting other cultures, in building mutual concern among our populations. That will be our strongest and most effective long-term defence policy.

(v) *Would unilateral British nuclear*   OR *Does the British deterrent encourage*
disarmament have no effect on other   *proliferation and do nothing to enhance*
countries and only serve to weaken British   *British prestige? Would British*
influence and allow France unchallenged   *disarmament within the context outlined in*
ascendancy in Europe?   *B help to break the nuclear log-jam?*

Britain's nuclear weapons have brought her no prestige or influence. This whole idea is inappropriate and completely out of place. If Britain wants to be more significant internationally, she would do well to detach herself from a lame dependence upon the United States and to achieve it through a policy of non-alignment.

(vi) *Is investment in Trident the best way to*   OR *Would commitment to Trident exacerbate*
continue to ensure effective British strategic   *all the drawbacks listed above?*
defence into the 21st century?

The Trident programme is ludicrous. But, unfortunately, like many ludicrous things, it is also very dangerous and expensive.

2 *NATO Forces and US Bases*

(i) *Must Britain continue to share*   OR *Should British obligations to NATO be*
responsibility for manning NATO nuclear   *met by strengthening conventional forces*
systems upon which her security depends?   *where necessary within an overall non-*
Would refusal to do so fatally weaken the   *nuclear strategy as recommended in B?*
alliance?

We have already seen why the argument in the left-hand column is spurious. Britain's long-term security does not depend upon NATO, still less upon NATO nuclear systems. I want to see NATO and the Warsaw Pact dismantled. I can understand why the Labour Party argues as on the right-hand side. Conventional forces do not need to be strengthened for defence purposes. But, after years of propaganda to the contrary, by both Labour and Tory governments, this is too difficult to get across quickly. They'd have a hard task explaining how they've conned us and wasted our resources not for defence but to appease our masters in the Alliance. So I understand why political considerations mean that the Labour Party has to approach the question of

NATO and conventional weapons build-up rather delicately. That's the problem with acquiescing in expenditure on successive falsehoods – it comes back and haunts you!

(ii) *Would the forced withdrawal of US nuclear bases from Britain make US defence of the West impossible? Is American interference in British affairs negligible?*   OR *Do the large numbers of nuclear facilities yielded to the US erode British sovereignty? Would their removal do no more than restore a normal peacetime relationship?*

The response of the American administration to the decisions taken during the recent Labour Party conference clearly showed up what the real situation is. Listening to the American Secretary of Defense gave me a surreal feeling that our apparent ally was all at once a potential enemy, threatening the withdrawal of economic favours and the deliberate destabilization of this country, if we dare to try to escape from its sphere of influence. Will America do everything it can to undermine a democratically elected government, which wants a very sane and rational defence policy that is not in accordance with American interests? I think that Labour Party policy will force the Americans out into the open about what really is the underpinning of the NATO Alliance – American economic and security interests. This will show what has been going on for the past forty years in Europe.

And our own governments have up until now been prepared to play along with this. With Cruise missiles, which are said to be protecting our freedom, they are prepared to deny people living in our towns and villages freedom of movement on our own roads when there is a Cruise convoy moving through, freedom of protest, freedom of access to common land and the sacred land of Salisbury Plain. So what price our sovereignty and independence?

(iii) *Will Britain continue to be targeted by Soviet warheads whether or not she disarms unilaterally?*   OR *Is Britain seen as an American aircraft carrier and targeted by the USSR accordingly? Will Britain fall an early victim in any superpower confrontation unless bases are removed?*

I think that the right-hand side is true. The mobility of Cruise missiles means the blanket targeting of most of southern England. If Britain gets rid of nuclear weapons, the Soviet Union has explicitly said that it will take Britain out of its primary list of targets. Obviously, if there were a general nuclear war, we would be killed eventually, by fallout or by nuclear winter, if by nothing else. But, without US bases or weapons targeted threateningly on the Soviet Union or other countries, we would be protected from first or second strikes.

(iv) *Can non-nuclear defences only safely be*   OR *In a nuclear-free Europe, decoupled from*
afforded by powers prepared to shelter   *the superpower nuclear confrontation,*
beneath the American strategic umbrella?   *would Britain no more expect to depend*
                                             upon the US 'umbrella' than any other
                                             Western ally – or than Eastern Europe
                                             upon the USSR?

It cannot be called an umbrella. On the contrary, we are all implicated in the terrible risks of American first-strike planning, without having any influence over it. We are endangered, not protected.

Moral Considerations

I would rather respond to all of these questions at once.

I feel very strongly that there is a rational aim to human life. It is survival. And not just survival on any terms, but survival with an increasing quality of life. I believe that the conditions for that survival are our recognition of the degree to which we are mutually dependent upon one another, and upon the birds, the animals, the fish, the plants, the foodstuffs, the resources of the earth. And that is why I believe that to poison the possibility of our future by the indiscriminate build-up of industry and weapons manufacture in the present is a fundamentally irrational course of action for the human race to be undertaking. It is irrational for us to be building up weaponry that deliberately threatens the immediate annihilation, or slow desecration, of all the earth's natural living systems. Any act which tends in that direction is, if you like, irrational in evolutionary terms. And that is also to say that it is immoral. I get very irritated with people who try to separate rationality and emotion, and tell us at Greenham that we are being emotional and should be more rational. On the contrary, we should all be more emotional about the death of a child, our own child or someone else's, about the death of a friend, about the death of a soldier. Only in that way can we begin to understand the significance of what it means to threaten the deaths of millions of people. The two cannot be separated, and it is very dangerous to try to do so. We know at a very gut level that to kill another person is wrong, and that to plan to kill another person is wrong. So to plan to kill on a large scale by making and deploying nuclear weapons is that much more wrong. We know that all of these things are wrong. We are not prepared, either to do this ourselves, or to have it done in our names. And simply saying 'no' is not enough, because it is assumed in our political system that our silence, and our acquiescence, and our vote every five years, is a sort of blank cheque to our governments to perpetrate these acts of atrocity. If we know that this is wrong, then we must take those kinds of action that will prevent governments from doing it in our name, otherwise we are hypocrites. That is what we are trying to do at Greenham by taking nonviolent direct action. We are trying to bring home the implications of what they are doing to the workers who are producing the weapons of mass destruction – the research workers at Aldermaston, the military workers at bases like Greenham, Welford, or Upper Heyford, those who drive the launchers for Cruise missiles, each convoy of which carries about 200 times the destructive power of the Hiroshima bomb. What I do is to place my own body in front of them and say, '*No. Stop. Are you prepared to follow through the logic of what you are doing, and run me down and kill me? Are you yourself prepared to do this act of bestiality and barbarism?*' And, if they did run me down, they would at least be consistent and show that they thought that it was all right to kill those they disagree with. But most, in fact, stop. And then we ask them, '*If you are not prepared, consciously, and in front of your own eyes, to murder another human being, what on earth are you doing playing your part in a system designed to destroy large numbers of human beings far away?*' We are trying to bring the morality of what they are doing close to them. That is one of the main troubles with nuclear weapons. In the First World War everyone was aware of the shattered, disfigured men who came back from the Front. Even the commanding officers were sickened. That was why it was to be 'the war to end all wars'. But now those who plan, prepare, and build for war are psychologically distanced from it. The destruction will take place a long way away and they expect to be safe in their bunkers. Those who suffer will be the women, the children, the civilians, those in the cities, those trying to live off the land, the animals, the birds, the fish. The innocents. There is this huge gap between the military's targeting and strategic thinking, and the actual act of killing. It is a very dangerous gap for the survival of the world. By taking nonviolent direct action we are trying to close that gap. We say '*Are you prepared to kill me? Because I am telling you that you cannot kill someone else in my name*'. So for me that is the starting point of my morality.

And that is why Greenham is women only. This whole desire to control, to dominate, to repress, and eventually to destroy, those who are different from you, is a male response. It is the view that 'might is right', that the person with the loudest voice, or the biggest bomb, has a right to impose his will on other cultures, other needs, other ways of looking at the world. It is no accident that the only women who are allowed to gain power in this very male system, are women, like Thatcher, who play the game in the ways that the most right-wing men want the game to be played. And women who approach things in a different way, who do not want to discuss these questions in the purely rational ways that men recognize, but think that to separate reason and emotion is to have lost touch with part of what makes human beings human, are just not listened to. Their views and needs simply don't get a hearing. Then the women lose confidence in themselves and do not recognize the validity of their own instinctive responses, because they have been so conditioned to being shouted down or ignored. For example, I see that I am the only woman you are interviewing. This happens again and again. If the peace camp had been mixed, it would have been a man who would have been listened to as a spokesperson, because you would have regarded his views as more important. So the decision to make Greenham women-only is not a decision to exclude men, but a decision to *include* women, all women. In Greenham, women's views can be heard, and in this way what was at first ridiculed has now come to be adopted in other parts of the peace movement. Women's understanding of peace is not just an absence of weapons or war, but is something that has to be created positively through nonviolence, imaginative risk, commitment, and a readiness to change ones own ways of working and inter-relating. It requires much more courage and hard work than any war-fighting would require. War-fighting is a passive response to conflict, which simply perpetuates the whole thing. Peace means struggling towards a completely different way of living and looking at the world, in which the language and political categories which make war possible are transcended. Peace cannot be separated from justice, freedom and independence. There are no short cuts. We all have to take responsibility for making the changes and refusing to benefit from abuse of our own power. But the future is so precious that it is worth going to prison if that jolts one more person out of the lethargy of hopelessness.

We are often told that we must be realistic and begin from where we are. I agree. But, in order to know what the first steps are, we need to know where we want to go. So let's begin by imagining what the world would have to be like if we are to survive, and are to be able to look forward to healthy, fulfilled lives for ourselves, and for our children and grandchildren. Imagine that we have succeeded in getting there. Then turn round, and retrace the path, step by step, until we reach where we are now – our starting point, this huge, paralysing mass of problems, which so many people feel so utterly powerless to change. And now we know what the first step is that we *have* to take, because there is no alternative if we are to reach the goal of survival. It is the step we *have* to take, not the easiest or the one that looks most convenient or most politically plausible. And it is the step that women, not only at Greenham, but all over the world, *are* taking.

Recommendations

1 Yes.
2 Yes (See **A2(A)(v)**).
3 Yes.
4 Yes (See **B(iii)**).
5 Yes.
6 Yes (See **B(vi)**).
7 Yes.
8 Yes (See **A2(B)**).
9 And start the whole thing off again? No.
10 Yes.
11 Yes (See **B(iii)**).
12 Yes (See **B(iv)**).

13 Yes.
14 Yes (See **B(vi)**).
15 Yes (See **B(vi)**).
16 Yes (See **C1**).
17 No (See **C1(iv)**).
18 No. Britain should leave NATO (See **C2(1)**).
19 Yes. And the American military presence should be removed entirely (See **B(vi)** & **C2(ii)**).
20 See 18.

Dr. Anthony Kenny

F.B.A.

Biographical Note

Born in 1931, Anthony Kenny was ordained as a Roman Catholic priest in 1955, but returned to lay state eight years later. Between 1963 and 1978 he was a lecturer in Philosophy at Oxford University and since 1978 has been Master of Balliol College. He has also been a Visiting Professor at a number of American universities.

Among his many publications on philosophy and public affairs, particular mention should be made here of *The Logic of Deterrence*, published in 1985 by the Firethorn Press.

Editorial Comment

These answers were communicated in an interview at Balliol College on June 3, 1986. They represent the thinking of a philosopher who, among other things, has for over twenty-five years been concerned, both with questions of human intention and purpose in general, and with how this bears on the morality of nuclear weapon deployment in particular. Dr Kenny does not see professional philosophy as an enterprise which is divorced from the practicalities of public life, but has consistently emphasized the importance of its rôle in clarifying the concepts used by decision-makers and others when they formulate, justify, and criticize, official policy. Perhaps of particular interest here is the strictness of the conditions upon which he is prepared to allow that the continued deployment of nuclear weapons is morally justified. This can be found in his answers to questions (iv) and (vi) under *Moral Considerations*, and in his response to *Recommendation 9*.

DR ANTHONY KENNY

A *Global Policy*

1 *The History of the Past Forty Years*

(i) *Has it been nuclear deterrence that has*   OR *Has it mainly been other factors?*
kept the peace between the great powers
since 1945?

I think that nuclear deterrence has been one of the factors that have kept the peace, but there have been other factors, too. If you like, it has been overdetermined, so that these alternatives are not mutually exclusive.

(ii) *Does mutual possession of an invulnerable* OR *Does the threat of strategic nuclear*
second-strike strategic nuclear force prevent   *retaliation, particularly against a similarly*
war?   *armed enemy, lack credibility and invite*
                                                                                       sub-deterrent encroachment?

Mutual possession of an invulnerable second strike nuclear strategic force does, I think, make full-scale war between the great powers less likely. But it means that smaller powers, like Libya or Vietnam, are more difficult for the great powers to deal with, because they are inhibited from using their full military potential against them, for fear of being drawn into a nuclear confrontation with one another. To this extent I think that it does invite sub-deterrent encroachment.

iii) *Have limited nuclear options at strategic and theatre levels enhanced deterrence by dramatically raising the threshold between peace and war?*   OR *Have most military planners from the start been aiming for nuclear war-fighting superiority? Has 'flexible response' dangerously lowered the threshold between conventional and nuclear war?*

The limited options introduced in order to enhance strategic deterrence are dangerous. Flexible response has, indeed, dangerously lowered the threshold between conventional and nuclear war. But I do not agree with the opening statement on the right: I don't think that, on the whole, military planners have been aiming for nuclear war-fighting superiority, if that means actually intending to plan seriously for a nuclear war. At least, not during the years when Mutual Assured Destruction was official doctrine. Although there has been a definite change of policy with the advent to power of those in favour of the recommendations of the Committee on the Present Danger.[1] They do seem to be talking about the possibility of nuclear war-fighting.

iv) *Has the size and variety of the nuclear arsenals held by the superpowers stabilized deterrence?*   OR *Has the logic of nuclear confrontation and worst-case analysis generated a dangerous and strategically pointless superfluity of weapons systems?*

I would certainly agree with the right-hand side here.

v) *Has the idea of nuclear balance between the superpowers been essential to stability and have arms-control negotiations helped to achieve it?*   OR *Have ideas of 'nuclear defence' and 'parity' proved illusory and is 'multilateral negotiation from strength' a contradiction in terms? Has 'arms-control' been just another name for the arms race?*

I agree with the statement implied in the first question on the right. The idea of 'parity' is illusory, and 'multilateral negotiation from strength' self-contradictory. As a result, although there have been perfectly genuine people working for arms-control, the constraints within which they have had to move, have meant that arms-control has never slowed down the arms race, and has in some cases even speeded it up.

vi) *Has force-planning been controlled by strategic thinking?*   OR *Has the self-reinforcing impetus of technology and vested interest dictated policies subsequently justified post hoc?*

I agree with the right-hand side here – mainly as a result of having read Lawrence Freedman's book, 'The Evolution of Nuclear Strategy'.

---

1. Formed in 1976 to warn Americans of the danger of the Soviet military build-up. A number of Committee members subsequently joined President Reagan's administration.

2 *The Prospect for the Future*

(A) WITH NUCLEAR WEAPONS
 (i) *Does the threat of an enemy first strike* OR *Is there an increasing threat from accurate*
     remain inconceivable for the foreseeable   *and time-urgent first-strike weapons?*
     future?

Yes, I think that new generations of nuclear weapons do significantly increase
the threat of a first strike. Weapons such as Cruise or Pershing II may not
have been intended as first strike weapons by the West, but I am sure that
they are seen as such by the East.

(ii) *Are command, control, communication and* OR *Does the amount of information to be*
     intelligence facilities likely to remain   *processed, pressure of time and fear of*
     secure?   *preemption put command and control*
                                                        systems under intolerable strain and make
                                                        inadvertent war more likely?

I agree with the implication on the right-hand side here.

(iii) *If nevertheless there were a limited nuclear* OR *Is the idea that nuclear war could be*
      exchange would it be likely to end   *limited once it had broken out a dangerous*
      hostilities swiftly?   *illusion?*

Here, we really don't know, do we? I doubt that anyone would deliberately
intend to fight a limited nuclear war, because of the enormous risk of escalation. But, if it came to it, escalation is not inevitable – both sides might draw
back as a result of the initial shock. In their Pastoral Letter[1] the American
bishops had rather a good qualified phrase on this: '*To cross this divide (ie from
the conventional to the nuclear arena) is to enter a world in which we have no
experience of control, much testimony against its possibility and therefore no moral
justification for submitting the human community to this risk.*'

(iv) *Do new generations of battlefield and*   OR *Do new battlefield and theatre weapons*
     theatre nuclear systems reinforce   *threaten a dangerous lowering of the*
     deterrence?   *nuclear threshold?*

Yes, I do think that new generations of battlefield and intermediate nuclear
weapons dangerously lower the nuclear threshold.

(v) *Does the Strategic Defence Initiative offer* OR *Is the Strategic Defence Initiative simply*
    the hope of an effective defence against   *the most recent and destabilizing example*
    nuclear weapons?   *of the process outlined in 1?*

I think that, if SDI began to look at all plausible, if it seemed to offer an
effective defence of centres of population against nuclear attack, as President
Reagan still argues, then it would be extremely destabilizing. One of the
regular defence correspondents in the American *Harper's* magazine has
pointed out how extraordinary it is that nobody seems to have noticed that, if
it worked, it would be a most effective *offensive* weapon.

---

1. *The Challenge of Peace*, May 1983.

But, since it is unlikely to do more than provide some defence for a limited number of nuclear weapons, it is probably more of a red herring than a serious threat. A surprisingly large number of American scientists say that they do not believe in it, and for this reason refuse to take money for it – which is a most unusual thing for university faculties to do!

vi) *Is the threat of 'horizontal' nuclear* OR *Is continuing reliance on nuclear deterrence*
proliferation best met by a continuation of *by the great powers bound to accelerate the*
past policies? *process of proliferation and make nuclear*
war more likely?

I don't really think that there is a close link between the continued build-up of nuclear weapons systems by the established powers, and the spread of nuclear weapons to potential nuclear powers. They are, I think, separate dangers. Of course, the fact that the major nuclear powers are continuing to build up their arsenals, makes it seem pretty hypocritical when they call for others to sign Non-Proliferation treaties, and so on. But the risk of nuclear war between, say, India and Pakistan, Iran and Iraq, or Israel and Syria, is influenced by local factors, which would not be much altered by even quite sweeping changes in superpower policies.

vii) *Do multilateral arms-control negotiations* OR *Is 'arms-control' an illusion which diverts*
offer the best prospect for future stability? *attention from the only safe policy –*
nuclear disarmament?

I do not hold out much hope for the current arms control and disarmament talks. The way ahead is, as implied on the right, by unilateral disarmament initiatives offered as part of a general process of nuclear disarmament. But it is not true to say that this is the 'only safe policy'. No policy is safe in these circumstances. We are talking about relative risk, about the probability of various evils happening, and the size of those evils. On prudential grounds I subscribe to the Pascalian calculation here: we should prefer nuclear disarmament to continued nuclear deployment, because the worst case with the latter is so much worse than the worst case with the former.

But it's principally for moral, rather than for prudential, reasons that I prefer nuclear disarmament.

8) WITHOUT NUCLEAR WEAPONS

i) *If nuclear arsenals were dismantled would* OR *Would nuclear disarmament remove the*
war between the great powers again *incentive for nuclear preemption while not*
become a rational option and therefore *affecting the reluctance of the great powers*
more likely? *to initiate a third world war?*

I have to admit that global nuclear disarmament might make a major conventional war slightly more likely.

(ii) *Would a major conventional war be likely*   OR *Is conventional war, however terrible,*
in itself to be as terrible as a limited   *preferable to nuclear war?*
nuclear war?

A major conventional war might well be as destructive as a nuclear war, which
was limited to a restricted number of exchanges (after all, the last war was in
a sense a limited nuclear war). But I do think that, in general, a conventional
war, however terrible, would be preferable to a nuclear war, because of the
risk of the latter becoming an all-out nuclear war.

(iii) *Because nuclear weapons cannot be*   OR *As with nerve gases in the last war, would*
uninvented would they not be bound to be   *there be no incentive to resort to*
used sooner or later once war had broken   *capabilities which the other side has as*
out?   *well?*

As I have said, there is no safe policy. There is no way that we'll ensure that
there will never be war. It might well be that, if a major war broke out between
the superpowers after there had been apparent nuclear disarmament, each
side would take steps to redevelop nuclear weapons before the other. But the
essential strategic planning on both sides would have been for conventional
war, so I think that even in that case the risks would be lower than they would
be if war broke out now.

(iv) *Is global nuclear disarmament only*   OR *Is to argue that even multilateral nuclear*
feasible in a world where war itself is no   *disarmament is not desirable to give up all*
longer a possibility?   *hope of a rational world-order?*

The terrible risks involved in the continuing deployment of nuclear weapons
by the great powers, means that we should certainly move in the direction of
global nuclear disarmament as fast as we can safely do so.

(v) *Is peace only preserved when we are seen*   OR *Do the years before 1914 show what*
to be prepared for war, as failure before   *happens when military planning and the*
1939 and success since 1945 show? Under   *arms race control political choices? Do*
likely future conditions would global   *present strategies make nuclear war almost*
nuclear disarmament make war, including   *inevitable under likely future conditions?*
nuclear war, more likely?   *Is global nuclear disarmament the only*
                                                    rational policy?

Global nuclear disarmament might make a major conventional war slightly
more likely, but it would make nuclear war less likely. A continuation of
current policies does not make nuclear war almost inevitable, although it is
potentially very dangerous. I see the present situation as relatively stable, but
highly vulnerable. We are not so much sliding down a slope towards a precipice, as standing near the edge of a cliff. As long as we stand where we are,
we will be all right. But something which pushes us a little in the wrong
direction, like an unexpected political crisis, could make us fall very fast. This
is not a state of affairs that we would be wise to live with.

But argument from historical analogy is seldom reliable. Examples can often
be used to support opposite conclusions. The Munich crisis can be said to

show that it's very important to stand up to dictators, but it can also be said to show the danger of being obsessed by the threat from world Bolshevism. In any case, analogies drawn from the pre-nuclear era are quite unreliable when applied to the post-nuclear age, because the kind of decisions, which it was then rational to take, no longer are.

B *NATO Policy*

(i) *Does the Soviet Union, together with her*   OR *Are NATO and WTO forces relatively* *Warsaw Pact allies, enjoy a strategically*   *evenly matched?* *dangerous military superiority in Europe?*

I do think that the Soviet Union and her allies enjoy quite a large military superiority. I don't think that the two sides are in this sense evenly matched. But, since it seems that you need a three-to-one advantage in order to be able to take the offensive confidently, the West is not too badly placed defensively. I would not myself be against a strengthening of Western conventional forces, if this was needed, so long as it was done in a non-provocative way.

(ii) *Is the Soviet Union an expansionist power* OR *Is the Soviet Union an encircled and* *which will take advantage of unilateral*   *threatened power trying to keep up with* *Western concessions and is only restrained* *Western technology and likely to respond* *and forced to accept arms-control*   *positively to unconditional offers of* *agreements by Western determination and* *Western restraint within a general context* *strength?*   *of detente?*

I tend to agree with the right-hand side here. I do not think that the Soviet Union is at the moment anxious for territorial expansion. But that is not to say that, if there were a rush to disarm by the West, she would not take advantage of it, and perhaps as a result again become more expansionist.

(iii) *Is Soviet chemical and conventional*   OR *Is NATO dependence on the early use of* *preponderance such that NATO must*   *nuclear weapons unnecessary and* *continue to be able to threaten early use of* *strategically suicidal?* *nuclear weapons?*

I am firmly on the right-hand side here.

(iv) *Does the growing size of the Soviet nuclear* OR *Does the West initiate nearly all phases of* *arsenal threaten the delicate theatre and* *the nuclear arms race and continue to enjoy* *strategic balance? Would Western failure* *a substantial lead in most areas? Is the* *to match Soviet systems be destabilizing?* *nuclear 'overkill' such that the West could*   *offer a nuclear 'freeze' or unconditional*   *cuts without risk?*

The idea on the left, that the balance is delicate, and that the West has to match every Soviet system, is quite wrong. If deterrence works at all, it is very crude, and depends upon uncertainty, not the kind of intricate numerical balancing that is characteristic of war-games. It is also true, I think, that the West has initiated most phases of the arms-race, and that the overkill is such that a freeze could be offered or cuts made without risk.

(v) *Are NATO 'forward defence' and 'deep*   OR *Should NATO exploit her lead in*
    strike' strategies essential for effective   *'emerging technology' to explore less*
    deterrence?   *provocative alternative strategies?*

The question of whether to persist with 'forward defence' and 'deep strike' strategies would remain, even if the nuclear components were removed. They are conventional, as well as nuclear, strategies. I do think that they are unnecessarily provocative, and my response is to agree with the implication on the right. I don't think that we should put too much trust in 'emerging technology'.

(vi) *Is it the presence of American front-line*   OR *Is it domination by the two super-powers*
    troops and the tying-in of theatre nuclear   *that poses the greatest threat to European*
    forces to the American strategic deterrent   *integrity? Would Europe be safer*
    that guarantees W. European security?   *decoupled from the super-power nuclear*
    Should American policies therefore be   *confrontation? Should Europe be made a*
    supported?   *nuclear weapon-free zone?*

I would say 'no' to what is implied on the left. The fact that, at the moment, American troops are essential to European security, does not reflect much credit on Europe. I have come round to the view of Hedley Bull, who used to be Head of International Relations here and died last year. In one of his last articles he argued that, although it was appropriate that immediately after the war the shattered and separated states of Western Europe should become clients of America, now that they are comparatively united, and, in terms of population and economic power, comparable to either of the two superpowers, they should take on responsibility for their own defence. It might be objected that Russia would not like two great power blocs ranged against her, but, if China were brought into the equation as well, we could move towards some rough kind of balance between the four, with no one power dominant, and no two in alliance with one another. In a commencement address I was giving in Ohio the other day, I said that this should be a prospect which might please the Americans, many of whom resent the way they feel that they contribute disproportionately to the defence of an ungrateful Europe. I think that the Libyan raid may prove to have been a turning-point in the relations between America and her Allies. Even in the middle of the Vietnam war, I do not remember such a divergence of views. Every European government, except our own, and the majority of the population in every country, including our own, disowned the American action. I would like to see Western Europe take on more of her own defence.

vii) *Would Western unilateral nuclear*   OR *Are unilateral initiatives as part of a*
disarmament invite Soviet blackmail? Are   *general programme of nuclear disarmament*
suggestions that the West should take the   *the only way to reverse the arms race? Is*
lead in offering unilateral disarmament   *talk of 'multilateral disarmament' insincere*
initiatives the thin end of this wedge? Do   *in the mouths of those who reject all*
radical nuclear disarmers consciously or   *suggestion of a Comprehensive Test Ban*
unconsciously serve Soviet interests and   *Treaty, a Nuclear Freeze, a European*
threaten to undermine Western defences?   *Nuclear Weapon-Free Zone, or a*
                                                declaration of No First Use?

I would imagine that some multilateralists are sincere, and some are not. But it has always struck me as remarkable, that, for some reason, everybody claims to be a multilateral disarmer – including even those who actually want to increase our armaments. Nobody admits to being an 'armer'!

As for the accusations on the left, I have openly said in my book that I would like us to go much further than a freeze. I also explained that clearly to those who are organizing the 'Freeze!' campaign, when I was asked to be a spokesman for it. They said that this would not embarrass them at all. The campaign deliberately embraces unilateralists and anti-unilateralists, who can combine together to work for the intermediate goal of a nuclear weapons freeze. This happens all the time in politics. There is nothing insincere in collaborating with people on a particular shorter term goal, even though, having achieved that goal, you may then have to walk your separate ways.

C British Policy

1 The British Deterrent

(i) *Is Britain's deterrent a weapon of last*   OR *Would all possible uses of Britain's*
resort which guarantees her sovereignty and   *'deterrent' be suicidal? Is its only effect to*
independence and protects her from nuclear   *encourage proliferation?*
blackmail?

I take the right-hand alternative here.

ii) *Are British nuclear forces valuable to*   OR *Is the 'second centre of decision making' an*
European allies because they provide a   *illusion when the weapons are dependent*
specifically European second centre of   *upon the US and there is no independent*
decision making?   *strategic role to be played? Are European*
                                                   allies unenthusiastic about a parochial
                                                   British force likely to inhibit her
                                                   commitment to European defence?

I suppose that, whether we like it or not, we are a 'second centre of decision-making'. It is possible, for example, that Mrs Thatcher left open the option of using nuclear weapons during the Falklands war. But I don't think that this has any significance, so far as the global superpower confrontation goes.

As to the question, whether, following on from my answer to **B(vi)**, a more independent Western Europe, responsible for its own defence, would need a strategic nuclear deterrent, held on the strictly conditional terms laid out in my book – I'm not sure. When I wrote my book, I was thinking within a NATO context, and there European nuclear weapons don't serve a helpful purpose at all. Since the Libyan adventure, I have come to favour the idea of detaching Western Europe from American interests, but I haven't thought through the implications for nuclear weapons policy. I would like to think more about that.

(iii) *Does the US favour shared responsibility*   OR *Are US forces committed anyway and*
and do British nuclear forces guarantee   *independent British initiatives more likely*
full US commitment to Europe and Soviet   *to trigger Soviet retaliation than US*
recognition of it?   *involvement?*

I am inclined to agree with the implication on the right.

(iv) *Is the cost of the British deterrent small in*   OR *Can Britain's nuclear forces only be*
view of the vital defence role it plays? Are   *afforded at the expense of conventional*
alternatives likely to be more expensive?   *strength and of other more important*
*   economic priorities?*

I think that the past costs of the British deterrent have been comparatively small. But, if we move on to Trident, this will eat more and more into the budget. I must say that I would prefer an overall reduction in the defence budget – but, if the only two alternatives were, either to remain nuclear, or to increase the defence budget slightly, I would favour the latter.

(v) *Would unilateral British nuclear*   OR *Does the British deterrent encourage*
disarmament have no effect on other   *proliferation and do nothing to enhance*
countries and only serve to weaken British   *British prestige? Would British*
influence and allow France unchallenged   *disarmament within the context outlined in*
ascendancy in Europe?   *B help to break the nuclear log-jam?*

Too much importance is attached to prestige. I would prefer it if France, like other countries, gave up her nuclear weapons capabilities, but I have no fear of France gaining prestige at Britain's expense, if she did not.

On the other hand, I do not attach much credence to the idea that British nuclear disarmament would be a 'good example' to others, who would then want to emulate her altruism. As recent talks in Moscow suggest, a unilateral British disarmament gesture could on its own achieve quite a substantial Russian reduction. But this would be the result of concrete bargaining. It is possible that this might initiate a general process of nuclear disarmament.

(vi) *Is investment in Trident the best way to*   OR *Would commitment to Trident exacerbate*
continue to ensure effective British strategic   *all the drawbacks listed above?*
defence into the 21st century?

The implication on the right is correct here.

2 NATO Forces and US Bases

(i) *Must Britain continue to share responsibility for manning NATO nuclear systems upon which her security depends? Would refusal to do so fatally weaken the alliance?*

OR *Should British obligations to NATO be met by strengthening conventional forces where necessary within an overall non-nuclear strategy as recommended in B?*

I agree with what is implied on the right, with the single qualification, that, for reasons that I have already given, I am no longer conviced that membership of NATO serves our interests best. So I would rephrase that as 'British obligations to the defence of Europe and the West . . .', instead of 'British obligations to NATO . . .'.

(ii) *Would the forced withdrawal of US nuclear bases from Britain make US defence of the West impossible? Is American interference in British affairs negligible?*

OR *Do the large numbers of nuclear facilities yielded to the US erode British sovereignty? Would their removal do no more than restore a normal peacetime relationship?*

The presence of American bases does erode British sovereignty, although probably less so than her membership of the European Economic Community. And, if a major war broke out or was in prospect, I don't think that the putative British 'veto' would deter the American President from using those bases. It would be better were they withdrawn.

(iii) *Will Britain continue to be targeted by Soviet warheads whether or not she disarms unilaterally?*

OR *Is Britain seen as an American aircraft carrier and targeted by the USSR accordingly? Will Britain fall an early victim in any superpower confrontation unless bases are removed?*

I agree with what is said on the right, although I do not think that the Soviet Union would lose all interest in Britain, if she were unilaterally to disarm and American facilities were removed.

(iv) *Can non-nuclear defences only safely be afforded by powers prepared to shelter beneath the American strategic umbrella?*

OR *In a nuclear-free Europe, decoupled from the superpower nuclear confrontation, would Britain no more expect to depend upon the US 'umbrella' than any other Western ally – or than Eastern Europe upon the USSR?*

I don't want to be sheltered by anyone's nuclear weapons, American or British. But I certainly think that, if we tell the Americans to leave, we will have to depend upon ourselves much more.

Moral Considerations

(i) *Is it morally right to pursue the policy least* OR *Are there actions which are in themselves likely to cause human suffering? May this wrong no matter what the situation? Is the sometimes involve doing things which in alternative to excuse almost any act of other circumstances would be wrong? barbarism?*

I endorse what is implied by the questions on the right.

(ii) *In formulating policy should we weigh up* OR *Is the only relevant point here that a the probability of success and the relative nuclear exchange of almost any kind costs in terms of human suffering of would in itself cause unimaginable alternative nuclear and non-nuclear suffering to largely civilian populations? strategies?*

Here again, I would agree with what is on the right, depending to some extent upon what goes into that 'almost'.

(iii) *So far as concerns intention, need we look* OR *Is there no such thing as a fully deployed no further than the fact that our sole aim in weapons system which is a bluff? Is to deploying nuclear weapons is to prevent deploy nuclear weapons to intend to use their use? them in certain circumstances?*

I think that to deploy nuclear weapons is to be *willing* to use them, rather than to *intend* to use them. It implies a conditional willingness that they should be used. In other words, it is an option that you have not ruled out. With that qualification, what is written on the right is correct.

(iv) *Are there possible uses of nuclear weapons* OR *Is a conditional intention to cause which are allowed by Just War theory, for indiscriminate and disproportionate example the bombing of Hiroshima and suffering of this kind, whether admonitory, Nagasaki in order to prevent worse preemptive or retaliatory, ruled out by Just suffering? Can there be a theory of Just War theory? Was it wrong to bomb Deterrence? Hiroshima and Nagasaki in 1945?*

So here, if we change 'intention' to 'willingness', I would accept the argument on the right. The continuing development and deployment of nuclear weapon systems is immoral in so far as it does involve such conditional willingness.

(v) *Is there no relevant connection between the* OR *Is it a scandal that such huge resources are development and deployment of nuclear devoted to the development and deployment weapons and world poverty and disease? of nuclear weapons and not to the alleviation of suffering?*

It is wrong to give the idea that nuclear weaponry is the most expensive part of the arms race. In some ways nuclear weapons are comparatively cheap. But, with that qualification, I agree with the implied statement on the right.

(vi) *Does Christian teaching allow the* OR *Does Christian teaching condemn the deployment of nuclear weapons? deployment of nuclear weapons?*

If by 'Christian teaching' we mean only what is in the Gospels, then this is very hard to answer, because so little is said about war, one way or the other.

But, if we take Just War theory to be an integral part of traditional Christian teaching, then I do indeed think that the use of nuclear weapons is condemned. So far as concerns their deployment, I would say that Christian teaching in the broader sense would only allow it on the terms outlined in my book. That is to say, temporarily, while the process of nuclear disarmament is being accomplished, and accompanied by a strict and explicit declaration that they will never be used under any circumstances, together with practical measures taken to ensure that this will be so.

Recommendations

1 Yes (See **B(vii)**).
2 Certainly on Anti-Satellite programmes. Not, perhaps, on all components of the Strategic Defence Initiative, because some are harmless and are likely to go ahead whether or not they are incorporated in SDI (See **A2**(A) (**v**)).
3 Yes.
4 (See **B(iii)**).
5 Yes. Although they do not all have to be immediate. They have to be seriously planned, seriously announced, and credibly put in train, so that the other side's intelligence knows that you really mean it.
6 I do not feel strongly either way about a European Nuclear Weapon-Free Zone.
7 I think that the powers who have not yet signed should do so. But I don't think that it makes a great deal of difference.
8 Yes, although I think that it is optimistic to expect anything like this earlier than well on into the next century. I would be happy if it was down to what I call a 'transitional deterrent' before the end of the century.
9 I accept the idea of a minimum nuclear deterrent on two conditions. First, that it is transitional to complete global nuclear disarmament. Second, that people really would have to mean that they would not use it, if the worst came to the worst.
10 Yes.
11 Yes (See B(iii)).
12 Yes (See **B(iv)**).
13 Yes, but see No. 16 below.
14 Yes.
15 See No. 6 above.
16 Yes, if we are talking about our continuing to be a member of the NATO Alliance. If we had an effective Western European alliance, then, if it was considered to be necessary, I would hope that Britain and France would hand over their nuclear capability to a European commmand (See **C1(ii)**).
17 Ideally, no. But, if the alternative was to keep nuclear weapons, yes (See **C1(iv)**).

18 I am coming round to thinking that Britain should not remain inside NATO (See **C2(i)**).

19 Yes to all of this (See **C2(ii)**).

20 Britain should be prepared to leave NATO if all else failed.

The Very Reverend
Monseigneur Bruce Kent

Biographical Note

Born in 1929, Bruce Kent served as a Second Lieutenant with the 6th Royal Tank Regiment between 1947 and 1949, and then took a Law degree at Oxford University. He was ordained in 1958, served as a curate in Kensington and Notting Hill, and, between 1964 and 1974, was chaplain at London University. Since then, as well as being at the Church of St John the Evangelist, Islington, until 1987, he has been Chairperson of War on Want (1974–6), and, first Chairperson, then General Secretary, of the Campaign for Nuclear Disarmament (1977–1985). He is now Vice Chairperson of CND and President of the International Peace Bureau.

Editorial Comment

These answers were given in an interview in Islington on March 6, 1986. They represent the response of someone who has been actively campaigning for peace for over twenty years, and has become widely influential as a spokesperson for CND and related organizations. The emphasis throughout is on the unusability of nuclear weapons, and on the consequent dangers inherent in defence policies based upon them. The answer to question **A2(B)(iv)** provides the wider conceptual setting for this. In addition, the central moral objection to nuclear weapon deployment is summed up in the answer to question **(iii)** under *Moral Considerations*. Of particular interest to the reader may be the answer to question **B(vii)**, in which Bruce Kent explains CND's central approach, and corrects a popular misunderstanding of it.

Mgr BRUCE KENT

A *Global Policy*

1 *The History of the Past Forty Years*

(i) *Has it been nuclear deterrence that has*   OR *Has it mainly been other factors?*
kept the peace between the great powers
since 1945?

Neither I nor anybody else can answer the main question conclusively here, because you cannot change individual factors and re-run history in order to find out. But, by the way, I will not call what has happened since 1945 'peace': the superpowers have worked out their wars in other people's countries at a cost of something like twenty million lives.

(ii) *Does mutual possession of an invulnerable* OR *Does the threat of strategic nuclear*
second-strike strategic nuclear force prevent   *retaliation, particularly against a similarly*
war?   *armed enemy, lack credibility and invite*
                                                     sub-deterrent encroachment?

I believe that, if nuclear weapons are possessed by two rational groups in opposition to one another, then the very possession of them, together with the threat to use them in retaliation, will actually prevent either side from initiating a nuclear attack. Each will know what the consequences would be. But I do not think that this has any effect on what you call 'sub-deterrent encroachment'. Since the nuclear option is so irrational, I think that both sides, through their satellites, and even by direct conflict, can risk sub-nuclear attack on one another.

(iii) *Have limited nuclear options at strategic and theatre levels enhanced deterrence by dramatically raising the threshold between peace and war?*	OR *Have most military planners from the start been aiming for nuclear war-fighting superiority? Has 'flexible response' dangerously lowered the threshold between conventional and nuclear war?*

I think that the attempt to get out of the irrationality of this mutual suicide position has actually created its own irrationalities. By lowering the threshold, by producing tactical nuclear weapons and so on, the military planners, particularly in the West, have made the boundary between nuclear and non-nuclear war much easier to cross. Since I do not believe that it makes sense for either side to attack the other, I think that war, if it occurs, will come about by some miscalculation. And, in that situation, we will be the first to use nuclear weapons, because we have relied on them as if we could win. I think that the logical nonsense of this policy of 'flexible response' is that there must be an assumption that you can have a limited nuclear war, that you can fire nuclear weapons and stop at a certain level. I can see no support for that at all, and therefore I think that the whole system of 'flexible response' is flawed in its very foundations. (I must say, though, that I am not sure that it's true that military planners have been deliberately aiming for nuclear 'war-fighting superiority'. Some have, like Weinberger, but in general it's worst-case analysis that leads planners always to want a bit more, in order to be able to negotiate from strength. But I don't think that this could fairly be called a 'war fighting' mentality.)

(iv) *Has the size and variety of the nuclear arsenals held by the superpowers stabilized deterrence?*	OR *Has the logic of nuclear confrontation and worst-case analysis generated a dangerous and strategically pointless superfluity of weapons systems?*

There is no sense in having a profusion of weapons unless you happen to believe that limited nuclear war has got some sense. For deterrence against nuclear attack, all you need is a very small number of invulnerable submarines facing one another. You don't need anything else, because every submarine is capable of delivering the most appalling second-strike retaliatory punishment, and, if people are not deterred by losing fifty of their cities, they they'll be deterred by nothing. So you certainly don't need additional nuclear weapons.

The build-up of nuclear arsenals has been very dangerous, because, together with improvements in technology, this has inevitably been seen as a move towards first use, and even first strike, policies.

(v) *Has the idea of nuclear balance between the superpowers been essential to stability and have arms-control negotiations helped to achieve it?*	OR *Have ideas of 'nuclear defence' and 'parity' proved illusory and is 'multilateral negotiation from strength' a contradiction in terms? Has 'arms-control' been just another name for the arms race?*

I think that 'parity' or 'balance' is the petrol of the arms race, because each side inevitably sees the other as ahead, and this impels both to try endlessly to 'catch up'. It is also plain that, although arms control has had a certain effect – for example the Partial Test Ban Treaty or SALT II could be said to be agreements in arms control, it has certainly not brought about a reduction in arsenals. The idea that there must be parity in numbers is part of a classic military approach, but is quite unnecessary if the aim is genuine nuclear deterrence.

So the idea of parity in numbers should be abandoned, and arms control measures should be pursued as steps on the way towards genuine disarmament, not as some kind of alternative to it.

(vi) *Has force-planning been controlled by strategic thinking?* OR *Has the self-reinforcing impetus of technology and vested interest dictated policies subsequently justified post hoc?*

Somebody described the situation as two giants in a cellar fighting in the dark. Neither side has much idea of what the other is doing, so each pursues its research projects in the laboratories, pressing forward with whatever new scheme has become a possibility for fear that the other is doing the same. For example, the Cruise missile again became feasible as a warhead carrier in about 1971 or 1972, and was then developed under its own impetus, not as a response to Soviet SS20s. It was only when it came to deployment that the SS20 was used as an excuse to hang it on. Both sides do that constantly. It is the technology that is dictating the policy rather than the other way round.

2 The Prospect for the Future

(A) WITH NUCLEAR WEAPONS

(i) *Does the threat of an enemy first strike remain inconceivable for the foreseeable future?* OR *Is there an increasing threat from accurate and time-urgent first-strike weapons?*

In any rational world a first strike remains inconceivable even for those who may think they have the capacity to attempt it, because they know that, if they did, atmospheric and other effects would cause incredible damage to themselves.

But the increasing threat to stability comes from the perception of the side which fears that it is at a disadvantage, and that the other side is gaining a superiority in first-strike capability. Greater accuracy and therefore counter-force capability, improved submarine detection, Star Wars (cloaking yourself in a lead jacket so you won't be vulnerable to the other side's attack) – put all those things together, and, if they follow a worst-cast analysis as they have to, then I think that a first-strike perception is bound to develop on the other side. They will have to say to themselves at some stage '*are we going to let them get into a first strike position or not?*' So it's the perception of the side that sees itself at a disadvantage that is, I think, the danger here.

(ii) *Are command, control, communication and* OR *Does the amount of information to be*
intelligence facilities likely to remain   *processed, pressure of time and fear of*
secure?   *preemption put command and control*
                                                   systems under intolerable strain and make
                                                   inadvertent war more likely?

Well, even now studies such as those by Desmond Ball[1] show that command
and control systems are much more archaic than I think people realize, and
much more dependent upon human error. As we move forward and produce
faster weapons with shorter flight-times, we are constantly making command,
control and communications more difficult with less time to respond. So I
would say that we are moving towards a position of intolerable strain, where
war by miscalculation does become more likely.

(iii) *If nevertheless there were a limited nuclear* OR *Is the idea that nuclear war could be*
exchange would it be likely to end   *limited once it had broken out a dangerous*
hostilities swiftly?   *illusion?*

I don't know who supports the idea that a nuclear exchange could be limited
now. And yet those who defend current policy have to argue that way. Carrington's speech in January was very interesting in this respect. He said that, as
well as having the function of deterring an enemy from using nuclear or other
weapons, nuclear weapons also have the operational function of bringing the
war to an end should deterrence fail. He has acknowledged the possibility of
the failure of deterrence as very few people do, and he thinks that nuclear
weapons can be used intelligently in that situation. I don't.

(iv) *Do new generations of battlefield and*   OR *Do new battlefield and theatre weapons*
theatre nuclear systems reinforce   *threaten a dangerous lowering of the*
deterrence?   *nuclear threshold?*

This has already been answered in **AI(iii)**. Any weapons system that has behind
it a strategy of first use lowers the threshold. It implies what is not possible.

(v) *Does the Strategic Defence Initiative offer* OR *Is the Strategic Defence Initiative simply*
the hope of an effective defence against   *the most recent and destabilizing example*
nuclear weapons?   *of the process outlined in 1?*

Well, it must be as on the right-hand side. Deterrence rests on the vulnerability
of the opponent. Once his vulnerability is removed, deterrence is brought to
an end, and that is very destabilizing. So there can be no argument but that
SDI is destabilizing.

Beyond that, of course, it's not going to work, apart perhaps from providing
some sort of protection for land-based missiles – which is destabilizing in a
different way, because it suggests progress towards first strike capability.

If the eventual elimination of nuclear weapons, or defence against them,
were genuinely the aim, then a far easier, cheaper and safer way of doing this
would be by starting to remove them!

---

1. For example, *Can Nuclear War be Controlled?* (International Institute for Strategic Studies
1981).

(vi) *Is the threat of 'horizontal' nuclear*   OR *Is continuing reliance on nuclear deterrence*
proliferation best met by a continuation of   *by the great powers bound to accelerate the*
past policies?   *process of proliferation and make nuclear*
                                                     war more likely?

If nuclear weapons are said to be essential for the defence of some countries, so must they be for the defence of others. It seems to me that logically proliferation is inevitable once the process has begun. It is true that it is remarkable that there are still only five countries that openly acknowledge possessing nuclear weapons, and perhaps two more that have them, and that proliferation is not moving faster than that. But, if we go on as we are, it will come. And the proliferation that no one is thinking about is the proliferation to sub-national groups – I see no reason why the PLO shouldn't acquire nuclear weapons of some sort or other.

(vii) *Do multilateral arms-control negotiations*   OR *Is 'arms-control' an illusion which diverts*
offer the best prospect for future stability?   *attention from the only safe policy –*
                                                      nuclear disarmament?

I repeat what I said in answer to **AI(V)**. A search for 'parity', a gentlemen's agreement to keep present high levels of nuclear weapons in a certain pattern, is not what I mean by 'arms control'. I see arms control as part of the process of nuclear disarmament.

(B) WITHOUT NUCLEAR WEAPONS

(i) *If nuclear arsenals were dismantled would*   OR *Would nuclear disarmament remove the*
war between the great powers again   *incentive for nuclear preemption while not*
become a rational option and therefore   *affecting the reluctance of the great powers*
more likely?   *to initiate a third world war?*

Well, I don't think that even with conventional weapons only, war between the great powers is a rational option, because the level of destructive power is so vast that both sides would suffer enormously. But I would agree that we can't just be leaving the world as it is, and simply remove the nuclear weapons from it. We have got at the same time to do a number of other things which will help to build confidence, interlock countries economically, and so on. But, even if present levels of distrust and hostility remain, I don't think that, with nuclear weapons out of the way, there would be an incentive to war.

(ii) *Would a major conventional war be likely*   OR *Is conventional war, however terrible,*
in itself to be as terrible as a limited   *preferable to nuclear war?*
nuclear war?

The assumption on the left-hand side is that there can be such a thing as a limited nuclear war, which, as I have said, I do not believe. But would a major conventional war be as terrible as, say, the accidental release of a flight of Cruise missiles? I don't know. I don't think that you can balance it. I don't think that there is any way in which you can answer that question.

(iii) *Because nuclear weapons cannot be*   OR *As with nerve gases in the last war, would*
uninvented would they not be bound to be   *there be no incentive to resort to*
used sooner or later once war had broken   *capabilities which the other side has as*
out?   *well?*

This takes me into a strange world, because it assumes that hostilities continue
in the absence of nuclear weapons, and that is not what we are working for.
But I suppose it's true that you cannot 'uninvent' anything – things like the
rack could be reintroduced, for example. If a third world war of a conventional
sort started, I am sure that both sides would think of manufacturing nuclear
weapons. But, if each side realized that the other had the capability as well,
then they would, as it were, cancel each other out.

But the main point is that you cannot altogether remove risk from the world.
At the moment the biggest possible risk is incurred by doing nothing about
ongoing technology, and letting the present situation continue. A policy of
proper nuclear disarmament would involve real, but much smaller, risks. If
the house is on fire, whatever way you escape, you'll face risks.

(iv) *Is global nuclear disarmament only*   OR *Is to argue that even multilateral nuclear*
feasible in a world where war itself is no   *disarmament is not desirable to give up all*
longer a possibility?   *hope of a rational world-order?*

To abandon even a programme of multilateral nuclear disarmament is to give up
hope of the future, which I think a lot of people are doing. Now we see people like
Michael Heseltine suggesting that nuclear weapons in their country are going to
be around as long as anyone else has got nuclear weapons. And I think that is
giving up hope of multilateral disarmament. It's a great pessimism. The assumption is that we have always got to do the worst in life. Human beings have always
got to behave in the most dreadful way. I don't think that's actually true in history. People do behave in other ways, and, once the general understanding has
been reached that nuclear weapons cannot produce any intelligent military
results, then we have a different sort of motivation for giving them up. We are
not talking about giving up rifles or anything that would traditionally be called
'weapons'. We have got something for which there isn't a word. That's why
Oliver Postage[1] used the word 'geddon' for them (from 'Armageddon') – he says
we shouldn't use the word 'weapon' at all. Vocabularies preserve ways of thinking. Once you use 'weapon' you've lost the argument. Even Reagan has now
acknowledged in his 'Star Wars' speeches that indefinite reliance on nuclear
'weapons' is irrational and a policy of despair.

(v) *Is peace only preserved when we are seen to*   OR *Do the years before 1914 show what*
be prepared for war, as failure before 1939   *happens when military planning and the*
and success since 1945 show? Under likely   *arms race control political choices? Do*
future conditions would global nuclear   *present strategies make nuclear war almost*
disarmament make war, including nuclear   *inevitable under likely future conditions? Is*
war, more likely?   *global nuclear disarmament the only*
                                                      rational policy?

---

1. '*The Writing in the Sky*' Trenard Press, 1983.

The assumption on the left-hand side is that there is a rational person who wants war, and, in the absence of nuclear weapons, would not be deterred from having a war. I don't think that's the situation. No rational person could want war, but, because of our current policies and our technology, we are moving towards war. So I think that we are in much more of a 1914 than a 1939 situation.

But I do think that there is a great deal of quite disgraceful propaganda about that run up to the 1939 war, that is widely believed. Our predecessors in the peace movements were actually supporting the League of Nations vigorously, whilst a number of Establishment figures were opposing the League and appeasing Hitler.

B *NATO Policy*

(i) *Does the Soviet Union, together with her Warsaw Pact allies, enjoy a strategically dangerous military superiority in Europe?*   OR *Are NATO and WTO forces relatively evenly matched?*

I'm not an expert, I just read the books. It's very difficult to know what you count and what weight you give to what you count. I would suggest that, if you put all the relevant factors into the soup bowl – such as, for example, the political unreliability of Poland, East Germany and Czechoslovakia, which is a major issue, then the situation is that the two sides are probably evenly matched. But it's not the kind of question that can be easily answered. You can say that they have got more of one thing – tanks, for instance – and we have got more of another – say, anti-tank weapons. But it is not an equation that on its own makes much sense, because, even if they do have more of this, that, or the other, it does not follow that they have got a dangerous superiority. Strategically significant superiority means that there would be hope of something called 'victory'. And there would not be.

(ii) *Is the Soviet Union an expansionist power which will take advantage of unilateral Western concessions and is only restrained and forced to accept arms-control agreements by Western determination and strength?*   OR *Is the Soviet Union an encircled and threatened power trying to keep up with Western technology and likely to respond positively to unconditional offers of Western restraint within a general context of detente?*

My inclination is to choose the right-hand side of the page. That's not to say that the Soviet Union cannot behave disgracefully, which it clearly can, as can be seen in Afghanistan, or in the appalling purges of its own people. But to me the overall picture is clearly one of an encircled power, which has from the beginning been deeply conscious of the Western aim to 'strangle the baby of Bolshevism' in its cradle. If the Soviet Union is an expansionist power, then it is doing extremely badly. It has been thrown out of far more countries than it has occupied. With the single exception of Afghanistan it has maintained its Yalta boundaries.

(iii) *Is Soviet chemical and conventional preponderance such that NATO must continue to be able to threaten early use of nuclear weapons?*
OR *Is NATO dependence on the early use of nuclear weapons unnecessary and strategically suicidal?*

I don't believe that any of the Institutes of Strategic Studies, or their equivalents, would claim that there was an overwhelming conventional preponderance of this kind. But, even if this were true, the early use of nuclear weapons is no counter to the threat, because it rests on the false assumption that there can be a limited nuclear war. It always comes back to that.

(iv) *Does the growing size of the Soviet nuclear arsenal threaten the delicate theatre and strategic balance? Would Western failure to match Soviet systems be destabilizing?*
OR *Does the West initiate nearly all phases of the nuclear arms race and continue to enjoy a substantial lead in most areas? Is the nuclear 'overkill' such that the West could offer a nuclear 'freeze' or unconditional cuts without risk?*

Well, indeed, both sides could offer unconditional cuts without risk. When you consider the number of nuclear weapons that there are – 50,000 or so – you can see that there is no 'delicate balance' at all. The numbers game just does not make sense. Both sides could make independent major cuts now.

(v) *Are NATO 'forward defence' and 'deep strike' strategies essential for effective deterrence?*
OR *Should NATO exploit her lead in 'emerging technology' to explore less provocative alternative strategies?*

If deep strike and forward defence strategies include a nuclear component, as they do, then I can only repeat what I said about the idea of limited nuclear war. If we're talking about conventional weapons only, then I would have thought that it would be much better to get away from the provocative nature of deep strike strategies, and concentrate on holding your own territory, not striking at other peoples'.

(vi) *Is it the presence of American front-line troops and the tying-in of theatre nuclear forces to the American strategic deterrent that guarantees W. European security? Should American policies therefore be supported?*
OR *Is it domination by the two super-powers that poses the greatest threat to European integrity? Would Europe be safer decoupled from the super-power nuclear confrontation? Should Europe be made a nuclear weapon-free zone?*

If you want Europe to be 'coupled' in this way, you don't need European-based nuclear weapons to do it. The Americans have got something like 300,000 troops and dependants in Western Europe, and, if that doesn't couple them, nothing will.

But I do not think that the threat is that one side will attack the other – what could either gain from direct assault on the other? The reality of the situation is that it is the superpowers who present the greatest possible danger to Europe, because their confrontation feeds and increases the technology of nuclear weaponry. I want a nuclear-free zone in Europe. I want American troops out of Western Europe and Russian troops out of Eastern Europe.

(vii) *Would Western unilateral nuclear disarmament invite Soviet blackmail? Are suggestions that the West should take the lead in offering unilateral disarmament initiatives the thin end of this wedge? Do radical nuclear disarmers consciously or unconsciously serve Soviet interests and threaten to undermine Western defences?*

OR *Are unilateral initiatives as part of a general programme of nuclear disarmament the only way to reverse the arms race? Is talk of 'multilateral disarmament' insincere in the mouths of those who reject all suggestion of a Comprehensive Test Ban Treaty, a Nuclear Freeze, a European Nuclear Weapon-Free Zone, or a declaration of No First Use?*

The right-hand side is my position. It is what CND is urging – unilateral disarmament initiatives by both sides as part of a general process of nuclear disarmament. We are not advocating immediate Western unilateral disarmament. You may ask why, if nuclear weapons are illegal, immoral, and suicidal, we are not advocating this. The answer is that for political reasons we have to compromise. In order to make some political gains, you have to accept the reality that you are not going to achieve these things straight away. In fact, it does not follow that, if one country has nuclear weapons and another does not, then the latter is likely to be open to nuclear blackmail – for example, the Americans did not try it in Vietnam. There is an inherent madness in threatening to use nuclear weapons against a non-nuclear power – although the popular psyche wouldn't accept this. But CND does not urge immediate and complete Western or Eastern nuclear disarmament. It urges unilateral *initiatives* where necessary, without which there is no hope of making any progress at all. The level of weaponry is such that we can all offer these initiatives without being unreasonable or putting stability at risk.

Opponents of CND deliberately foster the idea that we are in favour of immediate and complete unilateral Western disarmament – for example, Carrington and Howe have said as much in major speeches within the last 12 months. It is a fundamental point for CND to get across that this is quite untrue.

C British Policy

1 The British Deterrent

(i) *Is Britain's deterrent a weapon of last resort which guarantees her sovereignty and independence and protects her from nuclear blackmail?*

OR *Would all possible uses of Britain's 'deterrent' be suicidal? Is its only effect to encourage proliferation?*

I can think of no possible use that would not be suicidal. The single thing to be said in favour of British independent nuclear weapons is that they might deter the use of nuclear weapons by somebody else. That's all. They do not even deter an enemy from invading this country with conventional forces.

There are also all sorts of other disadvantages with them, such as that they make disarmament negotiations more difficult.

(ii) *Are British nuclear forces valuable to European allies because they provide a specifically European second centre of decision making?*   OR *Is the 'second centre of decision making' an illusion when the weapons are dependent upon the US and there is no independent strategic role to be played? Are European allies unenthusiastic about a parochial British force likely to inhibit her commitment to European defence?*

I don't think that we have heard from our European allies what they think of an independent British nuclear weapon. They seem just to leave us alone to do our own thing. If it meant that we had to cut down on our conventional contribution, that might be another issue – but at the moment we're also spending quite heavily on that, too.

But there's certainly no 'second centre of decision making' unless there is a prospect of doing what the capability is meant to suggest. Since that is not the case, there is no second centre.

(iii) *Does the US favour shared responsibility and do British nuclear forces guarantee full US commitment to Europe and Soviet recognition of it?*   OR *Are US forces committed anyway and independent British initiatives more likely to trigger Soviet retaliation than US involvement?*

Again, there is little evidence of serious American opinion about British independent nuclear weapons. As far as I can see, there is just a reluctant acquiescence that Britain wants to have them.

I don't see a link between an independent British nuclear force and American commitment to Europe, since I can find no function for an independent nuclear force. The Americans are here, and are substantially linked to Europe anyway. I think that it is just a nuisance in terms of disarmament negotiations. It's a joker in the pack. I don't think that it guarantees anything.

(iv) *Is the cost of the British deterrent small in view of the vital defence role it plays? Are alternatives likely to be more expensive?*   OR *Can Britain's nuclear forces only be afforded at the expense of conventional strength and of other more important economic priorities?*

It is certainly, as on the right-hand side, at the cost of more important priorities. The questions are slanted in the direction of assuming that security is only purchased by spending money on weapons, be they nuclear or non-nuclear, and I think that this is only a small part of the real security picture. But, on the left-hand side, the very word 'alternative' is one that I do not accept, because you cannot have an alternative to something that is not there. Money spent on Britain's independent nuclear weapons is money down the drain – it's not defence at all.

(v) *Would unilateral British nuclear disarmament have no effect on other countries and only serve to weaken British influence and allow France unchallenged ascendancy in Europe?*   OR *Does the British deterrent encourage proliferation and do nothing to enhance British prestige? Would British disarmament within the context outlined in B help to break the nuclear log-jam?*

At least British nuclear disarmament initiatives can't make proliferation *more* likely, and can only encourage those in other countries who are anxious to take similar steps themselves. I agree that we must not make too much of this, but example can help, as we have seen in New Zealand.

In any case, I don't think that genuine influence depends upon weapons. Some countries of very small size have more influence than we have here – the Five Continents Peace Proposal[1] is very important and has come from militarily small countries. Conversely, France may want to be the biggest arms-trader and nuclear dump in Europe. Fine. But that does not give her significant influence. There is nothing that France can do with all these things.

(vi) *Is investment in Trident the best way to continue to ensure effective British strategic defence into the 21st century?*   OR *Would commitment to Trident exacerbate all the drawbacks listed above?*

I deny the assumption behind the left-hand side. I think that Trident is not just a continuance of existing 'deterrent' forces, but has first-strike potential, violates the Non-Proliferation Treaty, and so on. There are many arguments against Trident, and, even for those like David Owen who want an independent nuclear weapon, it is not a good idea.

2 *NATO Forces and US Bases*

(i) *Must Britain continue to share responsibility for manning NATO nuclear systems upon which her security depends? Would refusal to do so fatally weaken the alliance?*   OR *Should British obligations to NATO be met by strengthening conventional forces where necessary within an overall non-nuclear strategy as recommended in B?*

Since all NATO nuclear systems in Europe are first use systems, deployed according to military strategy, which, as we have seen, would be suicidal, I think that we should not continue to man such systems. This will no doubt be seen as a betrayal of NATO by the Carvers of this world, in a way that the abandonment of our independent deterrent will not. But it is not treachery to the Alliance to object to policies that threaten to destroy it. While we are in NATO and are genuinely concerned about security, let us talk cooperatively about meeting whatever the threat is that we are supposed to be meeting. But not with nuclear weapons of first use.

---

1. An initiative launched in May 1984 by the Presidents of Argentina and Mexico, the Prime Ministers of Greece, India and Sweden and the First President of Tanzania.

(ii) *Would the forced withdrawal of US nuclear bases from Britain make US defence of the West impossible? Is American interference in British affairs negligible?* OR *Do the large numbers of nuclear facilities yielded to the US erode British sovereignty? Would their removal do no more than restore a normal peacetime relationship?*

American interference in British affairs is not negligible. There is legal interference, polilitical interference, and so on. Our sovereignty is certainly being reduced. Southern Ireland has got more sovereignty in these matters than we have.

And, since many of the bases are first use bases, I don't think that they contribute to the defence of the West. When they were set up, they were for planes like the B-29 which did not have the range to reach the USSR from the US, but now, with Trident submarines and so on, the original justification no longer exists.

(iii) *Will Britain continue to be targeted by Soviet warheads whether or not she disarms unilaterally?* OR *Is Britain seen as an American aircraft carrier and targeted by the USSR accordingly? Will Britain fall an early victim in any superpower confrontation unless bases are removed?*

So long as Britain remains in a nuclear alliance, we are going to be targeted. Since the accuracy of these weapons is so uncertain, even Sweden and Switzerland may be struck by nuclear warheads in a confrontation. Nobody is going to be safe. But I think that the removal of first use bases will make preemption much less likely, and will be a step in the right direction.

(iv) *Can non-nuclear defences only safely be afforded by powers prepared to shelter beneath the American strategic umbrella?* OR *In a nuclear-free Europe, decoupled from the superpower nuclear confrontation, would Britain no more expect to depend upon the US 'umbrella' than any other Western ally – or than Eastern Europe upon the USSR?*

The problems with the wording on both sides here is that the word 'umbrella' has been used. Once you use the word, you have won the argument. If, instead, you were to say *'Shall we shelter under the American lightning conductor?'*, then the whole argument changes. American nuclear weapons endanger us rather than give us security.

In going non-nuclear ourselves we would be recognizing that politically we can't get the superpowers to get rid of all their weapons immediately, and so we are doing what we can to take steps in that direction. But we are not saying that we want the Americans to remain nuclear indefinitely.

Moral Considerations

(i) *Is it morally right to pursue the policy least* OR *Are there actions which are in themselves*
likely to cause human suffering? May this *wrong no matter what the situation? Is the*
sometimes involve doing things which in *alternative to excuse almost any act of*
other circumstances would be wrong? *barbarism?*

I am obviously a 'right-hand side' person. There are some acts that are so
abominable that no prudential arguments advanced in their favour can justify
them. But, in addition to that, all such prudential reasons depend upon supposing things which have not, or have not yet, happened – for example: '*If
you do or don't do this, then that will or will not happen*'. I don't think that
this kind of speculation ever justifies the massacring of hundreds of thousands
of people.

(ii) *In formulating policy should we weigh up* OR *Is the only relevant point here that a*
the probability of success and the relative *nuclear exchange of almost any kind*
costs in terms of human suffering of *would in itself cause unimaginable*
alternative nuclear and non-nuclear *suffering to largely civilian populations?*
strategies?

I have already answered this.

(iii) *So far as concerns intention, need we look* OR *Is there no such thing as a fully deployed*
no further than the fact that our sole aim in *weapons system which is a bluff? Is to*
deploying nuclear weapons is to prevent *deploy nuclear weapons to intend to use*
their use? *them in certain circumstances?*

The right-hand side is correct. There is such an obvious gap in the argument
on the left. What are the *means* being employed? It's as if a burglar said '*My
sole aim is to feed my family*' – but what is he proposing to do in order to feed
his family? He is preparing to rob the bank. In the case of nuclear deterrence,
it may be your pious intention, as you formulate the terrible intention to do
these things in certain circumstances in your mind, to hope that it will not
come to this. But the fact remains that you have already constructed a grossly
immoral capability, over those implementation you have no control. Outside
circumstances may require you to do it one day, and you have already acquiesced in this. That is the key argument about the morality of deterrence.

(iv) *Are there possible uses of nuclear weapons* OR *Is a conditional intention to cause*
which are allowed by Just War theory, for *indiscriminate and disproportionate*
example the bombing of Hiroshima and *suffering of this kind, whether admonitory,*
Nagasaki in order to prevent worse *preemptive or retaliatory, ruled out by Just*
suffering? Can there be a theory of Just *War theory? Was it wrong to bomb*
Deterrence? *Hiroshima and Nagasaki in 1945?*

As far as the left-hand side goes, the bombing of Hiroshima and Nagasaki was
quite unjustified and wrong. Actually, if people wanted to make things difficult for me, they would use a different example – say, the elimination of an
enemy nuclear submarine base with a low-yield Pershing II warhead. Here we

have a discriminate weapon aimed at a military target. What is wrong with that? I think that there *is* something wrong with it, because all nuclear weapons, I'm told, produce radio-active material that is likely to go on damaging people for generations to come, so that, even in highly limited use like that, it is still an indiscriminate weapon. But this is playing around with the thing. There can be no Just War theory that justifies the use of nuclear weapons, so there can be no Just Deterrent theory, either.

(v) *Is there no relevant connection between the* OR *Is it a scandal that such huge resources are*
development and deployment of nuclear   *devoted to the development and deployment*
weapons and world poverty and disease?   *of nuclear weapons and not to the*
                                                   alleviation of suffering?

There is obviously a connection here, although, of course, it's not just nuclear weapons that are at fault, but all armaments in general.

It would undoubtedly be of far greater benefit to mankind if the resources now being squandered on the development, manufacture and deployment of nuclear weapons were instead to be channelled into a concerted assault on the causes of world poverty and disease.

(vi) *Does Christian teaching allow the*   OR *Does Christian teaching condemn the*
deployment of nuclear weapons?   *deployment of nuclear weapons?*

Christian teaching undoubtedly condemns the use of nuclear weapons. It therefore also condemns the conditional intention to use them, which is inseparable from their deployment.

Papal and other pronouncements make it clear that we must move vigorously towards the goal of nuclear disarmament, and that the continuing deployment of existing weapons is only tolerated temporarily, and under strict conditions, while that process is being swiftly accomplished.

Recommendations

1 Yes.
2 Yes (See **A2**(A)(**v**)).
3 Yes. And the West should undoubtedly have stopped testing at once and unconditionally in response to the Soviet testing moratorium.
4 Yes (See **B(iii)**).
5 Yes (See **AI(iv)**).
6 Yes (See **B(vi)**).
7 Yes (See **A2**(A)(**vi**)).
8 Yes (See **A2(B)**).
9 Yes. But not because either superpower is *entitled* to these 'weapons', but because, given the political realities of the world, there is no way that either side is going to get rid of theirs while the other still has some. To call, therefore, for what would amount to unilateral superpower nuclear dis-

armament is to my mind counter-productive, since it will stop people taking the steps which they could take here and now.

10 Yes.

11 Yes (See **B(iii)**).

12 Yes (See **B(iv)**).

13 Yes (See **CI(v)**).

14 Yes (See **B(vi)**).

15 Yes (See **B(vi)**).

16 Yes (See **CI**).

17 No (See **CI(iv)**).

18 Yes. But once again, as with No. 9, only because of the realities of the situation. We *are* going to stay in NATO, so let us by all means press for a non-nuclear strategy. Getting rid of American nuclear bases is going to be hard enough (See **C2(i)**).

19 Yes (See **C2(i)** & **C2(ii)**).

20 No.

Major-General
Yuri Lebedev

Biographical Note

Major-General Yuri Lebedev is Deputy Departmental Chief of the General Staff of the Armed Forces of the USSR. Born in 1925, he has been in military service since 1944, having graduated from military college and military-engineering academy. He subsequently served both in the field and in the central apparatus of the USSR Ministry of Defence. He is a specialist in the sphere of strategic arms, and took part in Soviet-American talks on the limitation and reduction of nuclear weapons.

Editorial Comment

This essay, entitled *The Arms Race and International Security*, has been written especially for this book, and translated by Natalia Mazitova. It represents the response of an experienced Soviet commentator to the questions sent. In order to help the reader to compare Major-General Lebedev's analysis with that of other contributors, the editor has taken the liberty of adding the appropriate sub-headings and lettering necessary to coordinate it with the questions under *Global Policy* in Section A.

Major-General Lebedev sees the nuclear arms race as having been created and sustained by the United States, as part of a bid for global dominance. The US nuclear arsenal is intended, either for direct use in a disarming first strike, or, by threatening it, as an instrument of nuclear blackmail during times of political crisis. The deterrent role of nuclear weapons is discounted by the author, and the stress throughout is on the increasing instability and danger which inevitably results from the continued US drive for permanent military superiority, and the Soviet refusal to permit it. Military solutions can no longer be found for problems which are largely political. Major-General Lebedev's central proposal is that this should now be recognized by both sides, so that political solutions can be found for political problems, and swift progress can be made towards the elimination of nuclear weapons altogether.

MAJOR-GENERAL YURI LEBEDEV

Mankind is entering the threshold of the twenty-first century with both concerns and hopes. The continued race for weapons, nuclear weapons above all, may lead to the incineration of our civilization in the nuclear flames.

A *Global Policy*

1 *The History of the Past Forty Years*

Having acquired nuclear weapons at the close of World War II, the United States military and political leaders thought that they could be used as the decisive instrument of foreign policy. This view appeared to dominate United States political philosophy and military strategy in the postwar history. The Americans initiated and continue to initiate every advance in the arms race. The development of nuclear weapons in the United States was followed by the production of thousands of nuclear warheads with which ever more sophisticated ground-, sea-, and air-based delivery vehicles were equipped for decades. Sophistication and build-up of other types of weapons – both mass destruction and conventional – were carried out in parallel without any interruption.

Let's analyse in retrospect the arms race unleashed by the Americans in the postwar period.

Stage One: Massive production of nuclear warheads and their delivery vehicles

The US had a nuclear monopoly from 1945 to 1949. By 1949 (when the Soviet Union staged its first nuclear test) the United States already had from 100 to 200 atomic bombs, and their carriers – B-29 bombers.

By 1957 – the time of United States rapid nuclear arms build-up – it had produced more than 2,000 nuclear bombs as compared with several hundred which the Soviet Union had.

At the same time the United States was stepping up the build-up of delivery vehicles – thousands of B-29, B-36, B-47, and B-52 bombers.

Stage Two: The race for nuclear missiles

In the period 1957–1962, America enhanced her nuclear arsenals from 2,000 to 4,000 nuclear warheads, and gave a powerful impetus to the development of fundamentally new delivery vehicles – intercontinental ballistic missiles of all basing modes. American scientists admit that as a result of this massive effort, United States supremacy in the nuclear field continued to be overwhelming in the early 1960s. The ratio between Soviet and American strategic weapons by 1963 was as follows:

Delivery vehicles	US	USSR
ICBM launchers	229	44
SLBM launchers	144	97
Ballistic missile Launchers of medium and intermediate range	105	(20–40)
Strategic bombers	1,300	155

So the American fostered myth about the 'Soviet missile threat' had no grounds whatsoever. Yet, it was used to impart an even more powerful impetus to the arms race in the US – hundreds of ICBMs and SLBMs were developed and deployed, and their sophistication continued.

Each time the Soviet Union had to react to the American escalation.

Importantly, the countermeasures taken by the Soviet Union were not aimed at gaining military superiority, but were strictly determined by the need to offset the threat.

Rough strategic parity was established in the early 1970s. But it did not suit Washington which resolutely pushed the arms race into a new channel by deciding to equip its missiles with MIRVs.

By the time Richard Nixon came to the White House, the United States had already carried out the programme for the deployment of offensive strategic arms, and tested MIRVed Minutemen-3 and Poseidons in 1968. From

1970, the United States began to MIRV its strategic missiles on a massive scale.

Stage Three: MIRVing of missiles

In 1970, the first ten MIRVed missiles were deployed in American ICBM silos. Somewhat later, Poseidon Submarine Launched Ballistic Missiles (SLBMs) were test-launched from a submerged submarine. Several months later, in the spring of 1971, the first atomic missile submarine, with new missiles, was placed on combat duty. The United States had launched a new round of the nuclear arms race, once again trying to gain military superiority over the Soviet Union.

In the estimate of American experts, the United States had thereby more than doubled its nuclear warhead total from 4,000 units in 1970 to 8,500 in 1977.

But even this did not seem enough to Washington. In the late 1970s the Americans continued to escalate the nuclear arms race. They modernized the Minuteman-2 and Minuteman-3 ICBMs, stepped up the development of anti-satellite (ASAT) weapons, and began to prepare for the re-equipment of twin atomic missile submarines with Trident-1 SLBMs. On June 30, 1977 the American Administration adopted a decision to deploy air-launched Cruise missiles. This new hard-to-control and dangerous type of weapon created serious difficulties for the conclusion of the SALT-2 Treaty.

And, finally, in the autumn of 1981 the new American President, Ronald Reagan, announced a programme of *'America's strategic rearmament'* aimed at placing the arms race on an entirely new foundation.

In this context it would be logical to ask: what effect did the Washington-launched nuclear arms race produce on United States security?

In brief it was as follows. As a result of the nuclear arms race which went on for decades, United States security was seriously jeopardized rather than strengthened. Indeed, American territory is no longer immune to enemy military operations as it was at the dawn of the nuclear age.

As a result of the nuclear arms race, the world has accumulated tens of thousands of nuclear warheads which can destroy all life on the planet. Washington has itself become hostage to nuclear weapons and its myopic postwar policy. Weapons themselves have become a politically senseless and militarily reckless instrument of foreign policy.

And, finally, the accumulation of huge stockpiles of nuclear weapons and their delivery vehicles has created such a dangerous factor for international security as a risk of unauthorized use of nuclear weapons. The price of technical error, or even the slightest inaccuracy in dealing with nuclear weapons has grown immeasurably. This has multiplied the threat to the security of the US and the rest of the world.

Stage Four: Giving a new dimension to the arms race

The current, fourth stage of the arms race which the US began in the late 1970s-early 1980s covers not only nuclear weapons, but all other types and systems of weapons and material, all forms of military activities. The race for offensive weapons – noth nuclear and space-strike weapons – is becoming especially dangerous.

Sometimes it is claimed that in the last decades the threat of mutual assured destruction was a factor which prevented an all-out war. Nothing is more dangerous than this illusion. It is not owing to, but despite, nuclear weapons that mankind has avoided a thermonuclear disaster so far.

2 The Prospect for the Future

(A) WITH NUCLEAR WEAPONS

The appearance of new types and systems of weapons and means of their control is bound to make the strategic situation even more precarious. An analysis of the peculiarities and potential consequences of the current stage of the arms race bears this out.

(i) *Does the threat of an enemy first strike remain inconceivable for the foreseeable future?*   OR *Is there an increasing threat from accurate and time-urgent first-strike weapons?*

To begin with, the United States is rapidly building a new strategic potential in addition to the existing one. It is planning to deploy new MX and Midgetman ICBMs, two new types of strategic bombers – the B-IB and Stealth ATB, an entirely new Trident system, and new-generation Cruise missiles of all basing modes with enhanced range, accuracy and speed. As a result of this massive development, Washington intends to have sited several thousand delivery vehicles and about 20,000 nuclear warheads by the early 1990s.

It should be stressed that all these nuclear weapons systems are much more effective than the existing ones and are designed for use in a first, 'disarming' strike against the Soviet Union and its allies. The military-strategic consequences of the United States effort to build such a potential may be extremely dangerous – it may upset the world's strategic stability and eventually trigger off a nuclear conflict. In other words, implementation of the American-planned programmes may precipitate a nuclear conflict which is bound to kill not only human civilization, but all life on earth. Now let's analyse the situation in more detail.

To begin with, trying to build a first-strike potential, Washington may develope an illusion that it will be in a position to use it. But this will be only an illusion, because the Soviet Union will never allow it to gain this potential for obvious reasons.

(ii) *Are command, control, communication and* OR *Does the amount of information to be*
      intelligence facilities likely to remain   *processed, pressure of time and fear of*
      secure?   *preemption put command and control*
                                                    systems under intolerable strain and make
                                                    inadvertent war more likely?

Secondly, a fundamentally new military-strategic situation is being created. The time for political decision-making is being reduced to the minimum, and weapons are being increasingly controlled by computers and other systems. At the same time, as the experience of the last few years has shown, even the most perfect technology is not guaranteed against mishaps which may spell disaster for all mankind.

(iii) *If nevertheless there were a limited nuclear* OR *Is the idea that nuclear war could be*
      exchange would it be likely to end   *limited once it had broken out a dangerous*
      hostilities swiftly?   *illusion?*

Thirdly, the United States has carried beyond any reasonable limits the sophistication of combat control, communication and intelligence systems. In effect, it wants to create an effective mechanism for controlling nuclear warfare.

Nothing is more dangerous than such calculations which encourage the development of adventurist plans for waging 'controlled', 'limited', 'sustained' and other nuclear wars. Under these plans a nuclear conflict can be 'controlled' and even 'won' if the corresponding weapons and combat control systems are developed. But nuclear war does not recognize any plans, scenarios and the like. Its consequences cannot be predicted, even with the latest computers.

(iv) *Do new generations of battlefield and*   OR *Do new battlefield and theatre weapons*
      theatre nuclear systems reinforce   *threaten a dangerous lowering of the*
      deterrence?   *nuclear threshold?*

Fourthly, deployment of first-strike weapons near Soviet borders (Pershing IIs and Cruise missiles have already been sited in Western Europe) inevitably enhances the risk of nuclear war, because missile travel time to targets is drastically reduced, as well as the time for decision-making on retaliation. Needless to say, in this case the USSR will increasingly mistrust the intentions of the United States ruling circles.

Apparently, the importance of this factor in the future will be growing, if the nuclear arms race is not curbed, and, all the more so, if the Americans deploy Trident II SLBMs capable of dealing high-accuracy strikes from a much closer range than the existing ICBMs. Understandably, such developments are extremely dangerous for international security because they can act as a catalyst of nuclear conflict, including an unsanctioned one.

The US-planned deployment of new types of strategic bombers and Cruise missiles inevitably leads to the lowering of the nuclear threshold, and can directly provoke it. Indeed, what is the Soviet Union supposed to do if it detects the launching of Cruise missiles or bombers which can carry both nuclear and conventional weapons?

Development of such weapons systems is a very destabilizing factor directly threatening international security, all the more so since the United States bluntly says that these systems are dual-purpose. The Americans want to turn these systems into an instrument of nuclear blackmail, using them whenever the world tensions are escalated to a very dangerous level.

Even a cursory glance at the prospects of the world with nuclear weapons makes it clear that the continuation of the nuclear arms race will lead in the near future to the elimination of a number of deterrence factors, and nuclear weapons will turn from deterrents into weapons of aggression. In this situation even military-strategic parity will not be a guarantee against nuclear war.

The military-strategic situation in the world may become even worse under the influence of other factors which are not directly related to the nuclear arms race and the future of strategic East-West relations. The influence of these factors is so great that it is simply pointless to speak about the prospects of military-strategic relations without considering them.

(v) *Does the Strategic Defence Initiative offer* OR *Is the Strategic Defence Initiative simply the hope of an effective defence against the most recent and destabilizing example nuclear weapons? of the process outlined in 1?*

One of the most dangerous factors for international security is the United States programme for the development of space strike weapons in the SDI framework. Deployment of these weapons, and even their development are the most dangerous catalysts of a potential nuclear conflict. This is so because the latest strategic weapons developed under SDI exactly meet the American requirements for first-strike weapons – an ability to deal strikes at a wide range of strategically important targets almost instantly. It is clear that their development, not to mention deployment, has nothing to do with mutual deterrence. It is also obvious that their deployment will rapidly escalate the race for nuclear and other weapons in a whole number of directions. The Soviet Union can clearly perceive the dangerous potential consequences of space strike weapons. This is exactly why it favours an overall ban on their development and deployment.

The American President's brainchild has one more dangerous trait. If space strike weapons are used, the other side will have practically no time left for retaliation. But, as the Soviet Union has repeatedly stated, it will not allow the United States to build military superiority over it and will be compelled to take effective countermeasures even under the pressure of time limitations. As a result of these developments, strategic stability, about which the West is talking today with such enthusiasm, will be reduced to strategic chaos in which cause-and-effect relations will be extremely confused, and in which it will be highly difficult to make reasonable political decisions.

Deployment of a large number of satellites, combat and auxiliary stations, communication means, and potential Anti-Satellite (ASAT) systems may lead to serious complications because the breakdown of a militarily important satellite may be interpreted as an attack. In many cases, it is very difficult to tell whether a satellite simply went out of action or was deliberately destroyed.

Deployment of a large-scale Anti Ballistic Missile (ABM) system with space-based elements also spells a whole number of negative consequences. To begin with, unilateral deployment of these systems leads to a sharp destabilization of the entire military-strategic situation. The side which deploys it will have a potential capability of launching a 'disarming' nuclear strike in the hope that anti-missile weapons will intercept what remains of the other side's retaliatory potential. But the other side is not likely to sit idly by and watch the deployment of an ABM system. It is bound to take countermeasures which may further aggravate the military-strategic situation.

But even if both states deploy their ABM systems in parallel, strategic stability won't be enhanced because even a small lead in the deployment of such a system implies a marked destabilization of the global strategic situation. Meanwhile, one side will inevitably gain the lead because the development of ABM systems cannot be an even process.

SDI implementation will exacerbate the global military-strategic situation also because the very opportunity of limiting the arms race will be called into question. And this is perfectly obvious since, for a number of years, the Soviet Union and the USA were trying to reach agreement on limiting offensive strategic weapons but to no avail, although the problem of nuclear balance was not yet complicated by the 'space factor'.

Another set of negative military-strategic consequences stemming from SDI implementation is linked with a sharp acceleration of the arms race, which may eventually go out of control. SDI implies not only a large-scale ABM system, but also a new round in the arms race. So its implementation will spell a broad range of hard-to-predict consequences of this race in both technological and military-strategic aspects.

It is obvious that SDI implementation will give a powerful impetus to the use of the latest advances in science and technology for military purposes. The United States Administration does not conceal that this is its aim. Weapons based on fundamentally new technologies, both nuclear and conventional, will be many times superior to the existing armaments. In these conditions it will be even more difficult to preserve military-strategic parity, mistrust between states will grow, and military-strategic stability will increasingly depend on how quickly this, that, or the other state will manage to use the latest scientific and technical gains for military purposes.

(vi) *Is the threat of 'horizontal' nuclear proliferation best met by a continuation of past policies?*   OR *Is continuing reliance on nuclear deterrence by the great powers bound to accelerate the process of proliferation and make nuclear war more likely?*

Military competition is growing more expensive all the time, arms spending is skyrocketing, and the priceless resources, which are rather limited, are being increasingly squandered on the arms race. This process will trigger off serious economic, commercial and financial difficulties which are bound to exert a negative effect on the political and military-strategic situation in the world.

(vii) *Do multilateral arms-control negotiations*   OR *Is 'arms-control' an illusion which diverts*
offer the best prospect for future stability?   *attention from the only safe policy –*
                                                      nuclear disarmament?

To sum up, SDI implementation will seriously prejudice international security, and sharply destabilize the political and military-strategic situation in the world. On the other hand, renunciation of the Star Wars programme will not aggravate the existing security problems in any way, but will create favourable conditions for arms limitation and disarmament. A graphic example is offered by Reykjavik. Its results were actually torpedoed by Washington's reluctance to abandon its plans for space militarization, making it clear that the present Administration does not want to curb the arms race and rid the world of nuclear weapons.

The arms race, above all the nuclear arms race, has entered a fundamentally new stage of its escalation. If it is not curbed today, tomorrow may be too late. Military confrontation will grow markedly, strategic stability will be done away with, and the very possibility of ensuring international security will be called into question. Military and technical processes will create a situation in which nuclear weapons will no longer be able to act as deterrents. They will be turned into weapons of suicide.

(B) WITHOUT NUCLEAR WEAPONS

Investing in the arms race, and staking the future on military-technical supremacy, are becoming not only absurd but suicidal. The Soviet leaders realize the danger full well. This is why they insist that military-technical methods of ensuring security should be renounced. These methods have been discredited once and for all. They may cost the world's nations not only their security, but even life itself.

The Soviet Union suggests settling the problem of security politically, above all, by reaching equitable and mutually acceptable agreements which would curb the nuclear arms race and lead to the complete destruction of nuclear arsenals.

Robert McNamara

Biographical Note

Born in 1916, Robert McNamara was Assistant Professor in Business Administration at Harvard between 1940 and 1943, served in the US army and airforce between 1943 and 1946, and was, first an executive, then President of the Ford Motor Company between 1946 and 1961. From 1961 to 1968 he was US Secretary of Defense. He moved on to become President of the World Bank between 1968 and 1981.

In *The Evolution of Nuclear Strategy*, Lawrence Freedman writes:

No single public figure has influenced the way we think about nuclear weapons quite as much as Robert S. McNamara . . . While he was in office many new concepts were introduced, of which the most important were *assured destruction, damage limitation* and *flexible response*, which remain central to this day to strategic debate.

An expanded version of the two lectures quoted from in these answers will be published by the *Pantheon Books division of Random House, Inc.*, New York, under the title *Blundering into Disaster*.

Editorial Comment

The answers recorded here are in part taken from an interview in London on November 18, 1986, but the bulk of the communication has been drawn from the two Sanford Lectures, delivered on November 8 and November 9, 1986, at Duke University, and arranged as was thought appropriate by the editor. They provide a detailed critique of the situation in which we now find ourselves by one of the principal architects of Western deterrent strategy. The answer to question **AIiv** describes the ad hoc nature of much of the decision-making, while answers to questions such as **AI(ii)**, **AI(iii)**, **A2(A)(i)**, **A2(A)(ii)**, and **B(iii)**, outline the disastrous consequences which result from continuing to rely for defence upon a deterrent threat which it can never be in the interest of either side to carry out. Four suggested alternative directions ahead are rejected or qualified in the answers to questions **A2(A)(v)**, **A2(B)**, and **B(ii)**, while Robert McNamara's own recommendation is explained in his answers to questions **A2(A)(vii)** and **B(vii)**.

ROBERT S. McNAMARA

A *Global Policy*

I *The History of the Past Forty Years*

(i) *Has it been nuclear deterrence that has*   OR *Has it mainly been other factors?*
    kept the peace between the great powers
    since 1945?

Although four decades have passed without the use of nuclear weapons, this is no guide to the future. We must differentiate clearly here between the period just after World War II (when the US had, first a nuclear monopoly, then an overwhelming nuclear superiority), and the situation as it is today. Nuclear weapons may have helped to keep the peace during times of crisis in the earlier period, but they can no longer be seen to be doing so now.

(ii) *Does mutual possession of an invulnerable* OR *Does the threat of strategic nuclear*
     second-strike strategic nuclear force prevent   *retaliation, particularly against a similarly*
     war?   *armed enemy, lack credibility and invite*
                                                           sub-deterrent encroachment?

From the moment we in the United States lost our nuclear superiority, nuclear deterrence has been clearly and fatally weakened. Mutual possession of nuclear weapons on these terms means that it can never be in the interest of either side to initiate their use. That was why, as Secretary of Defense, in long private conversations with successive Presidents – Kennedy and Johnson – I recommended, without qualification, that they never initiate, under any circumstances, the use of nuclear weapons. I believe they accepted my recommendations. That is also why in Brussels in 1979 Henry Kissinger said, in effect, that Europe should not expect us to launch strategic nuclear weapons against the Soviet Union in defence of Europe.

(iii) *Have limited nuclear options at strategic*   OR *Have most military planners from the start*
and theatre levels enhanced deterrence by   *been aiming for nuclear war-fighting*
dramatically raising the threshold between   *superiority? Has 'flexible response'*
peace and war?   *dangerously lowered the threshold between*
                                        conventional and nuclear war?

This is where the most dangerous illusions lie. First of all, there are no 'limited nuclear options'. No human mind has conceived of how to initiate the use of nuclear weapons with a high probability of limiting the subsequent exchange. Realistic plans for doing that simply do not exist – as political and military leaders will tell you, if they are honest. So this cannot possibly 'enhance deterrence'. One cannot build a credible deterrent on an incredible action.

And yet, for nearly twenty years, American strategists have attempted to formulate plans for the use of nuclear weapons that could move our strategy away from the targeting of Soviet cities and toward targeting of military forces. This trend has persisted to the present day, culminating in the view of Secretary of Defense, Weinberger, that the United States could actually achieve victory in such a war. According to Weinberger's 1984–88 defence guidance document: '*Should deterrence fail and strategic nuclear war with the USSR occur, the United States must prevail and be able to force the Soviet Union to seek earliest termination of hostilities on terms favourable to the United States.*' Similarly, in accordance with NATO strategy, 25,000 nuclear warheads have been deployed at sea and on land. They are supported by war-fighting strategies. Detailed war plans for their use are in the hands of field commanders. And the troops of each side routinely undertake exercises specifically designed to prepare for that use. General Bernard Rogers, the Supreme Allied Commander of NATO forces in Europe, has said it is likely that in the early hours of a military conflict in Western Europe, NATO commanders would in fact ask for the authority to initiate such use.

(iv) *Has the size and variety of the nuclear*   OR *Has the logic of nuclear confrontation and*
arsenals held by the superpowers stabilized   *worst-case analysis generated a dangerous*
deterrence?   *and strategically pointless superfluity of*
                                       weapons systems?

In the first half century of the nuclear age the world's inventory of nuclear weapons has increased from zero to 50,000. On average, each of them has a destructive power thirty times that of the Hiroshima bomb. A few hundred of the fifty thousand could destroy not only the United States, the Soviet Union, and their allies, but, through atmospheric effects, a major part of the rest of the world as well. This situation has evolved over the years through a series of incremental decisions. I myself participated in many of them. Each of the decisions, taken by itself, appeared rational and inescapable. But the fact is that they were made without reference to any overall master plan or long-term objective. They have led to nuclear arsenals and nuclear war plans that few of the participants either anticipated or would, in retrospect, wish to support. Because we lack a long-run plan for the nuclear age, the number of weapons continues to multiply. And now we appear on the verge of an escalation of the arms race that will not only place weapons in space, but will seriously increase the risk that one or the other of the adversaries will be tempted in a period of tension to initiate a preemptive nuclear strike before the opponent can get in the first blow.

(v) *Has the idea of nuclear balance between the superpowers been essential to stability and have arms-control negotiations helped to achieve it?*   OR *Have ideas of 'nuclear defence' and 'parity' proved illusory and is 'multilateral negotiation from strength' a contradiction in terms? Has 'arms-control' been just another name for the arms race?*

As I have said, I do not think that mutual deployment of nuclear weapons, as part of a strategy which threatens their use should deterrence fail, can ever be stable. Within this context, the idea of 'balance' lacks application, and therefore sense. During the past forty years, arms control has been a positive rather than a negative factor. But we cannot be surprised that it has not secured crisis stability, when that has not, unfortunately, been the main priority for the negotiators.

(vi) *Has force-planning been controlled by strategic thinking?*   OR *Has the self-reinforcing impetus of technology and vested interest dictated policies subsequently justified post hoc?*

Looking back over the first fifty years of the nuclear age, we see that we have reached our present position by way of a long series of unplanned, piecemeal, ad hoc, decisions, taken by military and civilian leaders of East and West. There has been no clear grasp of the longer-term implications of these actions, nor general agreement on the goals towards which they should be directed. As a result, overall objectives have been poorly framed, and rarely adhered to in relation to particular weapon developments. New technologies have been allowed to develop almost unchecked, however threatening, and force-planning has not been properly controlled by strategic thinking. It is a process which has led to a world in which the two great power blocs, not yet able to avoid continuing political conflict and potential military confrontation, face each other with nuclear war-fighting strategies and nuclear arsenals capable of destroying civilization several times over.

2 *The Prospect for the Future*

(A) WITH NUCLEAR WEAPONS
(i) *Does the threat of an enemy first strike*   OR *Is there an increasing threat from accurate*
remain inconceivable for the foreseeable   *and time-urgent first-strike weapons?*
future?

But it is when we look ahead to the deployment of the next generations of nuclear weapons that the greatest dangers threaten. Miniaturization is increasing the mobility, accuracy, and destructive power of weapons. In advanced stages of development are mobile land-based missiles; anti-satellite weapons; space-based systems; and land-, sea- and air-based Cruise missiles that are increasingly difficult to detect and hence increasingly difficult to limit by verifiable arms control agreements. Our current nuclear weapons-building programme, which is producing 2000 warheads annually, is the biggest in twenty years. And steps are underway to expand substantially, for the 1990s, both the production of the key nuclear materials – tritium, uranium, and plutonium – and the production of the warheads themselves. At the same time, our weapons laboratories are forecasting large increases in the number of underground tests required for the development of new types of nuclear arms. Above all, unconstrained weapons development and deployment over the next fifty years will lead, not only to increased numbers of weapons, but to greater danger of their use in time of tension – in other words, to greater 'crisis instability'.

There are two fundamental points to be made here.

First, the danger is not so much of a sudden attack 'out of the blue', when political conditions are in any case stable, but of the likely effect of new generations of nuclear weapons, deployed, as they are at the moment, as part of a war-fighting strategy, in times of tension and acute political crisis. Today we face a future in which for decades we must contemplate continuing confrontation between East and West. Any one of these confrontations can escalate, through miscalculation, into military conflict. In these circumstances, nuclear war-fighting strategies, integrally built into defence planning, will severely constrain political decision-making. In the tense atmosphere of a crisis, each side will feel pressure to delegate authority to fire nuclear weapons to battle-field commanders. As the likelihood of attack increases, these commanders will face a desperate dilemma: use them or lose them. And, because the strategic nuclear forces and the complex systems designed to command and control them are perceived by many to be vulnerable to a preemptive attack, they will argue the advantage of a preemptive strike.

The second point is that we are dealing in the first instance, not with *actual* plans for a first strike, but with each side's perception that there may be such plans on the other side. Americans often say that they find it incredible that the Soviets could suspect us of planning for a first strike. For example, Reagan has said, '*In 1946, when the United States was the only country in the world possessing these awesome nuclear weapons, we did not blackmail others with threats to use them. Doesn't our record alone refute the charge that we seek superiority, that we represent a threat to peace?*' But the Soviets recall, not only Hiroshima and Nagasaki, but subsequent threats to use nuclear weapons by, among others, Harry Truman (Korea), Dwight Eisenhower (also Korea), Richard Nixon (Vietnam), and Jimmy Carter (Persian Gulf). The danger is that, at a time of crisis, each side will *fear* that the other is planning a first strike, and that it will be this fear which will mutually increase the pressure to preempt.

(ii) *Are command, control, communication and* OR *Does the amount of information to be intelligence facilities likely to remain* *processed, pressure of time and fear of secure?* *preemption put command and control systems under intolerable strain and make inadvertent war more likely?*

This has already been substantially answered. The weapons are becoming more accurate, so to that extent command, control, communication and intelligence facilities are becoming more vulnerable. Clearly, not enough attention is being paid to this. It is correct to say that no well-informed, coolly rational, political or military leader is likely to initiate the use of nuclear weapons. But political and military leaders in moments of severe crisis are likely to be neither well-informed, nor coolly rational. During the seven years I served as Secretary of Defense, confrontations carrying a serious risk of military conflict developed on three separate occasions: over Berlin in August of 1961, over the introduction of Soviet missiles into Cuba in October of 1962, and in the Middle East in June of 1967. In no one of the three incidents did either side intend to act in a way which would lead to military conflict, but on each of the occasions lack of information, misinformation, and misjudgements, led to confrontation. And in each of them, as the crisis evolved, tensions heightened, emotions rose, and the danger of irrational decisions increased. In none of these cases did either side want war. In each of them we came perilously close to it.

(iii) *If nevertheless there were a limited nuclear* OR *Is the idea that nuclear war could be exchange would it be likely to end* *limited once it had broken out a dangerous hostilities swiftly?* *illusion?*

As I say, no human mind has conceived of how to initiate the use of nuclear weapons with a high probability of limiting the subsequent exchanges. There are no such realistic plans. Even someone like Al Haig,[1] who is convinced of the effectiveness of deterrence and opposed to a declared policy of 'no first use', has said that it is highly unlikely that nuclear war, once started, can be

---

1. Supreme Allied Commander Europe, 1974–79. Unites States Secretary of State, 1981–82.

limited. Any decision to use nuclear weapons would imply a high probability of the same cataclysmic consequences as a total nuclear exchange.

(iv) *Do new generations of battlefield and theatre nuclear systems reinforce deterrence?*   OR *Do new battlefield and theatre weapons threaten a dangerous lowering of the nuclear threshold?*

It is definitely not as implied on the left-hand side. New generations of battle-field and theatre nuclear systems are destabilizing. They do not enhance deterrence, for reasons already given.

(v) *Does the Strategic Defence Initiative offer the hope of an effective defence against nuclear weapons?*   OR *Is the Strategic Defence Initiative simply the most recent and destabilizing example of the process outlined in 1?*

Here we come to a very complicated subject. For the sake of clarity, I will distinguish between President Reagan's original proposal for the SDI, announced on March 23, 1983, which I will call Star Wars I, and subsequent alternative interpretations, which I will label Star Wars II.

Star Wars I is an attempt to reduce the long-term risks of nuclear war by substituting defensive for offensive forces. The aim is to create an impenetrable shield to protect the entire nation against a missile attack and therefore remove the need to threaten nuclear retaliation in order to deter attack. Indeed, with the shield in place, the President argued, we would be able to discard, not just nuclear deterrence, but nuclear weapons themselves. But, as Harold Brown, who succeeded Edward Teller as director of the Lawrence Livermore Laboratory, says, '*Technology does not offer even a reasonable prospect of a successful population defense. Both the United States and the Soviet Union will be able to undertake successful countermeasures against any system intended to defend urban-industrial centers and their populations, however many the layers of defense.*' In other words, until there are inventions that have not yet even been imagined, a defence robust and cheap enough to replace deterrence will remain a pipe dream.

What is common to the many versions of Star Wars II is that they would all require that we continue to maintain offensive forces, but add the defensive systems to them. The aim is to enhance deterrence. Former Secretary of State Henry Kissinger has written, '*Even granting – as I do – that a perfect defense of our population is almost certainly unattainable, the existence of some defense means that the attacker must plan on saturating it. This massively complicates the attacker's calculations. Anything that magnifies doubt inspires hesitation and adds to deterrence. The case grows stronger if one considers the defense of Intercontinental Ballistic Missile launchers. The incentive for a first strike would be sharply, perhaps decisively, reduced if an aggressor knew that half of the opponent's ICBMs would survive any foreseeable attack.*' But there is a fatal flaw in this. The Soviets are bound to interpret Star Wars II as being designed to support a first-strike strategy. Why? Because a leaky umbrella offers no protection in a downpour, but is quite useful in a drizzle. That is, such a defence would collapse under a full-scale Soviet first strike, but might cope adequately with the depleted Soviet forces that had survived a United States first strike. Nor are the Soviets likely to accept Reagan's pledge to share SDI technology with the Soviet Union in order to ensure that the programme will not lead to an American unilateral advantage. It was only two years ago that we refused to licence the sale to the Soviet Union of relatively simple personal computers. Are we likely to provide the Soviets with the technology that will help them to more effectively prosecute wars, whether they be with conventional or nuclear forces, in Afghanistan or Europe, or to undermine our competitive position in the commercial markets of the world? So, how will they react? Their promise to respond with a large offensive build-up is no empty threat. Each superpower's highest priority has been a nuclear arsenal that can assuredly penetrate to its opponent's vital assets. Such a capability, each side believes, is needed to deter the other side from launching a nuclear attack or using a nuclear advantage for political gain. We can safely conclude, therefore, from both the United States and Soviet statements, that any attempt to strengthen deterrence by adding strategic defences to strategic offensive forces will lead to a rapid escalation of the arms race. We cannot have both Star Wars and arms control. In sum, I can see no way by which American deployment of an antiballistic missile defence will strengthen deterrence. (It is sometimes argued that the threat of the SDI can be used as a bargaining chip. The claim is that it has already brought the Soviets to the negotiating table. If this is the case, then so much the better. But, by definition, bargaining chips are used to achieve a bargain, and so far there is no sign of this.)

Finally, there is the matter of cost. A full protective shield has been estimated at $1 trillion, with perpetual expenditure in the region of $100 to $200 billion a year thereafter to upgrade and modernize it. Thus, to deploy Star Wars would force us to divert massive amounts of money from conventional defence and from domestic programmes over a period of years extending well beyond the end of this century. The possibility of a cheaper alternative to Star Wars II will be considered in **B(iii)**.

So none of these rationales offer a satisfactory approach to reducing the risk of nuclear war in the decades that lie ahead. They combine unattainable technical goals with a policy rooted in concepts whose validity died at Hiroshima. And they carry the certainty of high cost and a dangerous escalation of the arms race.

(vi) *Is the threat of 'horizontal' nuclear*   OR *Is continuing reliance on nuclear deterrence*
proliferation best met by a continuation of   *by the great powers bound to accelerate the*
past policies?   *process of proliferation and make nuclear*
                                                       war more likely?

Let me just say this: If the United States and the Soviet Union were to move
as far as Reagan and Gorbachev discussed moving at Reykjavik – in other
words, the elimination of all nuclear weapons, except whatever was needed to
prevent cheating – then I think that this would have a very positive effect on
other powers and would reduce the danger of proliferation. It clearly could
not be done – and Reagan and Gorbachev indicated that it would not be done
– without the participation of Britain, France and China in the agreement.
But if all five powers were to agree that they would move toward elimination
of all nuclear weapons, then I think that this would increase the ability of
those five powers to put pressure on other states to avoid nuclear weapons
development.

(vii) *Do multilateral arms-control negotiations*   OR *Is 'arms-control' an illusion which diverts*
offer the best prospect for future stability?   *attention from the only safe policy –*
                                                       nuclear disarmament?

So today we face a future in which for decades we must contemplate continuing
confrontation between East and West. Any one of these confrontations can
escalate, through miscalculation, into military conflict. And that conflict will
be between blocs that possess 50,000 nuclear warheads – warheads that are
deployed on the battlefields and integrated into the war-plans. A single
nuclear-armed submarine of either side could unleash more firepower than
man has shot against man throughout history. If the superpowers continue to
weaken the arms control regime, as they have over the past six or seven years,
the risk of the world ultimately facing a nuclear conflagration will continue to
grow. We are on the verge of a dramatic escalation of the arms race – an
escalation to levels that will be more and more difficult, if not impossible, to
control. The risk that military conflict will quickly evolve into nuclear war,
leading to certain destruction of our civilization, is far greater than I am willing
to accept on military, political, or moral grounds. It is far greater than I am
prepared to pass on to my children or grandchildren. This is the unplanned,
and to me unacceptable, result of the long series of incremental decisions taken
by military and civilian leaders of East and West during the first half century
of the nuclear age. Can we work ourselves out of this position during the next
fifty years?

The conviction that we must change course is shared by groups and individuals as diverse as the Freeze movement, the President, the Catholic and
Methodist bishops, the majority of the nation's top scientists, Soviet leader
Mikhail Gorbachev, and such leaders of Third World and independent nations
as Rajiv Gandhi and the late Olof Palme. All agree that we need to plan to
reduce the long-term risk of nuclear war, but there is no consensus on what

course to take. The changes of direction being advocated follow from very different diagnoses of our predicament. There have been perhaps four main courses of action proposed recently, to which I want to add a fifth. Two of these, Star Wars I (the replacing of 'deterrence' with 'defence') and Star Wars II (the strengthening of deterrence by adding defensive forces to the offence), I have rejected. A third, the proposal of General Secretary Gorbachev to eliminate all nuclear weapons through negotiations, I will discuss in **A2(B)**. A fourth, the idea of achieving a broad political reconciliation between East and West, I will pursue further in **B(ii)**. Clearly, it is desirable and is the context within which responsible arms control negotiation should be conducted. But it cannot be stressed enough that this process will require time, patience and consistency of purpose. And there are limits to the results. It cannot be expected to eliminate the periods of tension and confrontation which have characterized East–West relations over the past four decades. It is not, therefore, a substitute for other actions designed to reduce the risk that military conflict, rising out of such confrontation, will lead to the use of nuclear weapons. Steps to control directly and reverse the arms race must go forward in parallel with efforts to reduce political tension.

We are left, then, to turn to our final option: a re-examination of the military role of nuclear weapons. We need a vision of long-term goals for nuclear force levels, military strategy, and arms control agreements, that will have as their main objective the minimizing of the risk of nuclear war. In the past we have failed to achieve crisis stability through negotiation, because nuclear weapons have been treated as if they could be deployed as part of traditional war-fighting strategies. What I suggest is that we acknowledge once and for all that this can no longer be the case. I propose that we accept that nuclear warheads are not weapons – they have no military use whatsoever, except to deter one's opponent from their use – and that we base all our military plans, our defence budgets, our weapons development and deployment programmes, and our arms control negotiations on that proposition. The ultimate goal should be that of mutual deterrence at the lowest force levels consistent with stability. If the Soviet Union and the United States were to agree, in principle, that each side's nuclear force would be no larger than was needed to deter a nuclear attack by the other, how might the size and composition of such a limited force be determined? The number required for a force sufficiently large to deter cheating should not need to exceed a few hundred warheads on each side – say, at most 500. Very possibly it would be far less. Two considerations would determine the ultimate size and composition of the deterrent force: that it deter attack with confidence, and that any undetected or sudden violation of arms control treaties would not imperil this deterrence. The policing of an arms agreement that restricted each side to a small number of warheads is quite feasible with present verification technology. With tactical nuclear forces to be eliminated entirely and the strategic forces having 500 or fewer warheads, the present inventory of 50,000 weapons could be cut to no more than 1000.

(Before such limited-force goals could be reached, other nuclear powers – China, France, Great Britain and possibly others – will have to be involved in the process of reducing nuclear arsenals lest their weapons disturb the strategic equilibrium.)

Several themes should govern our attitudes and policies as we move through these negotiations towards our long-term objectives. Each side must recognize that neither will permit the other to achieve a meaningful superiority. Attempts to gain such an advantage are not only futile, but dangerous. The forces pushing each side in the direction of a first-strike posture – whether real or perceived – must be reversed. A stable balance at the lowest possible level should be the goal. We must allay legitimate fears on both sides: Soviet fear of our technology, and our fear of their obsessive secrecy. These apprehensions provide an opportunity for a bargain: Soviet acceptance of more intrusive verification, in return for American constraints on applications of its technological innovation. Our technological edge should be exploited vigorously to enhance our security, but in a manner that does not threaten the stability of deterrence. Penetration of Soviet secrecy is to our mutual advantage, even if the Kremlin does not yet understand that. So is technological restraint, even though it runs against the American grain. We have reached the present dangerous and absurd confrontation by a long series of steps, many of which seemed rational at the time. Step-by-step, we can undo much of the damage.

The arms negotiations now underway, and in particular the discussions begun at Reykjavik, represent an historic opportunity to change course and to take the first steps towards the long-term goals which I have proposed. We can lay the foundations for entering the twenty-first century with a totally different nuclear strategy, one of mutual security instead of war-fighting; with vastly smaller nuclear forces; and with a dramatically lower risk that our civilization will be destroyed.

(B) WITHOUT NUCLEAR WEAPONS

I will take the first four questions together. Here we are dealing with the proposal of Mikhail Gorbachev that the United States and the Soviet Union should begin a phased transition aimed at achieving the total elimination of nuclear weapons by the year 2000.

Many – I would say most – United States military and civilian officials, as well as European leaders, hold the view that nuclear weapons are a necessary deterrent to Soviet aggression with conventional forces. Thus these individuals do not favour a world without nuclear weapons. Zbigniew Brzezinski, President Carter's national security advisor, said of Gorbachev's proposal, '*It is a plan for making the world safe for conventional warfare. I am therefore not enthusiastic about it.*' Other Western officials have responded to Gorbachev by suggesting that nuclear disarmament would not be desirable without dramatic changes in the superpower relationship, including the correction of the conventional force imbalances, full compliance with existing and future treaty obligations, peaceful resolution of regional conflicts in ways that allow free choice without outside interference, and a demonstrated commitment by the Soviet Union to peaceful competition throughout the world.

My criticism of Gorbachev's vision, however, is not that it is undesirable, but that it is infeasible under foreseeable circumstances. Although we might be able to verify the dismantling of Soviet nuclear weapons, we could not cleanse the minds of American and Soviet scientists of the knowledge of how to build them. Warheads might be eliminated, but the potential for recreating them would remain. And in a 'nuclear-free world' a single nuclear weapon, the production and storage of which would be impossible to detect, could alter the military balance. We would live with the fear of waking up one day to find Mr Gorbachev brandishing the world's only nuclear warhead, threatening to blackmail us into accepting his political demands. Thus we would have a strong incentive to stockpile secretly some nuclear bombs to protect ourselves against such a threat. The Soviets would harbour the same fears and would take the same kind of actions.

Unless we can develop technologies and procedures to ensure detection of any steps towards building a single nuclear bomb by any nation or terrorist group, an agreement for total nuclear disarmament will almost certainly degenerate into an unstable rearmament race. Thus, despite the desirability of a world without nuclear weapons, an agreement to that end does not appear feasible either today or for the foreseeable future.

(v) *Is peace only preserved when we are seen to be prepared for war, as failure before 1939 and success since 1945 show? Under likely future conditions would global nuclear disarmament make war, including nuclear war, more likely?* OR *Do the years before 1914 show what happens when military planning and the arms race control political choices? Do present strategies make nuclear war almost inevitable under likely future conditions? Is global nuclear disarmament the only rational policy?*

The parallel with 1914 is compelling. In 1962 President Kennedy insisted that each member of the National Security Council read Barbara Tuchman's *The Guns of August*. The book is the story of how the nations of Europe inadvertently blundered into World War I. President Kennedy reminded us of the 1914 conversation between two German chancellors on the origins of that war. One asked, 'How did it happen?' and his successor replied, 'Ah, if we only knew.' It was Kennedy's way of stressing the constant danger of miscalculation. Three recent events – the Soviet shoot-down of Korean Air-Lines Flight 007, leading to the death of 269 civilians; the explosion of the US space shuttle, Challenger; and the nuclear reactor accident at Chernobyl – serve to remind us all how often we are the victims of misinformation, mistaken judgements and human fallibility.

B *NATO Policy*

(i) *Does the Soviet Union, together with her*   OR *Are NATO and WTO forces relatively*
    Warsaw Pact allies, enjoy a strategically   *evenly matched?*
    dangerous military superiority in Europe?

During the twenty-five years I have been watching the scene, I think that we
in the West, and particularly the United States, have over and over again
overestimated the Soviet conventional force strength, underestimated the
NATO conventional force strength, and thereby exaggerated the imbalance
of forces between them. Secondly, when judging the strategic impact of an
existing imbalance of forces, we fail to recognize that an attacker requires
something of the order of a three-to-one advantage in conventional forces to
have a high confidence of success in an attack. And, finally, we frequently do
not understand that the Soviet Union feels that a portion of its force may be
unreliable, and/or be required to maintain order in the East. If we put all these
points together, the imbalance of force today is far less than it is perceived to
be by many in the West. And it is certainly within our power to correct it
within realistic political and financial constraints.

(ii) *Is the Soviet Union an expansionist power* OR *Is the Soviet Union an encircled and*
     which will take advantage of unilateral   *threatened power trying to keep up with*
     Western concessions and is only restrained   *Western technology and likely to respond*
     and forced to accept arms-control   *positively to unconditional offers of*
     agreements by Western determination and   *Western restraint within a general context*
     strength?   *of detente?*

I do not know what Soviet intentions are, but I am sure that Western objectives
can best be served through a process of 'sustained engagement' that will
increase markedly all areas of contact with the East. Our agenda should be far
more comprehensive than hitherto attempted. Narrow approaches focusing
primarily on one or another functional aspect of the relationship – for example,
arms control – are not enough. The dialogue needs to be broad-based, multi-
faceted, and continuous. The relationship must rest on the twin pillars of
firmness and flexibility. It is abundantly clear that both of these elements are
essential if our policies are to command public support and have a chance of
succeeding. There is not a contradiction here: detente without defence would
amount to surrender on the instalment plan; defence without detente would
increase tensions and the risk of conflict. The two are mutually reinforcing.

(iii) *Is Soviet chemical and conventional*   OR *Is NATO dependence on the early use of*
      preponderance such that NATO must   *nuclear weapons unnecessary and*
      continue to be able to threaten early use of *strategically suicidal?*
      nuclear weapons?

Most Americans are simply unaware that NATO strategy calls for early
initiation of the use of nuclear weapons in a conflict with the Soviets. Eighty
percent of them believe we would not use such weapons unless the Soviets
used them first. They would be shocked to learn they are mistaken. And they

would be horrified to be told that senior military commanders themselves believe that to carry out our present strategy would lead to the destruction of our society. But those are the facts.

If there is a case for NATO retaining its present strategy, that case must rest on the strategy's contribution to the deterrence of Soviet aggression being worth the risk of nuclear war in the event of deterrence failing. But there are two problems which stand in the way here. First, since the assumption is made that NATO will be responding to a Warsaw Pact invasion of Western Europe, and since the artillery has short range, the nuclear explosions would occur on NATO's own territory. Second, there is no reason to believe that the Warsaw Pact, now possessing tactical and intermediate-range nuclear forces at least comparable to those of NATO, would not respond to NATO's initiation of nuclear war with major nuclear attacks of its own. These attacks would probably seek most importantly to reduce NATO's ability to fight nuclear war by destroying command and control facilities; nuclear weapons storage sites; and the aircraft, missiles, and artillery that would deliver NATO's nuclear weapons. Thus the war would escalate from the battlefield to the rest of Western Europe (and probably to Eastern Europe as well, as NATO retaliated). So, as more and more Western political and military leaders recognize and publicly avow that the use of nuclear weapons would bring greater destruction to NATO than any conceivable contribution they might make to NATO's defence, there is less and less likelihood that NATO would authorize the use of any nuclear weapons except in response to a Soviet nuclear attack. As this diminishing prospect becomes more and more widely perceived – and it will – whatever deterrent value still resides in NATO's nuclear strategy will diminish still further. One cannot build a credible deterrent on an incredible action. And there are additional factors to be considered. Whether it contributes to deterrence or not, NATO's threat of first use is not without its costs. It is a most contentious policy, leading to divisive debates both within individual nations and between members of the Alliance, it reduces NATO's preparedness for conventional war, and, as I have indicated, it increases the risk of nuclear war.

So the costs of whatever deterrent value remains in NATO's nuclear strategy are substantial. Could not equivalent deterrence be achieved at lesser 'cost'? I believe the answer is yes. Compared to the huge risks which the Alliance now runs by relying on increasingly less credible nuclear threats, recent studies have pointed to ways by which the conventional forces may be strengthened at modest military, political, and economic cost. This would be in line with what was envisaged when flexible response first became NATO's official doctrine, while I was Secretary of Defense, nearly twenty years ago. The potential of any one of several proposals for increasing the strength of conventional forces, within reasonable financial constraints, is great. Unfortunately, not one of them has yet been accepted by any NATO nation for incorporation in its force structure and defence budget. NATO has not done so, because there is today no consensus among its military and civilian leaders on the military role of nuclear weapons. Once the bankruptcy of a nuclear war-fighting strategy is generally recognized and acknowledged, we can then set about substituting realistic and effective alternatives.

(iv) *Does the growing size of the Soviet nuclear* OR *Does the West initiate nearly all phases of arsenal threaten the delicate theatre and the nuclear arms race and continue to enjoy strategic balance? Would Western failure a substantial lead in most areas? Is the to match Soviet systems be destabilizing? nuclear 'overkill' such that the West could offer a nuclear 'freeze' or unconditional cuts without risk?*

It is the asymmetry of forces that makes arms control agreements designed to increase the stability of deterrence so difficult. But we should recognize, first, that there is rough overall parity today, and, secondly, that the width of the band of parity is sufficiently great to accommodate existing asymmetries and allow agreements which can bring about crisis stability. In 1962, for example, when we had roughly 5000 strategic nuclear warheads and the Soviet Union had 300, we were neverthless deterred from using our weapons in a first strike, because we feared the damage that surviving Soviet warheads would do. It did not matter to us at the time whether we had an advantage of 17 to 1, 5 to 1, or 2 to 1 – or even if they had an advantage of 2 to 1. That tells you that the width of the band of parity is very great. And that points to the great flexibility that there is in terms of arms control agreements.

(v) *Are NATO 'forward defence' and 'deep* OR *Should NATO exploit her lead in strike' strategies essential for effective 'emerging technology' to explore less deterrence? provocative alternative strategies?*

This has been answered under (iii). We should consider the types of conventional forces recommended by General Rogers, Professor William Kaufmann,[1] The European Security Study,[2] and others.

vi) *Is it the presence of American front-line* OR *Is it domination by the two super-powers troops and the tying-in of theatre nuclear that poses the greatest threat to European forces to the American strategic deterrent integrity? Would Europe be safer that guarantees W. European security? decoupled from the super-power nuclear Should American policies therefore be confrontation? Should Europe be made a supported? nuclear weapon-free zone?*

What is critical to Western Europe's security is the recognition by the Soviet Union that the US is committed to its defence. So the participation of US troops within NATO on the soil of Europe seems to me to be a major element in deterrence. On the other hand, as I have said, I do not think that tactical or intermediate nuclear forces contribute to European security, nor that Western Europe would want US strategic nuclear forces to be used in her defence.

---

1. Author of *The McNamara Strategy*. Harper 1964.
2. A study paper prepared in 1982 by Western defence experts, aiming, amongst other things, to assess the scope for harnessing new technology to NATO strategy.

(vii) *Would Western unilateral nuclear*
disarmament invite Soviet blackmail? Are
suggestions that the West should take the
lead in offering unilateral disarmament
initiatives the thin end of this wedge? Do
radical nuclear disarmers consciously or
unconsciously serve Soviet interests and
threaten to undermine Western defences?

OR *Are unilateral initiatives as part of a*
general programme of nuclear disarmament
the only way to reverse the arms race? Is
talk of 'multilateral disarmament' insincere
in the mouths of those who reject all
suggestion of a Comprehensive Test Ban
Treaty, a Nuclear Freeze, a European
Nuclear Weapon-Free Zone, or a
declaration of No First Use?

Having identified our goal, how can we move towards it? Some of our new policies would depend solely on the United States and its Allies; others would require Soviet cooperation. Within this context there is, therefore, room for particular unilateral nuclear initiatives, such as a further unilateral reduction in the numbers of tactical nuclear weapons deployed by NATO. But unilateral nuclear disarmament would be disastrous, and the main objective must be to secure multilateral agreement for policies which are clearly in the long-term interest of all parties. We should move quickly to refocus the arms control negotiations to accomplish what we cannot do by unilateral action alone. We can begin that process through the arms negotiations now underway.

In sum, to reduce the risk of blundering into disaster, I propose we adopt the view that the military role of nuclear weapons is limited to deterrence of one's opponent's use of such weapons, and that we move as rapidly as an Alliance consensus can be formed – it is likely to evolve gradually over the next five or ten years – to base all our military plans, our defence budgets, our weapons development and deployment programmes, and our arms nego-tiations, on that proposition. I realize that I am proposing a radical change in attitude towards NATO's present nuclear strategy. And I realize, too, that attitudes will not change quickly. They are based both on deep-seated feelings of mistrust of the Soviet Union and on misperceptions of how nuclear weapons can protect us against Soviet aggression. But through public debate, a debate in which citizens throughout the NATO countries – the potential victims of nuclear war – have both the capability and the responsibility to participate, we can reduce the risk of catastrophe by establishing long-term objectives that will underlie and shape all aspects of our nuclear programmes. That must be our goal.

C *British Policy*

This is a matter for the British people to decide. I want to make no comment.

Moral Considerations

It is a mistake to think that we can initiate the use of nuclear weapons without the process ending in the destruction of our societies. And therefore I believe that it is morally wrong ever to initiate the use of nuclear weapons. I say that without any qualification.

But it is also a mistake to think that we can eliminate the possibility of nuclear weapons. So, for the foreseeable future, minimum nuclear forces are necessary to deter any power or group from thinking that they can gain advantage by using, or threatening to use, nuclear weapons. I do not consider the deployment of such forces to be immoral, because there could be no deterrence without the intent to respond shown by deployment. Nor do I think that this is an un-Christian policy.

Selected Recommendations

1 I am not opposed to a freeze, if it contributes to rather than stands in the way of the kind of programme I have outlined.
2 No. Research programmes should continue.
3 I am not opposed to it. But nor would I be opposed to continuing tests, if this were part of a programme directed towards long-term stability. The important thing is the strategic objective.
4 What is crucial is not a declaration of no first use, but a radical shift of strategy away from dependence upon the use of nuclear weapons (see **B(iii)**).
5 Yes, if these are steps in the build-down of nuclear arsenals as described in **A2(A)(vii)**.
6 A European nuclear weapon-free zone does not mean very much, although I am not opposed to it.
7 Yes.
8 No (see **A2(B)**).
9 Minimum forces should be retained indefinitely as outlined in **A2(A)(vii)**.
10 See No. 2.
11 See No. 4.
12 See my answer to **B(vii)**.
13 No comment.
14 No. Such action should not be undertaken other than in agreement with our Allies and the Soviet Union.
15 See No. 6.
16–20 No comment.

Professor
James O'Connell

Biographical Note

Born in 1925, James O'Connell has been Professor and Head of the Department of Government at Ahmadu Bello University, and Associate Professor of Politics at the University of Ibadan, Nigeria. Between 1976 and 1978 he was Professor and Dean of the Faculty of Arts at Ulster College, Northern Ireland Polytechnic. He has been Visiting Professor of Politics at Warwick University, and Visiting Professor at Columbia University, New York. Since 1978 he has been the Professor of Peace Studies at Bradford University.

Editorial Comment

The answers recorded here were communicated in an interview in Bradford on July 21, 1986. Professor O'Connell is able to draw, not only upon his own work, but upon that of the other members of his department, and of the students whose research he supervises. This response, therefore, represents the thinking within the only university department in the country to be funded specifically for Peace Studies, that is to say for the study of all the ways in which just and peaceful relationships can be created and preserved between groups and nations. The reader may be interested in such conclusions as those that are drawn about the present conventional and nuclear balance between East and West (**B(i)** and **B(iv)**), about the scope for alternative strategies for NATO (**B(v)**), and about the impact of Britain's nuclear weapons programme on the defence budget (**CI(iv)** and **CI(vi)**). A central critique of current nuclear deterrent policies can be found in such answers as those under **A2(A)(i)** and **A2(A)(ii)**, and a suggested remedy under **A2(A)(vii)** and **B(vii)**.

PROFESSOR JAMES O'CONNELL

A *Global Policy*

I *The History of the Past Forty Years*

(i) *Has it been nuclear deterrence that has* OR *Has it mainly been other factors?*
kept the peace between the great powers
since 1945?

It is not possible to be categorical on this issue. It is probable that nuclear deterrence has been one of the restraining factors, but there have been others. For one thing, the countries of Western Europe have grown together politically and economically since 1945. This new-formed unity has removed a major source of instability from an area that has fought two major civil wars in this century. The creation of the European Economic Community owed little or nothing to nuclear deterrence. An indication of this fact is that Britain, which both possessed nuclear weapons and was more sensitive than most countries to a policy of deterrence, refused to join the Community in 1958 when it was formed. Furthermore, there has been no issue that would have led the great powers to accept anything like the costs of war, even as those costs were in 1939–45.

(ii) *Does mutual possession of an invulnerable* OR *Does the threat of strategic nuclear*
second-strike strategic nuclear force prevent *retaliation, particularly against a similarly*
war? *armed enemy, lack credibility and invite*
sub-deterrent encroachment?

It has manifestly been the case that the two superpowers have fought one another in a series of proxy engagements, notably in Indo-China, Africa and Afghanistan. Mutual possession of nuclear weapons has not prevented war. It may have restrained the superpowers from fighting one another directly, but their confrontation has helped to inflame rather than resolve regional conflicts. Moreover, the political immobilisation of the superpowers in their obsession with preventing one another from gaining political advantage has impeded their co-operating where they might have worked together to end regional conflicts. Finally, it seems worth saying that, in a world that is essentially multi-polar, the East-West divide has created an artificial bi-polarity.

(iii) *Have limited nuclear options at strategic and theatre levels enhanced deterrence by dramatically raising the threshold between peace and war?*   OR *Have most military planners from the start been aiming for nuclear war-fighting superiority? Has 'flexible response' dangerously lowered the threshold between conventional and nuclear war?*

I think that at tactical, intermediate, and strategic, levels there has been a trend within the military establishment to plan for nuclear war-fighting – and therefore for military superiority – even though the declaratory policy is one of deterrence through Mutual Assured Destruction. Indeed, the purpose of flexible response itself, when it was first thought out in the late 1950s and 1960s, was in a sense to restore the military superiority that the United States had grown used to and was reluctant to lose. Limited nuclear options may by and large increase the risk of nuclear conflict rather than decrease it. But I would not say that this is so much the result of a 'lowering of the nuclear threshold' (few now believe that a limited nuclear war could be contained) as of increasing the risk of inadvertent war. The danger is that fragile command and control structures will break down in the course of a mishandled crisis, in which, rather as in 1914, one power is impelled to strike first for fear that it will lose most if the other instead strikes first.

(iv) *Has the size and variety of the nuclear arsenals held by the superpowers stabilized deterrence?*   OR *Has the logic of nuclear confrontation and worst-case analysis generated a dangerous and strategically pointless superfluity of weapons systems?*

There is undoubtedly a great superfluity of nuclear weapons systems. The main reasons why this is dangerous are, first, that it increases the possibility of accidental warfare. Second, it is part of a process in which each side is perceived as moving towards a first strike position. Third, it creates a political climate which is dangerous because it increases tension and mistrust. For example, the debate in the 1970s in the United States about the 'window of vulnerability' influenced American political perceptions about the Soviet Union in ways which helped to create the dangerous mutual antagonism of the 1980s.

(v) *Has the idea of nuclear balance between*   OR *Have ideas of 'nuclear defence' and*
the superpowers been essential to stability   *'parity' proved illusory and is 'multilateral*
and have arms-control negotiations helped   *negotiation from strength' a contradiction*
to achieve it?   *in terms? Has 'arms-control' been just*
   another name for the arms race?

Insofar as there has been a measure of stability, it has not been a result of quantitative, or even of qualitative balance, in the sense of an equating of nuclear forces, but simply of the fact that each side has been able to damage the other beyond any acceptable level. 'Arms control', in the sense of a search for an agreement on parity, has not limited the growth of nuclear arsenals. Also, arms control negotiations have at times been little more than political gestures aimed to placate domestic opposition to nuclear weapons programmes. At the most, arms control agreements have edged arms growth in certain directions, but only within the constraints of the technology that was foreseen at the time. In any case, it seems to me that far too much is usually made of arms control negotiations. They cannot possibly carry the weight of public hopes for nuclear disarmament that is often placed on them. They are simply a narrow interface between the superpowers. What is important is the general political relationship between the superpowers from which arms control negotiations will emanate.

(vi) *Has force-planning been controlled by*   OR *Has the self-reinforcing impetus of*
strategic thinking?   *technology and vested interest dictated*
   policies subsequently justified post hoc?

I think that there has been a dialectical relationship between the technology, and strategic thinking and politics. On the one hand, I think that the basic decisions are still political. But, on the other hand, given that a weapons-system will take something like fifteen to twenty years to produce, if an American President or a Soviet Head of Government has it put to him by his military experts that the other is preparing a new weapons-system, then it is very difficult for him not to invest in similar preparations. The implication is that one must look a generation ahead in national security. To that extent there is a sense in which strategic thinking is technology-driven. But, in the last resort, there is still political control. Problems of political control over the weapons could, however, become problematic in a crisis, or in a limited nuclear conflict, because command-and-control capacities are fragile and inadequate on each side.

2 *The Prospect for the Future*

(A) WITH NUCLEAR WEAPONS

(i) *Does the threat of an enemy first strike*   OR *Is there an increasing threat from accurate*
remain inconceivable for the foreseeable   *and time-urgent first-strike weapons?*
future?

The whole trend in the evolution of nuclear arsenals is now clearly towards counterforce first-strike weapons – highly accurate ballistic and cruise systems. It still remains irrational for either side to launch a first strike from cold. But that is not so much where the risks lie. The great danger is that, in a situation of deep crisis, political leaders will be told by their military advisers that they must go first, because, if they do not, the other almost certainly will. It is unlikely that a nuclear power will deliberately strike first in the near future. But such action – to answer your question literally – is sadly not inconceivable. Existing command-and-control systems are exceedingly fragile and vulnerable. I also worry about the efficiency of Soviet computers in the event of a move towards 'launch-on-warning' policies as well as about the human factor on both sides. Let me add one further observation here: I think that as you go around with your questionnaire you will find two differing emphases in the replies that you will get. Those who favour nuclear weapons will insist on the stability that they bring. Those who are more uneasy about them or who are frankly hostile to them will emphasize the danger of the present complicated balance of terror. It seems to me that a curcial unifying theme should be that we had best use existing stability to move on towards greater political and military stability, which reduces present nuclear weapons to much smaller numbers, and to exercise control over the present unregulated arms race, in which the superpowers mirror one another in their distrust and in their profligate use of resources. In other words, we need to remain exceedingly sensitive to the existing danger. And, if we accept that there is a certain stability, we need to set out to build on it and to transform it and not just permit ourselves to hope that it will endure indefinitely.

(ii) *Are command, control, communication and* OR *Does the amount of information to be intelligence facilities likely to remain secure?* *processed, pressure of time and fear of preemption put command and control systems under intolerable strain and make inadvertent war more likely?*

In a politically stable situation there is probably relatively little danger. Moreover, there is, I think, a tacit agreement on both sides to respect each other's command, control and communications facilities. But, once again, it is in times of crisis that the problems are likely to multiply. As increasingly sophisticated time-urgent weapons with short flight times – like Trident and Pershing II – become available, this puts greater strain on command and control systems which are in any case themselves becoming more and more elaborate. We need only imagine a situation in which nuclear forces, or even just conventional forces, are put on the alert, to realize how fragile and vulnerable command and control facilities are. This situation may get worse. As Sir Geoffrey Howe pointed out in his speech of last March, we could well end up with automated decision-making by both sides, because there will be no other way of dealing with the information processing problem.

(iii) *If nevertheless there were a limited nuclear* OR *Is the idea that nuclear war could be*
exchange would it be likely to end   *limited once it had broken out a dangerous*
hostilities swiftly?   *illusion?*

Our hope may be that, if there were a limited nuclear exchange, the immediate
destruction and the panic among the civilian population would be such that
the exchange would be halted short of general conflagration. It is certainly
possible that there could be a limited nuclear war. But the pressures in the
other direction would also be very great, and we just cannot tell what would
be likely to happen.

(iv) *Do new generations of battlefield and* OR *Do new battlefield and theatre weapons*
theatre nuclear systems reinforce   *threaten a dangerous lowering of the*
deterrence?   *nuclear threshold?*

Here we reach the central difficulty in nuclear deterrent strategy. New generations of nuclear weapons are an attempt to convince your opponent that you
would be mad enough to use them if they ignored your threat, and your own
public that you are still sane. It is hard to see how this could be said to enhance
deterrence. It is rather like Denis Healey's 'law of holes' – if you are in a hole,
the wise thing to do is to stop digging. As it is, I think that the situation is
certainly more dangerous now than it was before, say, Pershing II was
deployed – because of the combination of its accuracy and short flight time.
The tendency of intermediate and tactical nuclear weapons towards greater
accuracy and lower collateral damage – in other words, towards greater
usability – contributes to lowering the nuclear threshold and to increasing the
risk that it will be crossed. One of the further problems with Cruise is that,
since it is a mobile weapon, you tend to put it out in the field in a crisis, and
that sends a signal to your opponent which makes him think that you are likely
to use it. It is the same with the SS20.

(v) *Does the Strategic Defence Initiative offer* OR *Is the Strategic Defence Initiative simply*
the hope of an effective defence against   *the most recent and destabilizing example*
nuclear weapons?   *of the process outlined in 1?*

There are so many strands to this. First of all, few people believe that the
more extravagant claims being made for SDI are technologically feasible.
Apart from anything else, both the Soviet Union and the United States are at
the same time developing the penetration aids and other devices to counter
any defensive system that may be deployed. In addition, defence stimulates
offence, so Strategic Defence is likely to trigger an acceleration in the arms
race. But, even if it were to prove even partially effective, it is likely to be seen
by the other side as part of a deliberate move towards a counter-force first
strike capability – there is clearly much more chance of warding off an enemy's
attempt at retaliation with the remnant of his nuclear force than of coping with
his entire arsenal. For this reason the threat of an effective or partially effective
defence might encourage preemption before it is fully operational. A shield is
as much a battle weapon as a sword. One of the most alarming aspects of the

whole thing is the way in which it is planned to be activated. There will no longer be any question of satellite information of a Soviet launch being checked by a second set of sensors, such as radar. Defences have to be triggered within, say forty seconds. There is simply no time for human decision-making. If it is ever invented in its presently proposed form, it will be a system which commits a nation to war automatically.

(vi) *Is the threat of 'horizontal' nuclear proliferation best met by a continuation of past policies?* OR *Is continuing reliance on nuclear deterrence by the great powers bound to accelerate the process of proliferation and make nuclear war more likely?*

To be logical, supporters of nuclear deterrence should argue that 'horizontal' proliferation is a good thing. If nuclear weapons deter from war, then the more countries which have them the better. In fact, few do argue like this. There is an obvious connection between 'horizontal' and 'vertical' proliferation. The immobility of the two superpowers *vis-à-vis* one another has meant that they have taken less interest in policing proliferation than they should have. Moreover, they have certain commercial and industrial interests in facilitating the spread of technology which makes it possible for proliferation to be underpinned. This probably applies more especially to the Americans. I think that it is utterly crucial that both powers take the problem of proliferation seriously, especially as the technology simplifies. I cannot see the problems of proliferation being brought under control unless the global climate favours nuclear disarmament – and the lead has to come from the superpowers.

(vii) *Do multilateral arms-control negotiations offer the best prospect for future stability?* OR *Is 'arms-control' an illusion which diverts attention from the only safe policy – nuclear disarmament?*

I think that the current bilateral and multilateral talks need to be kept up. But, judging by the lack of success of the past forty years, there seems little hope that they will bear fruit. The only way in which multilateral agreement to phase down nuclear arsenals can be reached is by individual countries being prepared to make significant unilateral concessions. Multilateralism only works when unilateral initiatives by either alliances or individual countries are made. What we need from several countries is a continuing endeavour to reduce tensions and to build confidence between governments and between peoples. We need at a minimum to be driven by the thought that deterrence in its existing shape cannot hope to last indefinitely. More positively, we need to appreciate our common humanity, our new and marvellous productive technologies, and our longer term converging interests.

(B) WITHOUT NUCLEAR WEAPONS

(i) *If nuclear arsenals were dismantled would* OR *Would nuclear disarmament remove the*
war between the great powers again   *incentive for nuclear preemption while not*
become a rational option and therefore   *affecting the reluctance of the great powers*
more likely?   *to initiate a third world war?*

I do not think that war between the great powers could again become a rational option. Even conventional technology is now so dangerous, and the advantages that can be gained from war are obviously so few, that the abolition of nuclear weapons would not make war more likely.

(ii) *Would a major conventional war be likely* OR *Is conventional war, however terrible,*
in itself to be as terrible as a limited   *preferable to nuclear war?*
nuclear war?

It is unlikely that a conventional war, even between industrialized countries, would be nearly as disastrous as a nuclear war. But it would still be unacceptably damaging.

(iii) *Because nuclear weapons cannot be*   OR *As with nerve gases in the last war, would*
uninvented would they not be bound to be   *there be no incentive to resort to*
used sooner or later once war had broken   *capabilities which the other side has as*
out?   *well?*

Did war break out, states would almost certainly consider a nuclear option. But it would still be as irrational and counter-productive as it is at present. What I think people must do is to live with the knowledge that these weapons can be put together again; and that they must so arrange disputes between nuclear-potential powers as to make it extremely unlikely that they would ever be tempted to put them together and use them.

(iv) *Is global nuclear disarmament only*   OR *Is to argue that even multilateral nuclear*
feasible in a world where war itself is no   *disarmament is not desirable to give up all*
longer a possibility?   *hope of a rational world-order?*

I think that we have to accept the fact that some level of arms will always be necessary to maintain order. But what we do want to reach is a situation in the world in which relations between countries on a global scale will be like, if not those between the United States and Canada, then at least like those between the states of the European Economic Community. Under those circumstances there would be disputes, but it would be most unlikely that the countries would ever go to war. Effectively the whole world is as small in technological terms today as Europe was in 1939 – and we have to make political and other arrangements accordingly.

(v) *Is peace only preserved when we are seen*   OR *Do the years before 1914 show what*
    to be prepared for war, as failure before   *happens when military planning and the*
    1939 and success since 1945 show? Under   *arms race control political choices? Do*
    likely future conditions would global   *present strategies make nuclear war almost*
    nuclear disarmament make war, including   *inevitable under likely future conditions?*
    nuclear war, more likely?   *Is global nuclear disarmament the only*
                                                                       rational policy?

It seems to me that 1939 was only the second phase of a conflict that started in 1914, and that the two phases should not be separated. Today's situation is much more like 1914 than 1939. However, technological conditions are so different now from either 1914 or 1939 that people have to think in greatly different ways. As Einstein said – with the invention of atomic weapons, everything had changed except our ways of thinking.

2 NATO Policy

(i) *Does the Soviet Union, together with her*   OR *Are NATO and WTO forces relatively*
    Warsaw Pact allies, enjoy a strategically   *evenly matched?*
    dangerous military superiority in Europe?

There have been a number of major contributions in the literature recently, which show quite clearly that the Soviet Union does not have overwhelming conventional superiority. The two sides are relatively evenly matched. In fact, if you take account of the unreliability of some of the non-Soviet members of the Warsaw Pact, then, if anything, the advantage lies with NATO.

(ii) *Is the Soviet Union an expansionist power* OR *Is the Soviet Union an encircled and*
    which will take advantage of unilateral   *threatened power trying to keep up with*
    Western concessions and is only restrained   *Western technology and likely to respond*
    and forced to accept arms-control   *positively to unconditional offers of*
    agreements by Western determination and   *Western restraint within a general context*
    strength?   *of detente?*

By and large the Soviet Union sees itself as encircled and threatened, while the West sees it as expansionist. The problem is one of mutual perception. The acquisition of an Eastern European empire was partly an attempt to prevent another attack from Germany, partly a reflection of where armies ended up in 1945, partly a revival of old Tsarist ambitions, and partly the Soviet leaders' instincts for conquest and expansion. At the moment, while still hanging on to the the shreds of ideological legitimacy, the USSR has lost its universalist confidence and feels somewhat under seige. It is the poorer of the two superpowers economically, and the more backward technologically. There is a good chance that under the present leadership it will reciprocate Western initiatives. It has already taken initiatives of its own, notably its curb on testing.

(iii) *Is Soviet chemical and conventional*   OR *Is NATO dependence on the early use of*
preponderance such that NATO must   *nuclear weapons unnecessary and*
continue to be able to threaten early use of   *strategically suicidal?*
nuclear weapons?

NATO dependence on the early use of nuclear weapons is militarily unnecessary and strategically suicidal in that it might lead to a 'limited' nuclear war, which for Europe would be total. Psychologically it also undermines NATO conventional defences by encouraging a combination of defeatism and trust in early and compensatory nuclear expedients. Finally, both sides need to take more seriously negotiations on mutual and balanced reductions in conventional forces.

(iv) *Does the growing size of the Soviet nuclear* OR *Does the West initiate nearly all phases of*
arsenal threaten the delicate theatre and   *the nuclear arms race and continue to enjoy*
strategic balance? Would Western failure   *a substantial lead in most areas? Is the*
to match Soviet systems be destabilizing?   *nuclear 'overkill' such that the West could*
offer a nuclear 'freeze' or unconditional
cuts without risk?

As I have said, I do not think that nuclear deterrence is stable. But there is a degree of overkill such that either side could make very generous concessions without affecting the level of risk. In terms of general military technology, the most recent Pentagon assessment says that the United States leads the Soviet Union in fourteen areas; they are equal in six; and the Soviet Union does not lead in any. It is also true that the United States has initiated most (but not all) of the phases of the nuclear arms race. There are certain areas where Soviet build-up has been disproportionate – particularly in certain classes of land-based ballistic missiles. But this is matched by American advantage in the other two arms of the strategic 'triad'. By and large there is a rough balance in capacity and a significant Western lead in technology.

(v) *Are NATO 'forward defence' and 'deep*   OR *Should NATO exploit her lead in*
strike' strategies essential for effective   *'emerging technology' to explore less*
deterrence?   *provocative alternative strategies?*

Current offensive strategies – whether Soviet operational manoeuvres or Western deep strike postures – are both unnecessary and likely to be dangerously destablizing in crisis. In addition, for political reasons, if confidence-building measures are to be undertaken, the arrangement of forces needs to be less provocative than it has traditionally been. In view of the present balance of forces, the West has the wealth, technology and reserve manpower to enable its forces confidently to explore alternative strategies. We should not, however, be tempted to place too much reliance on the technological 'fix' of Emerging Technologies. We should also be sceptical about the more extravagant claims of arms manufacturers.

(vi) *Is it the presence of American front-line troops and the tying-in of theatre nuclear forces to the American strategic deterrent that guarantees W. European security? Should American policies therefore be supported?*

OR *Is it domination by the two super-powers that poses the greatest threat to European integrity? Would Europe be safer decoupled from the super-power nuclear confrontation? Should Europe be made a nuclear weapon-free zone?*

In the immediate future, whether Europe is nuclear-free or not, it makes sense to keep American troops here because the NATO Alliance is not one that should be lightly unscrambled. Having said that, the crucial problem at the present moment is that Western Europe has not had an independent role but has simply lined up completely with one of the superpowers. What is important in the longer run is to make Europe nuclear-free; to re-work the Alliance in its present form; and to let European powers work out an independent common policy which stresses their friendship with the United States and their European kinship with the Soviet Union. I think that it would be unfortunate if Western Europe constituted itself a separate power bloc – as it were a third superpower alongside the other two. That would only continue the present set of strategies, while complicating them. I would certainly not see a reconstituted Western Europe arming itself with a nuclear capability.

(vii) *Would Western unilateral nuclear disarmament invite Soviet blackmail? Are suggestions that the West should take the lead in offering unilateral disarmament initiatives the thin end of this wedge? Do radical nuclear disarmers consciously or unconsciously serve Soviet interests and threaten to undermine Western defences?*

OR *Are unilateral initiatives as part of a general programme of nuclear disarmament the only way to reverse the arms race? Is talk of 'multilateral disarmament' insincere in the mouths of those who reject all suggestion of a Comprehensive Test Ban Treaty, a Nuclear Freeze, a European Nuclear Weapon-Free Zone, or a declaration of No First Use?*

There can be no doubt that the way ahead is for the West to be prepared to take significant initiatives – and to reciprocate those offered by the Soviet Union. In other words, to proceed by way of a series of carefully planned unilateral initiatives on both sides which are then consolidated by bilateral and multilateral treaties. Unilateralism of this kind is simply part of genuine multilateral disarmament. We now have plenty of evidence that the Soviet Union is ready to take part in such a process. What is the alternative? The question that people need to ask themselves is: 'Are we happy for the present situation to continue indefinitely?' Those who say 'yes' are genuine believers in indefinite nuclear deterrence. In which case they should be honest about it, and not, as so often happens, pose as 'multilateral disarmers'.

C *British Policy*

I *The British Deterrent*

(i) *Is Britain's deterrent a weapon of last*   OR *Would all possible uses of Britain's*
resort which guarantees her sovereignty and   *'deterrent' be suicidal? Is its only effect to*
independence and protects her from nuclear   *encourage proliferation?*
blackmail?

It seems to me that Britain has nuclear weapons because she was once an imperial power. They serve no military or strategic function. They cannot be used against a superpower – except possibly in the form of a final act of retaliation by some lonely submarine commander after Britain had already been destroyed. All that they do is encourage proliferation. Nobody, furthermore, has been able to sketch a plausible scenario of nuclear blackmail.

(ii) *Are British nuclear forces valuable to*   OR *Is the 'second centre of decision making' an*
European allies because they provide a   *illusion when the weapons are dependent*
specifically European second centre of   *upon the US and there is no independent*
decision making?   *strategic role to be played? Are European*
   allies unenthusiastic about a parochial
   British force likely to inhibit her
   commitment to European defence?

The second centre argument suggests that Britian would be likely to use her nuclear weapons in defence of Germany when the Americans were not prepared to use theirs. This seems inconceivable. If the Americans pulled out, so would the British. The argument is an unconvincing rationalization. In any case, multiple centres of decision-making imply greater uncertainty; and uncertainty implies greater crisis instability, not stability. That argument needs to be met head on.

(iii) *Does the US favour shared responsibility*   OR *Are US forces committed anyway and*
and do British nuclear forces guarantee   *independent British initiatives more likely*
full US commitment to Europe and Soviet   *to trigger Soviet retaliation than US*
recognition of it?   *involvement?*

My impression is that, if the British were in any way to threaten the Soviet Union, the Americans would very quickly extricate themselves from the resulting situation. They might well even move against British submarines and weapons did they come to believe that a British strike against a third power contained danger to American security. The funny thing about this kind of justification for British nuclear weapons is that, on the one hand, British governments argue that they must have them as part of solidarity with the United States, but they also argue that they need to have them when the United States no longer shows solidarity with them. And they have an in-between position, which I think is not even compatible with either, which is that they could threaten to use the weapons in such a way as to involve the Americans in the action. I think that the entire rationale is quite confused.

(iv) *Is the cost of the British deterrent small in* OR *Can Britain's nuclear forces only be*
view of the vital defence role it plays? Are *afforded at the expense of conventional*
alternatives likely to be more expensive? *strength and of other more important*
economic priorities?

Recent studies show that, if in the next ten years Britain retains nuclear weapons, the cost will make severe inroads into British conventional weapons and will weaken British conventional defence. Moreover, this will happen all the more quickly as Britain runs into balance of payments crises with the failure of its manufacturing industry and the decline of the petroleum industry. I would prefer it if nuclear spending was cut out of the defence budget altogether and the rest of the defence budget did not go up. The trouble at the moment is that defence priorities have not been properly worked out. There is defence of the island, defence of the North-East Atlantic, out-of-area operations, the Falklands, the army on the Rhine, and nuclear strategy. These six undertakings have not been prioritized against one another nor properly costed. It seems to me that one could work out a realistic set of defence propositions that were much less expensive, even in conventional terms, than the present ones. So the saving made by abandoning Britain's nuclear forces would go to strategic economic investment, as well as into the health service and the educational system.

(v) *Would unilateral British nuclear* OR *Does the British deterrent encourage*
disarmament have no effect on other *proliferation and do nothing to enhance*
countries and only serve to weaken British *British prestige? Would British*
influence and allow France unchallenged *disarmament within the context outlined in*
ascendancy in Europe? *B help to break the nuclear log-jam?*

Neither British nor French possession of nuclear weapons has given either a role of strategic counsel or a place 'at the top table'. If anything, West Germany has an ascendancy in Europe because of her economic strength. If British unilateral disarmament were part of the process described in **B(vii)**, it would be a significant contribution. But this depends upon the nature of the Soviet response and what follows from it. British disarmament could have a significant restraining effect elsewhere, too. It would certainly not diminish British influence, and could well enhance it.

(vi) *Is investment in Trident the best way to* OR *Would commitment to Trident exacerbate*
continue to ensure effective British strategic *all the drawbacks listed above?*
defence into the 21st century?

Trident has no strategic function for this country and is just a continuing form of proliferation. Its cost has helped to bring the public debate about British nuclear forces in general to a head. If Britain goes ahead with Trident, it will cut expenditure on new conventional equipment by at least thirty per cent during the late 1980s and severely damage army, air force and naval capabilities.

2 *NATO Forces and US Bases*

(i) *Must Britain continue to share* OR *Should British obligations to NATO be*
responsibility for manning NATO nuclear *met by strengthening conventional forces*
systems upon which her security depends? *where necessary within an overall non-*
Would refusal to do so fatally weaken the *nuclear strategy as recommended in B?*
alliance?

It seems to me that it is time that Britian distanced herself from nuclear
weapons in Europe, and worked out new political relations with the other
European powers and with the United States. She should be thinking in terms
of conventional strategies, working particularly with the Germans on alternative ways of strengthening non-provocative defences. The introduction of anti-
tank barriers, the mobilisation of reserve manpower – there are any number
of possibilities to be explored. For the time being we should stay in NATO.
There is a case for reworking the Alliance rather than breaking it up.

(ii) *Would the forced withdrawal of US* OR *Do the large numbers of nuclear facilities*
nuclear bases from Britain make US *yielded to the US erode British*
defence of the West impossible? Is *sovereignty? Would their removal do no*
American interference in British affairs *more than restore a normal peacetime*
negligible? *relationship?*

The Libyan raid has highlighted the question of sovereignty. Although the
Prime Minister's permission was given in that case, there can be no doubt that
a British veto would be brushed aside in the event of a nuclear war which
involved vital American interests. Apart from anything else, American law
does not allow the US president to give control of American nuclear weapons
to any non-national. The removal of American nuclear bases would in no way
alter the strategic balance between the superpowers, or, even in terms of
nuclear deterrent theory, make the 'defence of the West impossible'. The
bases play more of a political than a strategic military role.

(iii) *Will Britain continue to be targeted by* OR *Is Britain seen as an American aircraft*
Soviet warheads whether or not she *carrier and targeted by the USSR*
disarms unilaterally? *accordingly? Will Britain fall an early*
victim in any superpower confrontation
unless bases are removed?

Even if Britain ceased to be a nuclear power or to have American nuclear
weapons here, the island would still no doubt be targeted. Both the Soviet
Union and the United States almost certainly target neutral countries at the
moment. But it would no longer be so certain that, when it came to it, the
weapons would be used. What no country will escape will be the effects of a
nuclear winter or radiation fall out. Moreover, Chernobyl must at least warn
all of us what may happen once civil power stations are caught in the most
limited nuclear exchange.

(iv) *Can non-nuclear defences only safely be*   OR *In a nuclear-free Europe, decoupled from*
afforded by powers prepared to shelter   *the superpower nuclear confrontation,*
beneath the American strategic umbrella?   *would Britain no more expect to depend*
                                      upon the US 'umbrella' than any other
                                      Western ally – or than Eastern Europe
                                      upon the USSR?

As I have said, I do not think that nuclear weapons have brought stability or protection in the first place. It has been political arrangements that have been the main basis for stability. There is obviously nothing that a middle-ranking power like Britain can do to prevent the superpowers from continuing to deploy their nuclear arsenals. In any case, 'nuclear umbrella' is only a misleading metaphor for a policy that suggests that the US would start a nuclear war to protect its allies. One needs to remember Dr Kissinger's warning that no country can be expected to commit suicide on behalf of another. The only truth in the 'nuclear umbrella' theory is that both superpowers are not likely to use nuclear weapons incautiously against any power belonging to its opponent's alliance. However, as Palmerston said, countries do not have permanent allies but only permanent interests.

Moral Considerations

(i) *Is it morally right to pursue the policy least* OR *Are there actions which are in themselves*
likely to cause human suffering? May this   *wrong no matter what the situation? Is the*
sometimes involve doing things which in   *alternative to excuse almost any act of*
other circumstances would be wrong?   *barbarism?*

Under certain circumstances, which are usually difficult to spell out beforehand in any particular case, the most moral option may be to choose the lesser evil. Where one or the other of the evils is unavoidable, there may even be a moral obligation to choose the lesser. In this sense one may have to pursue a course of action that, in other circumstances, would be morally wrong. For example, I could conceive a moral use of tactical nuclear weapons against terrorists who had secured such weapons and were holding a population hostage. But one must retain a different sense of proportion in formulating policies that involve the destruction of entire populations by deliberate action.

(ii) *In formulating policy should we weigh up* OR *Is the only relevant point here that a*
the probability of success and the relative   *nuclear exchange of almost any kind*
costs in terms of human suffering of   *would in itself cause unimaginable*
alternative nuclear and non-nuclear   *suffering to largely civilian populations?*
strategies?

There is a prudential dimension in Just War decisions. The crucial factor in this connection is the principle of proportionality, in which a government weighs the probable success and relative cost of war against alternative costs in, for example, threats to security, justice and freedom. It is, consequently, reasonable to weigh the implications of nuclear and non-nuclear policies. It is not easy, however, to envisage a proportion between the evils of a nuclear war fought with strategic weapons, and other costs in lives and suffering. There is also the principle of discrimination in Just War theory. This principle is based on the acceptance of a common humanity, and argues that those not directly involved in combat should be spared destruction. Just War moralists accept that some collateral damage is inevitable in war. But any predictable form of strategic exchange between superpowers would involve destroying a large part of each other's population. It is difficult to accept the morality of decisions that involve the destruction of more than a hundred million persons with no practical involvement in governmental decisions or war effort, or with no effective animosity towards supposed enemies. At most one might conceivably accept the destruction of a limited number of persons in actions that saved many more from being destroyed. But the latter choice seems implausible in the present state of weaponry and strategy. I do not envy political leaders those war decisions that might confront them. But I do not think that any decision to destroy millions of people could be moral under any circumstances that I have heard any strategist describe, or any circumstances that I can conceive of. For my own part – and to state a personal choice rather than put an option to government – I would rather have myself, my family and my people perish than have, in the name of their survival, our government decide the destruction of millions of persons with whom I share a God-given humanity and against whom I have no grievance.

(iii) *So far as concerns intention, need we look no further than the fact that our sole aim in deploying nuclear weapons is to prevent their use?* OR *Is there no such thing as a fully deployed weapons system which is a bluff? Is to deploy nuclear weapons to intend to use them in certain circumstances?*

I think that, once one undertakes the strategic and technical devices needed for nuclear deterrence, then there is implicit in this the intention to use them, if only because the operatives are so conditioned. While in theory one may separate deployment from use, effectively one cannot separate them. If one deploys them, one thereby accepts the possibility of using them.

(iv) *Are there possible uses of nuclear weapons which are allowed by Just War theory, for example the bombing of Hiroshima and Nagasaki in order to prevent worse suffering? Can there be a theory of Just Deterrence?* OR *Is a conditional intention to cause indiscriminate and disproportionate suffering of this kind, whether admonitory, preemptive or retaliatory, ruled out by Just War theory? Was it wrong to bomb Hiroshima and Nagasaki in 1945?*

Yet on the issue of deploying weapons in a theory of Just Deterrence I hesitate to be categorical. For one thing, the situation of fear and distrust between the superpowers is such that they may justly – if in the context of a distorted world – retain their weapons. Yet on any but a most limited scale I do not think that they could rationally or morally prepare to use their already deployed weapons.

It is in their interest as well as in the interest of the rest of us to move out of the present impasse.

(v) *Is there no relevant connection between the* OR *Is it a scandal that such huge resources are*
development and deployment of nuclear   *devoted to the development and deployment*
weapons and world poverty and disease?   *of nuclear weapons and not to the*
                                                  alleviation of suffering?

I think that there is a moral link between the development of nuclear weapons and world poverty, because, first of all, resources are being deployed in respect of these weapons that could go elsewhere. And, secondly, the confrontation diverts attention from the plight of the poorer nations of the world. The will to use nuclear weapons in a strategic exchange, and the existence of extensive and profound poverty in the world, seem to me two great scandals of our time.

(vi) *Does Christian teaching allow the*   OR *Does Christian teaching condemn the*
deployment of nuclear weapons?   *deployment of nuclear weapons?*

It seems to me that practically all the authoritative Christian groups that have looked at this problem have up to now accepted the deployment of nuclear weapons. To take a most comprehensive review by the American Catholic bishops, *The Challenge of Peace*, I think that there is an ambiguity at the heart of its teaching. It accepts the deployment of the weapons, but it effectively condemns their use. The ambivalence lies in the acceptance of a deployment that is inseparable from the intention to use. The bishops seek a way out of their moral dilemma – which they do not seem sufficiently to recognize – by insisting on a moral obligation to work for arms control and relative disarmament. Yet there is evidence to suggest that they and their followers – and the same is true of other Christian bodies – have not accepted this moral imperative in practical life and politics.

Recommendations

1 Broadly speaking, Yes.
2 Ideally, yes (see **A2(A)(v)**).
3 Yes.
4 Yes (see **B(iii)**).
5 Yes (see **A1(iv)**).
6 Yes (see **B(vi)**).
7 Yes (see **A2(A)(vi)**).
8 Not necessarily (see **A2(B)**).
9 Yes.
10 Yes.
11 Yes (see **B(iii)**).
12 Yes (see **A2(A)(vii)** & **V(vii)**).
13 Yes.

14 Yes.
15 Yes (see **B(vi)**).
16 Yes (see **C1**).
17 No (see **C1(iv)**).
18 Yes (see **C2(i)**).
19 Yes (see **C2(i)** & **C2(ii)**).
20 No.

Dr. David Owen

P.C. M.P.

Biographical Note

Born in 1938, David Owen qualified as a doctor at St Thomas' Hospital, where he was Neurological and Psychiatric Registrar between 1964 and 1966. He has been Member of Parliament for Plymouth (Sutton) between 1966 and 1974, and for Plymouth (Devonport) since 1974. For fifteen years he was a Labour

Member of Parliament serving as Secretary of State for Foreign and Commonwealth Affairs between 1977 and 1979. In 1981 he became a founder-member
of the Social Democratic Party, and has been its leader since 1983.

Editorial Comment

Although Dr Owen was willing to contribute to this book, he was not able to
give an interview, so, with his permission, the responses which follow have
been selected and arranged by the editor from the sources cited at the beginning. Page references are provided throughout.

Readers will find a criticism of current nuclear deterrent policies in the East
and in the West in Section **A**, and an equally tranchant criticism of unilateralist
counter-proposals in Section **B** (see especially the answers to Questions **(iii)**
and **(vii)**). His own proposals, as interpreted by the editor, are summarized in
the *Recommendations* at the end. So far as concerns British policy, the broad
emphasis is on the importance of creating a powerful independent Western
European defence (see in particular the answer to question **C1(ii)**, against the
background of the answer to question **B(vi)**). Dr. Owen is critical, both of
Conservative Party plans to press ahead with the Trident option (**C1(iv)** and
C1(vi)), and with Labour Party proposals for a unilateral withdrawal from
NATO's nuclear deterrent strategy (**C2(i)** and **C2(ii)**).

Rt. HON. DR DAVID OWEN

Key to References

1 Effective Deterrence (Lecture 1981).
2 Common Security (Report of the Palme Commission on Dis-
    armament and Security Issues 1982).
3 A Total Test Ban (Speech 1984).
4 Europe's Nuclear Deterrence Strategy (Speech June 5, 1986).
5 Defence Debate (House of Commons June 30, 1986).
6 Transcript of Defence Fringe Meeting – Harrogate (Sept. 13,
    1986).
7 Why the Summit Succeeded (*Times* Oct. 16, 1986).
8 Plymouth Speech (Oct. 27, 1986).
9 What is to be Done? (Recommendations of the Palme Com-
    mission Oct 24–6, 1986).
10 Defence and Disarmament in Europe (SDP Policy Document
    No. 9, as amended June 1986).

A *Global Policy*

1 *The History of the Past Forty Years*

(i) *Has it been nuclear deterrence that has*   OR *Has it mainly been other factors?*
   kept the peace between the great powers
   since 1945?

Although a number of other factors have also contributed, there can be little doubt that, for forty years, nuclear deterrence has played a major role in helping to maintain an uneasy peace in Europe, and in preventing direct conflict between the Soviet Union and the United States world wide (*4.2,4.4*).

(ii) *Does mutual possession of an invulnerable* OR *Does the threat of strategic nuclear*
   second-strike strategic nuclear force prevent   *retaliation, particularly against a similarly*
   war?   *armed enemy, lack credibility and invite*
      sub-deterrent encroachment?

It has mainly been the mutual fear of nuclear devastation that has prevented war between the major powers (*4.2*). Peace has in the end rested on the deterrent value of a mutually assured second strike capability (*3.11*). This is what needs to be preserved (*3.23*).

(iii) *Have limited nuclear options at strategic*   OR *Have most military planners from the start*
    and theatre levels enhanced deterrence by   *been aiming for nuclear war-fighting*
    dramatically raising the threshold between   *superiority? Has 'flexible response'*
    peace and war?   *dangerously lowered the threshold between*
      conventional and nuclear war?

We must distinguish here between deterrence and defence. Deterrence is to convince an enemy that the burdens and risks of any attack far outweigh any possible gains. Defence is to reduce the likely burdens and risks if an enemy attacks, deterrence having failed. Deterrence aims at changing the intentions of the enemy, making it less likely they will decide to act. Defence aims at reducing the effectiveness of the enemy if they decide to act. Defensive and deterrent strategies must therefore interlink. In the early days of nuclear arsenals, the weapons were so devastating, the consequences of their use so appalling, that it was possible to envisage a purely deterrent force. The concept was one of mutually assured destruction. Then, as the technology of nuclear warfare developed, with miniaturization of the warheads, multiple independently-targeted re-entry vehicles and pinpoint accuracy from 4000 miles, with nuclear mines, nuclear depth-charges and short-range battlefield nuclear weapons, some saw nuclear deterrence as being merged with conventional deterrence. Nuclear weapons began to be part of the arsenal of war (*1.37–8*). It is a fact that military strategists in both the Warsaw Pact and NATO believe that nuclear weapons would be used in any war in Europe and that both sides expect to win such a war (*1.42*). This has been a very dangerous development. To set nuclear weapons within a seamless robe of defence decision-making in this way is to increase massively the risk that nuclear weapons will be used again (*1.46*). The battlefield nuclear war-fighting strategies of both East and West should be abandoned. Fortunately, a strong body of opinion on both sides, scientific, military and political, now recognizes this. And the main strategic argument for the original deployment of battlefield nuclear weapons no longer applies. The accuracy of new generations of longer-range weapons means that they could if necessary be used in a tactical role. So the abandonment of battlefield nuclear weapons does not mean that the option of a tactical battlefield response is foreclosed (*1.43*).

(iv) *Has the size and variety of the nuclear*   OR *Has the logic of nuclear confrontation and*
     arsenals held by the superpowers stabilized   *worst-case analysis generated a dangerous*
     deterrence?   *and strategically pointless superfluity of*
                                                          weapons systems?

Effective deterrence between the superpowers depends, not upon war-fighting superiority, nor upon the acquisition of an all-embracing defensive capability against nuclear war, but upon an absolute confidence on both sides in the invulnerability of powerful second strike forces. This defines the minimum level of nuclear weapons that are needed as a deterrent. China, France, and the UK can live with a more limited degree of confidence in the invulnerability of their deterrent, nor do they need as much power to give them the ultimate protection they need against nuclear blackmail. The overall levels of nuclear megatonnage and warheads that such a minimum capability represents is miniscule in comparison to the present absurd levels (*3.23*). We will not prevent the disaster of a nuclear exchange if we allow the nuclear arms race to continue to spiral sharply upwards. To go on proliferating and expanding nuclear stockpiles is to head towards doomsday. Present policies of increasing megatonnage and warheads carry a far greater risk than the calculated risks of decreasing nuclear megatonnage and warheads (*3.1, 3.24*).

(v) *Has the idea of nuclear balance between*   OR *Have ideas of 'nuclear defence' and*
    the superpowers been essential to stability   *'parity' proved illusory and is 'multilateral*
    and have arms-control negotiations helped   *negotiation from strength' a contradiction*
    to achieve it?   *in terms? Has 'arms-control' been just*
                                                         another name for the arms race?

The idea of a stable overall nuclear balance has been an important one. But it is not a purely mechanistic matter, nor just an arithmetical missile count; it should be a rounded assessment of overall capability that embraces conventional weapons and even involves general economic and political factors (*1.43*). Within this context, arms control negotiations have been significant, but can hardly be said to have been successful. In order to control and reverse the arms race, it is necessary first to understand the mechanisms that drive it. The psychology and the politics of arms control are every bit as important as the technology and science (*3.5*).

(vi) *Has force-planning been controlled by strategic thinking?*   OR *Has the self-reinforcing impetus of technology and vested interest dictated policies subsequently justified post hoc?*

The political, social and economic decisions that drive the arms race need to be understood in terms of human behaviour, of how political leaders and nations see each other, their motives, jealousies and pride. Above all, how feelings of national insecurity fed by military, scientific and industrial lobbying in democratic and communist systems, constantly undermine international security (*3.5*). Force planning has in the past been influenced too often by the military's wish always to have a comprehensive range of weaponry (*1.43*), while, for example, a Comprehensive Test Ban Treaty has been opposed by US and UK scientists working in cahoots because they sensed their jobs were threatened (*3.14*).

2 *The Prospect for the Future*

(A) WITH NUCLEAR WEAPONS

(i) *Does the threat of an enemy first strike remain inconceivable for the foreseeable future?*   OR *Is there an increasing threat from accurate and time-urgent first-strike weapons?*

The prospect of a deliberate all-out first strike by either side remains a very remote one so long as each continues to believe that it has a potent and invulnerable second strike capability (*3.11*).

(ii) *Are command, control, communication and intelligence facilities likely to remain secure?*   OR *Does the amount of information to be processed, pressure of time and fear of preemption put command and control systems under intolerable strain and make inadvertent war more likely?*

There are areas for concern here. The battlefield nuclear war-fighting strategies of both East and West, for example, are associated with acute command and control problems (*1.43*), while SDI could bring forward highly automated systems, even with a launch-on-warning response (*4.21*).

(iii) *If nevertheless there were a limited nuclear exchange would it be likely to end hostilities swiftly?*   OR *Is the idea that nuclear war could be limited once it had broken out a dangerous illusion?*

There are two dangerous misconceptions, which have done much to stimulate concern about nuclear deterrence. Firstly, the folly of stressing the significance of measures to protect civilian populations against thermo-nuclear war. Governments must do something to protect their citizens, but to pretend that civil defence can add to the deterrent effect of nuclear weapons is an absurdity; and to pretend that it is anything more than a palliative for the population is a cruel deception. Secondly, the folly of planning for a nuclear war-fighting strategy. Governments must plan for limiting nuclear war if, by inadvertence or design, nuclear weapons are even used, but loose talk of limited nuclear war has always been a contradiction in terms (*4.2*).

(iv) *Do new generations of battlefield and*   OR *Do new battlefield and theatre weapons*
theatre nuclear systems reinforce   *threaten a dangerous lowering of the*
deterrence?   *nuclear threshold?*

The predominant European motivation behind the 1979 theatre modernization decision was to lock the United States into deploying a new generation of ground launched nuclear missiles in Europe. President Carter's Administration did not think it was necessary to deploy a new generation of theatre nuclear weapons and were content to rely on strategic missiles, although in the end the Americans went along with the dominant wish of the Europeans (*4.13*). The effectiveness of the NATO deterrent, as of the Warsaw Pact deterrent, depends critically on its conventional component first, and secondly on its having an invulnerable second strike nuclear offensive component. If both these components can be assured, then the whole range of intermediate nuclear weapons could be negotiated away (*1.45*). In the meantime, the danger of the forward deployment of battlefield nuclear weapons, with its 'lose or use' dilemma, is now generally conceded (*4.16*).

(v) *Does the Strategic Defence Initiative offer* OR *Is the Strategic Defence Initiative simply*
the hope of an effective defence against   *the most recent and destabilizing example*
nuclear weapons?   *of the process outlined in 1?*

President Reagan's 1983 Strategic Defence Initiative (SDI) was announced by the United States Administration with no warning or prior consultation. Out of the blue, President Reagan decided to call in question, not just the value of deterrence, but its very morality. No wonder that a stunned Europe responded with widespread scepticism and not a little disguised anger. Whatever happens over deployment, SDI is triggering off a highly expensive new arms race, without providing invulnerable defence, nor obviously enhancing deterrence. It has so far damaged arms control prospects, and, as we have seen, could bring forward highly automated systems, even with a 'launch-on-warning' response (*4.19-21*). The philosophical case for the ABM Treaty, accepted by PresidentNixon and all his successors was that to attempt defensive invulnerability for all one's territory, as distinct from one's second strike installations or command and control centres, was to dangerously feed the arms race. The Strategic Defence Initiative opens up the same philosophical issue. If one attempts a comprehensive defence in space against all intercontinental nuclear missiles, most of which are part of a second strike system, it will just produce another twist in the arms race, this time in space, not just on earth (*3.13*).

(vi) *Is the threat of 'horizontal' nuclear*   OR *Is continuing reliance on nuclear deterrence*
proliferation best met by a continuation of   *by the great powers bound to accelerate the*
past policies?   *process of proliferation and make nuclear*
                                                         war more likely?

Sceptics say that concern over proliferation is exaggerated. Contrary to many pessimistic predictions, there are still only five declared nuclear weapon states. But all is not as it seems. Israel and probably South Africa are to all intents and purposes already nuclear weapon states. India's explosion of a nuclear device in 1974 puts pressure on Pakistan, which would in turn stimulate Iraq and Libya. In Latin America, Brazil and Argentina have modest nuclear weapons programmes underway. Article VI of the Non Proliferation Treaty, signed in 1968 and entering into force in 1970, put an obligation on nuclear weapon states to enter into good faith negotiations on effective arms control and disarmament. The only conceivable way of stopping clandestine proliferation is within the context of a changed international climate, with obvious moves from the nuclear weapon states to stop testing and to curb the arms race (3.6–10).

(vii) *Do multilateral arms-control negotiations offer the best prospect for future stability?* OR *Is 'arms-control' an illusion which diverts attention from the only safe policy – nuclear disarmament?*

The Reykjavik summit marks, not the end of serious arms control negotiations, but the beginning. I cannot understand why there is so much pessimism from sensible people about the outcome. All the ingredients are now present for a major arms deal, and I am confident it will happen. In Iceland, Mr Reagan and Mr Gorbachev took the sort of risks that distinguish the bureaucrat from the political leader (7). If the remaining three years of the 1980s repeat the first seven years of the decade, there will be no substantial agreement to control or reduce arms – but accelerating deployments of new and more dangerous weapons. Yet a basis has been laid for extraordinary progress. An opportunity exists for the 1980s to witness what only recently seemed to be a dream, but which now can become real: concrete accomplishments in disarmament, stability and peace. (*9.8*).

(B) WITHOUT NUCLEAR WEAPONS

(i) *If nuclear arsenals were dismantled would war between the great powers again become a rational option and therefore more likely?* OR *Would nuclear disarmament remove the incentive for nuclear preemption while not affecting the reluctance of the great powers to initiate a third world war?*

If there were global nuclear disarmament while current conventional forces remain intact, Western Europe would be exposed to the undoubted Soviet conventional superiority (*1.41*). This would clearly be dangerous. Global nuclear disarmament can only be realistically discussed against a background of political-military detente of the kind recommended by the Palme Commission (*2.xv*).

(ii) *Would a major conventional war be likely in itself to be as terrible as a limited nuclear war?* OR *Is conventional war, however terrible, preferable to nuclear war?*

We should not forget Field Marshal Lord Carver's warning about believing that conventional warfare is a comparatively harmless affair – one reason why some West German strategists accept even the risks of NATO's current tactical nuclear weapon strategy for their territory (*1.40*). As we recoil from the horror of nuclear war and the moral ambivalence surrounding nuclear deterrence, we should not let fading memories of the Second World War allow younger generations to forget that fifteen million in the Armed Services and between twenty-six and thirty-four million civilians, including six million Jews, lost their lives during that war. A new conventional war would be even more devastating to life and limb. Modern weapons have far greater destructive power, as experience in Vietnam and in the various Arab-Israeli were demonstrated (*4.2*).

(iii) *Because nuclear weapons cannot be uninvented would they not be bound to be used sooner or later once war had broken out?*   OR *As with nerve gases in the last war, would there be no incentive to resort to capabilities which the other side has as well?*

We should remember the fate of the Baruch Plan[1] in 1946. In seeking a world without nuclear weapons the plan was never able to overcome the fatal flaw which was the penalty of the Hiroshima explosion. Even if the US destroyed their atomic weapons everyone knew they would still retain knowledge of how to construct a bomb. The Soviet Union not unreasonably feared that the US could quickly reconstruct a bomb if political or military relations deteriorated (*3.3*).

(iv) *Is global nuclear disarmament only feasible in a world where war itself is no longer a possibility?*   OR *Is to argue that even multilateral nuclear disarmament is not desirable to give up all hope of a rational world-order?*

We share the urgent wish for greater progress towards the ultimate aim of general and complete disarmament (*2.xv*). But this can only be achieved as part of a much wider reordering of the world community along the lines recommended in the Report of the Independent Commission on Disarmament and Security Issues, chaired by Olof Palme.

B *NATO Policy*

(i) *Does the Soviet Union, together with her Warsaw Pact allies, enjoy a strategically dangerous military superiority in Europe?*   OR *Are NATO and WTO forces relatively evenly matched?*

The Soviet Union has had conventional superiority in Europe since 1945. Although, somewhat surprisingly, both the US and Canada have continued to base forward forces in Europe, it has not been in such numbers that they can be described as anything more than a crucial contribution to a conventional delaying force, not by any stretch of the imagination a conventional holding

---

1. See Note on p. 242

force. The Warsaw Pact forces, on the other hand, are clearly strong enough to sustain a NATO conventional attack (*1.40*).

If you talk to the NATO military commanders, the number one anxiety is ammunition stocks and the capacity to reinforce (6.18).

(ii) *Is the Soviet Union an expansionist power* OR *Is the Soviet Union an encircled and which will take advantage of unilateral threatened power trying to keep up with Western concessions and is only restrained Western technology and likely to respond and forced to accept arms-control positively to unconditional offers of agreements by Western determination and Western restraint within a general context strength? of detente?*

Some non-nuclear strategists sidestep arguments over Western conventional forces by saying that the Soviet Union has no intention of crossing the by now agreed East/West frontier in Europe; that Hungary in 1956, Czechoslovakia in 1968, and the threat of invasion to Poland in 1980–81 was within their own direct sphere of influence; that even Afghanistan was in the grey area of Soviet influence and not comparable in any way to an attack on Western Europe. Honest unilateralists find such rationalizations no substitute for a strong conventional defence strategy (*1.41*). We must not forget the crunching of freedom on the other side of the East-West divide since the end of the war. The memory of the Berlin airlift, the unrest in East Germany, and the Berlin wall must not be erased by time. Nor can we grow deaf to the cries for help that we could only listen to impotently from Hungary in 1956, and from Czechoslovakia in 1968, and, more recently, from Solidarity in Poland. Recent history reminds us that we cannot take our present stability for granted. As Europeans, we know all too well the potential power and influence of the Soviet Union. Though the USSR is a European country in part, as it has grown to be a superpower, so has it become an alien force in a Europe of medium-sized and small countries (*4.4–5*).

(iii) *Is Soviet chemical and conventional* OR *Is NATO dependence on the early use of preponderance such that NATO must nuclear weapons unnecessary and continue to be able to threaten early use of strategically suicidal? nuclear weapons?*

It is the acknowledged inbalance of conventional forces which has meant that the United States, France and Britain have never been prepared to sign a 'no first use' nuclear weapons agreement. We are not confident that our conventional defence can stop a Warsaw Pact attack and we have felt it necessary to say that, if attacked in overwhelming numbers, we reserve the right to threaten the first use of nuclear weapons against a Warsaw Pact which has nuclear weapons (*1.40*). NATO countries also believe that, despite the Soviets' public position that they would not use nuclear weapons first, the Soviet Union nevertheless plans and exercises on the basis of the first use of nuclear weapons (*2.xvi*). It is an awesome reality that, as a result, Britain is one of many countries committed to the illusion of a limited battlefield nuclear war-fighting strategy. There should be an urgent reassessment of that strategy in both NATO and Warsaw Pact countries (*2.xvi*). But this can only be achieved if the central problem of the conventional imbalance is tackled at the same time, by negotiating a reduction in Warsaw Pact conventional forces, and a strengthening where necessary of Western conventional capabilities. This is something that few non-nuclear strategists are prepared to face up to, and, until they do, their non-nuclear strategy lacks all credibility (*1.40*).

More significant than a premature declaration of 'no first use' of nuclear weapons would be the creation, step by step, of a functional battlefield nuclear weapon-free corridor, eventually reaching 150 kilometres either side of the East-West frontier. The significance of this proposal is that it tackles, at the root, the very doctrine of limited nuclear war. By removing the weapons, it reduces substantially the chance of the early use of nuclear weapons and the likelihood of a conventional attack immediately triggering the first use of nuclear weapons. No longer could nuclear weapon installations twenty kilometres from the border be overrun within hours of a conventional attack. It deliberately makes it harder to progress from conventional war to nuclear war. In this sense it demands a radical change in the conventional military wisdom that sees a seamless robe of escalation running across conventional and nuclear strategies (*2.xvii*).

(iv) *Does the growing size of the Soviet nuclear* OR *Does the West initiate nearly all phases of*
arsenal threaten the delicate theatre and *the nuclear arms race and continue to enjoy*
strategic balance? Would Western failure *a substantial lead in most areas? Is the*
to match Soviet systems be destabilizing? *nuclear 'overkill' such that the West could*
offer a nuclear 'freeze' or unconditional
cuts without risk?

What is essential to effective deterrence is mutual confidence in the invulnerability of powerful second strike nuclear forces. We should not believe that there has to be a matching, at every level and in every area, of every Soviet weapon system or strategy (*4.3*). In particular, a specifically Euro-strategic balance has never been necessary if there is a stable overall nuclear balance (*1.43*). To recognize this means adopting a political judgement about military sufficiency and rejecting the military wish for superiority. It means recognizing that such a wider judgement of the national and international good is bound to be easier with a democratic government than a totalitarian government and that is why the United States must not match every Soviet folly. It is a sign of immaturity, not virility, every time the Soviet military impose a new twist in the arms race for the Americans to respond. The military are part of the Soviet government's political decision-making. We should not be surprised in the West if the dynamics for the arms race appear stronger in the USSR at times. It should be the strength of our democracies that we do not feel bound to follow them blindly. We must be sufficiently skilled to de-escalate the arms race while preserving our security (*3.12*).

(v) *Are NATO 'forward defence' and 'deep*   OR *Should NATO exploit her lead in*
strike' strategies essential for effective   *'emerging technology' to explore less*
deterrence?   *provocative alternative strategies?*

If dependence on the early use of nuclear weapons could be removed, and a reasonable conventional balance achieved, we should be able to agree a US-European conventional fighting strategy on the Central Front fairly easily (*4.14*).

If we go for the so-called 'smart' bombs and new technology, there is no doubt that we will be beginning to develop the conventional capacity to stop the Soviet and Warsaw Pact forces massing, which at the moment is said to require tactical nuclear weapons. But there is a considerable price-tag on this (*6.19*).

(vi) *Is it the presence of American front-line*   OR *Is it domination by the two super-powers*
troops and the tying-in of theatre nuclear   *that poses the greatest threat to European*
forces to the American strategic deterrent   *integrity? Would Europe be safer*
that guarantees W. European security?   *decoupled from the super-power nuclear*
Should American policies therefore be   *confrontation? Should Europe be made a*
supported?   *nuclear weapon-free zone?*

The security of the West will continue to depend upon the presence of US troops in Europe, and on the potency of the US retaliatory nuclear second strike capability. But American perceptions have to be married with the differing perceptions of their European partners. The Alliance no longer gives the United States automatic authority; something President Carter understood and President Reagan initially did not understand (*1.44*). Nor can we assume in perpetuity that senators and congressmen will still be able to persuade United States voters and taxpayers to fund 300,000 members of the United States Armed Forces on the mainland of Europe (*5.735*). So, to help check the influence and pressure of the Soviet superpower, it has always been inevitable that a force would emerge from under the shadow of the United States that was fundamentally European in outlook and in interest. As nuclear weapons became more controversial within European politics, so the need to develop an inner European core within NATO to influence US nuclear strategy became urgent. What has been crucial for European security in the past is that at least two of three countries – Germany, France and the UK – have been bound together by relations of trust and intimacy. What cannot be gainsaid is that if there could be a tripod of Franco-German-Anglo understanding instead of a mere bipod, the so-called European pillar within NATO would be immensely strengthened. This must include a nuclear component, because the present imbalance in NATO is essentially because of the United States dominance over nuclear strategy (*4.5–7*). Would this not be a more effective way of standing up to the United States when we dislike their strategy on nuclear arms control? Would not Europe be in a much firmer and clearer position when arguing for maintaining SALT 2 limits if it also had its own worked-out view on NATO's nuclear strategy? Would not the partnership be more equal if, instead of the United States speaking separately to the French, Germans, Italians and British, it could feel that there was an underlying cohesion on nuclear strategic matters among the main European partners? That is the logical development (5.740).

But I am not postulating a European deterrent on the basis of replacing or excluding the United States, and the United States should certainly not be encouraged to withdraw. I would do everything in my power to hold the United States to the concept of the Atlantic Alliance for as long as humanly possible. If, as I hope, its forces remain for twenty, thirty or forty years, history will show that one of the reasons why they did stay was because there was a more equitable balance in the defence commitment to NATO by the European partners and the United States (5.737).

(vii) *Would Western unilateral nuclear disarmament invite Soviet blackmail? Are suggestions that the West should take the lead in offering unilateral disarmament initiatives the thin end of this wedge? Do radical nuclear disarmers consciously or unconsciously serve Soviet interests and threaten to undermine Western defences?*

OR *Are unilateral initiatives as part of a general programme of nuclear disarmament the only way to reverse the arms race? Is talk of 'multilateral disarmament' insincere in the mouths of those who reject all suggestion of a Comprehensive Test Ban Treaty, a Nuclear Freeze, a European Nuclear Weapon-Free Zone, or a declaration of No First Use?*

For Western unilateralists to give up the ability to threaten a second strike nuclear response in the face of a nuclear-armed Soviet Union is a decision of quite awesome dimensions. It goes against all past experience of how political leaders or nations actually act (1.41). The first nuclear arms race, it is worth recalling, was not between the Soviet Union and the United States, but was between Nazi Germany and the Allies. Those who in the Western democracies now challenge our possession of nuclear weapons as a deterrent, while the Soviet Union has theirs, should ask themselves what would have happened if Hitler's scientists had been able to test a nuclear bomb before Hitler had taken his life on 30 April 1945? Can anyone doubt it would have been a very different world? (3.1). No sane person can be content to live in a world where peace between the great powers is preserved mainly through the mutual fear of nuclear devastation. Yet no sane person can allow their emotions to suspend their reason. We may instinctively want to stop our nuclear world and get off, but we know we cannot. Nuclear weapons exist. They cannot disappear or be wished away. The task is, painstakingly, to negotiate them away (4.2).

C *British Policy*

1 *The British Deterrent*

We are one of the world's five nuclear-weapon states. Our membership of NATO means we have our own conventional and nuclear forces on the East-West frontier in Germany, and as a permanent member of the Security Council and a member of the Commonwealth we have many global responsibilities. No longer a superpower, we nevertheless hold a pivotal position and are capable of playing a constructive role over disarmament (*2.xv–xvi*).

(i) *Is Britain's deterrent a weapon of last*   OR *Would all possible uses of Britain's* *resort which guarantees her sovereignty and*   *'deterrent' be suicidal? Is its only effect to* *independence and protects her from nuclear*   *encourage proliferation?* *blackmail?*

Although the British deterrent can be said to provide ultimate protection against the possibility of nuclear blackmail (*3.23*), this does not make the suggestion that Britain should give up her independent deterrent intellectually untenable, so long as we accept that NATO should still retain nuclear and conventional deterrents, and provided also that we are content to rely upon the United States nuclear guarantee (*5.734*).

(ii) *Are British nuclear forces valuable to*   OR *Is the 'second centre of decision making' an* *European allies because they provide a*   *illusion when the weapons are dependent* *specifically European second centre of*   *upon the US and there is no independent* *decision making?*   *strategic role to be played? Are European*   *allies unenthusiastic about a parochial*   *British force likely to inhibit her*   *commitment to European defence?*

Many of us who believe in the need for nuclear deterrence for NATO find the case for Britain remaining a nuclear weapon state and contributing to NATO's nuclear deterrent strategy has been substantially enhanced by political events and US attitudes over the last twenty-five years. Few, if any, for instance, would argue against replacing Polaris on the grounds that were deployed in 1962 against the purchase of Polaris, that the capability was unnecessary, because we could rely totally on the US nuclear guarantee. There is too much concern about successive responses by the President of the United States to the Soviet Union and to Europe across the UK political spectrum for that to carry conviction (*4.10*). We must consider the changes that are taking place in the United States. At one time, one in four of the United States population had their origins in Europe. Now it is one in ten. There has been a massive shift of population towards the western and southern states. Nobody who knows and loves the United States can fail to appreciate that the Pacific orientation is much stronger than it was ten, let alone twenty years ago (*5.735*). In these circumstances, as we have seen, the European defence pillar must be strengthened. But it is impossible to see how this can be confined to conventional deterrence and deliberately exclude strengthening nuclear deterrence. A United Kingdom decision to abandon or phase out our own nuclear weapons would not, to put it mildly, be the most convincing way of starting to strengthen the European pillar within NATO (*4.11*).

For all these reasons, greater Anglo-French cooperation makes the utmost sense, not as an exclusive realtionship, but as an inclusive European relationship. The core of such an arrangement would be to build on existing Franco-German cooperation over nuclear strategy on the continent. At the moment, those who scoff at the concept of a European minimum deterrent are trying to have it both ways. They are arguing for British independence while tying themselves in for the next thirty years to American hardware. Yet they would only ever use that American hardware independently if the American nuclear guarantee did not exist. When one considers the potential for the Americans to interfere with that Trident missile hardware, in a situation where their guarantee had been withdrawn, one must question how independent such a system really is. Certainly it is a question, with Britain a member of the European Community and arguing for strengthening political cooperation, that is far more relevant in the latter part of the 1980s than it ever was in the early part of the 1960s (*8.6–7*). In future, the UK must moor permanently alongside continental Europe, instead of merely swinging at anchor in the Channel (*4.7–8*).

(iii) *Does the US favour shared responsibility*   OR *Are US forces committed anyway and*
and do British nuclear forces guarantee   *independent British initiatives more likely*
full US commitment to Europe and Soviet   *to trigger Soviet retaliation than US*
recognition of it?   *involvement?*

If Europe is more self-sufficient in its defence, the United States will not pull out of the NATO alliance. It will strengthen those in the United States who wish to remain in NATO if they feel that Europe is making a strong conventional and nuclear commitment. That view is held by many Americans, and many Americans stationed in Europe who are responsible for defence decisions in NATO also hold that view. The Supreme Allied Commander in Europe is only one example arguing that a stronger European defence commitment makes it easier for senators and congressmen to retain the American commitment to Europe (*5.737*).

I passionately believe that strengthening the European pillar is the mechanism whereby the United States nuclear guarantee will actually be upheld. It is the mechanism whereby we will see a continued United States' presence in Europe and a significant one. Everything I heard in Europe confirmed this belief. For do not believe that in five years' time there will be 325,000 US troops in Europe. Congress will reduce that upper limit within that period. Far better for such a change to be done by agreement, and for it to be introduced in a way that is coherent and planned, than for it to be done as a result of unilateral decision by the US Congress out of frustration. We know this is likely to happen, and it is obvious common sense to anticipate it happening (*6.2*).

(iv) *Is the cost of the British deterrent small in*   OR *Can Britain's nuclear forces only be*
view of the vital defence role it plays? Are   *afforded at the expense of conventional*
alternatives likely to be more expensive?   *strength and of other more important*
                                                      economic priorities?

This is a time for rethinking the budget. During the next three years there will be a reduction in real terms in defence spending of more than four and a half per cent. All of us should be prepared to reconsider past positions and to think long and hard about the future of our armed services, and, in particular, about how we strengthen the European pillar of NATO (*5.732, 743*). We have seen why it is essential that there is an effective nuclear component in Europe defences. But if on no other grounds, we should reconsider the Trident programme on grounds of expense. Despite the money already allocated, I still believe that it is possible to cancel Trident. If we do not do so, it will cut savagely into our defence capacity (*5.736*). The 'Towpath Papers'[1] puncture the Government's repeated claims that they are planning for a fifty-strong surface fleet, and show that provision will not be made for building Hunter Killer submarines during the Trident submarine construction programme. So Trident not only eats into the surface fleet and endangers new amphibious provision, but it will reduce the Hunter Killer submarine fleet, which is the equivalent in firepower and effectiveness to the battleships of the past (*8.4*). For that reason, I am prepared to look at less powerful, but nevertheless effective, alternatives (*5.737*).

(v) *Would unilateral British nuclear disarmament have no effect on other countries and only serve to weaken British influence and allow France unchallenged ascendancy in Europe?*
OR *Does the British deterrent encourage proliferation and do nothing to enhance British prestige? Would British disarmament within the context outlined in B help to break the nuclear log-jam?*

If Britain were ever to give up nuclear weapons, it should only be as part of a consensus calculated decision really contributing to the end of ridding the whole world of nuclear weapons. (*4.23*). In present circumstances it would have little effect in that direction: for example, the decision of France or Britain or both to give up their nuclear weapons would not affect the Soviet or US arsenals (*1.45*).

As it is, one of the arguments for Britain remaining a nuclear weapons state is that it is thereby able to use its influence in some areas to achieve arms control – for example, our relationship with the US is sufficiently robust for Britain to maintain an independent position on a test ban (*3.22*). But the critical factor is European. What is vital to Europe is that France should not be left as the only European nuclear weapon state. For the European Community, particularly in political cooperation, depends on a balance between the member states – large and small, nuclear and non nuclear. Apart from developing new missiles, there is no good reason why France and the UK should not discuss the theory behind their existing strategic weapons, and to widen those discussions to include the Federal Republic. Discussions would not compromise the independent control of forces. But it would mean that slowly, through the habit of working together, Britain and France would build up a similar perception about nuclear strategy. This would give a solidity to the way Europe approaches the United States. It would reinforce the vital hinge which must link Europe to North America (*4.11–12, 18*).

---

1. Naval documents dropped by mistake on a towpath in Sonning, Berkshire, and found by a freelance journalist.

(vi) *Is investment in Trident the best way to*   OR *Would commitment to Trident exacerbate*
     continue to ensure effective British strategic   *all the drawbacks listed above?*
     defence into the 21st century?

We have already mentioned cost. In addition, Trident represents a very substantial increase in nuclear capability over and above Polaris. It is a very good
system, and I am pleased that the United States has it, because the Soviet
Union has the same capabilities as those that are contained in the Trident
system. But it represents a dramatic 800 per cent increase in the number of
warheads – from 64 to 512, and a 1,200 per cent increase in the operational
availability of warheads – from 32 to 384. The question for Britain is whether
we can afford it, and whether, in arms control terms, it makes any sense for
a country that has always believed in a minimum deterrent. It is whether we
can get a reasonable nuclear minimum deterrent that will make a contribution
to Europe's minimum deterrent for less money than we would have to spend
on Trident. There are a number of options and we should look seriously at
them. There are existing systems like the American Tomahawk missiles, or
the possibility of building similar French or British cruise missiles. And there
are other alternatives. (5.736–7).

My own view is that the submarine option is still the best, and Tomahawk
cruise missiles the cheapest. Nothing has done more harm than those people
who have tried to argue that it is Trident or nothing. Some of the most senior
military figures in this country now worry that we are getting ourselves into a
situation where, if we go on insisting that it is Trident or nothing, then it may
be that 'nothing' is the answer (6.12, 16).

2 NATO Forces and US Bases

(i) *Must Britain continue to share*   OR *Should British obligations to NATO be*
     responsibility for manning NATO nuclear   *met by strengthening conventional forces*
     systems upon which her security depends?   *where necessary within an overall non-*
     Would refusal to do so fatally weaken the   *nuclear strategy as recommended in B?*
     alliance?

There is a logical inconsistency and moral weakness in the Labour Party's
case. The logic of disowning nuclear weapons – not just our own but our
allies – leads progressively to the justification of neutralism and to a lesser
commitment to NATO, and it leads eventually through a grave impact upon
the cohesion of NATO, to its dismemberment as we know it (5.735).

(ii) *Would the forced withdrawal of US*   OR *Do the large numbers of nuclear facilities*
     nuclear bases from Britain make US   *yielded to the US erode British*
     defence of the West impossible? Is   *sovereignty? Would their removal do no*
     American interference in British affairs   *more than restore a normal peacetime*
     negligible?   *relationship?*

It should be matter of concern to us all, irrespective of our political position,
that Northern European Socialist International parties have developed such a
hostile attitude to nuclear weapons. France can change governments from

Right to Left and back to the Right with a barely perceptible shift in nuclear strategy. The advent of the SPD to government in the Federal Republic of Germany, or the Dutch Labour Party in Holland would, however, lead to a perceptible tremor in the NATO Alliance. Whereas, the advent of the British Labour Party into government would, in marked contrast, trigger an earthquake within NATO. The creation of the SDP in the UK owed much to the dangerous defence policy progressively adopted by Labour since 1980. That policy is, in 1986, even more irresponsible and damaging to the collective strength of NATO. Now Labour is challenging the basic NATO strategy of nuclear deterrence. They are pledged to throw the United States out of all nuclear bases in the United Kingdom, as well as cancelling Trident and decommissioning Polaris. The effect of such a decision on opinion in the United States would be devastating (*4.15–16*). We should consider what has happened to the ANZUS treaty[1], which has been effectively set aside because the United States was not prepared to be a member of a treaty organization when one member of it had said that ships carrying nuclear weapons could not go through its ports (*5.728*). Hopefully, Labour will never be allowed to put such a policy into practice (*4.16*).

(iii) *Will Britain continue to be targeted by Soviet warheads whether or not she disarms unilaterally?*
OR *Is Britain seen as an American aircraft carrier and targeted by the USSR accordingly? Will Britain fall an early victim in any superpower confrontation unless bases are removed?*

The decision of France or Britain to give up their nuclear weapons would not ensure that either country avoided nuclear weapons being used on their territories. France has always been an extension of the European battlefield, Britain a strategic military island that would have to be towed away into the Southern Atlantic before it would be inviolate. A non-nuclear Britain would be just as subject to nuclear blackmail, and possibly to nuclear attack (*1.45*).

(iv) *Can non-nuclear defences only safely be afforded by powers prepared to shelter beneath the American strategic umbrella?*
OR *In a nuclear-free Europe, decoupled from the superpower nuclear confrontation, would Britain no more expect to depend upon the US 'umbrella' than any other Western ally – or than Eastern Europe upon the USSR?*

It is the deterrent value of the mutually assured second strike capability held by the superpowers that underpins peace in Europe (*3.11*). So it is dishonest of the Labour Party to claim that it will not depend on the American guarantee. It knows perfectly well that it is only because of the American nuclear guarantee that is can even pretend to indulge in the luxury of unilateralism. How can it justify throwing the United States out of its nuclear bases here, while still

---

1. The ANZUS Treaty of 1951 between the US, Australia and New Zealand, set aside because of the anti-nuclear policy adopted by New Zealand in 1984.

relying on membership of a NATO Alliance whose strategy is firmly based on conventional and nuclear deterrence? (*5.728*).

Moral Considerations

Some allege that the consequences of nuclear weapons are so morally outrageous that it is immoral even to threaten their use, when the threat, to be credible, must carry a readiness to act and risk an uncontrolled escalation. Some argue that there is no morality to killing of any kind and therefore none in war. In this sense the arguments of the pacifist have an absoluteness that no argument can easily confound, and deserve respect. Religious thought has through the ages tried to wrestle with the moral dilemma of war, and many compromises have evolved over time, some even to be blessed. But there has always been a sense that there is some undefined limit to the extent of the compromise. To many, nuclear weapons cross that threshold, and they rightly demand verifiable reductions by multilateral negotiations.

But those who advocate a non-nuclear defence strategy in terms of morality or practicality must rebut the argument that nuclear deterrence is the only way of preventing war between the great powers, including nuclear war. If it is possible to show that there is any other way of doing this, while potential enemies still possess a nuclear capability and a dangerous conventional superiority, then there is no possible justification for their retention (*1.39*). But at the moment there is no other way. The horror of nuclear war and the moral ambivalence surrounding nuclear deterrence should not blind us to the appalling devastation of conventional war, or to the fact that precipitate unilateral nuclear disarmament on moral grounds might make nuclear war itself more likely. The main problem of a unilateralist strategy is that it does not try to understand war, and by its impatience can provoke war (*4.2, 1.42*). Nuclear disarmament can only safely be achieved by painstaking multilateral negotiation. It cannot be achieved by moralizing (*3.5*).

Recommendations

NOTE. *These recommendations are deduced by the editor from the sources already cited. In each case references are given.*

In Britain, those who argue for multilateral negotiations and those who advocate unilateral disarmament measures, those who wish to remain fully committed to NATO and those who espouse neutrality, have more in common than they often realize. The 'Programme of Action' detailed in the Palme Commission Report is a coherent package of measures around which all can rally to reverse the present deeply disturbing trends (*2.xv*).

  1 Yes – if current negotiations for deep cuts fail (*10.11–12*).

2 Yes, there should be an immediate moratorium on weapons testing in space (*3.13*). The ABM Treaty should be clarified and reinforced (*9.2–4*).

3 Yes. There should be a complete ban over a three- or preferably five-year period on all testing, and an immediate moratorium on all tests once agreement is reached and prior to the treaty being ratified (*2.xix*). Arguments against this do not hold up.

(a) *Can a test ban be verified to give a sufficiently credible guarantee that there will be no cheating?* This is a complex technical subject, but most of the problems that seemed insurmountable in the 1960's have now been overcome. There is widespread agreement that this is no longer a reason for not pressing ahead (*3.16–22*).

(b) *Would a ban damage the safety and reliability of the existing nuclear stockpile?* The 'stockpile' or 'shelf-life' argument only surfaced within the context of a CTB as a major issue in 1977–8, when coincidentally for the first time it looked as if the breakthrough in verification was such that a CTB might actually be signed. Up until 1980, not a single American or British nuclear test had been undertaken on stockpiled weapons. The self-life argument was a deliberate diversion, the protection of a vested interest by the nuclear testing laboratories at Los Alamos, Livermore and Aldermaston (*3.14*).

(c) *Would a ban prevent new weapon development as part of assuring an invulnerable second strike capability?* The US and the Soviet Union have such a vast backlog of detailed and wide ranging knowledge of all likely new warhead designs that a CTB would impose few inhibitions to their continuing to develop new weapons systems. In any case, computer simmulation techniques are now available in compensation (*3.15–16*).

A comprehensive Test Ban Treaty could be a crucial stage in preventing further proliferation and moving towards minimum deterrence.

4 For reasons explained in **B(iii)** this is not critical. What is important is a shift of NATO strategy away from reliance on the early use of nuclear weapons.

5 Yes, within the context proposed in **AI(iii)** and **(iv)**. There should be a fifty per cent cut in strategic systems. INF systems should be, first reduced, then removed from Europe west of the Urals (*9.4, 6.19*).

6 A functional battlefield nuclear weapon-free corridor should be established along the East-West frontier in Europe (see **B(iii)**).

7 Yes (See **A2(A)(vi)**).

8 This should be part of a move towards minimum deterrence (see **AI(iv)**). The eventual goal of complete nuclear disarmanent depends upon other, wider factors (see **A2(B)(iv)**).

9 See 8.

10 Yes (see **A2(A)(v)**).

11 See 4.

12 Yes, within the context of **A1(iii) A2**(A)**(iv)** & **B(iv)**.

13 No (See **B(vi)** & **C1(ii)**).

14 No (See **B(vi)** & **C2(ii)**).

15 See 6.

16 No. But Britain should be prepared to give up her independent forces as part of a general settlement aimed at global nuclear disarmament (see **CI(v)**).

17 So far as concerns any money saved by abandoning the Trident programme, yes (**C1(iv)**).

18 Yes, as part of a general settlement with the Warsaw Pact (see **A1(iii)** & **B(iii)**).

19 No (See **C2(ii)**).

20 Yes (See **C2(i)**).

James Schlesinger

Biographical Note

Born in 1929, James Schlesinger was a professor at the University of Virginia between 1955 and 1963. First a senior staff member, he was then Director of Strategic Studies at the RAND Corporation between 1963 and 1967. Between 1971 and 1973 he was chairman of the US Atomic Energy Commission. He served as Secretary of Defense between 1973 and 1975, and as Secretary for Energy between 1977 and 1979. Since then, among other things, he has been at the Center for Strategic and International Studies at Georgetown University.

As Secretary of Defense under President Nixon, James Schlesinger is associated with a move away from explicit reliance upon the threat of direct attack on enemy centres of population, often referred to in shorthand as 'Mutual Assured Destruction', and towards the elaboration of a varied range of selective options aimed principally against enemy military forces.

Editorial Comment

This set of answers was given in an interview in London on November 14, 1986. It is full of interest for readers who want to understand something of the thinking of a distinguished strategist and statesman, who has helped to shape current American nuclear policy, but is at the same time critical of a number of aspects of it. He has been involved with questions of nuclear strategy since the 1950s, and, as his answers under *Moral Considerations* show, with its morality. The moral dimension to the move away from a policy of assured destruction is stressed. James Schlesinger's response is informed by the experience of having been responsible for the conduct of public policy at a time when many Americans felt that the Soviet Union took advantage of a period of notable United States restraint (for example, see the answer to question **B(ii)**). But he is as impatient with what he regards as the alarmism of critics on the political right in the United States, as he is with what he describes as the fantasies indulged in by critics on the political left in Britain.

The answers to questions such as **B(vi)** and **C1(ii)** give British readers an American perspective on European defence, while the answers to **C1(iii)**, **C2(i)** and **C2(ii)**, show how much room there is or is not seen to be for proposals to abandon an independent British deterrent, and to withdraw unilaterally from NATO's nuclear dispositions.

JAMES SCHLESINGER

A *Global Policy*

1 *The History of the Past Forty Years*

(i) *Has it been nuclear deterrence that has*   OR *Has it mainly been other factors?*
    kept the peace between the great powers
    since 1945?

Without nuclear deterrence we might have had far greater instability in the world. Particularly in the years immediately after World War II, the American strategic nuclear advantage provided stability for Western Europe in the face of what was believed to be overwhelming Soviet conventional military superiority. Nuclear weapons were seen as the great equalizer. To be sure, there are always other factors involved in such complex historical processes, and, even without nuclear deterrence, we might not have come to blows. But nuclear weapons have been the principal element in the post-war military scene, and, as such, have reinforced the condition of peace. Without them, the maintenance of peace might have been bought, if at all, then only at the cost of greater Soviet influence, if not domination, over much of continental Western Europe.

(ii) *Does mutual possession of an invulnerable*   OR *Does the threat of strategic nuclear second-strike strategic nuclear force prevent retaliation, particularly against a similarly war? armed enemy, lack credibility and invite sub-deterrent encroachment?*

The critics of current policy on the right-hand side in your analysis (who are on the political left) have here taken over a position that has long been of concern to prudent military planners in the West. Before there was mutual possession of invulnerable second-strike forces, that is for the first twenty-five or thirty years after World War II, American nuclear superiority offset Soviet military advantage elsewhere, so that the Soviets had no desire to test American resolve. And the Americans, given the nature of the American democracy, had no ambitions to expand by pressing the Soviet Union into territorial concessions. But the establishment of an invulnerable second-strike force on the part of the Soviet Union has removed that security, and there has, it seems to me, been appropriate concern that the Soviets might take advantage of what could be seen to be a stalemated condition to encroach at lower levels. It is, indeed, a serious problem. But it is, perhaps, ironical that this issue has been raised by some of those on the political left over here, because it suggests a malevolent intent on the part of the Soviet Union, which in other areas they are loath to concede.

(iii) *Have limited nuclear options at strategic*   OR *Have most military planners from the start and theatre levels enhanced deterrence by been aiming for nuclear war-fighting dramatically raising the threshold between superiority? Has 'flexible response' peace and war? dangerously lowered the threshold between conventional and nuclear war?*

The possession of an invulnerable second-strike force remains for the West a necessary condition for deterrence, but, as we have just seen, not a sufficient condition. We need something in addition to that second strike force, preferably conventional, but in view of Soviet conventional strength, also a strategy of selective nuclear strikes, in order to maintain the credibility of the deterrent. This is particularly important for the effectiveness of *extended* deterrence – especially for the protection of those parts of Western Europe which are contiguous to the Soviet Union and therefore lie most open to Soviet military pressure.

By broadening the concept of how theatre or strategic nuclear weapons may be deployed in this way, we have dramatically enhanced deterrence for the West, and thereby raised the threshold which represents the barrier between peace and war. The critics represented in the right-hand column are right when they say that a strategy of selective strikes lowers the threshold between conventional and nuclear war. It is this that enhances deterrence. Where they are wrong is to imply that this is more dangerous than the alternative. They do not seem to understand that it is the lowered threshold between conventional and nuclear war that, by offsetting the lack of credibility of an exclusively second strike force, thereby at the same time offsets the invitation to sub-deterrent encroachment. The proof of the pudding is in the eating, as the English might say, and the reality is that the strategy of flexible response has been sufficient to deter the Soviet Union.

(iv) *Has the size and variety of the nuclear arsenals held by the superpowers stabilized deterrence?* OR *Has the logic of nuclear confrontation and worst-case analysis generated a dangerous and strategically pointless superfluity of weapons systems?*

On the whole, the variety of nuclear weapons systems has stabilized deterrence. One would not want to be dependent on a single type of system that could, for example, only go after Moscow. That would lack credibility. It is the richness of the Western deterrent, provided primarily by the United States, that provides its credibility. The notion of having a very simplistic strategy – a minimum deterrent – which afflicts those who argue as in the right-hand column, would be dangerous. The critics do have a point about numerical redundancy. I think that the sizes of the two forces could be cut. That is why we are engaged in arms control discussions. But the numerical redundancy is relatively trivial when set against the overall picture. Insofar as the Soviet Union has aggressive intentions, it is the richness of the Western deterrent that restrains those ambitions.

(v) *Has the idea of nuclear balance between the superpowers been essential to stability and have arms-control negotiations helped to achieve it?* OR *Have ideas of 'nuclear defence' and 'parity' proved illusory and is 'multilateral negotiation from strength' a contradiction in terms? Has 'arms-control' been just another name for the arms race?*

Let me state very clear that we would not prefer rough equivalence. We would prefer to have an edge. But the Soviet Union is unlikely to be generous enough to provide us with that edge, so we must settle for rough equivalence. And that rough equivalence could be achieved by unilateral appreciation of mutual dependence. But it is much more likely to be achieved through arms control negotiations. That is why we pursue arms control negotiations. Let me address myself to the issues raised in the column on the right, because I find myself bemused by the fact that the attack on arms control, which in Britain tends to come from the political left, happens to be precisely the attack on arms control that in the United States comes from the political right.

In the United States arms control negotiations with the Soviet Union have been under attack, because it is said that arms control has never worked and that it has simply been a way of adjusting to the arms race. My response to both the political left in the UK and the political right in the United States is the same. Arms control has been a visible success, albeit a partial success. One has only to think of what the expansion of offensive weapons would have been on both sides if we had not had the ABM treaty of 1972. We in the United States had planned to respond to the Soviet Moscow defence system by expanding our number of strategic warheads if necessary to 50,000. Surely those on the political left in the UK can understand the difference between 10,000 and 50,000 warheads, just as their counterparts on the political right in the United States should be able to.

(vi) *Has force-planning been controlled by strategic thinking?*   OR *Has the self-reinforcing impetus of technology and vested interest dictated policies subsequently justified post hoc?*

As in so much of this there are no black-and-white answers. There are only shadings. In this case the critics represented in the right-hand column have a point. It is only a half-truth, to be sure, but it is a point. Technological developments have at times had an impact on strategic force structure that was not clearly perceived in advance. We have not always controlled deployment as well as we should have done in this respect. Incidentally, in the West this problem comes in part from the nature of democracy, which is something that we value for other reasons. The rapid turnover of governments in the West, the rapid turnover of senior officials in defence and foreign policy, means that the continuity is provided elsewhere, and the preservation of a strategic vision which dominates deployment is difficult to achieve. But critics should not forget the power of the Soviet military-industrial complex here. It varies from time to time, shrinking when there is a long-established leader like Stalin or Brezhnev, but sometimes playing a critical role in periods of transition. So there is some truth in what the critics say. But it is only a half-truth. In the United States the role of these so-called 'vested interests' is much less than it is in the Soviet Union. They can influence judgements at the margin, but they do not create and remove governments, and do not determine overall policy. And critics should reflect more carefully on the role of technology. Those who say that, once we have achieved an invulnerable second strike force, we can relax and stop competing in arms, should recall how we acquired such a force and how hard we have to work to maintain it. If they would think back to the 1950s, when we were dependent upon bombers, all soft and all located on a very small number of bases in the United States, and when we were frightened to death at the thought of a Soviet surprise attack, they will know that it was the technology of the ICBM and the SLBM that provided the invulnerability that they now so rightly praise. And this would never have come into existence if their views about the impetus of technology and the power of vested interests had prevailed.

2 *The Prospect for the Future*

(A) WITH NUCLEAR WEAPONS

(i) *Does the threat of an enemy first strike*   OR *Is there an increasing threat from accurate*
remain inconceivable for the foreseeable   *and time-urgent first-strike weapons?*
future?

It seems to be intriguing that the political left in Britain, which, so far as I know, has not had the deepest admiration for Mr Reagan, should here be campaigning under his slogan from 1980 – the 'window of vulnerability'. In the United States it has been the right wing that has talked about the increasing threat from time-urgent first-strike weapons. Some might think that we have a 'Pearl Harbor complex' – that suddenly, one bright morning, there will be a nuclear Pearl Harbor. I regard all of this as much exaggerated, whether it comes from the British left or the American right. This would be a decision taken only by irrational people. There will be no such nuclear bolt from the blue, either from the East or from the West. But I share the desire of the critics to improve the stability of the balance, and to avoid anything that increases, however modestly, the capability and therefore the temptation to initiation.

(ii) *Are command, control, communication and* OR *Does the amount of information to be*
intelligence facilities likely to remain   *processed, pressure of time and fear of*
secure?   *preemption put command and control*
                                                      systems under intolerable strain and make
                                                      inadvertent war more likely?

To those who argue as in the right-hand column here I answer with an English phrase – balderdash! Command and control systems will never be perfect, but they will probably be good enough, even under wartime conditions, and even though they may be damaged, to transmit the necessary minimum of orders. But, more important that this, each side knows that the command and control system on the other will be capable of this, and therefore both will refrain from those actions that would inevitably put their own societies at risk. Whether they be here or in the Soviet Union, and whatever their public professions, the political leaders that I have observed tend to be extraordinarily prudent men. They will not recklessly get themselves involved in nuclear war.

(iii) *If nevertheless there were a limited nuclear* OR *Is the idea that nuclear war could be*
exchange would it be likely to end   *limited once it had broken out a dangerous*
hostilities swiftly?   *illusion?*

I always appreciate clairvoyance. There is no guarantee that a nuclear exchange would be limited. But it is clear that it is in the interest of both sides that such an exchange be terminated without major damage to either society. An initial, very limited, employment of nuclear weapons will make the leaders on both sides very sober people. I find it odd that those who parade under the banner of the rationality of man should come to such negative conclusions regarding the rationality of the leaders.

(iv) *Do new generations of battlefield and*   OR *Do new battlefield and theatre weapons*
theatre nuclear systems reinforce   *threaten a dangerous lowering of the*
deterrence?   *nuclear threshold?*

Here I must pay tribute to the admonition of the critics in the right-hand column. We must always try to make sure that there is a clearly marked boundary line between conventional and nuclear war. There have been those in the atomic energy laboratories in the United States, and in the military establishments, who have tried to erode that boundary. In the 1950s, happily once for a brief period, it was American and NATO policy that nuclear weapons were to be treated like conventional weapons. We should not allow the advances in the technology of nuclear weapons to erode what is a very important political line of distinction. I am delighted to be able to pay some tribute to the critics here.

(v) *Does the Strategic Defence Initiative offer*   OR *Is the Strategic Defence Initiative simply*
the hope of an effective defence against   *the most recent and destabilizing example*
nuclear weapons?   *of the process outlined in 1?*

This is an immensely complicated subject in which one must deal with nuances of meaning. Both sides represented here have taken too black-and-white an attitude to it. The President of the United States, to my mind regrettably, jumped the traces and turned the whole strategic defence issue on its head. Normally, in research and development programmes, we try to resolve the technical questions before we draw conclusions about strategy and force structure. In this case, radical conclusions were drawn, even though there are innumerable technical problems that have not been resolved. That is very imprudent. And it is ironical that such imprudence comes under the banner of Conservation. On the other hand, the critics represented in the right-hand column have rejected clearly required research and development activities. Why clearly required? Because, whatever the claims of the Americans, the initiative happens to come from the Soviet Union. The Soviets have been vigorously working in this area for some time. It is indispensable that we at least match what they are doing. Does the SDI offer the hope of an effective defence against nuclear weapons? The answer is simply, no. This is an illusion which may have captivated American society, but the fact that an illusion captivates American society does not transform it into reality. It remains an illusion.

Can Strategic Defence enhance deterrence? Possibly. If it could be used to protect second-strike forces and were guided by arms control, it might have such a result. But, until we know what we are doing, the burden of proof rests upon anyone who wants to upset the ABM treaty.

But the most important benefit of Strategic Defence is that it provides enormous impetus to the Arms Control process. The Soviets are deeply concerned about the SDI, and this is very useful in eliciting a response for them, particularly with regard to offensive weapons. Of course, for those on the political left in Britain and on the political right in the United States, who curiously enough reject arms control for the same reasons, the role of the SDI in arms control negotiations is not, as I would see it, beneficial, but pernicious.

(vi) *Is the threat of 'horizontal' nuclear*   OR *Is continuing reliance on nuclear deterrence*
proliferation best met by a continuation of   *by the great powers bound to accelerate the*
past policies?   *process of proliferation and make nuclear*
    war more likely?

The first point to be made is that the maintenance of the nuclear deterrent by the two major powers is essential for the preservation of the civilization that they represent. So, even if there is a link between the threat of proliferation and continuing dependence by the great powers on nuclear deterrence, this does not have any policy implications. There is no way that we are going to give up the deterrent in order to ease whatever indignities the non-nuclear powers may feel have been heaped upon them.

The second point is that the link is much more complex than critics are inclined to suggest. The nuclear capable signatories to the Non Proliferation Treaty have agreed to come to the aid of any non-nuclear state threatened by nuclear attack. So a well-protected nuclear deterrent of the kind we have now is what provides deterrence against nuclear attack against the non-nuclear states. In the emotional diatribes on these issues, this kind of underlying reality is sometimes forgotten.

No doubt for those who have refrained from acquiring nuclear capabilities it is somewhat psychologically disturbing to see the superpowers steadily expanding their nuclear arsenals. But this is a state of affairs with which they simply have to live – and it is one with which they have so far been prepared to live. There is no inevitability about the pace of nuclear proliferation. It is a serious problem. But it is a problem that is not adequately dealt with by hand-wringing.

(vii) *Do multilateral arms-control negotiations*   OR *Is 'arms-control' an illusion which diverts*
offer the best prospect for future stability?   *attention from the only safe policy –*
    nuclear disarmament?

The notion that arms control is an illusion is one shared by the political left in Britain and the political right in the United States. But they come to conclusions which are diametrically opposed. For the former, the conclusion points towards nuclear disarmament; for the latter, it points towards a technologically perfect strategic defence which will make the United States invulnerable. Both sides operate on the basis of a rejection of reality.

B WITHOUT NUCLEAR WEAPONS

As you suggest, I will take the first four sets of questions together. Let me start with a personal observation. I have always been something of a maverick, and therefore I find it rather disquieting to identify myself with the views of the establishment, which are usually somewhat simplified. But in this case the establishment views, as you have outlined them down the left-hand column, are utterly sound on all four points. There is no way of eliminating nuclear weapons. The nuclear genie has been let out of the bottle, and there is no way of policing his reinsertion into it. If we were to have nuclear disarmament, whichever side cheated or was close to cheating, would have a great strategic advantage. Moreover, a world without nuclear weapons is not only one that cannot be brought into existence, but one that would carry very great risks for the West even if it could. We have already seen why this is so. Apart from everything else, the vast Soviet advantage in terms of chemical weapons would still terrify those who are concerned about frightful things.

So, why do leaders, like President Reagan, nevertheless say that global nuclear disarmament would be a good thing? As an actor, which is what his whole experience makes him, President Reagan knows that he must throw himself entirely into his role and persuade himself that the lines he is uttering are those that he sincerely feels. In this sense he believes what he says. And he is responding to the American public, whose mood he can understand almost viscerally. He is responding to critics on the political left, who demand an end to nuclear deterrence, by stealing their clothes; he is responding to a deep-seated desire to be rid of this threat. That is why he is so successful as a politician. But what he means by these remarks is something largely in the world of symbolism, which ought not to be interpreted as a guide to policy.

(v) *Is peace only preserved when we are seen to be prepared for war, as failure before 1939 and success since 1945 show? Under likely future conditions would global nuclear disarmament make war, including nuclear war, more likely?*

OR *Do the years before 1914 show what happens when military planning and the arms race control political choices? Do present strategies make nuclear war almost inevitable under likely future conditions? Is global nuclear disarmament the only rational policy?*

One must always look to history, but history never repeats itself precisely. The appropriate inference from 1939 is that one must not encourage a potentially aggressive power by seeming to be weaker or less resolute than one in fact is. The appropriate inference from 1914 is, as critics on the political left say, to prevent the kinds of instabilities that helped to precipitate war at that time. So both in a sense are right. But, so far as concerns the parallel with 1914, how are we to prevent those kinds of instabilities? The critics of the political left do not recognize that there are two mechanisms above all that enable us to do this – technology, which they fear, and arms control, which they deride. It is the combination of technology effectively employed, and arms control effectively executed that provides us with a protection against the instabilities of 1914, to which the critics quite rightly point.

B Nato Policy

(i) *Does the Soviet Union, together with her*   OR *Are NATO and WTO forces relatively*
    Warsaw Pact allies, enjoy a strategically   *evenly matched?*
    dangerous military superiority in Europe?

It is maintained in some circles in Britain that the two sides are relatively evenly matched in non-nuclear capabilities? That is touching. The eye of faith can discern things that an observer of reality cannot discern, I wish that these people, who can equate 200 Pact divisions with forty NATO divisions, together with all the problems of deployment, organization and reinforcement, would in addition look at some of the regional disparities. On the north flank of NATO, along the Norwegian-Soviet border, the Norwegians have a couple of companies forward and a brigade some hundreds of miles back at Bodo, up against six Soviet divisions, which can be rapidly reinforced. Only the eye of faith can discern equality in such circumstances. There is some truth in the claim that at times we have exaggerated Soviet advantages. But this notion of equality is a much greater exaggeration the other way.

(ii) *Is the Soviet Union an expansionist power*   OR *Is the Soviet Union an encircled and*
     which will take advantage of unilateral   *threatened power trying to keep up with*
     Western concessions and is only restrained   *Western technology and likely to respond*
     and forced to accept arms-control   *positively to unconditional offers of*
     agreements by Western determination and   *Western restraint within a general context*
     strength?   *of detente?*

Reality is more complex than any simple formulations of this kind. The critics are right, insofar as the Soviets *feel* themselves to be encircled and threatened. But the conclusion is wrong. The whole of history since 1945 shows that the Soviets do not respond positively to unconditional offers, but take them to be a sign of disunity and weakness in the West. They are an opportunistic power and take advantage of such opportunities. Indeed, it is because the Soviet Union feels itself to be threatened that it responds in this way, rather than striking a final accommodation. Afghanistan can be seen in this light – and the whole protective cordon in Eastern Europe is such an insulation. A true detente would of course be desirable. But, when the Soviets had it all rolling their way with regard to the climate of detente in the 1970s, they took gross advantage of it. These first-strike weapons, which those whose views are recorded in the right-hand column criticize, were deployed by the Soviet Union during the 1970s, when the United States was standing fast. The Soviets are only likely to be induced to accept balance and detente by an appreciation of Western strength.

(iii) *Is Soviet chemical and conventional*   OR *Is NATO dependence on the early use of*
    preponderance such that NATO must   *nuclear weapons unnecessary and*
    continue to be able to threaten early use of   *strategically suicidal?*
    nuclear weapons?

NATO's dependency upon nuclear weapons has been excessive. NATO has used nuclear weapons as a kind of crutch. It is to be regretted. In my judgement it should be lessened. We should move further and further away from the early use of nuclear weapons, as circumstances and the build-up of conventional capabilities permit. It would be delightful if those, particularly in Western Europe, who have been most vigorous in their criticism of NATO's dependency on nuclear weapons, would also be the foremost proponents of a major build-up of non-nuclear forces. That is the obvious logical conclusion. Do we discern that here in the United Kingdom or on the Continent? Regrettably, no. These countries in Western Europe are spending three per cent, four per cent of their GNP on defence: to have a conventional balance they would have to spend eight or nine per cent. That is not where those on the political left want to spend their money, so they indulge in these fantasies of a pre-existing conventional balance. They are right about the desirability of moving away from dependency upon nuclear weapons, but they fail altogether to see and advocate those measures that are necessary in order to do so.

(iv) *Does the growing size of the Soviet nuclear* OR *Does the West initiate nearly all phases of*
    arsenal threaten the delicate theatre and   *the nuclear arms race and continue to enjoy*
    strategic balance? Would Western failure   *a substantial lead in most areas? Is the*
    to match Soviet systems be destabilizing?   *nuclear 'overkill' such that the West could*
                                        offer a nuclear 'freeze' or unconditional
                                        cuts without risk?

The critics in the right-hand column here stress the robustness of the nuclear balance which they earlier saw as unstable. In order to form a judgement on the real world, one needs to eliminate inconsistencies. Generally speaking, we need to match the Soviet Union in the gross – not in each and every component. The fact that the West has initiated most of the innovations in the nuclear area once again reflects Western weakness in non-nuclear forces. We have seen what the remedy for that is.

As for the recommendation of a freeze – stability is more important than numerical ceilings. For example, had there been a freeze before hardened silos and submarine-based forces had been developed, the result would have been that second-strike forces would today be more vulnerable, an outcome which I would not want to see. A mutual freeze leading to something valuable near-term could be useful, but a unilateral freeze by the West would be likely simply to increase overall Soviet advantage and weaken the stability that protects us.

Similarly, had we had a Comprehensive Test Ban in 1963, our stockpile would be far less secure and far less safe than it is today. We will need a limited number of low yield tests in the future in order to validate the stockpile. That is why I talk about Test Limitation, not a Comprehensive Test Ban.

(v) *Are NATO 'forward defence' and 'deep*   OR *Should NATO exploit her lead in*
strike' strategies essential for effective   *'emerging technology' to explore less*
deterrence?   *provocative alternative strategies?*

A Soviet perception of our ability to strike deeply weakens Soviet confidence in the superiority of their conventional forces and, to that extent, reduces our reliance on nuclear weapons. This logic should induce critics of NATO nuclear policy to approve deep strike strategies. Certainly alternative strategies, in the form of stronger defences, can be explored. But they tend to come up against political difficulty in Germany, because they suggest the permanent division of the nation. Emerging Technologies have, of course, been proposed by the Reagan administration. I would not count my chickens before they are hatched. I would not want to become dependent upon Emerging Technologies before they have emerged!

(vi) *Is it the presence of American front-line troops* OR *Is it domination by the two super-powers that*
and the tying-in of theatre nuclear forces to the   *poses the greatest threat to European integrity?*
American strategic deterrent that guarantees   *Would Europe be safer decoupled from the*
W. European security? Should American   *super-power nuclear confrontation? Should*
policies therefore be supported?   *Europe be made a nuclear weapon-free zone?*

I am not sure that I am the most objective commentator on this matter. I spent some years fighting the Mansfield amendment for the withdrawal of American troops from Europe.[1] and it was in my years as Secretary of Defense that I developed the concept of the NATO triad, in which the three legs of the triad mutually supported one another. American troops in Europe are an essential ingredient in European security, because these small and medium-sized states need the backing of the only available Western superpower if they are to withstand the pressures of the Soviet Union. That is fundamental. Any challenge to that is based upon a misunderstanding.

Now, with regard to the issue of the two superpowers providing the greatest threat to European integrity, these critics apparently cannot distinguish between the superpower that threatens them, and the superpower that protects them. I pity them in their inability to make such an elementary distinction. I would remind them that the reason why American forces are here in Europe is the fear and desperation that came over Europe, particularly at the time of the Korean invasion, when it was felt that the Soviet Union, having unleashed forces in the Far East, would soon unleash forces here in the West. They begged at that time that the United States provide meat on the skeleton of the NATO Alliance. That judgement was and is essentially correct.

There are, of course, understandably, irritations with the United States, and a fear that American global responsibilities will feed back in a way that is detrimental to detente in Europe itself. All of that is true. But one should not throw the baby out with the bathwater. The reason why Western Europe can feel secure enough even to raise these kinds of question today is because of

---

1. A recurrent demand from the later 1960s sponsored by the Senate Majority leader, Michael Mansfield.

American protection. That is why the competition between East and West has turned to the Third World, instead of Western Europe as it was in the 1940s and 1950s. That is why the critics have been provided with the intellectual playing-room, if I may call it that, to indulge in these fantasies.

(vii) *Would Western unilateral nuclear disarmament invite Soviet blackmail? Are suggestions that the West should take the lead in offering unilateral disarmament initiatives the thin end of this wedge? Do radical nuclear disarmers consciously or unconsciously serve Soviet interests and threaten to undermine Western defences?*

OR *Are unilateral initiatives as part of a general programme of nuclear disarmament the only way to reverse the arms race? Is talk of 'multilateral disarmament' insincere in the mouths of those who reject all suggestion of a Comprehensive Test Ban Treaty, a Nuclear Freeze, a European Nuclear Weapon-Free Zone, or a declaration of No First Use?*

From time to time there is the possibility that a unilateral initiative may have a useful effect in catalysing arms control discussion. But one can hardly regard unilateral initiatives as the centre-piece of Western strategy. That is simply a formula for serial disarmament by the West with inevitable consequences. Unilateral measures of this reckless kind will increase risks and must obviously be rejected out of a sense of prudence.

C British Policy

1. The British Deterrent

(i) *Is Britain's deterrent a weapon of last resort which guarantees her sovereignty and independence and protects her from nuclear blackmail?*

OR *Would all possible uses of Britain's 'deterrent' be suicidal? Is its only effect to encourage proliferation?*

I should say at the outset that this is a subject upon which I speak with less authority, because I cannot speak as a Britisher. This is a matter that must be decided ultimately by the British themselves. In terms of overall alliance strategy, the view in the United States has historically been an ambivalent one about the British deterrent, save in this one respect: that the British must themselves decide, and we would support that decision. The view that the use of the British deterrent would very likely be suicidal is, of course, correct. But it is also irrelevant. The use of the great Western deterrent against Soviet cities would also very likely be suicidal. But the underlying fallacy of this objection is the notion of the *use* of the deterrent. The deterrent is there to deter – to avoid the use. This simple reality is what is ignored in the rhetoric of the critic. Having witnessed forty-one years of non-use through successful deterrents, one might think that they would be prepared to see at least the possibility that deterrence deters. Now the British deterrent has the advantage that, although in itself small, it receives reinforcement against the backdrop of the larger Western deterrent. This strengthens the argument for the effectiveness of the British deterrent – but may also, of course, be interpreted as meaning that there is less of a need for it.

(ii) *Are British nuclear forces valuable to*   OR *Is the 'second centre of decision making' an*
European allies because they provide a   *illusion when the weapons are dependent*
specifically European second centre of   *upon the US and there is no independent*
decision making?   *strategic role to be played? Are European*
                                                    allies unenthusiastic about a parochial
                                                    British force likely to inhibit her
                                                    commitment to European defence?

It is an exaggeration, at best, to talk about the British deterrent as part of a second, European, centre of decision-making, as if, given the very small force that the United Kingdom has, and the very large force that the Soviet Union has, the British force would be launched against Soviet cities in the event of a massive conventional attack against West Germany. That is an argument designed to impress those who are impressed by that kind of argument! It is not really sound. The reason for the British force is that it gives comfort to Britain that her national interests will ultimately be protected – and that is a position that the United States has respected.

I think that the broader idea of the British and French nuclear forces being coordinated, if not integrated, into a European force is a long road, though a desirable road to follow. It would take many years and a great deal of expenditure before an adequate force could be built up with second strike capabilities and the perceived capacity to respond to the invasion of another state in Western Europe, namely West Germany, that did not have its own nuclear force. Until such problems are solved, these forces have great national value, great symbolic value, but they are not central to the overall security of the North Atlantic Treaty. Until such time as Europe in its totality has put together a truly European force, it will be dependent upon the American strategic forces, and Europe will depend upon a single centre of nuclear decision-making.

(iii) *Does the US favour shared responsibility*   OR *Are US forces committed anyway and*
and do British nuclear forces guarantee   *independent British initiatives more likely*
full US commitment to Europe and Soviet   *to trigger Soviet retaliation than US*
recognition of it?   *involvement?*

The long-term position of the United States has been that an independent deterrent for the United Kingdom is not an essential condition. The concern has been, however, that the abandonment of the deterrent would be part of a general weakening of determination and commitment to Western defence policy.

(iv) *Is the cost of the British deterrent small in*   OR *Can Britain's nuclear forces only be*
view of the vital defence role it plays? Are   *afforded at the expense of conventional*
alternatives likely to be more expensive?   *strength and of other more important*
                                                       economic priorities?

This is a matter for the British to decide. But we have all recognized that a British nuclear force detracts from the resources that might otherwise be available for conventional defence.

(v) *Would unilateral British nuclear*   OR *Does the British deterrent encourage*
disarmament have no effect on other   *proliferation and do nothing to enhance*
countries and only serve to weaken British   *British prestige? Would British*
influence and allow France unchallenged   *disarmament within the context outlined in*
ascendancy in Europe?   *B help to break the nuclear log-jam?*

Britain's undoubted influence with the United States depends, not upon her independent nuclear forces, but upon an overall political relationship that has by now become traditional. Thus the stated policy of the British Labour Party to wind down the British independent deterrent, but increase Britain's contribution to conventional forces, is not, as such, damaging to relations with the United States. But the appropriate fear here is that those commitments that are made to strengthening expenditures on conventional forces, taken while one is getting rid of the nuclear deterrent, will suddenly, if not surprisingly, disappear after one has got rid of it.

(vi) *Is investment in Trident the best way to*   OR *Would commitment to Trident exacerbate*
continue to ensure effective British strategic   *all the drawbacks listed above?*
defence into the 21st century?

This goes to the heart of the question of whether or not the investment of British resources in a viable independent nuclear capability is desirable. This is a question for the British to decide. If the decision is to maintain a viable independent nuclear capability, it points towards Trident as being necessary for the modernization of Britain's forces.

2 *NATO forces and US bases*

(i) *Must Britain continue to share*   OR *Should British obligations to NATO be*
responsibility for manning NATO nuclear   *met by strengthening conventional forces*
systems upon which her security depends?   *where necessary within an overall non-*
Would refusal to do so fatally weaken the   *nuclear strategy as recommended in B?*
alliance?

In the large, what is written in the left-hand column is correct. I myself have great confidence in the protection afforded by the strategic nuclear forces of the United States that are not European-based. To that extent this is a political, rather than an essential military issue. It is the European allies who have not been satisfied with the protection provided by American's overall strategic capability, and who have demanded, and are demanding, that there should be European-based nuclear forces as well. (In what follows, I treat the French nuclear capability as separate from NATO assets.) Now, if there are to be European-based nuclear forces, then someone has to man them. It is true that some European countries have never participated in this, such as Norway, and that some governments have desired to opt out from time to time, such as the Danish and Dutch governments. But there is a difference between this, and what I will call the defection from the nuclear deterrent by a major Western European state, such as the United Kingdom. The result of the withdrawal of the United Kingdom would be to leave the whole burden to be

borne by West Germany. The political cohesion of the Alliance is more important that the building-blocks of military strategy. The defection of the UK
from the nuclear deterrent must inevitably weaken the Alliance.

(ii) *Would the forced withdrawal of US*   OR *Do the large numbers of nuclear facilities*
nuclear bases from Britain make US   *yielded to the US erode British*
defence of the West impossible? Is   *sovereignty? Would their removal do no*
American interference in British affairs   *more than restore a normal peacetime*
negligible?   *relationship?*

Military requirements change. In the age of the Poseidon, and particularly of
the Trident, the requirement for Holy Loch, for example, is much less than
it was in the period when we depended upon the short-range Polaris forces.
So again the critical questions here are more political than military. A unilateral
British decision to opt out will in this case also shift the burden to European
allies, while exposing them to some of the distrust that at the moment is
directed against the Americans West of the Atlantic. This will be a further
erosion of the European concept.

As to the repercussions in the United States of such a forced withdrawal of
American nuclear bases from Britain, I have lived too long, and have seen too
many prophesies of disaster proved groundless, to predict dramatic consequences. The outcome would depend upon circumstances. If this were read
as an irresponsible and anti-American action by those who have long enjoyed
American protection, the reaction might be disastrous. Inevitably it would be
unfavourable. But it might be mitigated if the reduction were taken in the
right spirit and spaced over time. I would hope that sensible people within the
British Labour Party would be able to mitigate the political consequences of
such an action. Let us just say that the special relationship between the United
States and the United Kingdom would be placed in cold storage for an
extended period. As for the idea that British sovereignty has been eroded, the
very fact that these policies are being realistically proposed shows that it has
not. No. British sovereignty is alive and well.

(iii) *Will Britain continue to be targeted by*   OR *Is Britain seen as an American aircraft*
Soviet warheads whether or not she   *carrier and targeted by the USSR*
disarms unilaterally?   *accordingly? Will Britain fall an early*
                                                  victim in any superpower confrontation
                                                  unless bases are removed?

Britain will continue to be targeted by the Soviet Union, so long as she is part
of NATO and part of a Europe protected by the United States. The Soviets
will target British cities, British military bases, command-control centres,
intelligence centres. Elimination of American bases and the independent
British deterrent would reduce Soviet concern sharply, but her targets only
slightly.

(iv) *Can non-nuclear defences only safely be afforded by powers prepared to shelter beneath the American strategic umbrella?*   OR *In a nuclear-free Europe, decoupled from the superpower nuclear confrontation, would Britain no more expect to depend upon the US 'umbrella' than any other Western ally – or than Eastern Europe upon the USSR?*

It may make sense politically within the context of the United Kingdom electoral process to say that Britain does not want to shelter under the American umbrella. But it does not make any sense if it is remembered that the United States umbrella is providing protection for Norway, for the Federal Republic, for Italy, for Greece, for Turkey. If one is a beneficiary of the American nuclear umbrella, one can safely say that one rejects dependency upon the umbrella, as long as, happily, it is above ones head.

Moral Considerations

Let us take these questions together, as you suggest.

In this world we must always deal with moral perplexities and moral ambiguities. Many people, apparently, think that moral ambiguity can be eliminated simply by decree. I do not.

Now, it is true that a strategy designed to attack civilians and urban areas is, as such, immoral. I have always felt such a strategy to be morally repugnant. It was embraced in the 1950s under the label 'Massive Retaliation', which was directed against Soviet cities, and its only moral justification was that it worked and did not require execution. Actual execution would have been morally repugnant – and perhaps for this reason Secretary Dulles drew back some of the original outline of Massive Retaliation, and stated that our policy would be to respond at times and places of our own choosing. Similarly, I have always had reservations about 'Mutual Assured Destruction' in its original form. It is for that reason that, when I was Secretary of Defense, we moved away from the threat against Soviet cities, to the threat of precise elimination of selected military targets in order to achieve city avoidance. In nuclear matters we should always make the punishment fit the crime. As the Catholic bishops and others have rightly said, massive retaliation is disproportionate and immoral. So, if the Soviets were to engage in a massive conventional attack on the West, the response would be small-scale selective nuclear targeting against the East. I share the moral doubts of the critics and have done something to deliver Western strategy from dependence upon what I regard as the unethical targeting of civilians as an appropriate response. But those who argue that we must rid ourselves of nuclear weapons unilaterally on moral grounds, are taking what to me is a most immoral position. They are saying that we should surrender the free societies of Western Europe to the goodwill of the Soviet Union, which, neither in its present form, nor in its prior form as Imperial Russia, ever demonstrated much respect for the Western notion of liberty. Are English liberty, the spirit of the French revolution, the hard-won West German democracy, the freedom of the Scandinavians and the Low Countries, to be sacrificed simply because of correct doubts about the moral ambiguities of nuclear weapon deployment? I would say – no. To make that reckless decision would be an immoral act.

We are left with the question of whether it is immoral to retain a capability of attacking Soviet cities in order to deter the Soviets from attacking or threatening to attack our cities. To this again I say 'no'. That is clearly not the case. What is, indeed, an intriguing question is whether, if the Soviets nevertheless struck our cities, we would be morally entitled to strike at theirs. This has troubled those of us who have been analyzing nuclear weapons since the 1950s – long before the moral discoveries of some of the more recent critics. All that we can say is that in the entirely hypothetical conditions of a prior Soviet attack against our cities, the decision would be taken, as it were, existentially, in a way that we cannot now anticipate. We can do no more than ruminate about the moral aspects of such a decision taken under those circumstances.

(v) *Is there no relevant connection between the* OR *Is it a scandal that such huge resources are development and deployment of nuclear devoted to the development and deployment weapons and world poverty and disease? of nuclear weapons and not to the alleviation of suffering?*

Nuclear weapons represent only a small proportion of our total expenditure on military capabilities. So to say that this money should be spend on the relief of poverty (which, I may say, is an historically novel judgement) is to advocate pacifism. Pure pacifism must be respected, but to argue this only in terms of nuclear weapons seems to me to be illogical and unjustifiable.

(vi) *Does Christian teaching allow the* OR *Does Christian teaching condemn the deployment of nuclear weapons? deployment of nuclear weapons?*

None of the churches has condemned what I have just outlined, and some have endorsed it contingently. They would, quite rightly in my judgement, like to move away from it. But once again, this requires the creation of those forces that will reduce or eliminate Western reliance upon nuclear weapons. There is a difference between captious criticism and responsible action. And the only responsible action, if this is what one desires, is to develop the alternative that will face down Soviet non-nuclear forces, before one throws away the shield that for so long has protected the West.

Recommendations

1 No (See **B(iv)**).
2 No (See **A2(A)v)**).
3 No (See **B(iv)**).
4 No (See **B(iii)**).
5 Deep, but not unconditional cuts (See **A1(iv)**).

6 No.

7 Yes (See **A2**(A)(**vi**)).

8 No (See **A2**(**B**)).

9 No (See **A1**(**iv**)).

10 No.

11 No (See **B**(**iii**)).

12 No (See **B**(**iv**) & **B**(**vii**)).

13 This would be up to the British and the French (See **C1**).

14 No, for political rather than for military reasons (See **C2**(**ii**)).

15 No.

16 As for No. 13.

17 If the decision is to give up the British deterrent, yes (See **C1**(**iv**)).

18 No (See **C2**(**i**)).

19 No (See **C2**(**i**) & **C2**(**ii**)).

20 Does not apply.

E. P. Thompson

Biographical Note

E. P. Thompson is a writer and historian. He was one of the founders (in 1980) of END (European Nuclear Disarmament) and is a Vice-President of CND.

Among his writings on peace and international relations are *Zero Option* (1982), *The Heavy Dancers* (1985), and *Double Exposure* (1985), and he has co-edited and contributed to three Penguin Specials: *Protest and Survive* (1980), *Star Wars* (1985) and (with Dan Smith) *Prospectus for a Habitable Planet* (1987).

Editorial Comment

These answers were given in an interview in E. P. Thompson's home near Worcester on December 15, 1986. They represent the thinking of one of the most influential figures in the peace movement. Readers may find answers, such as those to questions **A2**(A)(**vii**), **A2**(B)(**iv**), B(**vi**), and **B**(**vii**), characteristic in the breadth of their ecumenicism. A champion of diversity and cultural variety, E. P. Thompson contrasts the cold war antagonisms associated with superpower confrontation and condominium, with the historic compromise between different traditions which is necessary if mankind is to survive the nuclear age. British policy is seen to be part of this wider process.

E. P. THOMPSON

A *Global Policy*

1 *The History of the Past Forty Years*

(i) *Has it been nuclear deterrence that has*   OR *Has it mainly been other factors?*
kept the peace between the great powers
since 1945?

This is what historians call a 'counter-factual' proposition. It cannot be answered. It's like asking if the Industrial Revolution could have taken place without railways. You can play around with these games, but it's not real history. There are multiple factors at work, and in any case you can't remove one supposed factor and 'replay' the thing in order to find out. Most historians don't believe in counter-factual history.

In this case, there may have been one or two crises, such as the Berlin airlift, when war might have occurred if there had not been a threat of nuclear retaliation. On the other hand, this so-called 'stabilizing factor' has also had the effect of freezing and perpetuating the post-Yalta confrontation of blocs and of deterring the resolution of underlying political differences, with a resulting steady and dangerous build-up of tension on both sides. What is the final account that we will be brought to for all this?

(ii) *Does mutual possession of an invulnerable*   OR *Does the threat of strategic nuclear*
second-strike strategic nuclear force prevent   *retaliation, particularly against a similarly*
war?   *armed enemy, lack credibility and invite*
   sub-deterrent encroachment?

On the left-hand side here we have an example of anthropomorphic projection – the 'pathetic fallacy' of attributing human intentions, in this case those of one or another ruling group, to things, in this case weapons. What we have is a weapon of inconceivable destructive power. To call it a 'deterrent' is a statement of faith in human intentions, and not one that is usually accredited to the other side. For them it is not a 'deterrent', but a possible first-strike weapon. Similarly, it is nothing more than a statement of strategic intention or motivation to distinguish between 'first' and 'second-strike' weapons. NATO, for example, pretends that *all* its weapons, nuclear and non-nuclear, are 'second-strike' weapons, but claims that WTO weapons are 'first-strike'. And yet NATO refuses to make a declaration of 'no first use' of nuclear weapons. It's a very strange kind of double-talk. This is all part of what I regard as latter-day scholasticism. Deterrence theory is the scholasticism of contemporary times. Arbitrary and elaborate distinctions are made and quarrelled over, endless disquisitions are written, and proposals to reform the deterrent system in this or that way are put forward. And all this does is to distract us from tackling the central problem of the political confrontation of the blocs.

(iii) *Have limited nuclear options at strategic and theatre levels enhanced deterrence by dramatically raising the threshold between peace and war?*   OR *Have most military planners from the start been aiming for nuclear war-fighting superiority? Has 'flexible response' dangerously lowered the threshold between conventional and nuclear war?*

'Yes' to the proposition on the right-hand side.

The arguing on the left-hand side is what I meant when I referred to scholasticism. 'If this, then that' – these endless theoretical extrapolations and extensions lead to a ceaseless elaboration of menus and options and levels. Deterrence theory is an in-built accelerator to the nuclear arms race. One of the most common theoretical devices here is the 'worst-case hypothesis', by which planners on both sides have to envisage and imagine the worst possible case and evolve answers to it. This constantly worsens the situation, and feeds and exaggerates the next phase of worst-case projection. I once called this 'Deterrence as Addiction'. This just would not be allowed in other areas of social or political thinking, such as, for example, criminology. The result would be to fill the entire nation with prisons and police forces 'in case' the crime rate increased to the maximum that could be conceived. On the other hand, any attempt to operate on the 'better-case hypothesis' – to say 'if such-and-such happened we would be in a better situation, so let's work for it to happen' – is dismissed as utopian, romantic, and moralistic, by the monks and hermits of the defence community. And yet, if you look at past human history, it is only where people did work for better-case hypotheses that real progress has been achieved – such as, for example, in the securing of civil liberties. In the 1920s Ghandi would have seemed a romantic utopian, to be written off as 'unrealistic'.

(iv) *Has the size and variety of the nuclear arsenals held by the superpowers stabilized deterrence?*   OR *Has the logic of nuclear confrontation and worst-case analysis generated a dangerous and strategically pointless superfluity of weapons systems?*

I think that the superfluity of nuclear weapons systems is not only strategically pointless, but very dangerous. And this is not just because of their instability as weapons, but because they are also symbols. As symbols, these weapons systems are a great blast of halitosis in the other side's face. They represent the foulest sort of human message that you can send. All the business about SS20's and Euro-missiles, for example, was simply symbolic political confrontation. It had very little to do with the actual use to which these weapons could be put.

(v) *Has the idea of nuclear balance between the superpowers been essential to stability and have arms-control negotiations helped to achieve it?*   OR *Have ideas of 'nuclear defence' and 'parity' proved illusory and is 'multilateral negotiation from strength' a contradiction in terms? Has 'arms-control' been just another name for the arms race?*

'Yes' to the proposition on the right-hand side.

As I have explained, it is precisely the idea of 'balance', as interpreted through worst-case analysis, which has been accelerating the nuclear arms race in recent decades. It can almost be called the characteristic obsession of the nuclear mentality. For example, Brezhnev and Andropov were ardent believers in balance and parity, and constantly tried to inject it into their end of what they called the 'peace movement'. Contrary to what a number of those in the Western establishments claim, they used to be embarrassed at the fact that sections of the Western peace movement should be advocating unilateral measures. 'The necessary thing is to establish balance and parity' was their refrain. We in END had terrible rows with the Russians at conferences about this. And the same, of course, is true of the monks and hermits on the other side.

What is interesting now is that, with Gorbachev's more flexible approach, all of this seems to be falling away. Joan Ruddock[1] was in the Soviet Union a couple of weeks ago, and I understand that she found a far greater readiness to talk, instead of these blanket po-faced arguments about 'parity'.

(vi) *Has force-planning been controlled by strategic thinking?*   OR *Has the self-reinforcing impetus of technology and vested interest dictated policies subsequently justified post hoc?*

I think that there is considerable force in Solly Zuckerman's[2] arguments. The right-hand side is nearer to the truth. I have recently looked into this in relation to Star Wars, and there is a clear correlation between the firms making Trident, MX, B1 bombers, Cruise, Pershing, and so on, whose order books are running out in the early 1990s, and the industrial lobby pressing for SDI as prospective prime contractors. Then there are what Solly Zuckerman called 'the alchemists of the laboratories', such as the scientists of the Lawrence Livermore laboratory. This is part of what some commentators call 'technological creep'. Finally, as I have already said, there is also an 'ideological creep', which does not just come along behind and endorse what the tehnologists are doing, but actively spurs them on.

---

1. Until recently Vice-Chair of CND. Now prospective parliamentary candidate for Deptford.
2. Chief Scientific Adviser to the Secretary of State for Defence, 1960-66.

2 *The Prospect for the Future*

(A) WITH NUCLEAR WEAPONS

(i) *Does the threat of an enemy first strike*   OR *Is there an increasing threat from accurate*
remain inconceivable for the foreseeable   *and time-urgent first-strike weapons?*
future?

This is all a question of perception. In my own judgement, neither party at
the present time has any serious strategy or policy of first-strike, but in the
perception of the other, this can always be seen as a possibility. The SDI is
inducing these fears in the Soviet Union at the moment, for example. In
this context, everything which tends to computerize decision-making is very
dangerous. It is undoubtedly a highly unstable situation, where, as now, for
military-technical reasons, at a certain point in an acute political crisis, a side
which thinks that the other is planning a nuclear strike of some kind must as
a result itself strike first.

(ii) *Are command, control, communication and* OR *Does the amount of information to be*
intelligence facilities likely to remain   *processed, pressure of time and fear of*
secure?   *preemption put command and control*
                                                     systems under intolerable strain and make
                                                     inadvertent war more likely?

The right-hand side is correct. It must be so. Greater time-urgency increases
dependence upon the computer, and pushes the whole system further towards
launch-on-warning. There simply is no such thing as a bug-free programme at
that level of sophistication. And everything to do with SDI and EDI (European
Defence Initiative) will be computer-dependent. The time-lag between the
first sensor information of an enemy launch, and the projected reply, will be
so short that there cannot possibly be room for any kind of political consultation. The response will be virtually automatic. It will be some computer ana-
logue of Colonel North which will be taking the decision.

(iii) *If nevertheless there were a limited nuclear* OR *Is the idea that nuclear war could be*
exchange would it be likely to end   *limited once it had broken out a dangerous*
hostilities swiftly?   *illusion?*

'Yes' to the proposition on the right-hand side.

There seems to be quite widespread agreement that it is not feasible to
envisage a limited nuclear war being fought with weapons dependent upon
cruise or rocket technology. What some people appear to think is feasible is
the use of nuclear land-mines and nuclear artillery. But, once these things go
off, they will not have clear messages tied to them. The situation will be one
of general panic, communications systems will be disrupted, and so on. The
whole idea of a limited nuclear war is unrealistic and irresponsible.

Perhaps the place where a nuclear war is becoming every year more possible
is the Middle East. It is not hard to see a situation in which Israel used its
nuclear arsenal against Iraq or Syria, because it felt its existence threatened.
If this did happen, depending upon the political circumstances, it would prob-

ably be something that the two superpowers would stand back from. And over the grave of the Middle East the human species might perhaps learn a bit of sense.

(iv) *Do new generations of battlefield and*   OR *Do new battlefield and theatre weapons*
theatre nuclear systems reinforce   *threaten a dangerous lowering of the*
deterrence?   *nuclear threshold?*

'Yes' to the proposition on the right-hand side.

(v) *Does the Strategic Defence Initiative offer*   OR *Is the Strategic Defence Initiative simply*
the hope of an effective defence against   *the most recent and destabilizing example*
nuclear weapons?   *of the process outlined in 1?*

The proposition on the right-hand side is undoubtedly correct. The American SDI certainly offers no hope of effective defence for the population at large (Star Wars I). And, to the extent that it may provide partial protection for land-based nuclear forces (Star Wars II), this can only further accelerate the nuclear arms race. The hawks in the Soviet Union are bound to want to multiply the numbers of their warheads so as to overcome this. To call it 'enhancing deterrence' is just the usual kind of nuclear double-talk. In the meantime, of course, the SDI is clearly undermining arms talks. It may not succeed in shooting down missiles, but it is already shooting down disarmament. It has done this very effectively at Reykjavik. To call it 'defence' is a complete misnomer. Apart from the fact that, in terms of nuclear confrontation, to threaten to disarm the enemy is in itself highly aggressive, there is always the likelihood that these technologies will be adapted for offensive purposes later on. We can envisage exotic new generations of weapons, such as lasers, being put on permanent station in space.

(vi) *Is the threat of 'horizontal' nuclear*   OR *Is continuing reliance on nuclear deterrence*
proliferation best met by a continuation of   *by the great powers bound to accelerate the*
past policies?   *process of proliferation and make nuclear*
                                      war more likely?

'Yes' to the proposition on the right-hand side.

This is obviously so. The possession of nuclear weapons by some powers puts pressure on others to follow suit. For example, in India, despite a long history of commitment by Congress Party to anti-nuclear non-aligned positions, there is considerable national feeling that the attempt to prevent India from developing her own nuclear arsenal is a way of symbolically downgrading the country. This pressure seems to be becoming harder to resist.

There is also the clear obligation laid on existing nuclear weapon powers which signed the Non-Proliferation Treaty to build down their own nuclear arsenals. The fact that they have not done this, but have, on the contrary, built them up, is in breach of the Treaty.

(vii) *Do multilateral arms-control negotiations*   OR *Is 'arms-control' an illusion which diverts*
     offer the best prospect for future stability?   *attention from the only safe policy –*
                                                                  nuclear disarmament?

If the human species is to survive, then somewhere along the road there will have to be agreements of this kind. To that extent, we should not write off the possibility of them. If I am asked to confine myself to the question of arms reduction, then I believe that, in order to get the process going, we need, not negotiations, but actions. I favour independent initiatives, along the lines suggested by Charles Osgood in *'An Alternative to War or Surrender'*.[1] There is plenty of fat that can be cut on both sides without danger, and these would be friendly signals, awaiting a response in kind. At some point, also, a phased reduction of conventional forces must no doubt be part of the settlement. But what I obejct to here is the way in which those who are in fact opposed to reductions of all kinds use this as a last resort in order to block any agreement on nuclear weapons. They use the 'conventional' card, not in its own right, but simply as a way of preventing movement elsewhere.

But in fact I find the whole of this line of argument much too restricted. It is too exclusively weapon-based. What is needed is a much broader political confidence, not necessarily anything to do with weapons. We want to work towards an historic compromise between the two blocs, which must be achieved at all levels and in all kinds of ways. The reduction of weapons is likely to be a consequence rather than a cause of this. Nuclear weapons are the most graphic symbol of what we are trying to get away from. They may, therefore, be the hardest point at which to begin to do so.

(B) WITHOUT NUCLEAR WEAPONS

(i) *If nuclear arsenals were dismantled would*   OR *Would nuclear disarmament remove the*
     war between the great powers again   *incentive for nuclear preemption while not*
     become a rational option and therefore   *affecting the reluctance of the great powers*
     more likely?   *to initiate a third world war?*

The proposition on the left-hand side is taken completely out of context. The dismantling of nuclear arsenals is not going to happen without far-ranging political, cultural, and economic agreements at the same time. I really refuse to discuss one apart from the other.

(ii) *Would a major conventional war be likely*   OR *Is conventional war, however terrible,*
     in itself to be as terrible as a limited   *preferable to nuclear war?*
     nuclear war?

The objective of the peace movement has always been to prevent both nuclear and conventional wars. I am not interested in trying to distinguish between them. Those who argue as on the left-hand side seem incapable of imagining an end to the confrontation between the blocs. But I can envisage the possibility that this might be transformed remarkably rapidly – as rapidly as the

---

1. University of Illinois Press 1962.

old colonial empires disappeared and thawed like snow after World War II. Once the process begins, it will not be limited to negotiations about arms. It will be a total political process involving the healing of cultures. It is not a climate in which a conventional war will come about.

(iii) *Because nuclear weapons cannot be uninvented would they not be bound to be used sooner or later once war had broken out?* OR *As with nerve gases in the last war, would there be no incentive to resort to capabilities which the other side has as well?*

In a certain sense it is not possible to 'disinvent' nuclear weapons. But it might be within reach of human culture to disinvent the capacity to use them. That is, to make them outlaws to human culture.

There have been suggestions that each side might keep a handful of nuclear armed submarines during this process. It's very hypothetical. But I don't object.

(iv) *Is global nuclear disarmament only feasible in a world where war itself is no longer a possibility?* OR *Is to argue that even multilateral nuclear disarmament is not desirable to give up all hope of a rational world-order?*

I agree that those who refuse to contemplate even multilateral nuclear disarmament are giving up hope of a rational world order. What is important is not guessing what the end process might be, because that will happen beyond our time, but beginning to put the thing into reverse now. The repair of human culture will no doubt lead to all kinds of emergencies, hazards and political accidents along the way. A real thaw in the Eastern bloc would not proceed evenly or tidily. What is important is that neither side should try to take advantage of difficulties which the other might encounter on the passage back to normality. I do not see an abrupt transition to non-alignment, but a slippage in both blocs towards de-alignment. It is not synchronization that is needed, but some 'give' on both sides. If you like, an increasing Finlandization of the countries in Eastern Europe, and a Swedenization or Austrianization of the countries in Western Europe.

(v) *Is peace only preserved when we are seen to be prepared for war, as failure before 1939 and success since 1945 show? Under likely future conditions would global nuclear disarmament make war, including nuclear war, more likely?* OR *Do the years before 1914 show what happens when military planning and the arms race control political choices? Do present strategies make nuclear war almost inevitable under likely future conditions? Is global nuclear disarmament the only rational policy?*

The proposition on the right-hand side is nearer to the truth, with the two heavily-armed camps, and war-fighting plans which could so easily dictate policy in a time of political crisis. Historians are always being asked '*What lessons can we learn from the past?*' Well, one of the lessons that we can learn is that the immediate past is often a misleading paradigm for the present. Our memories are based on experiences from thirty, forty, or fifty years ago – and very often that is exactly what is not being repeated. The Soviet Union's historical memory is still overwhelmingly of Nazi aggression in World War II, and therefore their image of the future is of aggression from the West of the same kind. For the Americans it's more the fear of another Pearl Harbour – a sudden and unexpected first strike out of a blue sky. It is the trauma of the immediate past which often misleads the present, and immobilizes it. If you want to look at historical parallels you usually have to look further back. I think that 1914 is much more of a paradigm of our present predicament – the arms race, the inflexible alliances, the involuntary drift to some 'Sarajevo'.

B *Nato Policy*

(i) *Does the Soviet Union, together with her Warsaw Pact allies, enjoy a strategically dangerous military superiority in Europe?* OR *Are NATO and WTO forces relatively evenly matched?*

The proposition on the right-hand side is nearer to the truth. There is gross and deliberate exaggeration of Soviet bloc force strength on the part of NATO apologists here. Large numbers of Soviet troops are there for police purposes in the East European countries. Many of the WTO forces are liable to be disloyal or ineffective. Numbers of Soviet tanks are always mentioned, but little reference is made to their battle-worthiness. And so it continues. This is all part of what Dan Smith[1] describes as a 'con trick', which has been going on since the 1960s – the counting game with conventional forces. Assessments such as those made by the Institute of Strategic Studies,[2] for example, are more modest.

(ii) *Is the Soviet Union an expansionist power which will take advantage of unilateral Western concessions and is only restrained and forced to accept arms-control agreements by Western determination and strength?* OR *Is the Soviet Union an encircled and threatened power trying to keep up with Western technology and likely to respond positively to unconditional offers of Western restraint within a general context of detente?*

I am much more in agreement with the proposition on the right-hand side here. It is true that the Soviet Union is still saddled with the legacy of Stalinism, is overripe for internal reform, and is encumbered by a periphery of increasingly restless client states. It is also true that there is as yet little evidence that Gorbachev and his associates are in any sense democrats. But they do represent the new generation of modernizers and technocrats, and the West should be prepared to encourage and support them as such. If Western governments do not reciprocate friendly gestures made by the Soviet Union or offer independent initiatives of their own, there is a great danger that Gorbachev will be discredited and the opportunity for further peaceful progress lost. The trouble is that there are a number of very dangerous people around the American President who are finding it hard to play against Gorbachev's hand at the

---

1. A member of the *Alternative Defence Commission*, and Vice-Chair of CND.
2. For example, the widely influential annual *The Military Balance*.

moment, and would far rather be dealing with someone like Brezhnev. They would like to discredit the present leadership for that reason.

(iii) *Is Soviet chemical and conventional preponderance such that NATO must continue to be able to threaten early use of nuclear weapons?* OR *Is NATO dependence on the early use of nuclear weapons unnecessary and strategically suicidal?*

The proposition on the right-hand side is correct. As the Welsh saying has it, '*Granny was never ill until she died*'.

(iv) *Does the growing size of the Soviet nuclear arsenal threaten the delicate theatre and strategic balance? Would Western failure to match Soviet systems be destabilizing?* OR *Does the West initiate nearly all phases of the nuclear arms race and continue to enjoy a substantial lead in most areas? Is the nuclear 'overkill' such that the West could offer a nuclear 'freeze' or unconditional cuts without risk?*

'Yes' to the proposition on the right-hand side. Within this context I am very much in support of CND's general strategy for Britain. It is possible for a small nation to take an initiative of this kind.

(v) *Are NATO 'forward defence' and 'deep strike' strategies essential for effective deterrence?* OR *Should NATO exploit her lead in 'emerging technology' to explore less provocative alternative strategies?*

There is a Penguin Special coming out in February on this, called '*Prospectus for a Habitable Planet*'. The chapter on non-aggressive defence strategies is written by April Carter, who is on the Alternative Defence Commission. She comes down very much on the right-hand side here, and I agree with her. This is all part of the wider process of working towards measures which might provide common security to both blocs.

(vi) *Is it the presence of American front-line troops and the tying-in of theatre nuclear forces to the American strategic deterrent that guarantees W. European security? Should American policies therefore be supported?* OR *Is it domination by the two super-powers that poses the greatest threat to European integrity? Would Europe be safer decoupled from the super-power nuclear confrontation? Should Europe be made a nuclear weapon-free zone?*

'Yes' to the proposition on the right-hand side. This is a principal platform of END policy now. We want to see the withdrawal of all Soviet troops and bases from East Europe, and all American troops and bases from West Europe. In broad terms, this is bound to be the direction in which we move, so the question simply is – how can we do it with minimum risk of upheaval and instability? The great enigma in all of this is the pace of change in the Soviet Union. This is something which none of us can predict. The process will no doubt evolve at different speeds and in different ways in different parts of Europe. And the West will have to be part of it.

If you travel in Eastern Europe, there can be no question at all but that this is the direction in which people want us to go. Youthful opinion in Hungary, for example, wants Soviet forces withdrawn, but knows that this cannot happen if there is not comparable movement in the West. It is a highly sensitive subject. After a recent talk I gave in Hungary, an old man stood up and said that Soviet troops should leave, and the young people in the audience turned their backs on him. They thought he was an 'agent provocateur'. Either that, or one of the 'wounded' of 1956, who had never recovered from that trauma.

But the same is also true in the West. Although, unlike Eastern Europe, Western Europe is in a sense occupied by consent, the results are still pernicious. As in the East, there is the great danger of being caught up in the superpower nuclear confrontation, which does not relate to European interests. And another development, which depresses me tremendously, is the creeping authoritarianism in a number of Western societies. Britain is a particularly bad case. This country is much less democratic and open in spirit than it was in 1945. Organs like the security services, the Association of Chief Police Officers, the Ministry of Defence, and so on, are removed from accountability, and what is left of the democratic process is becoming increasingly ritualistic. American penetration into the establishment in this country is part of the whole process.

So the main priority is to end the present exaggerated and unnatural bipolarity of world politics. It is the global hegemony of the two superpowers which must be dismantled, because their political and military confrontation represents the greater danger to the survival of the human species at the moment. We must encourage the development of alternative centres of initiative and influence, and work towards far more plural diplomacies. I see great hope and immense potential in the non-aligned world, which now easily outnumbers those still under the tutelage of the two power blocs. Particularly if China is added to its weight, this represents, not only a majority of the world's population, but huge potential markets, alternative areas of cultural exchange, and so on. The superpowers are going to have to take notice – particularly if more and more countries walk out of the theatre, because they are no longer prepared to be an audience for these Reykjaviks and Genevas.

vii) *Would Western unilateral nuclear disarmament invite Soviet blackmail? Are suggestions that the West should take the lead in offering unilateral disarmament initiatives the thin end of this wedge? Do radical nuclear disarmers consciously or unconsciously serve Soviet interests and threaten to undermine Western defences?*

OR *Are unilateral initiatives as part of a general programme of nuclear disarmament the only way to reverse the arms race? Is talk of 'multilateral disarmament' insincere in the mouths of those who reject all suggestion of a Comprehensive Test Ban Treaty, a Nuclear Freeze, a European Nuclear Weapon-Free Zone, or a declaration of No First Use?*

The trap in the proposition on the left-hand side lies in the second word – 'Western'. It is this continual insistence on seeing everything in terms of the two power blocs, and on identifying with one of them, which perpetuates the present system, prevents gradual and carefully managed change, and allows the water to build up behind the dam until eventually it breaks. As I have said, I do not want just to talk in terms of weapons-systems at all. We should be thinking much more broadly about all the interchange needed to bring about the historic compromise. But, if I was forced to confine myself to the question of disarmament, and argue in terms that would be understood by the defence community, I would suggest that the GRIT[1] strategy, worked out in Osgood's book, and recommended in the Church of England working party report *'The Church and the Bomb'*,[2] is a very reasonable one. This is not 'unilateral disarmament', but graduated independent initiatives aimed at reducing tension and creating the atmosphere for further measures. Every upward movement in the arms race is one-sided. We don't ask the other side *'Can we introduce Trident?'* – we just introduce it. So the downward movement can be taken one-sidedly, also. And then the ratchet can be held at that point, and you can wait for a response. If there is no response, then it would evidently become increasingly difficult politically to hold it. But, unless such unconditional initiatives are offered, and responded to, on both sides, it is hard to see how there can be any hope for arms control. I know of two reasons for believing that this is the right moment for the West to offer signals and actions of this kind. First of all, there are the Soviet Union's manifest economic difficulties. And, second, there is the fact that their entire diplomatic strategy is now based upon their trying to present themselves as the peace-loving pioneers. It would be almost impossible for them not to respond in some way. They have, after all, been making their own unilateral initiatives, especially their long-sustained Test Moratorium. The ball is now in the court of 'the West'.

C *British Policy*

I *The British Deterrent*

(i) *Is Britain's deterrent a weapon of last resort which guarantees her sovereignty and independence and protects her from nuclear blackmail?*   OR *Would all possible uses of Britain's 'deterrent' be suicidal? Is its only effect to encourage proliferation?*

'Yes' to the proposition on the right-hand side. A 'weapon of last resort' simply means a suicide weapon. And I just do not see a scenario in which the question of the nuclear blackmail of Britain would arise. Yugoslavia has not been blackmailed, nor even has Finland, a tiny country on the border of the Soviet Union.

(ii) *Are British nuclear forces valuable to European allies because they provide a specifically European second centre of decision making?*   OR *Is the 'second centre of decision making' an illusion when the weapons are dependent upon the US and there is no independent strategic role to be played? Are European allies unenthusiastic about a parochial British force likely to inhibit her commitment to European defence?*

---

1. Graduated and Reciprocated Initiatives in Tension-Reduction.
2. Hodder and Stoughton, 1982.

The statement on the left-hand side is just not in my mind-set at all. They are talking about the destruction of Europe. Why should one want to participate in that?

(iii) *Does the US favour shared responsibility* OR *Are US forces committed anyway and*
and do British nuclear forces guarantee   *independent British initiatives more likely*
full US commitment to Europe and Soviet   *to trigger Soviet retaliation than US*
recognition of it?   *involvement?*

I do not want 'US commitment to Europe' in the first place. In the second place, it is *not* to 'Europe', but to NATO partners (or clients) only.

(iv) *Is the cost of the British deterrent small in* OR *Can Britain's nuclear forces only be*
view of the vital defence role it plays? Are   *afforded at the expense of conventional*
alternatives likely to be more expensive?   *strength and of other more important*
                                                   economic priorities?

We must include the question of disarmament with the questions of foreign policy, and of cultural and economic relations in general. We must pursue measures which will reduce the state of confrontation between the blocs, and allow both nuclear and conventional disarmament to proceed together. I'm not going to argue this like a shopkeeper.

(v) *Would unilateral British nuclear* OR *Does the British deterrent encourage*
disarmament have no effect on other   *proliferation and do nothing to enhance*
countries and only serve to weaken British *British prestige? Would British*
influence and allow France unchallenged   *disarmament within the context outlined in*
ascendancy in Europe?   *B help to break the nuclear log-jam?*

Getting rid of British nuclear weapons, and the adoption of an independent foreign policy, would be the first steps towards increasing British influence in the world since the end of the Second World War. At the moment, Sweden probably has more influence than we do, because we are seen to be little more than the most dependent of all the client states of the USA. With our long historical connections with Europe, Africa and Asia, our resumption of independence of movement, so far from weakening us, would make us a great deal stronger.

(vi) *Is investment in Trident the best way to* OR *Would commitment to Trident exacerbate*
continue to ensure effective British strategic   *all the drawbacks listed above?*
defence into the 21st century?

'Yes' to the proposition on the right-hand side.

2 Nato Forces and US Bases

(i) *Must Britain continue to share* OR *Should British obligations to NATO be*
responsibility for manning NATO nuclear   *met by strengthening conventional forces*
systems upon which her security depends?   *where necessary within an overall non-*
Would refusal to do so fatally weaken the *nuclear strategy as recommended in B?*
alliance?

I welcome the Labour Party's stand on nuclear weapons, but I wish they had also adopted a more independent foreign policy. I think that it is the Americans who should be expelled from NATO. Or, failing that, we should act as we want to act, and, if other members of NATO want to expel us, let them. Our policy should be one of non-alignment with either of the two blocs, and mediation between them in association with other non-aligned powers.

(ii) *Would the forced withdrawal of US nuclear bases from Britain make US defence of the West impossible? Is American interference in British affairs negligible?*

OR *Do the large numbers of nuclear facilities yielded to the US erode British sovereignty? Would their removal do no more than restore a normal peacetime relationship?*

'Yes' to the proposition on the right-hand side. The existence of American bases in this country is, indeed, a major component in the serious erosion of British sovereignty. The American penetration of the British establishment, which I was mentioning earlier, has gone much further than many people realize. I do not mean the American people, I mean very nasty Americans. Some of the things that have been going on in the security services, and possibly inside the Ministry of Defence, are quite scandalous. There is direct nobbling of individuals within these organizations by the American CIA, American multi-nationals, and so on. If this were summarily removed, it might induce a measure of rationality into American thinking about their role in Europe.

(iii) *Will Britain continue to be targeted by Soviet warheads whether or not she disarms unilaterally?*

OR *Is Britain seen as an American aircraft carrier and targeted by the USSR accordingly? Will Britain fall an early victim in any superpower confrontation unless bases are removed?*

In view of recent findings about the 'nuclear winter', these questions are somewhat abstract. So I would not advocate a non-nuclear policy for Britain on the grounds of safety. The reason for declaring Bradford, for example, a 'nuclear free zone' is not in the expectation that as a result Bradford would not be hit, but as a symbol.

(iv) *Can non-nuclear defences only safely be afforded by powers prepared to shelter beneath the American strategic umbrella?*

OR *In a nuclear-free Europe, decoupled from the superpower nuclear confrontation, would Britain no more expect to depend upon the US 'umbrella' than any other Western ally – or than Eastern Europe upon the USSR?*

'Yes' to the proposition on the right-hand side. We can't stop the Americans persisting with nuclear weapons. But we will be no more 'sheltering' under a 'nuclear umbrella' than is Austria, say, or Sweden. Or than Yugoslavia is 'sheltering' under a Russian one.

Moral Considerations

(i) *Is it morally right to pursue the policy least* OR *Are there actions which are in themselves*
likely to cause human suffering? May this *wrong no matter what the situation? Is the*
sometimes involve doing things which in *alternative to excuse almost any act of*
other circumstances would be wrong? *barbarism?*

(ii) *In formulating policy should we weigh up* OR *Is the only relevant point here that a*
the probability of success and the relative *nuclear exchange of almost any kind*
costs in terms of human suffering of *would in itself cause unimaginable*
alternative nuclear and non-nuclear *suffering to largely civilian populations?*
strategies?

(iii) *So far as concerns intention, need we look* OR *Is there no such thing as a fully deployed*
no further than the fact that our sole aim in *weapons system which is a bluff? Is to*
deploying nuclear weapons is to prevent *deploy nuclear weapons to intend to use*
their use? *them in certain circumstances?*

(iv) *Are there possible uses of nuclear weapons* OR *Is a conditional intention to cause*
which are allowed by Just War theory, for *indiscriminate and disproportionate*
example the bombing of Hiroshima and *suffering of this kind, whether admonitory,*
Nagasaki in order to prevent worse *preemptive or retaliatory, ruled out by Just*
suffering? Can there be a theory of Just *War theory? Was it wrong to bomb*
Deterrence? *Hiroshima and Nagasaki in 1945?*

'Yes' to the second proposition in each case. The deployment of nuclear
weapons corrupts culture at its source. The rocket-pad from which nuclear
weapons are launched is the human mind. The very term 'deterrence' is an
evasion. It apparently sweetens what is a very foul thing. The deployment of
nuclear weapons pollutes culture, it pollutes language, it pollutes children's
minds. In that sense I do accept the argument about intention.

More broadly, the deployment of nuclear weapons threatens the existence
of the human species, and is immoral for that reason. What I have called 'the
ecological imperative of the species – survival' must involve the rejection of
them. My sympathies lie with people like the Greenham women, who really
act this out in their lives. But I do accept that there are thoughtful and rational
people who actually think that nuclear deterrence has prevented war, and I
do not want to call that immoral as an attitude.

(v) *Is there no relevant connection between the* OR *Is it a scandal that such huge resources are*
development and deployment of nuclear *devoted to the development and deployment*
weapons and world poverty and disease? *of nuclear weapons and not to the*
alleviation of suffering?

'Yes' to the proposition on the right-hand side, although nuclear weapons are
only part of this. In general, what is so pernicious is the whole cold war system,
together with its armament industries and military infrastructures, through
which both blocs try to infiltrate, pervert, and turn to their own advantage,
every indigenous movement in the Third World.

(vi) *Does Christian teaching allow the deployment of nuclear weapons?*   OR *Does Christian teaching condemn the deployment of nuclear weapons?*

Christianity is such a contradictory historical phenomenon. The deployment of nuclear weapons is certainly un-Christian according to the sort of belief that William Blake had – and Blake is one of my heroes. But, on the other hand, one also comes across some horrific apologists for war in the Christian tradition. So I think I'll leave this to the Christians.

Recommendations

1 Yes.
2 Yes (See **A2**(A)(**v**)).
3 Yes.
4 Yes.
5 Yes (See **A2**(A)(**vii**)).
6 Yes (See **B**(**vi**)).
7 Yes (See **A2**(A)(**vi**)).
8 Yes (See **A2**(B)).
9 No comment. But see **A2**(B)(**iii**).
10 Yes.
11 Yes (See **B**(**iii**)).
12 Yes (See **B**(**iv**)).
13 Yes.
14 Yes (See **B**(**vi**)).
15 Yes.
16 Yes (See **C1**).
17 No. The recommendations of the Alternative Defence Commission[1] as to strictly defensive armaments should be taken into account by the Ministry of Defence.
18 No. The best solution would be for NATO to expel the United States. Failing that, Britain should do as she pleases, and challenge NATO to expel her.
19 Yes. All American military facilities should be removed (See **C2**(**ii**)).
20 No.

---

1. Established in 1980. Report *'Defence Without the Bomb'*, published in 1983 by Taylor and Francis.

Caspar Weinberger

Biographical Note

Born in 1917, Caspar Weinberger graduated at Harvard in 1938, and then served with the US Army in the Pacific between 1941 and 1945. He was a member of the California State Legislature, 1952-1958, and subsequently Vice-Chairman, then Chairman, of the California Republican Party Central

Committee, 1960-1964. From 1970 to 1975 he served successively as Chairman of the Federal Trade Commission, Director of the Office of Management and Budget, Counsellor to the President, and Secretary for Health, Education and Welfare. He was with Bechtel Corporation between 1975 and 1980. Since 1981 he has been Secretary of Defense.

Editorial Comment

The Secretary of Defense prepared these answers in response to the questions sent to him, and has given permission for them to be published. They represent the thinking of the person most immediately in charge of Western strategic defences, and therefore reflect constraints and pressures, which are, perhaps, not easily appreciated by those, particularly in Western Europe, who do not carry that responsibility. It is at once striking, for example, that the Secretary of Defense does not recognize a distinction between '*Global*' and '*NATO*' perspectives. The threat posed by the nature of the Soviet régime, and the disproportionate strength of Soviet forces, *is* the global setting for all defence considerations. It is the Soviet non-nuclear military advantage which necessitates a continuing nuclear component in Western defence strategy (see, for example, the answers to questions **A2(B)(i)**, **B(ii)** and **B(iii)**); and it is the massive and sustained build-up of Soviet strategic and theatre nuclear forces, particularly during the 1970s, which necessitates the modernization of the Western nuclear deterrent (see, for example, the answers to questions **A1(iv)**, **A1(v)**, **A2(A)(i)**, **A2(A)(iv)**, and the charts accompanying the answer to question **B(iv)**). In general, the idea that the strengthening of the Western deterrent makes its use more likely is rejected, and it is maintained that, on the contrary, it is only Soviet perception of its manifest potency that can protect Western freedom and independence, assure future stability and prevent both nuclear and non-nuclear war.

CASPAR WEINBERGER

A *Global Policy*

1 *The History of the Past Forty Years*

(i) *Has it been nuclear deterrence that has kept the peace between the great powers since 1945? – OR – Has it mainly been other factors?*

It would be difficult to argue that the existence of nuclear weaponry has not been essential both to continued peace and to the political freedom of our NATO allies – particularly if one considers continuing Soviet efforts to build overwhelming conventional forces. The Soviets' brutal suppression of democratic movements within the Warsaw Pact and their adventurism elsewhere around the world serve as stark reminders of what the Soviet leadership will do when it believes the risk to the USSR is low. Further, in any such discussion, one must remember that, given Soviet determination to build nuclear weapons and refusal to forgo them when the US offered to do so through the Baruch plan,[1] there has never been, in reality, a choice for Western nations as to possession of nuclear weapons.

(ii) *Does mutual possession of an invulnerable second strike strategic nuclear force prevent war? – OR – Does the threat of strategic nuclear retaliation, particularly against a similarly armed enemy, lack credibility and invite sub-deterrent encroachment?*

In our present world, our possession of a secure retaliatory force is critical to preventing Soviet attack. It is important that the Soviet leaders should not perceive that they could attack the United States or her Allies successfully. Our forces and plans must be adequate to respond appropriately to any level of Soviet aggression, and hence deter any attack. A mix of flexible options, each of which would provide a credible and effective response to a potential Soviet attack is necessary, therefore. This means that we must have adequate conventional forces to be able to pose a credible deterrent to Soviet non-nuclear attack as well as possessing flexible nuclear capabilities. In the future, we may be able to reduce the requirement for nuclear retaliatory forces if we are able to develop and deploy effective defenses against ballistic missiles.

(iii) *Have limited nuclear options at strategic and theatre levels enhanced deterrence by dramatically raising the threshold between peace and war? – OR – Have most military planners from the start been aiming for nuclear war-fighting superiority? Has 'flexible response' dangerously lowered the threshold between conventional and nuclear war?*

Flexible response – the ability to respond appropriately to any level of Soviet aggression – has been the cornerstone of the free world's deterrent posture since the 1960s. It clearly has worked.

(iv) *Has the size and variety of the nuclear arsenals held by the superpowers stabilized deterrence? – OR – Has the logic of nuclear confrontation and worst-case analysis generated a dangerous and strategically pointless superfluity of weapons systems?*

We have designed a force posture, the Triad,[2] to minimize the chance that an unforeseen technical breakthrough would destroy our deterrent, and in this

---

1. The proposal presented by Bernard Baruch on behalf of the US Government at the first meeting of the Atomic Energy Commission in 1946 to hand over all potential nuclear war-making activities to an international authority, and to destroy existing stocks of nuclear weapons. The USSR turned the proposal down, probably on the grounds that it would make US technological superiority in that area permanent.

2. Intercontinental Ballistic Missiles, Submarine-Launched Ballistic Missiles, and munitions dropped or launched by Long-Range Bombers.

sense, a diverse force structure adds to stability. In any discussion of stability, however, it is important to distinguish between the United States and the Soviet Union. The United States had unquestioned nuclear superiority for many years after World War II. We did not have any political desire to attack the Soviet Union and the Soviet Union could not attack us. That was stability in a very real sense. Today, the democracies of the West still have no reason to attack the Soviet Union. Further, we believe that there could be no winners in a nuclear war, and that such a war must never be fought. For stability, we must ensure that Soviet leaders also understand this basic fact. Unfortunately, some of the Soviet weapons – such as the powerful SS-18 missile – are designed explicitly to destroy United States forces and prevent a United States response, and they have been deployed in such numbers as to pose a clear first strike threat to America's land-based systems. Such Soviet forces clearly threaten stability. Thus it is both the type of systems deployed, and the number of those systems which affect strategic stability. As a result, our arms reductions proposals seek not only to reduce dramatically the size of the American and Soviet nuclear arsenals, but to place particular limits on the more destabilizing systems.

(v) *Has the idea of nuclear balance between the superpowers been essential to stability and have arms-control negotiations helped to achieve it? – OR – Have ideas of 'nuclear defense' and 'parity' proved illusory and is 'multilateral negotiation from strength' a contradiction in terms? Has 'arms-control' been just another name for the arms race?*

Previously negotiated arms control agreements did not restrain effectively Soviet strategic programs. After a decade of relative neglect – in which the Soviet Union built new and more powerful strategic forces deliberately designed to upset the strategic balance – the United States has determined to modernize United States strategic forces precisely to redress a developing imbalance. Such an imbalance, if allowed to persist, could undermine stability. Contrary to critics' charges, the United States modernization program is not designed to produce strategic superiority, nor will it; it will however, restore a strategic balance. At the same time, the President has proposed deep, mutual and verifiable reductions in strategic forces. Such reductions, particularly in the more threatening systems, could lead to an increase in stability.

(vi) *Has force-planning been controlled by strategic thinking? – OR – Has the self-reinforcing impetus of technology and vested interest dictated policies subsequently justified post hoc?*

Strategic weapons systems have very long lives – during which both technology and policy may change. Capabilities of systems developed several decades ago may, in fact, not meet current policy goals. For instance, the hardening of key Soviet installations requires modernized United States weapons to hold these

targets at risk and to continue thereby to deter the Soviet leadership effectively. As a general rule, however, United States weapons development has
been led by policy requirements and not the other way around (and, I believe,
Soviet development of a first strike force posture resulted from Soviet military
policy and doctrine). In the Reagan Administration we have made a particular
point of ensuring that our force modernization decisions are tailored specifically to achieving national policy objectives. We have also sought to make
certain that our acquisition programs provide weapons systems that, over their
expected lifetimes, will serve policy interests.

2 The Prospect for the Future

(A) WITH NUCLEAR WEAPONS

(i) *Does the threat of an enemy first strike remain inconceivable for the foreseeable
future? – OR – Is there an increasing threat from accurate and time-urgent first-
strike weapons?*

As in questions of stability, one must distinguish between the West and the
Soviet Union in considering the first strike issue. Even when it had a first
strike capability, the U.S. did not attack the Soviet Union. Today, it is inconceivable that any Western leader could believe that he could attack the Soviet
Union and avoid retaliation. Given their vastly different motives, Communist
leaders must remain persuaded that they could not attack the United States
and avoid retaliation. The SS-18 and follow-on Soviet missiles are an obvious
effort to pose precisely that type of threat – an attempt to destroy the United
States systems which would be required for effective retaliation. The United
States modernization program is intended to defeat such attempts by reducing
the overall vulnerability of United States forces. The answer, then, is that the
threat of a Soviet first strike will be low – provided that the West modernizes
its strategic deterrent.

(ii) *Are command, control, communication and intelligence facilities likely to remain
secure? – OR – Does the amount of information to be processed, pressure of time
and fear of preemption put command and control systems under intolerable strain
and make inadvertent war more likely?*

It is fundamental to deterrence that we must be able confidently to detect and
assess a Soviet attack and then respond effectively. While our capabilities
today support effective use of our forces, programmed C^3 (Command, Control
and Communications) improvements are designed to both improve and
extend reliable control of our strategic forces into the future.

(iii) *If, nevertheless, there were a limited nuclear exchange would it be likely to end hostilities swiftly? – OR – Is the idea that nuclear war could be limited once it had broken out a dangerous illusion*

The course of a war, once begun, is uncertain. It is not possible to be certain that our efforts to limit escalation and terminate a conflict once begun would succeed. But it is imperative that we take every step possible both to deter war and to limit the destruction of any conflict, despite all our efforts to prevent it. Without credible limited options, our critics' view that any response to a Soviet attack would automatically lead to mutual suicide could become a tragic self-fulfilling prophecy. In short, while our policy cannot guarantee success, our critics' policy can only guarantee failure. Deterrence must not fail at any level.

(iv) *Do new generations of battlefield and theater nuclear systems reinforce deterrence? – OR – Do new battlefield and theater weapons threaten a dangerous lowering of the nuclear threshold?*

Theater nuclear systems, like strategic systems, also require modernization to counter the many years of unconstrained Soviet deployments of such systems at the SS-20. Again, there must not be a Soviet perception of Allied weakness to invite aggression at any level. Further to the question, however, modernized theater nuclear systems do not lower the nuclear threshold. To argue that they would implies that both the use of non-strategic nuclear weapons does not carry great risk, and that the use of modern nuclear weapons is easier to contemplate than was the case with the systems they replace. Neither is true. As the answer to question A2(A)(iii) indicates, the use of any nuclear weapons is fraught with profound uncertainties which can be balanced only by the extreme consequences which would befall the West if those weapons were not used to halt Soviet aggression. As a result, the key is to defer any such questions by continuing to deter Soviet aggression at any level. As a final point, it is important to note that, by improving its conventional capabilities across the board, NATO is actually seeking to raise the nuclear threshold.

(v) *Does the Strategic Defense Initiative offer the hope of an effective defense against nuclear weapons? – OR – Is the Strategic Defense Initiative simply the most recent and destabilizing example of the process outlines in 1?*

The Strategic Defense Initiative is essential if we are ever to free the world of the threat of nuclear war. SDI is a research initiative whose goal is to destroy weapons after they are launched. Since such research, should it prove fruitful, would remove rather than increase an aggressor's incentive to attack it is clearly not 'destabilizing'.

(vi) *Is the threat of 'horizontal' nuclear proliferation best met by a continuation of past policies? – OR – Is continuing reliance on nuclear deterrence by the great powers bound to accelerate the process of proliferation and make nuclear war more likely?*

Both the United States and the Soviet Union discourage the proliferation of nuclear weaponry. Both nations encourage others to join them as signators to the nuclear Non-Proliferation Treaty, and both support the oversight roles of the International Atomic Energy Agency. These responsible actions by both the United States and the Soviet Union should continue.

(vii) *Do multilateral arms-control negotiations offer the best prospect for future stability? – OR – Is 'arms-control' an illusion which diverts attention from the only safe policy – nuclear disarmament?*

Multilateral arms control efforts may bear fruit in certain areas. The central dilemma of the nuclear balance can only be resolved by the United States and the Soviet Union. If the Soviet Leaders truly are prepared to agree to deep, mutual, verifiable reductions then we are ready to work with them to reduce dramatically nuclear weapons on both sides.

(B) WITHOUT NUCLEAR WEAPONS

(i) *If nuclear arsenals were dismantled would war between the great powers again become a rational option and therefore more likely? – OR – Would nuclear disarmament remove the incentive for nuclear preemption while not affecting the reluctance of the great powers to initiate a third world war?*

Total nuclear disarmament – in the face of Soviet conventional force superiority – would be a highly dangerous, destabilizing, policy for the West because we would not retain an adequate deterrent to Soviet conventional aggression. Nuclear weapons are only part of the overall problem faced by the West. The central feature of this problem is that the Soviet leadership considers democracy and freedom anathema, and that, in the absence of high risk to themselves, they are prepared to use military force against those who enjoy the fruits and blessings of liberty.

(ii) *Would a major conventional war be likely in itself to be as terrible as a limited nuclear war? – OR – Is conventional war, however terrible, preferable to nuclear war?*

This question attempts to set a level of 'desirability' for either conventional or nuclear war. No war is 'preferable'. Conventional war could be devastating on a scale not yet experienced by humanity. We must have the strength to deter all plausible aggression against our Alliance.

(iii) *Because nuclear weapons cannot be uninvented would they not be bound to be used sooner or later once war had broken out? – OR – As with nerve gases in the last war, would there be no incentive to resort to capabilities which the other side has as well?*

Same as (**ii**).

(**iv**) *Is global nuclear disarmament only feasible in a world where war itself is no longer a possibility? – OR – Is to argue that even multilateral nuclear disarmament is not desirable to give up all hope of a rational world-order?*

As long as the Soviet Union poses a military threat to the West, we must maintain a deterrent which will assure, to the maximum degree possible, that the Soviet leaders must never decide to attack us. Global nuclear disarmament which did nothing to remove the Soviet non-nuclear threat to the Free World would be a dangerous, destabilizing step.

B *Nato Policy*

(**i**) *Does the Soviet Union, together with her Warsaw Pact allies, enjoy a strategically dangerous military superiority in Europe? – OR – Are NATO and WTO forces relatively evenly matched?*

The Soviet Union maintains an extremely large standing army which provides a dangerous degree of military superiority in Europe. Soviet investment in all areas of military force continues, including such capabilities as chemical and biological warfare – which they deploy in violation of treaty. The Allies must therefore continue to modernize conventional capabilities to ensure that deterrence of conventional attack does not fail.

(**ii**) *Is the Soviet Union an expansionist power which will take advantage of unilateral Western concessions and is only restrained and forced to accept arms-control agreements by Western determination and strength? – OR – Is the Soviet Union an encircled and threatened power trying to keep up with Western technology and likely to respond positively to unconditional offers of Western restraint within a general context of detente?*

Clearly the former. Soviet actions after World War II and today in Asia, Africa, and Central America confirm Communist ideological intent to expand throughout the world. The Soviets have clearly demonstrated that they are restrained only by Western unity and strength.

(**iii**) *Is Soviet chemical and conventional preponderance such that NATO must continue to be able to threaten early use of nuclear weapons? – OR – Is NATO dependence on the early use of nuclear weapons unnecessary and strategically suicidal?*

The whole goal of Flexible Response is to *deter* by maintaining a credible capability to respond appropriately to any level of Soviet attack. The West will certainly attempt to meet aggression with conventional forces, but cannot forgo the possible use of nuclear weapons in the face of a major attack by Soviet forces. Given the massive nature of Soviet forces, the West must continue to rely on nuclear weapons as an essential element of deterrence. The Soviets must not see any possibility for success in initiating a war, conventional *or* nuclear.

(iv) *Does the growing size of the Soviet nuclear arsenal threaten the delicate theater and strategic balance? Would Western failure to match Soviet systems be destabilizing? – OR – Does the West initiate nearly all phases of the nuclear arms race and continue to enjoy a substantial lead in most areas? Is the nuclear 'overkill' such that the West could offer a nuclear 'freeze' or unconditional cuts without risk?*

As the attached charts indicate, it is simply not true that the United States has initiated developments in what the question calls 'the nuclear arms race'. The massive growth in Soviet nuclear capabilities, clearly designed to achieve a first strike capability, threatens the entire global balance, and can only be offset by Western modernization. A nuclear freeze would codify the current Soviet advantages, and could result, therefore, in a less stable world. Unilateral cuts by the West would have a similar effect, although their destabilizing nature would be felt far more quickly than would those of a nuclear freeze. Furthermore, either a freeze or unilateral cuts would remove any Soviet incentives to negotiate seriously for mutual arms reductions.

STRATEGIC NUCLEAR MISSILE PROGRAMS

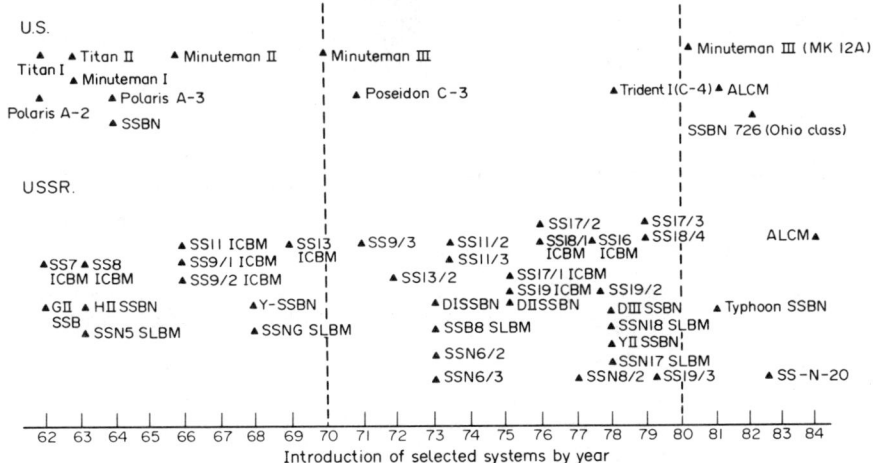

COMPARISON OF U.S. AND SOVIET LONGER-RANGE INF WEAPONS
HOW TODAY'S LRINF IMBALANCE DEVELOPED
AND SOVIET PUBLIC DESCRIPTIONS OF US-USSR FORCE POSTURE

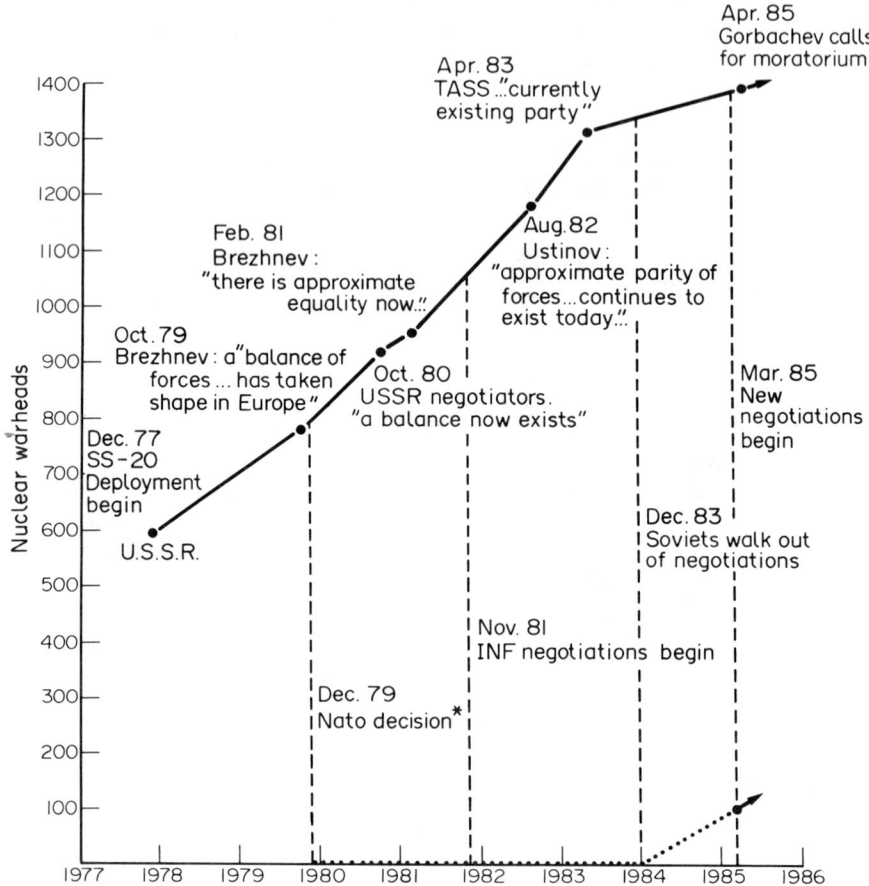

* This decision called for LRINF deployments at end of 1983 unless an arms control agreement were reached which made them unnecessary

(v) *Are NATO 'forward defense' and 'deep strike' strategies essential for effective deterrence? – OR – Should NATO exploit her lead in 'emerging technology' to explore less provocative alternative strategies?*

The NATO forward defense strategy is designed to prevent the Soviet Union from perceiving that it can attack NATO successfully without major military risk. As such it is an essential element of NATO's deterrence of war. The US and other NATO nations are, in fact, exploring the possible benefits that might accrue from emerging technologies. Highly capable conventional weapons can, for instance, better deter the Soviets by increasing the probability that NATO could deny Soviet war aims – and lessen Western reliance upon nuclear weaponry at the same time. It is not justifiable to call weapons which would help blunt a Soviet attack which was already in progress 'provocative'. Nor can it reasonably be suggested that NATO, using forward defense and deep strike, poses a conventional military threat to the Soviet Union or the Warsaw Pact.

(vi) *Is it the presence of American front-line troops and the tying-in of theater nuclear forces to the American strategic deterrent that guarantees W. European security? Should American policies therefore be supported? – OR – Is it domination by the two super-powers that poses the greatest threat to European integrity? Would Europe be safer decoupled from the super-power nuclear confrontation? Should Europe be made a nuclear weapon free zone?*

The fundamental problem which lead to the creation of the NATO alliance was that the Soviet Union was taking over the countries of Eastern Europe, and free nations of Western Europe could not expect to defend themselves from a Soviet attack without American involvement. The forward deployment of American forces guarantees the Soviet Union that they will indeed face full American involvement in the defense of Europe. The physical presence of American troops has helped deter the Soviets for over forty years. It is difficult to see how Europe – or America – would be safer without the NATO Alliance. It is even more difficult to see how Europe would remain free from Soviet coercion.

(vii) *Would Western unilateral nuclear disarmament invite Soviet blackmail? Are suggestions that the West should take the lead in offering unilateral disarmament initiatives the thin end of this wedge? Do radical nuclear disarmers consciously or unconsciously serve Soviet interests and threaten to undermine Western defenses? – OR – Are unilateral initiatives as part of a general programme of nuclear disarmament the only way to reverse the arms race? Is talk of 'multilateral disarmament' insincere in the mouths of those who reject all suggestion of a Comprehensive Test Ban Treaty, a Nuclear Freeze, a European Nuclear Weapon Free Zone, or a declaration of No First Use?*

Unilateral disarmament would not provide any incentive for the Soviets to reduce their forces. Responsible arms control policies leading to mutual verifiable reductions could well increase the security of the entire world. Calls for unilateral disarmament – which can only be voiced in the West – are simply not productive or helpful. Neither a No First Use declaration, nor a Nuclear Freeze, nor a European Nuclear Weapon Free Zone are in the security interests of the West: all would serve to codify existing Soviet advantages.

c BRITISH POLICY

1 THE BRITISH DETERRENT

(i) *Is Britain's deterrent a weapon of last resort which guarantees her sovereignty and independence and protects her from nuclear blackmail? – OR – Would all possible uses of Britain's 'deterrent' be suicidal? Is its only effect to ensure Soviet targeting?*

First, one should have no illusion that if the Soviet Union uses nuclear weapons against the Alliance, some NATO countries would not be targeted – regardless of the presence or absence of nuclear weapons on their soil. Further, much of Britain's nuclear capability is at sea and cannot be easily destroyed. That capability is a very powerful guarantor of British freedom – and contributes significantly to the overall security of the West.

(ii) *Are British nuclear forces valuable to European allies because they provide a specifically European second centre of decision making? – OR – Is the 'second centre of decision making' an illusion when the weapons are dependent upon the US and there is no independent strategic role to be played? Are European allies unenthusiastic about a parochial British force likely to inhibit her commitment to European defense?*

British nuclear forces are valuable to the *entire* Alliance because they provide an important part of NATO's overall deterrent capability. Britain's nuclear forces do play both an Alliance role and a genuinely independent one – both of which deter Soviet aggression. This case for the UK deterrent – and its modernization – was made quite conclusively in the two UK Ministry of Defence white papers with which we fully agree: '*The Future United Kingdom Strategic Nuclear Deterrent Force*' (July 1980) and '*The United Kingdom Trident Programme*' (March 1982).

(iii) *Does the US favour shared responsibility and do British nuclear forces guarantee full US commitment to Europe and Soviet recognition of it? – OR – Are US forces committed anyway and independent British initiatives more likely to trigger Soviet retaliation than US involvement?*

The NATO Alliance is based upon the shared capabilities of the members – each contributing to ensure the denial of Soviet war aims if required – to provide an overall deterrent to Soviet attack. The United States and Britian both contribute large forces – some of them nuclear, but all of them vital – to the Alliance. It is important that the Alliance as a whole remain strong and firmly committed for effective deterrence, and all Alliance capabilities, including nuclear, must be kept modern and effective.

(iv) *Is the cost of the British deterrent small in view of the vital defense role it plays? Are alternatives likely to be more expensive? – OR – Can Britain's nuclear forces only be afforded at the expense of conventional strength and of other more important economic priorities?*

The United States government fully supports the continued existence of the United Kingdom independent deterrent. The firm commitment of British forces – both conventional and nuclear – is vital to the Alliance. The exact allotment of British resources is, of course, a question on which I defer to the British Government. In that regard, however, I would note the points in both the July 1980 MoD White Paper ('*No alternative use of British resources would provide a comparable strengthening of collaborative Alliance deterrence to aggression.*') and the Statement on the Defence Estimates 1983 ('. . . *no equivalent spending on conventional weapons could possibly have the same value* [as the UK Trident] *in preventing war or offer a better assurance for the long term*'). So I would agree the cost of the British deterrent *is* small in view of the role it plays.

(v) *Would unilateral British nuclear disarmament have no effect on other countries and only serve to weaken British influence and allow France unchallenged ascendancy in Europe? – OR – Does the British deterrent encourage proliferation and do nothing to enhance British prestige? Would British disarmament within the context outlined in B help to break the nuclear log-jam?*

First, unilateral British nuclear disarmament would not provide any incentive for any other government to reciprocate. Second, there is a need to deter the Soviet Union, not France. Nor does any UK/French contest for Western European nuclear ascendancy exist. Finally, unilateral nuclear disarmament by any of the Western allies would undercut NATO's overall deterrent posture – it would greatly weaken the West's military capabilities without reducing the threat posed by Soviet nuclear and conventional forces.

(vi) *Is investment in Trident the best way to continue to ensure effective British strategic defense into the 21st century? – OR – Would commitment to Trident exacerbate all the drawbacks listed above?*

Yes, investment in Trident is the best way to ensure effective British strategic defense into the 21st century.

2 NATO FORCES AND US BASES

(i) *Must Britain continue to share responsibility for manning NATO nuclear systems upon which her security depends? Would refusal to do so fatally weaken the Alliance? – OR – Should British obligations to NATO be met by strengthening conventional forces where necessary within an overall non-nuclear strategy as recommended in B?*

The British contributions to NATO – both conventional and nuclear – must be considered from an Alliance viewpoint. They are essential. Regrettably, faced with Soviet conventional and nuclear capabilities, the Alliance does not have the option to resort to a full non-nuclear strategy.

(ii) *Would the forced withdrawal of US nuclear bases from Britain make US defense of the West impossible? Is American interference in British affairs negligible? – OR – Do the large numbers of nuclear facilities yielded to the US erode British sovereignty? Would their removal do no more than restore a normal peacetime relationship?*

U.S. presence in Europe – at significant cost to this country – is intended both to demonstrate to the Soviet Union that America is firmly committed to NATO defense and to give us the advantages of forward deployment for our defending forces. Should any NATO nation request withdrawal of American support, it would send a signal to Moscow that NATO unity – absolutely essential to deterrence – could be fragmented. The United States does not – and has no desire or intention to – intrude in internal British affairs or impair British sovereignity in any way. This applies equally to US forces based in the UK as well as to US foreign policy.

(iii) *Will Britain continue to be targeted by Soviet warheads whether or not she unilaterally disarms? – OR – Is Britain seen as an American aircraft carrier and targeted by the USSR accordingly? Will Britain fall an early victim in any super-power confrontation unless bases are removed?*

Britain possesses military and industrial power. There is no reason to believe that, should the Soviet Union use nuclear weapons in attacking the West, Britain would be spared gratuitously. Rather, schemes such as unilateral disarmament and foregoing Allied support could only fracture Alliance unity and heighten Soviet perceptions of military success – thereby weakening deterrence.

(iv) *Can non-nuclear defenses only safely be afforded by powers prepared to shelter beneath the American strategic umbrella? – OR – In a nuclear-free Europe, decoupled from the super-power nuclear confrontation, would Britain no more expect to depend upon the US 'umbrella' than any other Western ally – or than Eastern Europe upon the USSR?*

One must state up front that NATO can in no way be compared to the Warsaw Pact. NATO nations freely agree to cooperate in common defense against possible Soviet aggression. The non-Soviet Warsaw Pact nations do not 'depend' upon the Soviet Union for defense against a threat that the West does not pose. They are forced to submit to Soviet hegemony due solely to brute Soviet force. Not only can Britain, freely joined in the NATO Alliance, depend upon the US, but the US depends upon Britain. It is foolish to speak of a '*nuclear free Europe, decoupled from the super-power nuclear confrontation*'; it is the political and military threat posed by the USSR to the free nations of Western Europe which is a major cause of super-power tensions, and not the other way around.

Moral Considerations

The policy of the Western nations is to jointly preserve their freedoms and cultural values while preventing aggression and war – all war. The security provided by a strong defense provides the environment in which education, business, religion and freedom can flourish. Even conventional war would be devastating to all our nations, and all of these areas would suffer greatly if war erupted. It would be a cruel 'economy' to jeopardize our national values by weakening our deterrence of the Soviet Union. In that our policy seeks to prevent war, and to ensure the continued existence of the Western political tradition which fosters and protects individual and human rights, democratic government and religious freedom and toleration, it is clearly and manifestly a most moral policy.

Recommendations

NOTE These recommendations have been deduced by the editor from the text (except for No. 3), and appropriate references have been given. They were not made by the Secretary of Defense himself.

1. No (See **B(iv)** & **B(vii)**).
2. No (See **A2(A)(v)**).
3. No, because the introduction of modern safety and security devices into the two-thirds of our stockpiled weapons that do not yet have them would be halted by a test ban (Quoted in the *Times* September 11, 1986).
4. No (See **B(iii)** & **B(vii)**).
5. Yes, if the cuts are mutual and verifiable (See **A2(A)(vii)**).
6. No (See **B(vi)** and **B(vii)**).
7. Yes (See **A2(A)(vi)**).
8. No (See **A2(B)(i)**).
9. Does not apply.
10. No (See **A2(A)(v)**).
11. No (See **B(iii)**).
12. No (See **B(iv)** & **B(vii)**).
13. No (See **B(i)**).
14. No (See **A2(A)(iv)** & **C2(ii)**).
15. No (See **B(vi)** & **B(vii)**).
16. No (See **CI**).
17. Does not apply (See **CI(iv)**).

18 In present circumstances the Alliance does not have the option to resort to a full non-nuclear strategy (See **C2(1)**).

19 No (See **C2(i)** & **C2(ii)**).

20 Does not apply.

The Rt. Hon.
George Younger

T.D., P.C., D.L., M.P.

Biographical Note

Born in 1931, George Younger read Modern History at New College, Oxford, and, from 1950, served with the Argyll and Sutherland Highlanders in the Regular and Territorial Army. He was elected Conservative MP for Ayr in 1964. Following the general election of 1970 he was appointed Parliamentary

Under-Secretary of State, Scottish Office, later serving as Minister of State for
Defence. In Opposition between 1974 and 1979 he was, among other things,
Chief Opposition Spokesman on Defence (1975-1976). From 1979 to January
1986 he was Secretary of State for Scotland, and has been Secretary of State
for Defence since then.

Editorial Comment

These answers were communicated in an interview in the Ministry of Defence
on December 16, 1986. The reader is presented here with a complete rationale
for current policy. In Section **A1** the Secretary of State gives a reasoned exposition of what he calls 'Mutual Assured Deterrence'. In Section **A2**(A) he
refutes the suggestion that current policy is likely to lead to a greater risk of
instability. In Section **A2**(B) he rejects global nuclear disarmament as a desirable short-term option for reasons further explained in the answers to questions **B(i)** and **B(ii)**. Particularly important here is the justification for NATO's
Flexible Response and Deep Strike strategies to be found in the answers to
questions **B(iii)** and **B(v)**. The modernization of Britain's independent nuclear
forces is defended in Section **C1**, while the criticism in the answers to questions
C2(i) and **C2(ii)** of Opposition proposals to move towards non-nuclear defence
within NATO Alliance should be seen against the background of answers such
as those to questions **B(vi)** and **B(vii)**.

THE RT. HON. GEORGE YOUNGER

A *Global Policy*

1 *The History of the Past Forty Years*

(i) *Has it been nuclear deterrence that has*   OR *Has it mainly been other factors?*
kept the peace between the great powers
since 1945?

No doubt many factors have contributed to the preservation of peace between
the great powers during the past forty years. But, given the tensions that exist
between East and West, and in particular the huge imbalance of conventional
forces, it would be wrong to overlook the part that fear of nuclear retaliation
has played in ensuring that tensions did not spill over into war. For the past
forty years our security has depended on nuclear weapons. And it still does.

(ii) *Does mutual possession of an invulnerable* OR *Does the threat of strategic nuclear*
second-strike strategic nuclear force prevent   *retaliation, particularly against a similarly*
war?   *armed enemy, lack credibility and invite*
                                                    sub-deterrent encroachment?

Mutual possession of an invulnerable second-strike strategic nuclear force is
the ultimate underpinning of deterrence. But on its own it is not enough to

ensure the prevention of war. If all we had was the American strategic nuclear deterrent, the Soviet Union might be tempted to contemplate adventure at lower levels on the grounds that the leap to a full strategic nuclear exchange would be too disproportionate for the United States to risk. It might lack credibility.

(iii) *Have limited nuclear options at strategic and theatre levels enhanced deterrence by dramatically raising the threshold between peace and war?* OR *Have most military planners from the start been aiming for nuclear war-fighting superiority? Has 'flexible response' dangerously lowered the threshold between conventional and nuclear war?*

That is why, ever since the tripwire strategy ceased to be credible, the West has regarded a range of nuclear options within a strategy of flexible response as essential for effective deterrence. The importance of a graduated capability of this kind is that it denies the Soviet Union the perception that it might be possible to secure a swift advantage at one level without incurring unacceptable damage in reply.

To attempt to infer from this that, by doing this, NATO is planning for nuclear war, is to try to make a false distinction. Deterrence is only effective when the enemy perceives that you have the capability and the will to carry out your threat if he ignores it. The purpose behind our dispositions is the *prevention* of war, and it can be done in no other way. Flexible response has added credibility to the deterrent.

(iv) *Has the size and variety of the nuclear arsenals held by the superpowers stabilized deterrence?* OR *Has the logic of nuclear confrontation and worst-case analysis generated a dangerous and strategically pointless superfluity of weapons systems?*

Within these terms, it is important that nuclear arsenals are diverse enough to offer these options. Extended deterrence demands more than a minimum strategic force. Looked at globally, the size of current arsenals is excessive, which is why, among other things, we favour fifty percent cut in strategic weapons on both sides. But that is not to say that it is dangerous. Deterrence is stable.

(v) *Has the idea of nuclear balance between the superpowers been essential to stability and have arms-control negotiations helped to achieve it?* OR *Have ideas of 'nuclear defence' and 'parity' proved illusory and is 'multilateral negotiation from strength' a contradiction in terms? Has 'arms-control' been just another name for the arms race?*

The idea of balance is an important one. The West is not aiming for nuclear superiority, but for balance. That does not mean exact parity, system by system, in any mechanical way; it means a balance of Mutual Assured Deterrence. Arms control contributes by helping to orchestrate this. It facilitates mutual understanding of how the system works, and curbs escalation and proliferation. But we must not suppose that arms control is a substitute for proper defence, nor that it can achieve anything very significant unless carried on within a wider context of military and political negotiation. We must not become so preoccupied with nuclear weapon number counting that we neglect the broader situation which gives nuclear weapons their significance.

(vi) *Has force-planning been controlled by*   OR *Has the self-reinforcing impetus of*
     strategic thinking?   *technology and vested interest dictated*
                                                            policies subsequently justified post hoc?

We must not let technology drive policy. Nor must we allow it to undermine stability. There is always a threat that this might happen, which is why it must be firmly controlled. But the idea of those represented on the right-hand side here that there is a runaway system is a gross exaggeration. In general, force-planning is controlled by strategic thinking. Despite what a number of the critics seem to suggest, it is, in fact, in the Soviet Union, rather than in the West, that political restraint on military spending is harder to achieve.

2 *The Prospect for the Future*

(A) WITH NUCLEAR WEAPONS
(i) *Does the threat of an enemy first strike*   OR *Is there an increasing threat from accurate*
    remain inconceivable for the foreseeable   *and time-urgent first-strike weapons?*
    future?

For our part, we have undertaken quite clearly that there are no circumstances in which we will use *any* weapons first. But fear of an enemy first strike is to do with perceptions, and it is true that at times there are expressions of alarm on this score on both sides. But the fact is that there is nothing in the pipeline which is remotely likely to threaten the present perceived mutual inhibition against a first strike. The prospects for Mutual Assured Deterrence are stable.

(ii) *Are command, control, communication and* OR *Does the amount of information to be*
     intelligence facilities likely to remain   *processed, pressure of time and fear of*
     secure?   *preemption put command and control*
                                                           systems under intolerable strain and make
                                                           inadvertent war more likely?

I am surprised by those represented on the right-hand side here, who suggest that the modernization of command and control systems will make inadvertent war more likely. It seems to me that the reverse is the case. Had there been nuclear weapons in the days when Admiral Nelson set off on a six-month mission with no more communication that some brief instructions in his pocket, we would be in trouble. But the instantaneous communications that we have today prevent that.

(iii) *If nevertheless there were a limited nuclear* OR *Is the idea that nuclear war could be*
      exchange would it be likely to end   *limited once it had broken out a dangerous*
      hostilities swiftly?   *illusion?*

None of us can know what would happen if deterrence broke down. Clearly we have to make plans to limit the damage should that happen, and it would be irresponsible not to do so. But it is absurd to criticize this as 'planning for limited nuclear war'. The purpose is to deter war, and the fear on both sides that, if deterrence failed, neither would be able to limit what the other did, is part of that deterrence. It is a potent component in ensuring that it does not fail. Our ability to make a flexible response is the best way of effecting this.

(iv) *Do new generations of battlefield and theatre nuclear systems reinforce deterrence?* OR *Do new battlefield and theatre weapons threaten a dangerous lowering of the nuclear threshold?*

Given the threatened Soviet preponderance in Long Range Intermediate Nuclear Forces, the Western deployment of land-based Cruise and Pershing II missiles has clearly helped to stabilize deterrence. Failure to have done so is what would have been destabilizing. As to the possibility of a 'zero' option, in which all of these systems would be removed by both sides, if this could be achieved, we would of course, welcome it. Such an outcome would, of course, have implications for deterrence, and it would be essential to have adequate constraints on Soviet shorter-range intermediate forces.

(v) *Does the Strategic Defence Initiative offer the hope of an effective defence against nuclear weapons?* OR *Is the Strategic Defence Initiative simply the most recent and destabilizing example of the process outlined in 1?*

It is hard to believe that Mr Gorbachev expected the proposals on SDI that he made at Reykjavik to be accepted. They would have placed severe new constraints on US research while comparable Soviet activities remained unacknowledged. SDI is only a research programme. We cannot yet tell what options it may open up – or whether it is going to produce anything at all. But we must continue to explore the possibilities that technology offers, because, as has often been demonstrated in the past, these may turn out to enhance our security. The essential question is whether defensive systems have a role to play in maintaining deterrence and ensuring strategic stability, or whether we should continue to deter strategic nuclear attack solely by the threat of retaliation.

But the programme should be conducted within the terms jointly endorsed by the President and the Prime Minister at Camp David[1] two years ago. It has been made clear that, in its research phase, it will not infringe existing agreements, such as the ABM treaty, and that, if and when it comes to deployment, this will be subject to negotiation, both with Allies, and with the Soviet Union. The aim is to enhance deterrence.

(vi) *Is the threat of 'horizontal' nuclear proliferation best met by a continuation of past policies?* OR *Is continuing reliance on nuclear deterrence by the great powers bound to accelerate the process of proliferation and make nuclear war more likely?*

We should go on containing the threat of nuclear weapon proliferation as we

---

1. The Camp David Accord, December 1984.

have done, surprisingly successfully, up until now. But I do not accept the link implied in the question on the right-hand side, between the continued reliance on nuclear deterrence by the existing nuclear powers, and the likelihood of the spread of nuclear weapons to others. If nuclear weapons could be abolished entirely, then proliferation would evidently be ended as part of it. But this is not going to happen. Short of that, I do not think that current nuclear deterrent policies affect the issue of proliferation.

(vii) *Do multilateral arms-control negotiations* OR *Is 'arms-control' an illusion which diverts*
     offer the best prospect for future stability?   *attention from the only safe policy –*
                                       nuclear disarmament?

No real consensus has emerged on whether Reykjavik was a blind alley from which we must all now retreat, or a break-up in the ice-floes of arms control, or even a fundamental shift in the international security framework. I take a hopeful view. So far as concerns arms control, we would welcome fifty per cent reductions in strategic weapons, an INF agreement, and further constraints on weapon testing (the problem with a Comprehensive Test Ban, which we would otherwise favour, is verification). If Reykjavik proves to be a sign of a fundamental shift, then, as the Prime Minister and the President agreed the other day, this must include a settlement to the whole range of issues that divide East and West. If there is such a shift, how marvellous. But we must wait and see.

In the meantime, we can be confident that, if present policies are continued, deterrence will remain stable.

(B) WITHOUT NUCLEAR WEAPONS

(i) *If nuclear arsenals were dismantled would* OR *Would nuclear disarmament remove the*
   war between the great powers again   *incentive for nuclear preemption while not*
   become a rational option and therefore   *affecting the reluctance of the great powers*
   more likely?   *to initiate a third world war?*

If Mr Gorbachev's proposal to eliminate nuclear weapons by the year 2000 means leaving everything else as it is now, then clearly it is not desirable. The first worry would be that we would have no way of proving that Mr Gorbachev had in fact given up his nuclear weapons. And the second worry would be that in any case this would make the conventional imbalance very much more dangerous. It would be possible to concentrate troops for a conventional attack without having to fear a nuclear response. To replace the current situation of strategic stability with the unstable international environment that would result from a world made safe for conventional war is not an attractive proposition.

(ii) *Would a major conventional war be likely* OR *Is conventional war, however terrible,*
   in itself to be as terrible as a limited   *preferable to nuclear war?*
   nuclear war?

A conventional war in Europe today, even in the unlikely event that it remained at the conventional level, would, indeed, be terrible. It is important to remember that what properly maintained nuclear deterrence does is to ensure the prevention of war of all kinds. It is a serious mistake to concentrate so much on nuclear weapons all the time that we overlook the appalling threat of modern conventional war.

(iii) *Because nuclear weapons cannot be uninvented would they not be bound to be used sooner or later once war had broken out?*   OR *As with nerve gases in the last war, would there be no incentive to resort to capabilities which the other side has as well?*

But, since we cannot uninvent nuclear weapons, were a conventional war to break out in this way, then both sides would be hurrying to redevelop them. Hasty nuclear disarmament makes nuclear war more, not less, likely.

(iv) *Is global nuclear disarmament only feasible in a world where war itself is no longer a possibility?*   OR *Is to argue that even multilateral nuclear disarmament is not desirable to give up all hope of a rational world-order?*

The vision of a non-nuclear world, to which we should all aspire as an ultimate goal for general disarmament, should not be allowed to obscure what we need for effective deterrence now, or the modest but real steps that we can take to secure reductions in weapon levels and improve East–West relations. It would be nice to wish away both the Soviet threat and the need for a nuclear deterrent. That would be the best of all possible worlds. But, until such dreams have more substance than they do at present, we shall continue to depend on nuclear weapons to ensure our security. We must work towards our goal painstakingly, realistically, and responsibly. To rush recklessly ahead towards some supposed Utopia is to put our security at risk.

(v) *Is peace only preserved when we are seen to be prepared for war, as failure before 1939 and success since 1945 show? Under likely future conditions would global nuclear disarmament make war, including nuclear war, more likely?*   OR *Do the years before 1914 show what happens when military planning and the arms race control political choices? Do present strategies make nuclear war almost inevitable under likely future conditions? Is global nuclear disarmament the only rational policy?*

I do not see our situation today as comparable to that in 1914. Nuclear deterrence is stable. It is not a system which is running out of control. The key difference in the nuclear age is that nuclear war is totally unacceptable to all decision-makers in all countries, and for that reason they will do almost anything to avoid it. In 1914 there were a number of advisers recommending war. Today that is no longer the case.

b *NATO Policy*

(i) *Does the Soviet Union, together with her Warsaw Pact allies, enjoy a strategically dangerous military superiority in Europe?*   OR *Are NATO and WTO forces relatively evenly matched?*

The Soviet threat is the starting point for all we do in defence. There can be no doubt that, at the moment, there is a serious non-nuclear military imbalance between the two sides, and those who deny this are, for whatever reason, simply ignoring the facts. Soviet spending on armed forces has risen by some sixty percent in real terms over the past fifteen years and is still rising. As the annual White Paper makes clear, and indeed other publications (for instance, the recently published IISS assessment), we are speaking of a wide imbalance in terms of numbers of men and divisions in favour of the Warsaw pact, a two-to-one advantage in numbers of main battle tanks and of fix-wing tactical aircraft, a three-to-one advantage in artillery, and so on. The Soviet navy is smaller, but more than enough to disrupt vital transatlantic supply routes. These are ready forces. We must also consider the Soviet ability to create even greater local superiority by a sudden massing of troops, and her longer-term advantage in reinforcement and supply. In addition, there is the near Soviet monopoly in chemical weapons. To say this is not to be alarmist. NATO has certainly made progress in strengthening her conventional forces. But the serious non-nuclear military imbalance is an undeniable fact. To ignore it, for example to try to claim that the two sides are evenly matched, is an irresponsible refusal to recognize the reality of the world we are living in.

(ii) *Is the Soviet Union an expansionist power* OR *Is the Soviet Union an encircled and which will take advantage of unilateral threatened power trying to keep up with Western concessions and is only restrained Western technology and likely to respond and forced to accept arms-control positively to unconditional offers of agreements by Western determination and Western restraint within a general context strength? of detente?*

We must not, of course, confuse what we know of Soviet capabilities, with what we can only guess about Soviet intentions. I do not think, for example, that the Soviet Union has any direct desire to attack the West. But two points need to be made here. First, Soviet ideological hostility towards the West remains fundamentally unchanged. It is no more than stating the facts to say that, because the Soviet system depends upon repression, the free West is a standing threat to its continued existence. Secondly, there is the Soviet record. This shows that the way to handle the Soviet Union is to be strong and united, while at the same time exploring the possibilities for mutual accommodation and agreement. It is striking that in those areas in which the West has been relatively weaker, there has been no incentive for the Soviet Union to give anything away. It is disappointing that after thirteen years, agreement has not been reached at the MBFR[1] negotiations, nor have the negotiations for a global ban on chemical weapons so far produced concrete results. This contrasts with the situation where the introduction of Cruise and Pershing II has led to suggestions of a mutual giving up of INF weapons. The fundamental factor remains the underlying imbalance in non-nuclear forces. While that remains

---

1. The Mutual and Balanced Force Reduction talks which have been going on since 1973 in Vienna between the WTO and NATO countries.

so, we do not want to depend for our security on Soviet good will – on some vague supposition that the Soviet Union does not intend to take advantage of her superiority. We do know that the forces exist. We do not know what Soviet intentions are. Prudent and responsible defence in the West has to make proper provision accordingly.

(iii) *Is Soviet chemical and conventional*   OR *Is NATO dependence on the early use of*
preponderance such that NATO must   *nuclear weapons unnecessary and*
continue to be able to threaten early use of   *strategically suicidal?*
nuclear weapons?

Flexible response is the only credible strategy for the West in the face of the Soviet threat as it now stands. As the statement issued after the recent meeting between the President and the Prime Minister made clear, it will continue to require effective nuclear deterrence based on a mix of options. But two popular misconceptions need to be corrected here.

In the first place, flexible response includes conventional as well as nuclear options. NATO keeps open the option of using nuclear weapons in order to deter the Soviet Union – but that does not mean that this would have to be invoked at any particular stage of a conventional conflict were deterrence neverthless to fail. It could be that we would be able to hold a conventional attack with conventional forces. That would clearly be our aim. The nuclear option remains precisely that – an option. Secondly, the reason for keeping the option open is in order to deter. It is to demonstrate to the Soviet leaders that they cannot undertake aggression against NATO territory without putting their own homeland, their forces and those of their Warsaw Pact allies, at risk. A 'declaration of no first use' of nuclear weapons would be counter-productive and meaningless. It would be counter-productive insofar as it weakened deterrence. And it would be meaningless for the same reason that the Soviet declaration is meaningless – no matter what Soviet official spokesmen may say, their nuclear forces are trained to preempt an anticipated attack.

The fundamental fact is that NATO is a purely defensive alliance. We have made the only significant declaration – that we will on no account use *any* weapon first.

(iv) *Does the growing size of the Soviet nuclear* OR *Does the West initiate nearly all phases of*
arsenal threaten the delicate theatre and   *the nuclear arms race and continue to enjoy*
strategic balance? Would Western failure   *a substantial lead in most areas? Is the*
to match Soviet systems be destabilizing?   *nuclear 'overkill' such that the West could*
                                                 offer a nuclear 'freeze' or unconditional
                                                 cuts without risk?

The West does not have to match the Soviet Union system-by-system, but does need to make sure that the Soviet Union does not achieve a preponderance at any one level, which might invite a dangerous attempt to exploit it. That is why the West was right to respond to the Soviet build-up in LRINF forces. Within these terms, although there is room for unilateral adjustments, such as the current reductions being made in NATO's battlefield weapons, more sweeping unilateral moves would clearly be destabilizing.

(v) *Are NATO 'forward defence' and 'deep*   OR *Should NATO exploit her lead in*
strike' strategies essential for effective   *'emerging technology' to explore less*
deterrence?   *provocative alternative strategies?*

It is militarily meaningless to make the kind of distinction between 'offensive' and 'defensive' weapons and strategies proposed by the critics represented in the right-hand column. In view of Soviet plans for concentrating massive successive waves of attack along a particular axis, NATO must be able to strike at the follow-on echelons, airfields, and lines of communication. But, once again, the crucial point is to do with deterrence. The enemy will only be deterred from attacking when he knows that, if he does, he will not be vulnerable only in the territory that he is occupying.

Emerging technologies are supplements to, not substitutes for, NATO's overall defence. They do, indeed, offer the hope of a significant strengthening of NATO non-nuclear forces, and therefore of a welcome deferral of the likelihood of having to invoke the nuclear option. That is why NATO is developing them. But they are no panacea. The gestation period for many of these systems is a long one, they are expensive, and, of course, the Soviet Union is also developing similar capabilities.

(vi) *Is it the presence of American front-line*   OR *Is it domination by the two super-powers*
troops and the tying-in of theatre nuclear   *that poses the greatest threat to European*
forces to the American strategic deterrent   *integrity? Would Europe be safer*
that guarantees W. European security?   *decoupled from the super-power nuclear*
Should American policies therefore be   *confrontation? Should Europe be made a*
supported?   *nuclear weapon-free zone?*

It is indeed the presence of American front-line troops, and the tying-in of those troops, by whatever stages, to the American strategic deterrent, that continues to underpin Western security. We nearly lost two world wars because the Americans were not in. Their commitment to the security of Western Europe is now made tangible by their presence. But that is not, of course, to say that European states are going to see eye-to-eye with their ally on every issue. For one thing, the United States is a global power, and has no land frontier with the Soviet Union. There are bound to be differences of perspective. Unlike the Warsaw Pact, which is a vehicle for the imposition of Soviet control, NATO is a free association of partners for mutual advantage. It is also important to remember that the United States is not opposed to a stronger and more united Europe. On the contrary, many Americans would welcome it. The essential point is that, at a time of change, when it is possible that old Cold War configurations may be beginning to shift, it is all the more important that Western cohesion and strength is maintained. NATO needs to adapt, but must not lose the unity and sense of common purpose that has so far preserved our freedom. It is fundamental to Western security that the

Transatlantic Alliance remains strong. To put this at risk is to my mind irresponsibility of the worst kind.

(vii) *Would Western unilateral nuclear disarmament invite Soviet blackmail? Are suggestions that the West should take the lead in offering unilateral disarmament initiatives the thin end of this wedge? Do radical nuclear disarmers consciously or unconsciously serve Soviet interests and threaten to undermine Western defences?*

OR *Are unilateral initiatives as part of a general programme of nuclear disarmament the only way to reverse the arms race? Is talk of 'multilateral disarmament' insincere in the mouths of those who reject all suggestion of a Comprehensive Test Ban Treaty, a Nuclear Freeze, a European Nuclear Weapon-Free Zone, or a declaration of No First Use?*

One-sided measures of the kind proposed in the right-hand column have failed in the past. The way forward is a combination of continued nuclear deterrence, together with bilateral and multilateral negotiations. This is a long and difficult road, but one which we must go on travelling down. Our policies have brought us to this point and are beginning to bear fruit. To make the kind of rash unilateral gestures that have been suggested in some quarters, would be to throw all of this in jeopardy. It would just create instability.

C British Policy

1 The British Deterrent

(i) *Is Britain's deterrent a weapon of last resort which guarantees her sovereignty and independence and protects her from nuclear blackmail?*

OR *Would all possible uses of Britain's 'deterrent' be suicidal? Is its only effect to encourage proliferation?*

Seen from a purely British point of view, the independent British nuclear deterrent is an ultimate safeguard against nuclear blackmail in a world of nuclear weapon powers. It is an ultimate option, but, for that reason, a remote one. Of more immediate significance, therefore, is the importance of the British deterrent within the Western Alliance. British nuclear forces are committed to NATO.

(ii) *Are British nuclear forces valuable to European allies because they provide a specifically European second centre of decision making?*

OR *Is the 'second centre of decision making' an illusion when the weapons are dependent upon the US and there is no independent strategic role to be played? Are European allies unenthusiastic about a parochial British force likely to inhibit her commitment to European defence?*

The fact that the British nuclear force is European, that is to say, non-American, is significant, because of its effect on Soviet perceptions. It is important that the Soviet planner sees that there is a European component to the Western nuclear deterrent, in case he might otherwise be tempted to suppose that the United States might be inhibited from using her nuclear forces in defence of Europe. It is a further complication for the planner. His work is not done when he has made a judgement about America – he must also assess the threat from Britain and France. A British nuclear force also helps European partners to see the deterrent as not only an American contribution. It means that there is a diversification of commitment, from a country like Norway which would only allow nuclear weapons on to her soil in wartime; through those countries which allow American nuclear weapons on their soil; to Britain which also has her own forces. But this is not to suggest that a European force is an alternative to an American force. There are those who suggest that we should somehow unilaterally switch nuclear partners from the United States to France – with little or no consultation with either, it seems. But this would produce no advantage over our present arrangements and would probably end up being more expensive. The British and American nuclear forces are complementary within the overall framework of the Western Alliance.

(iii) *Does the US favour shared responsibility*   OR   *Are US forces committed anyway and*
      and do British nuclear forces guarantee   *independent British initiatives more likely*
      full US commitment to Europe and Soviet   *to trigger Soviet retaliation than US*
      recognition of it?   *involvement?*

The United States favours a British force because it favours shared responsibility. It also fears that British unilateral nuclear disarmament will be part of a general down-grading of the British defence effort. We have had these forces for so long now that there is scepticism about claims that we can give them up and compensate by being all the more vigorous elsewhere. It would make NATO look like one great big daddy and a lot of little hens running behind. At the moment it is not like that. America is the biggest partner, certainly, but Britain is also one of the major contributors.

(iv) *Is the cost of the British deterrent small in*   OR   *Can Britain's nuclear forces only be*
      view of the vital defence role it plays? Are   *afforded at the expense of conventional*
      alternatives likely to be more expensive?   *strength and of other more important*
                                                                 economic priorities?

Arguments about the cost of the British nuclear deterrent are a red herring. If it was not a nuclear weapon, nobody would be complaining that it was expensive. For example, Tornado is costing more, but there is no comparable 'Ban the Tornado' campaign. This is just a useful handle for the anti-nuclear brigade to hang their argument on.

(v) *Would unilateral British nuclear*   OR   *Does the British deterrent encourage*
      disarmament have no effect on other   *proliferation and do nothing to enhance*
      countries and only serve to weaken British   *British prestige? Would British*
      influence and allow France unchallenged   *disarmament within the context outlined in*
      ascendancy in Europe?   *B help to break the nuclear log-jam?*

If Britain gave up her independent deterrent, it would have no effect on the Soviet Union. The disparity in power is too great. The fact that at the time of Reykjavik Mr Gorbachev dropped the precondition that he had previously been insisting on with regard to the British and French deterrents, shows that this had just been a ploy aimed at dividing the West.

Although it is not enough in itself to constitute a major reason for Britain to keep her deterrent, it is certainly true that it serves to give her an important measure of influence with the United States as the Camp David Accords showed.

(vi) *Is investment in Trident the best way to continue to ensure effective British strategic defence into the 21st century?*   OR *Would commitment to Trident exacerbate all the drawbacks listed above?*

There can be no doubt that, for the role it has to play, Trident is the best system. Alternatives such as Cruise missiles would be more expensive – for example, to acquire a deterrent force based on Cruise missiles that would be as effective as one based on Trident could cost up to twice as much.

Nor will Trident represent an enormous escalation in firepower over Polaris. We have made it plain that we will not be using the full warhead-capacity. Our objective remains for it to be a minimum deterrent, although it has to be a rather larger minumum in order to get through what are now more sophisticated defences.

2 *NATO Forces and US Bases*

(i) *Must Britain continue to share responsibility for manning NATO nuclear systems upon which her security depends? Would refusal to do so fatally weaken the alliance?*   OR *Should British obligations to NATO be met by strengthening conventional forces where necessary within an overall non-nuclear strategy as recommended in B?*

This is of great importance. To refuse to do this would undoubtedly divide and weaken the Alliance, throwing the burden in particular onto the West Germans. It is nonsense to suggest that Britain's obligations to NATO can be met by '*strengthening conventional forces within an overall non-nuclear strategy*'. There is no overall non-nuclear strategy, nor can there be while the situation is as it is.

(ii) *Would the forced withdrawal of US nuclear bases from Britain make US defence of the West impossible? Is American interference in British affairs negligible?*   OR *Do the large numbers of nuclear facilities yielded to the US erode British sovereignty? Would their removal do no more than restore a normal peacetime relationship?*

First of all, our sovereignty is not eroded. We have control over how American bases are used. No operation is conducted from an American base in Britain without the Prime Minister's approval – as the Libyan raid showed.

But, once again, the main thing to stress is that the Atlantic Alliance is the foundation on which European security is built. The transatlantic partnership is based on pragmatic mutual self-interest, underpinned by a common heritage, shared experience, and a joint commitment to the principles of freedom and democracy. It is a unique bargain, and not one that we should take for granted. There are already signs of resurgent neo-isolationism in America, and a shift in US attention towards the Pacific basin, so that Europe is no longer the automatic first concern of many Americans today. If we put in doubt the value to America of its continued involvement in Europe – for example, by depriving their conventional forces of the nuclear umbrella they require to meet the Soviet threat – then we put in doubt also the foundations on which our security is based. It would be a profoundly misguided and irresponsible thing to do.

(iii) *Will Britain continue to be targeted by Soviet warheads whether or not she disarms unilaterally?* OR *Is Britain seen as an American aircraft carrier and targeted by the USSR accordingly? Will Britain fall an early victim in any superpower confrontation unless bases are removed?*

It is unrealistic to think that Britain could be a nuclear-free sanctuary, no matter what she did, Her geographical position alone means that she will be targeted.

(iv) *Can non-nuclear defences only safely be afforded by powers prepared to shelter beneath the American strategic umbrella?* OR *In a nuclear-free Europe, decoupled from the superpower nuclear confrontation, would Britain no more expect to depend upon the US 'umbrella' than any other Western ally – or than Eastern Europe upon the USSR?*

It means nothing for the Labour Party to say *'we are not going to shelter under the American nuclear umbrella'*. This is empty rhetoric. The American umbrella is there, and is recognized as such on both sides of the Iron Curtain. It is only because of it that the Labour Party can indulge in the luxury of such a policy at all.

Moral Considerations

Any moral discussion must be founded on the realities that we face; including the existence of nuclear weapons, and the realities of the measures nations have historically been prepared to take in pursuit of their objectives, including war. The moral repugnance at the thought of the effects of nuclear weapons is understandable, and, indeed, right. That must be the starting-point for serious discussion of defence and deterrence. I believe that the aim of preventing war is a moral one; and that the Government's duty to ensure the security of the people is a moral one. As far as resources are concerned, of course we have to weigh up the consequences on other programmes of spending on defence; but, as one of my predecessors put it, *'Peace is expensive – but it is never as expensive as war.'*

Recommendations

1 No, because this would freeze present imbalances, remove much of the incentive to achieve cuts, and be impossible to verify (SDE 1983, p8, para 2).[1]

2 No (see **A2(A)(v)**).

3 No (see **A2(A)(vii)**).

4 No (see **B(iii)**).

5 No, we should concentrate efforts on reductions in United States and Soviet arsenals.

6 No, not in Europe, because it would be militarily meaningless (SDE 1983, p8, para 4).

7 Yes.

8 No, because the British Government believes that total nuclear disarmament could only contribute to security if it was accompanied by reductions in conventional arms as part of the process of general and complete disarmament. It does not seem likely that this is achievable by the end of the century (see **A2(B)**).

9 I do believe that it will be necessary for the United States to retain a minimum strategic force unless or until more effective means can be devised for maintaining Western security. But it is of course difficult to comment on the specific weapon system that such a minimum strategic force might be based on (see **A1(iv)**).

10 No (see **A2(A)(v)**).

11 No (see **B(iii)**).

12 No (see **B(iv)**).

13 No (see **C1**).

14 No (see **A1(iii)** etc).

15 No. See No. 6.

16 No (see **C1**).

17 Does not apply.

18 No (see **C2(1)**).

19 No (see **C2(1)** & **C2(ii)**).

20 Does not apply.

---

1. Statement on the Defence Estimates.

12 Should NATO announce an immediate freeze on the deployment of new nuclear weapons systems and unconditional cuts in existing nuclear arsenals with a view to the eventual
   a. discarding of all battlefield and dual capable systems?
   b. phasing out of longer-range theatre systems?
13 Should Britain and France abandon their independent nuclear forces?
14 Should the United States announce a programme for the phased withdrawal of her nuclear and nuclear-related bases in Europe?
15 Should Europe be made a nuclear weapon-free zone?

C *British Policy*

Within this context:

16 Should Britain relinquish her independent nuclear capability?
17 Should the money saved be spent on strengthening conventional forces?
18 Should Britain remain inside NATO and press for a non-nuclear strategy?
19 Should Britain refuse to man NATO nuclear delivery systems and insist upon the withdrawal of US nuclear weapons from Britain?
20 In the absence of a change in US and NATO policy should Britain stay in the Alliance?

PART 3 POSTSCRIPT

We have reached the end of this stage of the investigation. In the search for what is rationally and morally the best policy, we have consulted humane, intelligent and informed people, and have discovered the extent and depth of their disagreement. When we look at the substance of the actual recommendations that they have made, it seems that mutually incompatible courses of action are being urged upon us. We are being told by some that it is essential for security, if not survival, that we broadly persist with current policies, and that to do so is morally right; and by others that this is clearly morally wrong, and that we are courting disaster unless we abandon all or some of them. Others again, suggest that the choices are not as clear-cut as this, but thereby appear to be contradicting those who say that they are. These are elaborate and impressive sets of arguments, a number of which are drawn from extensive experience in the conduct of public affairs, and all of which represent sustained, concentrated, and committed engagement with the subject in question. They are not to be lightly dismissed or set aside. But an adequate attempt to understand the implications of what is recorded in Part II would clearly demand extensive further enquiry, and a great deal more space than is available here. So we will confine ourselves to a few concluding remarks, and, in so doing, try to indicate something of the direction in which future investigation might go.

ɪ *Voting*

Let us say that we have been appealed to as voters. In that case, the alternatives between which we are being asked to choose do, indeed, appear to be clear-cut. Although in General Elections in the West the choice before the electorate is not one in which single issues are differentiated for separate decision in this way, we will for the moment ignore this fact. We will suppose that we are faced with the question, 'Should we continue to develop and deploy nuclear weapons systems?', and that a simple counting of the votes cast will decide the matter. As British voters, our decision will only directly affect British policy, and a number of commentators maintain that continued commitment by all the main British political parties to NATO, to the American presence in this country, and to high defence spending, means that even here the bulk of existing structures and traditions will remain unaffected. Inertia is likely to overcome innovation whatever the outcome. But that is not how the matter is being presented to the electorate, nor is it part of what is being argued by those whom we have consulted in Part II of this book. The choice that we are being asked to make is not only between alternative policies for Britain, but between alternative interpretations of the situation in which we find ourselves, and between alternative visions of the direction in which the whole of global politics should evolve. Within terms of the world as we understand it, we are voting for the world as we want it to be.

And the options open to us have been narrowed down by the party system. We are, effectively, offered a choice between three alternatives, although we will also mention a fourth.

We can choose *Alternative A*, which is to implement Recommendation (LEFT) and to continue to support current Western policy in general (Conservative).

We can choose *Alternative B*, which is to work towards non-nuclear defence as proposed in the 'Global' and part of the 'NATO' sections of Recommendation (RIGHT), but in the meantime to retain a nuclear option for Britain and for Europe and to continue to support Western deterrent strategy (Alliance).

We can choose *Alternative C*, which is to implement the proposals under 'British Policy', and to support the proposals under 'Global Policy' and 'NATO Policy' in Recommendation (RIGHT) (Labour).

Or we can choose the more radical *Alternative D*, which is to reduce defence spending, remove all American military facilities from Britain, withdraw from NATO, and join the non-aligned bloc.

So far as concerns voting, we have run out of time. We cannot go on indefinitely analysing, comparing and assessing. Sooner or later we have to make our minds up about how we are going to act. The moment of decision has now arrived. We should imagine that, as we turned the page at the end of Part II of this book, the voting slip and pencil were put into our hands and the ballot box was placed in front of us. We have been asked to mark one of the four alternatives below with a cross, and have been told that, if we choose none of them, we will be allowing current policies to continue. We are allowed just enough time to read to the end of this section, and then we must be prepared to commit ourselves. Whether by deliberate choice or by default we will have arbitrated, and the consequences and implications of our action or inaction will already be beginning to unfold.

ALTERNATIVE A	
ALTERNATIVE B	
ALTERNATIVE C	
ALTERNATIVE D	

2 *Arguing*

But have we made the right choice? Whatever our response, what we have or have not done is still part of the continuing debate. Political decision does not necessarily end controversy. So far as concerns voting, we have reached a point where, in one way or another, we have had to come to some kind of immediate conclusion about what we take to be the matter in question. Part II is in this sense the end of the process. But, so far as concerns the fact that the disagreement nevertheless continues, Part II is only a beginning. We have been presented with forceful and apparently self-consistent rationales, but we have not started to try to analyse the relationships between prior and subsequent points within each, nor to compare one with another, either as a whole, or part-by-part. So we cannot yet explain clearly and in detail why it is that we may want to prefer one set of recommendations to another. This is neither a straight-forward, nor an easy process. There are difficulties to do with what *is* recorded in Part II, and there are difficulties to do with what is *not*. We will begin with the latter.

First of all, it is evident that only a very few contributors have been consulted, and that a sample of this size is bound to be seen by some readers as unrepresentative – however that may be defined. But this is a shortcoming which can be overcome later, to the extent that it is thought to be necessary to do so, by the simple expedient of widening the sample. And the same applies to the fact that many of the questions here reflect Western, West European, and, in particular, British preoccupations, because of the nature of the audiences for which this book is intended. The range of questions can be broadened. Opinion can be canvassed from other quarters in this country, from other West European countries, from other contributors within the Eastern bloc, and from other parts of the world. Those who feel that the approach has been too narrow or too clear-cut to do justice to the range and complexity of the subject, can be asked what these broader issues are and how we should be responding to them. Those who feel that the approach has been too unspecific and general to do justice to the technical detail upon which much of the arguing depends (for example, over questions of verification, or of the exact interpretation of particular arms control agreements), can be asked to explain the importance of those technical points to us in as much detail as is considered to be appropriate. However diverse, intricate, or vast the subject, in searching for the best policy as readers and voters, we are dealing in the first instance only with what we are told. We are concerned with the *jusitification* for alternative proposed courses of action. So, if a particular factor or issue is said to be relevant by those who are thereby recommending certain policies to us, we can ask them to explain why. They cannot reasonably both say that this cannot be done, and at the same time appeal to us as voters to make an informed choice. Only what is not, or cannot, be rationally or intelligibly justified to us will be beyond our reach. And that also puts it beyond the reach of any democratic process which is said to include us as part of the electorate.

But what about Part II itself? How adequate is it as a record of the thinking of those whom we have consulted, and how much scope does it provide for us to understand, compare, and assess, the alternative sets of recommendations that they have made? As a record, it no doubt suffers from the fact that the imposition of a common framework of questions may have inhibited what would otherwise have been a different emphasis in each case. There may have been other things that would have been said. On the other hand, each of those interviewed has been free to criticize the framework of questions and to depart from it whenever he or she felt it to be necessary, and has been invited to revise and alter the text at the end. And there is no reason why we should not ask them to comment at greater length later. So, if we assume, as a result, that none of them is seriously dissatisfied with the outcome at this stage, then we can move on to the critical point where we begin to try to compare and assess the answers that we have received.

Readers will already have reacted in any number of ways. For example, some may have given up the attempt to determine what the best policy is, having become discouraged by the fact that those who are better informed and more experienced than we are seem to disagree so radically among themselves about so many aspects of it. Others may have had their original opinion further confirmed by what they have read. They may have found little difficulty in distinguishing between those sets of arguments that are sensible and convincing and those that are weak and implausible, and in explaining how the latter are nevertheless strongly advocated by coming to certain uncomplimentary conclusions about those who are advocating them. In neither of these cases is there likely to be much incentive to carry the investigation further. But we will not at this stage take either of these two courses. We will not take the former, and wash our hands of the whole affair, because none of those whom we have consulted has advised us to respond like this. But nor will we take the latter. We will not accept some of these arguments and dismiss others, because we do not feel that we are yet in a position to do so. We have not ourselves attempted to relate the answers to one another in order to determine exactly where the differences lie, nor have we asked those whom we have been consulting to assess the disagreement for us. We would like to ask them what they think are the most important issues that divide those who are disagreeing with one another here. Can these issues be resolved by further argument, and, if so, how? Will the appeal be to empirical fact? Or to broad political judgement? Or to rational consistency? Or to moral principle? And why is it that others come to such radically different conclusions about them? What kinds of mistakes are they making? Or is it more a question of their judgement being clouded by partisan interest, or prior political commitment? In short, the crucial thing that we would like to do now is to ask those who have contributed, and others, where the continuing disagreement lies, what its nature is, whether there is a hope that parts of it may eventually be resolved, and how we should respond to what still remains at issue.

There is little more that can usefully be said here, short of actually carrying through the enterprise. But we will end with a specific example, in order to show why it is worthwhile trying to do so. We have seen that disagreement about the relative strengths of NATO and Warsaw Pact conventional forces is a major component in the debate. Within the last few months, and with reference to precisely the same set of recently published and openly available figures and comments, official statements by representatives of the three main political groupings in this country have concluded: (A) that the figures show that *there is a serious military imbalance* between NATO and the Warsaw Pact in the latter's favour, which is *not quite the three to one advantage that an attacker is commonly thought to require, but rather too close for our comfort*; (B) that they show that *the conventional balance in Europe is still such as to make general military aggression a highly risky undertaking for either side*; and (C) that they show that *Warsaw Pact and NATO forces are fairly evenly balanced*. In each case, the statement is used to support broad policy recommendations, which, taken together, are mutually incompatible. What are we to make of this? And how can we determine which statement to believe? Let us suppose that we do not have direct access to the source itself (which is how things are for most of us in these cases). Then what we would like to do is to ask representatives from each of the three party groupings, first, to assess the relative importance of the judgement in question for the overall case being made, and, second, to specify exactly where and why the others have gone wrong. We would then like to be able to persuade each to respond to these criticisms in detail – and to continue in this way for as long as is needed until general agreement is reached that unnecessary misunderstandings have been cleared up, and the full rationales behind the rival positions have been mutually understood. And what will we find then? Will we find that a consensus has been reached about what the figures do and do not show, and about how this bears upon the disagreement in general? Will it turn out that much of what had before been referred to unequivocally as demonstrable fact, is now seen to be open to a legitimate variety of interpretation? Will this in turn seem to narrow, or to widen, the differences between the alternative policies on offer? And, in the light of all this, will each still continue as before to accuse the other of transparent deception and deliberate statistical manipulation?

Such a process is likely at times to be laborious and intricate, but it is possible to suggest that it is only in this kind of way that we can adequately assess what the choices are that we, as voters, are being asked to make. And it is, perhaps, only in this way that we can hope to expose the extent and depth of the conceptual gulfs which divide us. It may even be that to become aware of them is to begin to bridge them. But we must not indulge in speculation. We do not yet know if anyone will be prepared to take part in such an enterprise. Let us just say that the fact that those whose judgements are recorded in Part II have in each case responded to the same set of questions, may mean that we now have a chance to take an investigation of this kind further than would otherwise have been possible.

3 *Understanding*

And now, finally, how does what we describe in Section I of this Postscript relate to what we propose in Section 2? How does voting relate to arguing? This is a deep question. It is deeper than can be fathomed in these pages. We have been carried to the edge of it on a number of occasions in the course of this enquiry, and, in a sense, it underlies everything else that is written here. In the end, if we do not succeed in resolving the disagreement to general satisfaction, it seems to be what we are left with.

First, there is the fact of disagreement itself. How are we to understand it? We are almost bound to do so on the analogy of what we see when we look at what is contained in Part II. Those whom we have consulted live with one another in the world, and so the statements that they make, and, by extension, the beliefs that they hold, are seen to 'coexist' in a similar kind of way. There they are, set out beside one another in the pages of this book. Whether we call them 'statements' or 'beliefs' or 'opinions' or 'arguments' or 'judgements' or 'policies' or 'perspectives', we are happy to refer to them in the plural as familiar and commonplace entities. And, insofar as what is recorded in Part II can at the same time also be called a 'disagreement', it, too, is just such another familiar and commonplace feature of the world. We are quite used to the idea that there are arguments or opinions, which appear to be incompatible with one another. We have no difficulty in declaring '*I understand what you say, and I disagree with it*'. In this, and in other ways, we refer to disagreements as sets of coexisting, mutually incompatible, judgements.

But what does the fact of the implementation of public policy show? Let us imagine that I have won the vote, and am now able to put my own preferred policy into operation. How do I behave? I insist upon doing exactly what, in the disagreement, you have been imploring me not to do with all the eloquence at your command. I impose as public policy what you have clearly said is both grossly immoral and inexcusably reckless and dangerous. I do this, despite the fact that you have repeatedly told me that it will put the lives and well-being of millions of people at risk, including not only those who have voted the other way or abstained, but also those who have not had the chance to vote at all. It is not so much that actions speak louder than words, as that what I am *doing* shows you what it is that I have been *saying*. My 'statements' and 'beliefs' are no longer familiar and commonplace. They are something horrifying and beyond your comprehension. Conversely, the fact that your appeals, however apparently politely received, are entirely set aside with seeming equanimity, shows you that I feel nothing of their force. I demonstrate how much I appreciate what you say by riding rough-shod over it without apparent disquiet. You realize that what I refer to as 'your beliefs' are in the important sense simply not your beliefs. I just have not seen what you have been pointing at. In the world as defined by the implementation of my policy, you discover to your cost that your opinion does not exist at all.

We have reached the edge of the central discontinuity, which lies beneath all the others. The fact that only one of two incompatible policies is implemented shows the sense in which the rationales behind those policies do not coexist either. What had before seemed familiar and commonplace, all at once becomes bewildering and strange. When we look back at what is contained in Part II of this book, we are no longer confident that we can understand it. Beneath the reassuring fact that here, side by side, we have statements and beliefs to be analysed and compared, lies the alarming fact of what happens when the vote goes one way rather than another. It calls in question the sense in which they *do* lie 'side by side', or can be referred to in the plural at all. It calls in question what 'they' are. The discontinuities, which again and again threatened to interrupt our comprehension of what we were reading, were perhaps after all not just unfortunate peripheral discrepancies, to be ironed out at leisure if possible, and, if not, to be set aside as incidental. It may turn out that they are intimations of what lies at the very heart of the disagreement itself, signposts to guide us towards an understanding of what it can mean to say that we share the world with one another as fellow-citizens, and that we want above all to live in it together in justice and in peace.